NEW DIRECTIONS IN SCANDINAVIAN STUDIES

Terje Leiren and Christine Ingebritsen, Series Editors

NEW DIRECTIONS IN SCANDINAVIAN STUDIES

This series offers interdisciplinary approaches to the study of the Nordic region of Scandinavia and the Baltic States and their cultural connections in North America. By redefining the boundaries of Scandinavian studies to include the Baltic States and Scandinavian America, the series presents books that focus on the study of the culture, history, literature, and politics of the North.

Small States in International Relations, edited by Christine Ingebritsen, Iver B. Neumann, Sieglinde Gstohl, and Jessica Beyer

Danish Cookbooks: Domesticity and National Identity, 1616–1901, by Carol Gold

Crime and Fantasy in Scandinavia: Fiction, Film, and Social Change, by Andrew Nestingen

Selected Plays of Marcus Thrane, translated and introduced by Terje I. Leiren

Munch's Ibsen: A Painter's Visions of a Playwright, by Joan Templeton

Knut Hamsun: The Dark Side of Literary Brilliance, by Monika Žagar

Nordic Exposures: Scandinavian Identities in Classical Hollywood Cinema, by Arne Lunde

Icons of Danish Modernity: Georg Brandes and Asta Nielsen, by Julie K. Allen

Danish Folktales, Legends, and Other Stories, by Timothy R. Tangherlini

Church Resistance to Nazism in Norway, 1940–1945, by Arne Hassing

Church Resistance to Nazism in Norway

1940–1945

———

ARNE HASSING

———

University of
Washington Press

SEATTLE AND LONDON

*This publication is supported by a grant from
the Scandinavian Studies Publication Fund.*

© 2014 by the University of Washington Press
Printed and bound in the United States of America
Design by Dustin Kilgore
Composed in Sabon, a typeface designed by Jan Tschichold
17 16 15 14 13   5 4 3 2 1

All rights reserved. No part of this publication may be reproduced
or transmitted in any form or by any means, electronic or mechanical,
including photocopy, recording, or any information storage or retrieval
system, without permission in writing from the publisher.

University of Washington Press
PO Box 50096, Seattle, WA 98145, USA
www.washington.edu/uwpress

Library of Congress Cataloging-in-Publication Data
Hassing, Arne.
Church resistance to Nazism in Norway, 1940–1945 / Arne Hassing. —
1st [edition].
    pages   cm. — (New directions in Scandinavian studies)
Includes bibliographical references and index.
ISBN 978-0-295-99308-9 (cloth : alk. paper)
1. Lutheran Church—Norway—History—20th century.
2. Anti-Nazi movement—Norway.   3. Norske kirke—History—
20th century.   4. Norway—Church history—20th century.   I. Title.
BX8037.H37   2014   940.53'481—dc23
2013019968

The paper used in this publication is acid-free and meets the minimum
requirements of American National Standard for Information Sciences—
Permanence of Paper for Printed Library Materials, ANSI Z39.48–1984.∞

For Ruthanne

CONTENTS

Preface   ix

Acknowledgments   xvii

Map of the Church of Norway's dioceses in 1940   xx

PART I. PRELUDES

1. German Prelude   5
2. Norwegian Preludes   18

PART II. INVASION,
ACCOMMODATION, COLLABORATION

3. *Weserübung*   37
4. Forging a Front   52

PART III. RESISTANCE

5. In Defense of a Just State   69
6. The NS Church System   83
7. Against Nazification   95
8. In Defense of the Church   108
9. The Resignation of the Bishops   119
10. In Defense of the Young   130
11. Easter 1942   155

PART IV. CONTESTING NS LEGITIMACY

12. Negotiations?   169
13. The Autonomous Church   180
14. The NS Church   191

PART V. FINAL PROTESTS

15. In Defense of Jews   205
16. Against Compulsory Labor Service   216

PART VI. HOLDING OUT

17. Between the Times   229

PART VII. LIBERATION

18. The Reckoning   243
    Epilogue: Legacies   256

Abbreviations   277
Notes   279
Bibliography   325
Index   351

Image gallery follows page 142

PREFACE

During World War II, Allied propaganda and the free press celebrated Christian resistance to Nazism in German-occupied Norway. A few observers also understood its larger importance. The great Swiss theologian and leader of the German church resistance, Karl Barth, wrote in 1943 that "the scope and significance of the church struggles in Holland and Norway" were "greater than those of the one in Germany." After the war, Norwegian church resistance changed Lutheran political ethics and became a case study in civil resistance.[1]

In spite of its significance, the sources that non-Norwegian authors draw on to write about the church resistance are still limited to wartime books, the occasional postwar article, and books that deal with church resistance as part of a broader subject. A typical example is the excellent comparative study of European civilian resistance by French scholar Jacques Semelin. In that book, the church is central to his presentation of the "particularly active" Norwegian resistance.[2] Yet his account is based on translations of one article (Skodvin 1969) and one book (Gjelsvik 1979), neither primarily about the church resistance. Compared to the extensive English-language literature produced on the German church struggle, the neglect of Norway—and the Netherlands—is puzzling. Perhaps it is simply "the great powers" ignoring small nations in scholarship as in politics.

Norwegian scholars, however, have written extensively on the topic. The first books appeared in 1945, written by participants, and their books have special merit as both primary and secondary sources. The standard account became H. C. Christie's *Den norske kirke i kamp* (The Church of Norway in Struggle). Among the book's virtues are details not available in other sources. Ingvald B. Carlsen's *Kirkefronten i Norge* (The Church Front in Norway during the Occupation) is briefer and more popular, and at a few points it supplements Christie's book. Kristian Hansson's book, *Stat og kirke: Fredstider og kampår i Norge* (State and Church: Times of Peace and Years of War in Norway), is important because Hansson was the legal consultant to the church's leadership until his arrest in 1942; he places the church's resistance in the context of prewar church-state relations. Finally, Oscar Handeland's *Kristent samråd i kirkekampen* (The Christian Consultative Council in the Church Struggle) tells the story of the church's leadership council from 1940 to 1942, its accuracy verified by members of the council. Other books published in 1945, by Eivind Berggrav, Ludwig Schübeler, and Wollert Krohn-Hansen, provide valuable first-person accounts.[3]

After 1945, shorter surveys of the church's resistance continued to be published. Einar Molland wrote on "Kirkens kamp" (the Church's Struggle) for the official three-volume history of the war, *Norges krig* (Norway's War), published in 1950. In 1971, Carl F. Wisløff wrote a chapter on the resistance for the third volume of *Norsk kirkehistorie* (Norwegian Church History). Both were overviews by historians who had participated in the events, but, as single chapters they were inherently limited.

The scholar who has done most to give the topic a high profile is Torleiv Austad, Professor of Theology Emeritus at the Norwegian School of Theology. He engaged in groundbreaking research for his dissertation, published as *Kirkens grunn: Analyse av en kirkelig bekjennelse fra okkupasjonstiden 1940–45* (The Foundation of the Church: Analysis of a Confession from the Occupation Era, 1940–45) in 1974, and thereafter he has published shorter surveys and many articles on the history and theology of the church's resistance. His book, *Kirkelig Motstand: Dokumenter fra den norske kirkekamp under okkupasjonen 1940–45 med innledninger og kommentarer* (Church Resistance: Documents from the Norwegian Church Struggle during the Occupation 1940–45 with Introductions and Commentary), introduces, reprints, and analyzes the main documents of the church's resistance, and as such it is the most systematic analysis to date, particularly on the theological dimension. His book and mine are intended to be read as companion, complementary volumes, and, to facilitate cross-referencing between the two, whenever possible this book cites documents printed in Austad's book, rather than referring to documents in archival collections. At almost every point, the Norwegian language reader will find additional details in Austad's book.

Ragnar Norrman's Swedish book, *Quislingkyrkan: Nasjonal Samlings kyrkopolitik 1940–1945* (The Quisling Church: Nasjonal Samling's Church Politics 1940–1945), is another detailed study, this time of the "Quisling Church" and its collaboration with the German and Norwegian Nazi authorities. Our two books are complementary as well, insofar as we examine opposite sides of the struggle. Together with Austad's book, Norrman's and mine offer three perspectives and approaches that form a comprehensive account of church collaboration and resistance during the German occupation.

A recent and more popular book is Pål Berg's *Kirke i krig: Den norske kirke under 2. verdenskrig 1940–45* (Church in War: The Church of Norway During the Second World War, 1940–45). It is exceptional in displaying the most extensive collection of photographs in a single volume.

A number of other works have contributed substantially to our understanding of the church's resistance. Two edited books contain valuable studies: *Kirken, krisen og krigen* (The Church, the Crisis, and the War), edited by Stein Ugelvik Larsen and Ingun Montgomery, was part of a collaborative project on the Scandinavian churches before and during World War II, and it includes useful studies on the Church of Norway's resistance to Nazism. Another valuable collection of articles was edited by Jan Ove Ulstein under the title *Kyrkja under krigen: Bokutgåve av TKRS 1 1995* (The Church During the War: Book Edition of TKRS 1 1995). Also in this category is *Die öffentliche Verantwortung der Evangelisch-lutherischen Kirche in einer Bekenntnissituation: Das Paradigma des norwegischen Kirchenkampfes* (The Public Responsibility of the Evangelical Lutheran Church in a Situation of Confession: The Paradigm of the Norwegian Church Struggle), a collection of articles by German and Scandinavian contributors on Norwegian church resistance in comparative theological perspective, edited by R. Heinrich Foerster. The most relevant contributions to these books appear in the bibliography.

Other works that contributed indirectly to this volume are too numerous to name here, but biographical studies of the three leading figures in the conflict—Vidkun Quisling, Eivind Berggrav, and Josef Terboven—

have helped more than the notes indicate. When I began research, only Quisling had been the subject of biographical studies, and none was recognized as definitive or standard. That changed in the course of my research, as several scholars published standard books: Oddvar Høidal's and Hans-Fredrik Dahl's biographies of Vidkun Quisling, Gunnar Heiene's biography of Berggrav, and Berit Nøkleby's biography of Josef Terboven. Robert Bohn's study of the Reichskommissariat filled another important gap.[4] For a more complete overview of the literature, readers are referred to the bibliography at the end of this book and to the volumes of Norrman (1998) and Austad (2005). Space considerations have limited my bibliography almost completely to sources cited.

When I began this book, my aim was to write the first critical book-length history of the church's resistance to Nazism. In spite of the intervening years, no such study has appeared, and this book thus fulfills my original intention. In addition to being a history of the Norwegian church struggle, I think this book advances understanding of the subject in five areas.

First, it is based on the most extensive archival research to date. I have consulted archival collections throughout Norway, including regional state archives, as well as church and state archive in Sweden, Germany, Switzerland, the United Kingdom, and the United States; sources cited represent only a fragment of the research.

Second, I show the ecumenical movement's influence on Bishop Eivind Berggrav's theology of church, state, and society. In early Norwegian postwar accounts, the rule was to lift up the specifically Lutheran aspects of the church's resistance, with only a mention, if any, of the ecumenical context and contribution. That tendency has been modified in subsequent accounts, beginning with Torleiv Austad's reference to ecumenical "impulses" in Berggrav's thought.[5] Austad's German student Arnd Heling has pursued Austad's insight by showing, in particular, the influence of the 1917 Uppsala and 1925 Stockholm conferences on Eivind Berggrav's thought.[6] Aud V. Tønnessen has also included a valuable analysis of the ecumenical dimension of the resistance in her book about the postwar church debate on the welfare state.[7] I have taken the analysis a bit further, showing that key ideas Berggrav used in the church struggle had predecessors in ecumenical documents and, in particular, in the conferences of the 1930s. As the late Nils Ehrenström, a Swedish Lutheran and former study director of the World Council of Churches, once said to me, "The Norwegian church struggle had an ecumenical context." It also had an ecumenical theological and ethical content.

A third contribution is to show the depth of the Church of Norway's tendency to accommodate to a Nazi state. In spite of its resistance to Nazism, the Church of Norway's instinct was accommodation, even to the Nazi state. Not only was the church comparatively late in adopting a posture of resistance, a few weeks after its separation from the Nazi state in 1942 it was willing to enter negotiation to reconcile with the same state. In Chapter 12, I disclose for the first time, to my knowledge, the unstated reason—the proverbial elephant in the room—for the church's willingness to risk its entire moral and political capital for the sake of retaining state ties, even to a Nazi state.

Fourth, this study situates the church's resistance within the pre- and postwar history of the church, seeking, first, to show the continuity between prewar church history and its resistance during the occupation and, second, the repercussions of the wartime resistance in the postwar era.

Finally, this book views the German Kirchenkampf, generally termed the "church struggle" in English, as the initial context of the Church of Norway's resistance. The German struggle was closely observed by Norwegian church leaders, and it served as both a prototype and an antitype for the Norwegian church. The Norwegian church struggle was not a continuation of the German one, as if, somehow, the German Evangelical Church's failures could be redeemed by the Church of Norway's resistance. Nevertheless, the lessons learned allowed the Church of Norway to chart a different course and show that Lutheranism could be understood and applied differently.

There is a limit to the scope of this book: it is about the resistance of the Church of Norway (Lutheran) and its national leadership. As the state church, the Church of Norway was the Nazi state's primary target for the "New Order" in church affairs. The non-Lutheran free churches supported the resistance, but they were not the initial or principal targets of Nazification. Until the very end, neither were the voluntary mission societies within the Church of Norway. For that reason, I have kept the focus on the national leadership of the Church of Norway.

A word about usage, abbreviations, and translations. It has been common in Norway to talk about "the church" and mean the Lutheran state

Church of Norway. The usage comes naturally, because it is still the dominant church, and few contemporary Church of Norway leaders and scholars would want to imply that other Christian churches are not "the church." I would prefer, however, not to perpetuate such usage or its theological implications, so my title is not "The Church's (or the Church of Norway's) Resistance to Nazism in Norway, 1940–1945," but *Church Resistance to Nazism in Norway, 1940–1945*. The title recognizes that church resistance was first and foremost the Church of Norway's resistance to Nazism, but without implying that the Church of Norway is the only "church" in Norway or excluding the resistance of other Christian denominations from the category of "church" resistance.

Nevertheless, to avoid repetitive references to "the Church of Norway," and for that reason alone, "the church" will generally refer to the Church of Norway. After the Church of Norway's separation from the state at Easter 1942, I shall use both "the church" and "the autonomous church" to mean the Church of Norway, in contrast to "the NS church" or "the NS state church." The term "free churches" will refer to the non-state (hence "free") Protestant churches, and "churches" applies to all Christian churches, usually meaning in Norway. Occasionally "the church" will refer to the church universal, with the context indicating that meaning.

For the ease of English-speaking readers, I have generally used English equivalents of names and titles. At the first mention of a name or title that would *not* be obvious to a Norwegian reader, I have included the Norwegian title. Thus, for a Norwegian-speaking reader "Christian Democratic Party" may not be the obvious English title of *Kristelig folkeparti*, although it is now the party's official English title, but Coordination Committee should obviously mean Koordinasjons komiteen without translation. I have made some exceptions throughout, such as Storting instead of Parliament, Reichskommissar and Reichskommissariat instead of Imperial Commissioner and Imperial Commissioners Office, Nasjonal Samling or NS for Quisling's National Union Party, and Wehrmacht instead of "German armed forces." For the constitutional Norwegian Labor Party government that was in power before 1940 and continued the war from exile in London, I use "Norwegian government." Although Germany had governing authority in occupied Norway, I use "NS government" or "NS state" to refer to the rule of its Norwegian surrogates, mostly to avoid cumbersome alternatives. For clerical titles in English, I have relied on *Church Word List: Norwegian-English*, published in 1995 by the Church of Norway's Information Service, even when I don't consider them the best alternatives.

Finally, for reasons of length, I have used abbreviated titles in the notes, but in no case should there be doubt about their identification in the bibliography, which includes full titles and translations of non-English titles. All translations are my own, unless otherwise indicated.

ACKNOWLEDGMENTS

In a book review published in 1945, Olav Valen-Sendstad observed that the Norwegian church struggle had already created "a huge and highly demanding task for *historians* (his italics)."[1] He was right. In attempting to meet the challenge, I have accumulated multiple debts.

To my family, I am most indebted, above all to my wife, Ruthanne, about whom I cannot say enough or thank enough; her love holds me together, her encouragement and support have never wavered, and she has been a discerning critic of the manuscript. My dedication of this book to her is but a token of my love, debt, and gratitude. My deep thanks and gratitude are also due to our daughter Kirsten (Howard) and son Erik, who never—not once—complained about the time taken from them for this project, though I live with regrets

My collaborator, friend, and author of the Norwegian companion volume, Torleiv Austad, has been unfailingly supportive, generous, patient, and gracious. Over many years, our discussions have clarified my thought and directed me to overlooked aspects of the subject. We originally planned that his book, *Kirkelig Motstand: Dokumenter fra den norske kirkekamp under okkupasjonen 1940–45 med innledninger og kommentarer* [Church Resistance: Documents from the Norwegian Church Struggle During the Occupation, 1940–45, with Introductions and Commentary] and mine would be a complementary two-volume set. They are still complementary, but Austad's book came out in 2005 and this one, for various reasons, did not. Austad's book is more directed toward specific theological issues, and it provides in depth analyses of many ideas that receive more cursory treatment in my book, or that I have had to omit altogether.[2]

Thanks, also, to friends and professional colleagues who offered suggestions and criticisms of the original and far longer manuscript: Ole Kristian Grimnes, Professor of History Emeritus, University of Oslo; Ivar Kraglund, Deputy Director, Norway's Resistance Museum; Bernt T. Oftestad, Professor of European Cultural History Emeritus, Norwegian School of Theology; the late Tore Meistad, associate professor, University of Agder; and my friend Jerry Gaither, who provided the perspective of a non-specialist.

For advice and letters of support, my thanks go to the late Fredrik A. Norwood, Professor of Church History, Garrett-Evangelical Theological Seminary; the late Franklin D. Scott, Professor of History, Northwestern University; Karl W. Luckert, Professor Emeritus of Religious Studies, Missouri State University; and the late Nils E. Bloch-Hoell, Professor of Missiology and Ecumenics, the Theological Faculty, University of Oslo.

I also have received generous support from friends, colleagues, and administrators in the Department of Comparative Cultural Studies at Northern Arizona University: the late Wayne W. "Bill" Mahan, C. T. Aufdemberge, Thomas J. Cleman, Dennis Rusché, and Jason BeDuhn. Thanks also to Henry Hooper for his grant of a laptop when I needed it the most.

A special thanks to a number of people, agencies, and institutions who have helped to secure or have supported me with grants: Northern Arizona University for a leave of absence in 1980–81, two one-semester sabbaticals, and several intramural grants; the Fulbright Program for a fellowship in 1980 and an extension grant in 1981; the National Endowment for the Humanities for a fellowship in 1980–81; the Norwegian Information Service and Norwegian Research Council for travel and research grants in 1985; and finally, numerous personnel of the archives and libraries listed in the bibliography who have offered their professional advice and service.

Louella Holter, editor, and Eve Paludan, associate editor, Bilby Research Center, Northern Arizona University were a joy to work with, and their thorough editing improved the text and saved me from errors. Many thanks as well to the staff of the University of Washington Press for their patience, encouragement, support, and professionalism, particularly the unfailingly helpful and understanding Tim Zimmermann and Sarah Cohen, copy editor extraordinaire.

Tony De Luz, Senior Scientific Illustrator, IDEALAB, Northern Arizona University, is responsible for the diocesan map.

Finally, a special thanks to Terje Leiren for encouraging me to submit this manuscript to New Directions in Scandinavian Studies, recommending it to the press, and, I am sure, being instrumental in the University of Washington's Department of Scandinavian Studies providing a publication grant from the Scandinavian Studies Publication Fund. To the Department itself, thank you.

Every effort has been made to check for errors, and those that remain are my responsibility.

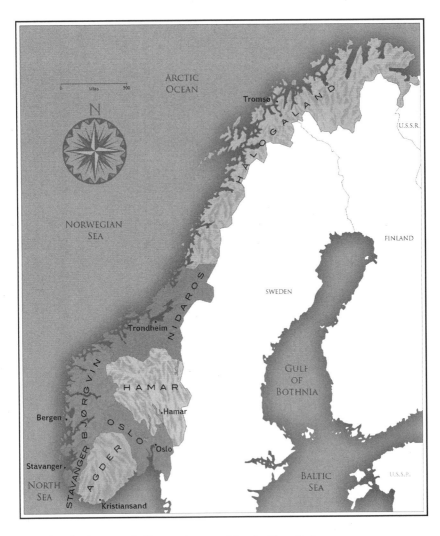

The Church of Norway's dioceses in 1940. Map by Tony De Luz, IDEALAB,
Northern Arizona University

*Church Resistance to Nazism
in Norway, 1940–1945*

———

PART I

Preludes

—

Chapter 1

German Prelude

———

A TROUBLING OBSERVATION

The year was 1936, and Adolf Keller, the Swiss Secretary of the European Central Bureau of Inter-Church Aid, delivered a series of lectures on church and state in Europe. He could not have chosen a more relevant topic. The "church struggle" (Kirchenkampf) between Adolf Hitler's National Socialist state and the German Evangelical Church was entering its fourth year. Keller knew the German church well and had followed the conflict from its inception, and one aspect particularly troubled him: the willingness of the Lutheran churches "to collaborate with the State and, following Romans 13, to go a long way even with an antagonistic Government."[1]

Norwegian church leaders also followed the German Evangelical Church's confrontation with Nazism and were troubled by it, but they did not expect to find themselves in the same situation. When they did, they drew on the lessons of the German experience. For that reason, the Protestant church struggle in Germany was the prelude to the Church of Norway's resistance to Nazism.[2]

GERMAN PROTESTANTISM BEFORE 1933

Before 1933, German Protestantism comprised 28 independent Lutheran, Reformed, and United (Lutheran/Reformed) state-supported territorial churches. Since the early nineteenth century they had dreamed of consolidating into a national church, but numerous political and ecclesiastical obstacles had stood in the way. In spite of their differences, in the early 1920s Protestants agreed that the common purpose of their churches was to mobilize "in behalf of the religious and moral world-view of the German Reformation," and their moral agenda was "an ever higher, ever more perfect morality" through Christianity. The connection of Christianity to a higher morality held such a "commanding position" in German Protestantism at the time that it can "scarcely be exaggerated." This point needs emphasizing in order to highlight the revolutionary nature of subsequent developments.[3]

The context of those developments was the crisis created by World War I, Germany's military defeat, the collapse of the monarchy, the punitive Treaty of Versailles, the runaway inflation and economic depression of the 1920s and early 1930s, and the Protestant sense of lostness in the democratic but ineffectual Weimar Republic (1919–1933).[4] The old was gone, the present was chaotic, and the future was unpredictable.

In search of answers, former monarchists and nationalists looked to *das Volk*, the German people, as an ethnic, racial, and national community. Amidst the forces of destruction, only *das Volk* seemed to remain, and the *völkisch* (ethnic German) movement that emerged was thus based on "the unity of blood."[5] National Socialism built on this ethnic base. As the preeminent scholar of the German church struggle, Klaus Scholder, put it, "no one can understand the power which National Socialism achieved without realizing that behind it stood the claim and the conviction to be fighting on the side of good against evil."[6] Chief among the evils to be fought were Communists and Jews, both viewed as direct threats to *völkisch* identity and culture.

In the 1930s, Lutheran theology thought of God's rule in the world in terms of orders of creation. Within that framework, a younger generation of German Protestants created a new political ethic in the 1920s that can be seen in a lecture on "Church and *Volkstum*" by Paul Althaus, professor at the University of Erlangen. He elevated the German people as a racial, ethnic, and national community to the preeminent order of creation, which meant that the church had "to be committed to it above all others and to the movement that translated the will of *das Volk* into political action."[7] The question for Althaus was not the consequences of a totalitarian state, but whether the state served the will of God. If it did, its intervention in all of life was not an issue.[8] The movement thus shifted the center of church consciousness from Jesus and his ethical demand to *das Volk* and their ethical demands, eventually subordinating Jesus and traditional Christianity to Nazism—*das Volk* in political action.

The German Protestant ideology that emerged was thus a fusion of Christianity, ethnicity, nationalism, and anti-Semitism, and it predisposed its adherents to Adolf Hitler's vision of a new Germany.[9] In July 1932, about 38 percent of the Protestant electorate supported the National Socialist German Labor Party, and "the greater the percentage of Protestants in an area, the greater its Nazi vote." Religion was thus "the best predictor of Nazi voting," and the Protestant vote made it so.[10]

THE GERMAN CHURCH STRUGGLE

Through free elections, but without an electoral majority, Hitler became Chancellor of Germany on 30 January 1933, and played on German fears to expand his power. The fateful turn came on 24 March, when he persuaded the Reichstag to pass the Enabling Act, authorizing him to rule by decree for four years. He used his authority to restore public order, guarantee personal security, clean up public pornography and prostitution, and revive the economy. He also initiated a policy of alignment (*Gleichschaltung*), based on the principle that whoever "does not convert must be subdued."[11] He then suppressed, dissolved, or imprisoned members of opposition political parties, trade unions, professional organizations, and political opponents. By mid-July 1933, the Nazi revolution was complete.

In 1931, the German Christian (*Deutsche Christen*) movement emerged. Based on *völkisch* ideology, Aryan theology, and anti-Semitism, its first objective was a single German Evangelical Church under one national bishop and synod; in the church elections of July 1933, it won two-thirds of the vote. The German Christians followed up by approving a Reich church constitution and at the first National Synod at Wittenberg elected Ludwig Müller as Reich bishop. As of September 1933, a national church was a reality. Next on their agenda was aligning the church with National Socialism—Nazification. They intended to incorporate all the territorial state churches into the Reich Church, strike the Old Testament from the Christian scriptures, eliminate Jewish themes from the New Testament, and purge non-Aryan (Jewish-born) pastors and members.

Two groups rose to oppose them. The first was the Young Reformation Movement led by Martin Niemöller, a Lutheran pastor in the Berlin suburb of Dahlem. He also organized the Pastors' Emergency League, which by January 1934 attracted over 7,000 pastors, about 37 percent of the Protestant clergy.[12] The other opposition group was from the Lutheran state churches of Württemberg and Bavaria, which had resisted incorporation into the Reich Church and thus remained "intact," meaning unified under their own bishops. This coalition opposed the German Christians in the name of scripture and the apostolic Christian creeds, plus distinctively Lutheran or Calvinist creeds known as "confessions."

Hitler had a longstanding policy of not provoking the churches, had supported a Reich Church for the sake of controlling it, and preferred to deal with the church from behind the scenes, but the conflict became too divisive for him to ignore.[13] On 25 January 1934, he convened 12 leaders of the Protestant churches, but instead of mediating the dispute he attacked Niemöller, charged his group with disloyalty, and demanded a declaration of solidarity with Bishop Müller. The intimidation worked. A few days later, the Lutheran bishops pledged their unconditional loyalty to Hitler and the Third Reich and signed a public declaration of support for Müller; following their lead, about 1,800 mostly Lutheran pastors subsequently withdrew from the Pastors' Emergency League. The declaration became the quintessential symbol of Lutheran collaboration with the Nazi state.

The Pastors' Emergency League, joined by the intact churches of Württemberg and Bavaria, responded by forming the Confessing Church as the true church of Jesus Christ and the legal Protestant Church of Germany. The Confessing Church's enduring act was the Barmen Declaration, written almost wholly by the Reformed (Calvinist) theologian Karl Barth and approved by the church's first synod in May 1934.[14] The declaration protested German Christian violations on the principle that "Jesus Christ, as he is attested for us in Holy Scripture, is the one Word of God which we have to hear and which we have to trust and obey in life and in death," there being no areas of life "in which we should not belong to Jesus Christ, but to other lords." In other words, Jesus Christ was the one "Word of God" and source of Christian faith and theology—not orders of creation, and not the *Volk*. The Barmen Declaration affirmed that the state had a "divine appointment" to uphold justice and peace and was entitled to the judicious use of force, but it rejected as "false doctrine" that the state "should and could become the single and totalitarian order of human life, thus fulfilling the Church's vocation as well." The Confessing Church was to be "a Nazi-free space."[15]

Ever since their meeting with Hitler in January 1934, Lutheran bishops in the Confessing Church had harbored suspicions about the national loyalty of advocates for a non-accomodationist church policy, particularly fellow Lutherans Martin Niemöller and Dietrich Bonhoeffer. They also disliked the Reformed tone of the Barmen Declaration and the Dahlem resolutions. That tone was Christ-centered, less willing "to see God's Will anywhere else in nature and history than in Jesus Christ and His Gospel alone."[16] On 25 August 1934, their suspicions led the intact Lutheran churches to form the Lutheran Council in order to give greater voice to Lutheran views.

The German Christian offensive continued, and in early October 1934 the Reich Church's chief administrator, August Jäger, forcibly incorporated the remaining intact churches into the Reich Church and placed bishops Theophil Würm of Würtemberg and Hans Meiser of Bavaria under house arrest. That was a miscalculation. In Stuttgart and Munich, ordinary Germans engaged in "the greatest and at the same time most remarkable protest demonstrations ever experienced in the Third Reich."[17] The repercussions forced the resignation of Jäger and the release of the bishops, whom Hitler cordially received in an audience on 30 October. The Confessing Church responded on 19 and 20 October 1934 at its second national synod, in the Berlin suburb of Dahlem, by urging pastors to resist the new church authorities. It also declared that the Confessing Church was the legitimate national church and used an ecclesiastical emergency law to establish a separate church.

In the course of 1935, the regime raised the stakes by promoting anti-Christian propaganda and demanding unquestioning loyalty and obedience to Hitler. It used the Gestapo to intimidate and arrest its church opponents. Government loyalists could now construe resistance on church issues as resistance to the state itself, forcing the Confessing Church to become a resistance organization against its will. At the Confessing Church's final synod in mid-February 1936, the more radical "Dahlemites" continued to disagree with Lutherans about how to respond to German Christians and their growing use of the Gestapo to impose their agenda. The differences proved insurmountable, leading to a permanent split in the Confessing Church.

One might have thought that the Dahlemites would reconstitute themselves as a free church, but they never contemplated such a step. Not only were the leaders still keen to profess loyalty to Hitler and the Reich, the state church tradition made the free church idea unthinkable. The Confessing Church simply wanted to be recognized, at home and abroad, as the true German Evangelical Church, not a political resistance movement or a "sect," the pejorative term for the free churches.[18]

The difficulty was that the Confessing Church's theological opposition itself became political as the state became increasingly ideological and totalitarian. A direct confrontation became unavoidable. In May 1936 the Dahlemites finally sent an unprecedented and wide-ranging protest to Hitler. They charged the state with attacking church autonomy, supporting a Nazi form of Christianity, closing church schools, restricting the media, attempting to impose an "anti-Semitic attitude," ordering extra-legal activities by the Gestapo, and creating concentration camps.[19] The Dahlemites' central charge, however, was the state's "suppression of the Evangelical Church, the perversion of its faith, the abandoning of Evangelical morality, and the nationwide process of 'de-Christianization.'"[20]

The protest was hard-hitting and courageous, but Hitler ignored it, perhaps because of the upcoming Olympic Games in Berlin. However, the international press published the text, and critics quickly charged the Dahlemites with conspiracy and treachery. In response, the Dahlemites backtracked. In August, they published an abbreviated version of their protest, limited to protesting attacks on the church, but they could not reverse the spreading stain of disloyalty.

In the final phase of the German church struggle, the regime was increasingly successful in silencing the church. The Gestapo targeted dissident clergy, culminating in the summer of 1937 with the arrests of Martin Niemöller, Otto Dibelius, and 48 other Confessing Church leaders. Intimidation silenced most of the rest. By 1938, not even the torching of 177 synagogues and arrest of 20,000 Jews on *Kristallnacht* provoked church reaction.

In April 1938, Protestant sins of omission turned into sins of commission—and complete ideological collaboration—when the German Christians issued the Godesberg Declaration.[21] Signed by a third of Protestant bishops, it affirmed that "native National Socialist ideology is a prerequisite" for all political power in the churches and that this ideology was the key "to a true understanding of the Christian faith in its religious aspects." Furthermore, Christianity by its nature was "irreconcilable opposition to Judaism," and "true Christian faith" could not develop with "supranational or international" churches like Roman Catholicism or "world-Protestant" movements. It only flourished within the given orders of creation—i.e., individual nations.

The next month, Lutheran bishops August Marahrens, Theophil Wurm, Hans Meiser, and Julius Kühlewein issued a similar declaration. They stated that Martin Luther had taught the Evangelical Church "to distinguish clearly between the realms of reason and faith, of politics and religion, of State and Church" and instructed church members "to enter with full devotion into the Führer's work of construction." The declaration went on to draw a sharp contrast between the Christian message and the Jewish religion, concluding that in "the realm of national life a serious, responsibly undertaken race policy is necessary, for the maintenance of the purity of our nationality."[22] This statement represented the total subordination of Christ and Christianity to the ethical imperatives of *das Volk* and Nazi ideology.

Quoting a German theologian (probably Dietrich Bonhoeffer), the Swiss Evangelical Press Service condemned the declaration as "nothing less than the Lutheran Church's declaration of bankruptcy."[23] The statement also implicated the Scandinavian Lutheran churches. Nils Ehrenström, the Swedish Lutheran director of the research division of the World Council of Churches in Formation, brought the declaration to the attention of Sweden's Archbishop Erling Eidem, noting the harm it did to Lutheranism and urging the Scandinavian bishops to publicly repudiate it, but Eidem and the other Scandinavian bishops kept their silence.[24]

Three months later, Germany invaded Poland. Well beforde the invasion and the start of World War II, German patriotism and fear of Communism led all but a few Christians to close ranks around their government and its policies. There was an occasional protest, such as that of the Prussian Confessional Synod (Breslau) in October 1943, which denied the state's right to annihilate various classifications of people, including Jews.[25] But by that time Germany was already in a life-and-death struggle, many clergy members had been drafted into the army, and clerical protests had no effect. Only a few Christians, such as Dietrich Bonhoeffer and the members of the future resistance organization the Kreisau Circle, moved into direct political opposition.

Hitler himself had decided on a detente with the churches at home and abroad for the duration of the war and so informed party officials on many occasions; he did not want unnecessary civilian distractions. But he was contemptuous of Christianity and the church, "that most horrible institution imaginable," and he viewed the clergy as "the evil that is gnawing at our vitals" whose eventual destruction he deeply desired. In the meantime, he had a war to wage and once Germany had won it, he would "clear up" the church problem and eliminate Christianity itself.[26]

ACCOUNTING FOR GERMAN LUTHERANISM

From the outset of the church struggle, the Lutheran relationship to the Nazi state raised questions that still haunt German Protestantism and challenge historians. Why did German Lutheranism accommodate so readily to Nazism? Why did Lutherans support the German Christian movement? Why did they fail to protest human rights violations, particularly the persecution of Jews? Was there a distinctively "Lutheran" explanation?

Early scholarship saw a direct line from Martin Luther to Hitler, while recent studies have tended to avoid grand explanations.[27] The truth probably does not lie in a single cause but a constellation of historical developments and theological ideas.

Klaus Scholder's analysis focuses on the fusion of religious, ethnic, and national identity in German Protestantism since the nineteenth century. In his view, the shaping feature of nationalistic Protestantism and its "new piety" was its concept of God. Neither the Christian God of love nor the Enlightenment God of the greatest good, Protestants worshipped "God the Father, the Lord of peoples and kingdoms, the great God of battles, the omnipotent Avenger and Judge." According to Scholder:

> Dogmatic qualifications are almost completely lacking; there is no trace of a trinitarian conception, and the Apostles' Creed is reduced to the first article ["I believe in God the Father"]. The concept of "das Volk" matches this concept of God. By being directly subordinated to God, Volk and

Volkstum are given the status of the supreme order of creation. The battle over Volkstum (and its concrete political form, the nation) becomes the battle for God's order, for God itself. Service of Volk and Fatherland logically becomes the true service of God, and dedication to society the supreme moral demand.[28]

The Christian God thus turned into the "German God," for whom Germans were "his chosen people, chosen for their piety, honesty, and loyalty," and for whom German history was "the place of his revolution." Political unity and freedom was thus "the fulfillment of his will and his order."[29]

This fusion of Protestant Christianity, ethnicity, and nationalism, with its conception of a Christian Germanic mission, meant that after 1918 Protestants aligned themselves with the most conservative political parties and turned the church itself into "a bastion of reaction." This nationalist Protestant conservatism cut across theological schools of thought, as German Protestants became caught up in the rush of national feeling induced by Hitler.[30]

That explanation is related to the insights of scholars such as William McGovern and of popular authors like William Shirer. In their view, endorsed by Scholder, German Protestants were conditioned by tradition and theology to support an authoritarian state. The resulting ideology, called "statism," claimed that the authoritarian national state was the ideal form of government and the most effective instrument of national transformation. Statism had its roots in the thought of Martin Luther, who intended to reform the church but ended up with a changed concept of the state.[31] Luther's call for the state to reform the church thus subordinated the church to the state and left the state unchecked by any other power. As the church-state relationship evolved, German Protestantism accepted that "the state had supreme power in religious matters" and its clergy became "completely servile to the political authority of the state."[32] The result was a "nation-statist" mentality that was anti-democratic, anti-individualistic, and against most forms of freedom, a mentality that feared and condemned resistance to the nation state. According to Michael Mann, "nation-statism" formed the ideological core of both Lutheranism and National Socialism.[33]

German Protestant identity and nation-statism are historical explanations, but at their root were theological constructs of traditional German Lutheranism: the orders of creation, inwardness, the authority of the state, the doctrine of the two realms, and anti-Semitism. According to Lutheran natural theology, God created "orders" of creation as a means to relate to and rule in the world. The concept of orders of creation framed the Lutheran understanding of society: there were biological orders, such as family and race, and cultural orders, such as economies and education, and they were all part of the "temporal realm," the order of human life.[34] Furthermore, each order existed as a hierarchy of authority and obedience—father and family, king and subjects—which God in his love had provided to check evil in the temporal realm.

After World War I, prominent German Lutheran theologians of the stature of Paul Althaus, Werner Elert, Friedrich Gogarten, Emanuel Hirsch, and Hermann Sasse accepted as fundamental propositions that God had revealed himself, above all, in three orders of creation: family, national community (*Volk*), and the state.[35] The orders were theoretically subordinated to God's revelation in Christ, but "by being directly subordinated to God," the *Volk* and *Volkstum* were "given the status of the supreme order of creation."[36] Once German Protestantism made the additional move, derived from Romanticism, of accepting the state as the expression of the organic life of the German *Volk*—a people constituted by race and embedded in the struggle for survival—the problem of the state as an order of creation becomes evident.[37] Not only does such a view mandate unqualified obedience to the state, it demands theological accommodation to state ideology. That was the path taken by the German Christian church movement.

The *Volkstum* movement and its theological supporters also adopted a racist ideology. The clearest examples of how racially determined concepts of *Volk* and *Volkstum* could override the primacy of Jesus in historic Christianity were two claims made by the German Christians: that Jesus was not a Jew but an anti-Semite who opposed "Jews," and that the Gospel was not about God's universal love but about his hatred of Jews.[38] Jesus' opposition to "Jews" was thus proof of his anti-Semitism, and contrary scriptural evidence was simply "fraudulent." Moreover, the Christian message was not about sin and grace or law and Gospel, the two traditional poles of Lutheran thought, but about heroic racial struggle.

How could the Jesus of the Sermon on the Mount so easily become the

Aryan Christ? The answer lies in the second problematic Lutheran construct: "Christ rules in the inner life, God in the outer."[39] The "Christ-determined" sphere was the inner subject and, to some extent, the family, but not society and certainly not the state. Thus two moral codes can co-exist, one for personal life and the other for collective life. By this thinking, sin rules in collective life, where the state functions according to the iron laws of necessity and coercion.[40] As the Swedish Lutheran theologian Nils Ehrenström put the issue in a 1937 survey of church and state, the "life of pure love was relegated to the inner world of the heart," while the political sphere "was severed from the suffering and self-sacrificing love which is at the heart of the Christian message."[41]

Reinforcing Lutheran inwardness and world negation was the influence of Pietism, which had experienced a revival in the 1920s. Pietism nurtured a profound spirituality, commitment to service, and consciousness of world mission. But Pietists were also convinced that "the world"—in other words, social and political life—was irredeemable. This intensified the Reformation tradition that the temporal realm was under the power of sin and that politics was of no concern to the church. Most of the clergy took a similar view and were thus "apolitical," which by default cast them as defenders of the status quo. As a result of this "inward spirituality," Lutheranism "abdicated responsibility for political and social problems and adjusted itself to whatever political regime happened to be in power."[42]

The third Lutheran construct was the theological authority it accorded to the state, leading to its state servility. If one could not apply Christian principles to the state, what was the appropriate Christian relationship to it? The Lutheran answer was found in St. Paul's letter to the Romans, chapter 13, verses 1 and 2 (New Revised Standard Version): "Let every person be subject to the governing authorities; for there is no authority except from God, and those authorities that exist have been instituted by God. Therefore whoever resists authority resists what God has appointed, and those who resist will incur judgment." Loyalty to the state was conditional in theory: in the Augsburg Confession's Article 16, Christians did not owe loyalty to state authorities and the law when the state ordered citizens to sin, and in such cases they were to obey God rather than human beings.[43]

There were two problems with this proviso that meant it had little application in practice. First, the temporal realm was by definition under the dominion of sin, which God had created law and the state to check. And second, Lutheran theology did not specify the kind of state "sin" that Christians could legitimately resist. The Lutheran propensity to accommodate the Nazi state can thus "be explained—if not explained away—by the traditional acceptance that 'the powers that be are ordained of God.'"[44]

The three Lutheran constructs discussed so far culminate in another doctrine credited with the German Evangelical Church's failure to resist Nazism: the doctrine of the two realms.[45] Formulated by Martin Luther and classically expressed in Article 28 of the Augsburg Confession, the doctrine of the two realms stated that for the sake of preserving social harmony God had ordained two realms, the spiritual and the temporal, and two institutions, church and state, each with its appropriate and distinctive authority, function, and mode of discipline. Christ ruled through the gospel in the spiritual realm—"the realm of eternal things and benefits"—whereas God (the Father) ruled through the secular state to protect "the body and goods against external violence."[46]

Both realms and their functions existed for the wellbeing of humanity, but they were not to be confused or mixed. In particular, the church was not to interfere with the secular state:

> It should not set up and depose kings. It should not annul or disrupt secular law and obedience to political authority. It should not make or prescribe laws for the secular power concerning secular affairs. . . . It should not usurp the other's duty, transfer earthly kingdoms, abrogate the laws of magistrates, abolish lawful obedience, interfere with judgments concerning any civil ordinances or contracts, prescribe to magistrates laws concerning the form of government that should be established. As Christ says [John 18:36]: "My kingdom is not from this world."[47]

When its own theology disqualified the church from checking the state, the state was freed to function without reference or accountability to Christian ethical norms or the church.

Finally, Luther and Lutheranism contributed to a central feature of Nazism that ultimately led to the Holocaust. Scholars disagree about whether Luther's diatribe, *On the Jews and Their Lies*, was a blueprint for the Holocaust, but not that anti-Semitism permeated German Lutheranism.[48] In combination with state servility and the divorce of ethical criteria from the temporal realm, pervasive anti-Semitism encouraged the Protestant Evangelical Church—including the Confessing Church—to remain silent in the face of the state's persecution of Jews. The "betrayal" of the Jews was systemic.[49] As late as December 1942, Lutheran leaders ignored their own doctrinal distinctions about the two realms and called for the state to enact "the severest measures" against Jews. As long as anti-Semitism was acceptable Lutheran theology, the path to National Socialism was through an open door.[50]

In sum, German Lutheranism's willingness to accommodate to the Nazi state did not have a single cause but a constellation of causes, each related to and reinforcing the other in the construction of a distinctive German Lutheran worldview. It was a worldview that could not resist Nazism.

THE QUESTION

In his analysis of church and state in northern Europe, Keller remarks that the "purest form of State Church to-day exists in the Scandinavian countries," and the "purely state character of the Church" was particularly pronounced in Norway.[51] For most of its history, the Church of Norway exhibited the classic Lutheran pattern of state submission and state servility, and its leaders and members had no difficulty accepting such a posture as desirable and distinctively Lutheran.[52] Any contemporary observer would have had reasonable grounds to predict that, faced with the same choices as German Lutherans, the Church of Norway would have gone "a long way even with an antagonistic government."

As it turned out, the Church of Norway did make compromises with the Nazi state before it finally rejected alignment. But its stance was in marked contrast to its German mother church, which raises the obvious question: why did the Lutheran encounter with Nazism in Norway have a different outcome? That is the question this book attempts to answer.

Chapter 2

Norwegian Preludes

——

A NORWEGIAN CHRISTIANITY?

In 1930, Norwegians celebrated nine centuries of Christianity. For a commemorative volume, a promising pastor named Johannes Smemo contributed an article on Norwegian Christianity that tried to pin down its distinctiveness. Smemo was sure that Christianity was the same always and everywhere, and he did not want to make too much of "the Norwegian," but he was also sure *something* distinguished Norwegian Christianity.

Forced to choose one word to define it, he picked "individualism," by which he meant living on "independent experience" and "a clear point of view," not "on the word and authority of others." He himself had witnessed "insightful and level-headed" mothers tell their 12-year old sons that it was about time for them to develop "a clear point of view," which, he thought, must place Norwegian Christians at the "extreme limits of individualism."[1] He did not think anyone would describe Swedish or Danish Christianity quite that way, and, he might have added, the same was true of German Christianity.

THE CHURCH OF NORWAY

In 1938, Norway had a population of 2,814,194, of whom 96.5 percent belonged to the Evangelical Lutheran Church.[2] The sources of the church's faith were the Bible, the Apostles', Nicene, and Athanasian creeds, the Augsburg Confession (also known as *Confessio Augustana* or simply Augustana), Martin Luther's *Short Catechism*, King Christian V's Danish Law of 1683, and the Norwegian Law of 1687. The Augsburg Confession of 1530 was particularly authoritative as a theological, legal, and political document.

The church consisted of seven dioceses (see map), 91 deaneries (*prostier*), and 1,017 parishes served by 730 pastors. The Oslo Diocese was the largest, with more than 200 clergy, while each of the rest numbered 100 or less. The authority of the seven bishops rested in their supervisory, advisory, and teaching duties, as well as in their rights of ordination and collation. Preeminent was Eivind J. Berggrav (1884–1959), a bishop since 1928 and Bishop of Oslo since 1937. A man of exceptional intelligence, energy, and flair, he was the natural leader of the bishops.[3] In the 1920s, the bishops convened informally for what was called the Bishops' Conference. Berggrav worked to elevate the Conference's purpose and status, driven partly by fear of a weak church leadership structure should Labor form a revolutionary government. His efforts culminated in 1934, when the state recognized the Conference as the bishops' official voice and its official church advisory body. The recognition strengthened the bishops' leadership within the church as well their influence on the state.[4]

The clergy were educated at the liberal Theological Faculty of the University of Oslo (Det teologiske fakultet) or, after 1908, at the orthodox Free Faculty of Theology (Det teologiske Menighetsfakultet)[5]. In the interwar decades, the latter accounted for two-thirds of the theological graduates.[6] Bishops and clergy were senior civil servants. Bishops had salaries comparable to Supreme Court justices and parish pastors (*sokneprest*) to heads of government departments; they could only be removed from office through legal proceedings that documented their incompetence.[7] Their primary state function was to maintain the civil register. Their pastoral duties were preaching, pastoral counseling and visits, administering the sacraments, and conducting the rites of passage—baptisms, confirmations, weddings, and funerals.

The church's polity (church order) was the product of the Reformation and of eighteenth-century Absolutism, both forms of statism, but the church underwent a democratization in the nineteenth century. Its polity, however, did not reflect the change until the Parish Council Law of 1920, which introduced publicly elected parish councils, followed in 1933 by a similar Diocesan Council Law. The councils advised the state on pastoral and episcopal nominations respectively.

In the early twentieth century, the Church of Norway thought of itself as "the folk church" (*folkekirken*), meaning a church of the people as well as a church in service to the people. It was of the people in the extent of its reach into every home, basically through the rites of passage and religious instruction in the schools. More than 95 percent of Norwegians were baptized, confirmed, or buried in the church; 89.5 percent were married there; and most believed in God, life after death, and the efficacy of prayer. Christianity and the church thus formed a "sacred canopy" over their lives, but 75 percent were passive members who constituted an "anonymous Christianity" that normally the church could not activate. To illustrate, in 1939 the Agder Diocese—part of Norway's Bible Belt—reported an average of only eight communicants (worshipers receiving communion) per service, and a few days before the German invasion church leaders in the Nidaros Diocese were pondering "the problem of the empty pews."[8]

Levels of church involvement might have been higher were it not for the 25 domestic and foreign mission societies that operated 17,371 chapters, employed hundreds of lay preachers, and engaged about 13.6 percent of the population.[9] Their membership was highest in the South, Southwest, and West. Usually called "the organizations," their members comprised a high proportion of active Christians, and some societies functioned independently of the state church, as churches within the church.[10] Theologically, they were orthodox, meaning they adhered to the classic Christian dogmas, tended to interpret the Bible literally, and accepted the Augsburg Confession as the authoritative distillation of scriptural faith. They accounted for most of Norwegian Christianity's individualism, and Ivar Welle, a clergyman and author, acknowledged their influence when he characterized the Church of Norway as a "distinctively laymen's church."[11] That characterization may have been too strong, but it indicates the significance of the lay mission societies in the church.

The person most responsible for the rise of the laity in the church was Hans Nielsen Hauge (1771–1824). He had a religious awakening in 1796, and until 1804 he traveled throughout Norway preaching personal conversion and the necessity of good works. As a lay preacher, however, he ran afoul of the Conventicle Law, which prohibited lay persons from preaching without the consent of the local state church clergyman, and for his temerity, Hauge spent 1804 until 1809 in prison. In the meantime, his activity initiated a rural folk movement that was both spiritual and economic, and many of his followers became key figures in the democratization of politics and the state. In the 1850s, his followers were largely absorbed into the organized mission societies, for whom he was the spiritual father and continuing inspiration.

In 1940, the mission societies had three outstanding leaders. Einar Amdahl (1888–1974) was the energetic general secretary of the largest, the Norwegian Mission Society (*Det Norske Misjonsselskap*), which engaged in foreign missions. Ole Hallesby (1879–1961) was the leader of the Norwegian Lutheran Home Mission Society (*Det norske lutherske Indremisjonsselskap*), which focused on domestic missions. He was an influential theology professor at the Free Faculty of Theology, a popular devotional author, and a scathing polemicist for confessional Lutheranism. Ludvig Hope (1871–1954) was a folksy and inspirational leader of the Norwegian Lutheran China Mission Association (*Det norske lutherske Kinamisjonsforbund*). His organization and the Western Home Mission Association (*Vestlandske Indremisjonsforbund*) were the most independent of the church and critical of it.[12] In 1938, the mission societies formed the Council of Autonomous Organizations (*Organisasjonenes Fellesråd*) to discuss common problems, coordinate their work, and make joint representations on church issues.

The Dissenter Law of 1845 granted non-Lutheran Christians toleration, but nearly a century later the so-called "free churches" were still struggling for religious and legal equality and many Church of Norway's leaders routinely referred to them as "sects," a term as pejorative in Norway as it was in Germany.[13] Most were of Anglo-American origin, notably the Society of Friends (Quakers), Methodists, Baptists, and Pentecostalists, with the largest non-Lutheran church of Norwegian origin being the Mission Covenant Church (*Misjonsforbundet*). Most of the free churches were members of the Dissenter Parliament (Dissentertinget), formed at the beginning of the century to provide a common voice in dealings with both the state and the Church of Norway. Although the free churches' influence was greater than their 2.7 percent of the population, they did not add up to as many active members as the largest Lutheran mission society.[14]

The Roman Catholic Church was small (less than 5,000 members) and was isolated by its own exclusivism.[15] Its exclusivism was matched by Lutheran exclusivism and hostility, and the conflicts of the sixteenth century reverberated still reverberated in the twentieth.

The Jewish community was also small (around 2,000 members), new, and largely unassimilated. Few Norwegians knew or had met Jews, and none of the churches had formal relations with either of Norway's two synagogues. (For more on the Jewish community, see chapter 15.)

"THE CRISIS?"

Historians of Scandinavia have analyzed the interwar era under a single rubric: "the crisis." The crisis was first a crisis of capitalism, and in Norway it started with the post-World War I depression of 1921, continued with another downturn in 1926–27, and ended with the depression of 1931–34.[16] One statistic is enough to convey its impact: unemployment among trade union workers rose from 2 percent in 1920 to 18 percent in 1921, 26 percent in 1927, and 33 percent in 1933. In the winters of 1932–33 and 1933–34 it reached 40 percent; in labor lore, these were "the hard thirties."

Two ideologies were ready to step in where the liberal state, parliamentary democracy, capitalism, and Christianity seemed to fail: Communism on "the Left" and Fascism on "the Right." Communism had its first success in the Russian revolution of 1917, and Fascism rose in the next two decades, partly in reaction to it. In Norway, both posed a challenge to Christianity and the church. Christians and their churches have accommodated without protest and in profound ways secular worldviews and the secularization of societies, but during the interwar era there were three threats that sectors of the church in Norway found too direct to ignore: liberal theology, the liberal state, and the labor movement. Their encounter with all three shaped the Church of Norway on its way to confronting a Nazi state.

CHURCH AND THEOLOGY

When Smemo tried to delineate Norwegian Christianity, he did not conceal that its individualism also produced less-than-desirable traits in its followers. Among these were self-satisfaction, one-sidedness, divisiveness, and a tendency to engage in conflict. Most of these qualities were in full display between the two world wars, especially in the arena most important to Lutheranism—theology.

Beginning in the early nineteenth century, Christian thinkers emerged in Europe and North America who thought modernity and Christianity could be reconciled. Their theology was called "modern" or, more commonly, "liberal." Liberals saw themselves as reinterpreting theology in order to preserve the credibility of faith in the post-Enlightenment world, but the orthodox viewed their project as the surrender of the faith itself.[17] Traditionalist Lutherans thus rejected liberal theology *in toto*. The opposition turned to crisis in the so-called "professor case" of 1903–6, in which a disputed faculty vacancy at the Theological Faculty concluded with the appointment of a liberal theologian, Johannes Ording. The orthodox New Testament professor, Sigurd Odland, resigned in protest, and in 1908 orthodox leaders established the rival Free Faculty of Theology. Once the two theologies were institutionalized, the conflict started seeping through the church.

A new stage of the conflict erupted in 1919, when orthodox professor Edvard Sverdrup offered peace if liberals would accept the Apostles' Creed "word for word." The New Testament professor at the Theological Faculty, Johan Lyder Brun, rebuffed the gesture, refusing to identify the faith with "temporally conditioned statements."[18] Christianity, he replied, had a divine origin and inspiration, but it also had a human dimension that history could explain. With that, the orthodox decided it was time to go on the offensive, led by Ole Hallesby, the Free Faculty of Theology professor who was also leader of the Norwegian Lutheran Home Mission Society. In mid-January 1920, Hallesby and his allies convened 950 elected delegates and many more deputies and observers at the Calmeyer Street Mission Hall in Oslo. To open their proceedings, Johan M. Wisløff laid down the gauntlet: liberal theology, he proclaimed, was not Christianity but another religion. The convention initiated a campaign to re-Christianize Norway by adopting a policy of non-cooperation with liberals, which in practice meant a boycott of liberal clergy and their ministries. This was Norway's fundamentalist revolt.[19]

The so-called "church conflict" (*kirkestriden*) permeated church life for the next decade. The secular public supported the liberals, but they were no match for the dominance of the orthodox within the church and the mission societies. By the close of the 1920s, the liberals had essentially

lost, unable to sustain their own institutions. Liberal theology still dominated the Theological Faculty, however, and it had representatives among
the bishops and the clergy, so the conflict simmered.

The 1930s proved to be a "remarkably peaceful" and "featureless"
decade.[20] The orthodox themselves grew tired of conflict and suffered
internal disagreements, and new theological perspectives directed attention to new issues. Karl Barth's neo-orthodox theology attracted students
and clergy on both sides of the theological divide. Other movements and
groups, such as the Oxford Group Movement, also tempered orthodoxy
without undermining its hegemony. Common to several of the new directions was a focus on "theology's collective and objective expression: the
church, office, confession, the dogmas and sacraments."[21]

Had the church conflict been solely an academic disagreement, it would
not have had the "church political" repercussions that it did.[22] It was an
unedifying display of theological acrimony that did nothing to attract an
increasingly secular public to Christianity and deflected attention from
serious intellectual challenges. Viewed from the perspective of what was
to come, however, orthodoxy and neo-orthodoxy created a theological
consensus that would prove as resistant to modern ideologies as to modern theologies.

CHURCH AND STATE

The repercussions of the theological conflict were complicated by liberalism in the state. Since 1845 the state had been transitioning from a confessional state, whose ideological purpose was to uphold the evangelical
Lutheran worldview, to a liberal state, whose purpose was to guarantee
the rights of all worldviews. As such, the state began to understand itself
to be the guardian of theological diversity in the church. The issue origi-
nated in the second article of the Constitution, which established that the
"Evangelical-Lutheran Religion shall be maintained and constitute the
established Church of the Kingdom." The article also stated that "inhabitants who profess the said religion are bound to educate their children in
the same."[23] Additional articles and laws guaranteed those provisions,
such as the requirements that the King and more than half the cabinet
had to be Evangelical Lutheran.

To understand the interwar church conflict and the church struggle (*kirkekampen*) with Nazism, it is necessary to grasp how profoundly the Church of Norway was the state church and, indeed, the state's church. The King was the constitutional head of the church (which by 1940 meant the King and the government cabinet); church legislation was the function of the Storting (Parliament); and the state's Ministry of Church and Education oversaw church administration. The Ministry had three divisions: church, school, and culture. The Church Division, generally referred to as the Church Department, was led by a director general (*ekspedisjonssjef*) and was subdivided into six offices, each with its own head.[24] The Church Department was responsible for episcopal and clerical appointments.

Although the church advised the state, the state made the decisions. The church was thus subsumed into the state and was not a separate legal entity. Predictably, people commonly called it "the state church."[25] The clergy, however, particularly Berggrav, preferred to think of it less bureaucratically as "the folk church," meaning the uniting institution of the country, particularly with respect to common ethical values.

The status of the doctrine of the two realms was essentially the same as in German Lutheranism. The Lutheran stance of submission to the state and the church's restriction of its scope to the "spiritual" realm went unquestioned. There was thus no tradition of the official church challenging the state, and neither the Russian Revolution, the rise of a militant Marxist labor movement at home, nor the rise of Fascism provoked a reevaluation of the traditional church-state relationship. The church, therefore, was not theologically prepared to face a totalitarian state.[26]

That did not mean, however, that it was a servile church when state decisions crossed orthodox interests. The flashpoint between church and state after World War I was the state's appointment of theological liberals to church offices, and Jens Gleditsch's appointment as Bishop of Nidaros in 1923 is illustrative of a pattern that persisted throughout the era. Gleditsch was an accomplished man, "a living synthesis of pastor and European" who symbolized "the liberal spirit."[27] As a liberal, he was not high on the list of the church's preferred episcopal nominees, but the government appointed him on the principle of equality: liberal theology had a constituency and ought be represented among the bishops. The orthodox were outraged that the state's commitment to equality took precedence over its constitutional obligation to uphold the Evangelical Lutheran religion, which was to be interpreted as they understood it.

Nor could the orthodox find redress in the courts, as a famous encounter revealed. Arnulf Øverland, a poet and at that time a Communist, lectured in 1931 on "Christianity—The Tenth National Plague." Øverland painted Christianity as a sinister religion that endorsed cannibalism and crippled young minds. It was time for Europe to put it behind and eliminate obligatory religion classes in the schools. Øverland's characterization of his faith offended Hallesby, who sued him for violating the country's blasphemy laws, which protected any legally recognized religion from offensive criticism. The court, however, found the defendant not guilty, leaving orthodox Christians disappointed and puzzled. If Øverland was not guilty, why were blasphemy laws on the books? What could Article 2 of the Constitution still mean? In retrospect, the answer is that the state was deconstructing the unitary religious state and reconstructing a pluralistic one.[28] For that project to succeed, the "Evangelical Lutheran Religion" as objective truth had to give way to its being one truth among many, within the church as without.

In spite of the conflicts, all parties in the church supported the church-state status quo because they benefited from it. Liberals retained legitimacy in the church and access to church positions they might not get otherwise, and the orthodox mission societies retained the primed mission field created by compulsory religion classes in the public schools.[29] But the church-state conflict demonstrated that a large segment of the church did not suffer from state servility, and general satisfaction with the status quo represented a kind of internal unity.

CHRISTIANS AND POLITICS

In 1940, Norwegians assumed that their nation and culture were "Christian." The evidence was in the Constitution, the laws, the state church, the school curriculum, and in moral norms, culture, and social life. Nevertheless, Christianity and a Christian culture had been under attack by the intellectual elite since the 1880s, and between 1920 and 1935 the assault was led by the Norwegian Labor Party.

At the core of the interwar conflict was the Christian attempt to maintain a limited, Christian, cultural state and the labor movement's intention to replace it with a social democratic secular one. In the church's view, a "good society" emerged from individuals exercising moral choice, forming a "right disposition," and having "right family and sexual morals." Unlike Labor Party ideology, this form of "individualistic" Christianity did not include a sense of social ethics.[30] Labor Party values, on the other hand, were rooted in the economically and politically disenfranchised labor class, which never saw its condition measurably altered by individual acts of Christian charity. The labor movement believed that only through systemic restructuring of the economy, society, and the state could the working class have a just share of society's goods. Marxism not only interpreted their condition, it provided a political program for economic justice. The primary question facing the labor movement in the early twentieth century was whether justice would be achieved by revolution or through the ballot box.

Differences between Labor and the church were initially sharp. The Labor Party of the interwar era was led by Marxist materialists. It believed that the revolution might be necessary to institute the Socialist state, but it competed simultaneously in democratic politics. It was opposed by Christians who considered Christianity and Marxism to be incompatible and by church leaders who were critical of the Labor Party's secular values and totalitarian tendencies. The arena of conflict was the ballot box.

In the Storting election of 1918, inspired by the Russian revolution of the year before, the Labor Party adopted a revolutionary platform that proposed eliminating religion classes from the public schools. Several Christian Labor Party leaders and members left the party in protest, and Christians organized to bring out the anti-Labor vote.[31] The result was an election setback that led to the Labor Party dropping the proposal. However, it was reinserted into the 1930 election platform in response to a widely read 1923 treatise called *Communism and Religion* by Edvard Bull, a militant Marxist professor. The party's official stance remained revolutionary, and the elections became a referendum on democracy and religion. Voter turnout rose 9.5 percent, including a 12.5 percent increase in female voters, of whom large numbers were Christians.[32] The result was a 25 percent drop in the Labor Party's Storting representation.

Some factions within the Labor Party's leadership had never been happy about their party's militant anti-religion stance, and the 1930 elections confirmed that anti-Christianity was an electoral liability, especially in the mission society strongholds of the South and West. For the 1933 elections, therefore, the Labor Party ran on preserving religion classes, without saying that they should be confessional.[33] The new policy bore immediate results. Labor won 40.1 percent of the vote and 69 of the 150 Storting seats. Two years later it increased its electoral share to 42.5 percent but added only one more Storting representative. The party leadership attributed the lower-than-expected increase in representation to "low church" (i.e., mission society) agitation in the South and West.[34]

Electoral success softened Labor's rhetoric, particularly after Johan Nygaardsvold formed a Labor government in 1935. The Labor Party government proved pragmatic and even conciliatory, symbolized by its appointment of the pro-church Nils Hjelmtveit as Minister of Church and Education.[35] Christian political engagement and resistance was one reason for the outcome, demonstrating that Norway's Christians could mobilize effectively when core values were at stake. Labor's pragmatic church policy did not mean, however, that it was going to be deflected from creating a social democratic welfare state based on secular values.

ON GERMAN NATIONAL SOCIALISM

Norway had deep and longstanding ties to Germany. The two countries had engaged in trade since the Middle Ages, Germany was the motherland of Lutheranism, and German was the dominant second language taught in the schools. Before World War II, Norwegians followed developments in Germany more closely than those in any other country, and every segment of society had contacts in the corresponding German segment. The best scholars among the bishops, clergy, and theological faculties had attended German universities, almost as a rite of passage.[36]

Some clerical voices expressed sympathy for the National Socialist revolution during its early stages. In April 1933, for example, a young scholar and clergyman, Thorleif Boman, wrote admiringly of the revolution in the Christian daily newspaper *Dagen*, and in January 1934 Hallesby praised Hitler and his renewal of Germany. In the course of 1933 and 1934, however, as the revolution revealed more of its character, church supporters of the Nazi revolution became isolated voices or joined the NS.

The reaction of these clergy supporters was in marked contrast to that of the laity. Journalist and author Ronald Fangen, for example, asserted that Nazism was a form of ethnic and national idolatry that was irreconcilable with Christianity.[37] More influential still was *Dagen*, which represented the low-church orthodoxy of the mission societies in the West. Its editor, Johannes Lavik, and foreign correspondent Arne Giverholt consistently condemned National Socialism's promotion of "paganism," racism, and, above all, anti-Semitism, as incompatible with Christianity.[38]

The pattern of increasing disillusionment among the clergy carried over to the German church struggle. Leading clerical observers reserved judgment in the first months of the church revolution, but opinion hardened once the German Christians took control. The pivotal event was the Prussian Union Church's "Brown Synod" on 5 and 6 September 1933, when the German Christians passed a law requiring clergy to commit to the "national government" and excluded clergy of non-Aryan descent from offices in the church. After the synod, Giverholt wrote that the German "Volk" church had become a "Nazi sect," and Ivar Welle returned from Germany feeling like he had visited another planet.[39] Virtually all Christian commentators thereafter sided with the Confessing Church.

The person whose opinion mattered most was Bishop Eivind Berggrav. He had been visiting Germany since 1907, had studied at Marburg, and spoke fluent German. He had deep sympathy for German suffering during World War I and a high regard for his German friends, the "decent" Germans. Their initial support for Hitler contributed to his own cautious optimism in the opening months of the Nazi revolution. As the German Christians took over the church, however, he condemned them as "a Nazi Church," and by the end of March 1934 he feared that "ruin may now be the only rescue for German Christianity."[40] He nonetheless derived lessons from observing the German church struggle that he would apply in his own church's encounter with a Nazi state.

ON "THE JEWISH QUESTION"

The Jewish community of Norway had only a short history, because the Constitution excluded Jews from the kingdom until 1851. In the next twenty-five years, only a handful of Jews immigrated, but after 1875 a few hundred came from Denmark, the north German province of Schleswig-Holstein, and central Europe. From the 1880s, Jews from the Baltic states and eastern Europe accounted for most of the influx, and in the 1930s, an additional few hundred German and central European Jews were granted asylum from Nazi persecution. Of the approximately 2,100 resident Jews in 1940, about 1,400 were Norwegian citizens, with most of the rest in transit to other countries.[41] The majority settled in Oslo and Trondheim, where they built the two synagogues in the country.

In spite of the country's exclusionary pre-modern history, Norwegians liked to think they did not have a so-called "Jewish problem."[42] In the 1930s, anti-Semitism was sufficiently unacceptable to public opinion, the media, and the major political parties that Norwegian Jews lived with a general sense of security.[43] But the country was also exceptionally homogeneous and correspondingly xenophobic. As a result, Norway had a highly restrictive interwar immigration and refugee policy, which affected Jews.[44] Norway did not want immigrants or a "Jewish problem," and it allowed only about 600 Jews into the country between 1933 and 1940, most on a temporary basis.[45]

In a recent study, Torleiv Austad summed up the predominant prewar attitude of Christians toward Jews as indifference, along with a strong current of anti-Judaism and a very small current of anti-Semitism.[46] But if there was indifference and anti-Judaism in the church, it was also rare for Christians to be anti-Semitic or condone persecution of Jews. An exhaustive study of literature about Jews between 1980 and 1940, for example, yielded virtually no instances of Christian anti-Semitism but several denunciations of anti-Semitism and the persecution of Jews.[47] Indifference did not mean condoning anti-Semitism or persecution of Jews, particularly among the laity tied to the mission societies.

Overt anti-Semitism generally appeared in extreme right-wing groups, and perhaps the most striking way to understand the degree to which church opinion rejected anti-Semitism is to consider the Christians who were members of Fascist National Union Party (*Nasjonal Samling*, hereafter NS) as it became an openly Nazi party.[48] Article 22 of the NS platform called for protection of Christianity's "fundamental values," and in 1933 politically right wing Christians joined the party thinking they had joined a conservative national party with a clear Christian and anti-Communist profile. Enough Christians were drawn to the party to form a distinct Christian faction, and anti-Semitism was initially confined to a rival National Socialist faction. In 1935, however, NS leader Vidkun Quisling adopted anti-Semitism as a political strategy, and in 1935 anti-

Semitic rhetoric began appearing in the NS media. Christian members registered the change, and when they understood that Quisling had sanctioned the anti-Semitic rhetoric, almost all of them left the party. For them, "National Socialism and racism were neo-paganism and irreconcilable with a Christian view of life."[49]

The NS Christian reaction was significant. When the most nationalistic and politically reactionary Christians could not reconcile Christianity with racism and anti-Semitism, the key condition for Christian support of Nazi ideology was absent, and a major condition for resistance was in play.

ECUMENICAL IMPULSES

Because no one in the Church of Norway found it necessary to rethink its traditional theology of the state, there was no Lutheran political ethic to draw on when the church faced a Nazi regime.[50] Within the international church community, however, the ecumenical movement—a Protestant movement for Christian unity—was engaged in a fundamental rethinking of church and state issues. This reconsideration began at the Uppsala Conference of 1917 and continued at the greatest ecumenical event of the modern era, the Stockholm Conference of 1925.

With the growth of Communist and Fascist states in the 1920s and early 1930s, the church-state issue forced itself to the foreground of ecumenical discussion, culminating in 1937 with the Oxford Conference on Church, Community, and State. It is striking how many themes from Oxford appeared in the Church of Norway's resistance to Nazism: the sovereignty of God and his will in all of life; God as the source of justice; the state as guarantor and servant of justice; the primacy of obedience to God over the state; the church's duty to criticize a state that departs from standards set out in God's Word; and, most importantly, the "duty" of disobedience to a state that fails to uphold "the standards of justice set forth in the Word of God."[51] The church was not called just to defend its own freedoms and rights within the state, as the German Confessing Church had done; it had a responsibility to hold the state accountable to "the standards of justice" for the sake of human freedom and rights.

The Oxford Conference also offered strategic guidelines and practical suggestions for churches confronting a totalitarian state. At issue was the church's right to fulfill its mission, and the conference spelled out the essential conditions for doing so.

> We recognize as essential conditions necessary to the Church's fulfillment of its primary duty that it should enjoy (a) freedom to determine its faith and creed; (b) freedom of public and private worship, preaching and teaching; (c) freedom from any imposition by the State of religious ceremonies and forms of worship; (d) freedom to determine the nature of its government and the qualifications of its ministers and members, and, conversely, the freedom of the individual to join the Church to which he feels called; (e) freedom to control the education of its ministers, to give religious instruction to its youths, and to provide for adequate development of their religious life; (f) freedom of Christian service and missionary activity, both home and foreign.[52]

If these and other conditions were not met, it was the duty of clergy and laity "to do all in their power to secure this freedom, even at the cost of disestablishment."

In the Church of Norway, a handful of church leaders were engaged in the ecumenical movement. Among them, Berggrav was the outstanding figure. His ecumenical initiation went back to 1903, and he attended the conferences at Uppsala in 1917 and Stockholm in 1925. He did not attend the Oxford Conference, but it is inconceivable that he did not read its reports.[53] After becoming Bishop of Oslo, in the very year of the Oxford Conference, he assumed leadership of the three branches of the ecumenical movement in Norway (Faith and Order, Life and Work, and the World Alliance for International Friendship Through the Churches). This consolidation vaulted him into the leadership of the ecumenical movement at home and abroad.

PREPARED TO RESIST?

Was the Church of Norway prepared to resist a Nazi state or would it, like the Lutherans of the German Evangelical Church, be prepared to go a long way toward accommodation? On the basis of its "individualism" as defined by Smemo, its active and anti-authoritarian laity, the laity's willingness to confront the state and take on moral and cultural issues in the public square, the laity's political engagement, and the general rejection of racism and anti-Semitism as anti-Christian, there were reasons to think not. But considering the church's failure to rethink the traditional interpretation of the two realms, the clergy's tradition of state servility, the clergy's embededness in the state's civil service, and the church's internal divisions, there were compelling reasons to think it would. On 8 April 1940, no one could have answered the question with confidence.

PART II

*Invasion,
Accommodation,
Collaboration*

—

Chapter 3

Weserübung

PEACE MEDIATION

Germany invaded Poland on 1 September 1939, and three days later the United Kingdom declared war on Germany. The United Kingdom, however, was not prepared to go to war on Polish soil, leading to the "Phony War," a pause in hostilities that would last over seven months. The bishop of Oslo was one of many who saw an opening and threw themselves into mediating a peace settlement.

Berggrav knew that he could use the ecumenical movement as a platform to promote reconciliation, but he faced a problem: as long as there was no reconciliation within his own church, he had no credibility attempting to reconcile the warring powers. This was another idea from the Oxford Conference on Church, Community, and State: the church had to embody the qualities on which it called the world to account.[1] It occurred to him that an appeal co-signed with Hallesby would be a dramatic gesture.

Berggrav and Hallesby had seen each other only once in the last dozen years, exiting and entering an Oslo streetcar.[2] Convinced that Berggrav was a theological liberal, Hallesby had famously declared in 1937 that until the new bishop of Oslo renounced his liberal past and unconditionally confessed the church's creed, "we shall pray."[3] Berggrav himself was reticent about placing himself in any camp, but his general mindset was certainly liberal. After consulting trusted colleagues, he set aside his apprehension at meeting his most severe critic and telephoned Hallesby with his proposal. To Berggrav's surprise, Hallesby agreed. On 6 September 1939, "God's Call to Us Now" appeared in major Scandinavian newspapers. It appealed for calm, responsibility, prayer, solidarity with both sides, and peace.[4]

"God's Call to Us Now" had immediate consequences. Leading Norwegians urged Berggrav to make a last-ditch effort to prevent war, and he threw himself into a round of Scandinavian and ecumenical peace initiatives between Holland, Berlin, and London that would not end until 31 January 1940. In the course of his personal diplomacy, he met and took the measure of both the English foreign minister, Viscount Halifax (Edward F. L. Wood), and Hitler's designated successor and commander-in-chief of the German Air Force, Hermann Göring. His efforts over several months ended in failure, because, in his judgment, neither side trusted the other.[5]

Berggrav did make a final trip to Berlin on 18 March, a last ditch effort at the urging of an English businessman, reputedly with close ties to the British Foreign Office, and the Swedish foreign minister, Christian Günther. The plan was unrealistic and the mission was utopian, but it was a measure of the desperation to avoid war. Hitler and Italy's Benito Mussolini were already meeting at the Brenner Pass, and, as Günther put it to Berggrav, "Go! The time is 10 minutes to 12."

In Berlin, Berggrav met with Secretary of State Ernst von Weizsäcker, who told him that not much could be done to prevent war. The doomsday clock was in fact at five minutes to twelve, but they scheduled another meeting at von Weizsäcker's home. The diplomat arrived late, his face ashen. Once they were alone, he leaned forward, as if about to fall, and burst out, "There's going to be *war! War! War!*" The scene, wrote Berggrav, was "overwhelming."[6] He flew back to Oslo thinking it must be midnight.

But it was not quite midnight, and in Oslo Berggrav faced unfinished business. On 30 November 1939, the Soviet Union had invaded Finland, starting the so-called "Winter War." The Finns had fought with extraordinary bravery and initial success, and the Norwegian public felt deep solidarity with their Scandinavian neighbors. More than 700 men volunteered to fight the Russians, the public contributed generous stocks of food and supplies, and there were numerous calls for the government to provide military aid.

The government, however, was cautious. It faced neutrality violations by both Germany and the United Kingdom and wanted to avoid being drawn into war. Military aid to Finland could lead to a Soviet alliance with Germany against Norway and the Allies, a possibility that Britain and France also feared. The government thus offered only token military aid to Finland, vetoed a possible transit of French and British troops through Norway to Finland, and interned Finns who strayed across the border.[7] The government of Sweden made similar calculations, and without outside military support Finland could not hold out.

When the Winter War finally ended on 12 March 1940, the Finnish defeat left many Norwegians, including the Church of Norway's bishops, ashamed at their country's failure to extend effective aid to the Finns. To show solidarity and mend fences with the Church of Finland, the bishops decided a visit from Berggrav was in order, and on 30 March he left for Finland. He was in talks with Bishop Aleksi Lehtonen in Helsingfors—now Helsinki—when midnight struck.

ENTER QUISLING

While Berggrav had been engaged on a peace mission between London and Berlin, the NS leader, Vidkun Quisling, had been in Berlin on a mission of his own. His name has already appeared, but he needs a fuller introduction if the rest of this story is to be understood.

Vidkun Abraham Lauritz Jonssøn Quisling was born on 18 July 1887 in Fyresdal, Telemark, the eldest son of the parish pastor. He was a precocious student, excelling in mathematics, immersing himself in Norwegian history, and graduating from Norway's army college with exceptional grades. He became a respected Army major, gained military and humanitarian relief experience during the Russian and Ukrainian famines of the 1920s, returned to Norway, and from 1931 to early 1933 served as a controversial minister of defense in the Agrarian Party government (*Bondepartiet*).

Finding no existing party suited to his escalating ambitions or his evolving ideology, on 16 May 1933 he launched the National Union (Nasjonal Samling or NS) party. It was an anti-democratic, anti-Communist, authoritarian national party, and in the 1933 Storting elections it attracted only 27,847 of the 1,248,236 votes cast (2.3 percent) and did not win a single seat. In 1935, the NS evolved into a racist and anti-Semitic imitation of German National Socialism, but that agenda did not produce better election results, and in 1937 a decimated NS contested its last election.

Quisling was led by vision more than facts. In his own mind, he was the prescient interpreter of an evolving universe and the prophet of an imminent new age. In the philosophical worldview he called Universism, some aspects of the old order would be absorbed into the new, but much would be left behind.[8] Thus Christianity would not endure, but its "fundamental values"—as the party platform put it—could be carried forward; Article 22 of the party's platform, which called for protection of Christianity's "fundamental values," thus had its real meaning in the context of Quisling's Universism. Even after he was reduced to the *Fører* (leader, as in the German *Führer*) of a few hundred true believers, Quisling trusted that Fate had chosen him as the prophetic and self-sacrificing Christ of "The New Age."[9]

In obedience to Fate, Quisling decided to commit treason, to use Germany to advance his political agenda at home. For Quisling, what he was about to do was anything but treason. He was simply trying to find a way to save Norway from itself—from a broken parliamentary democracy, from the dilution of its Aryan race and national culture, from the conspiracies of Anglo-American Jewish plutocrats, and, above all, from international Communism and Socialism, represented abroad by the Soviet Union and at home by the Labor Party. He wanted a pan-Germanic new order to which Norway would contribute as an independent nation, and the best chance to achieve that goal was to forestall a British invasion with a German one. His immediate need, however, was German financial support for his nearly defunct party, and that was the reason he was in Berlin on 10 December 1939.

Quisling very quickly became a pawn in other people's plans, above all Admiral Erich Raeder. Raeder had been trying to persuade Hitler that an invasion of Norway would secure bases for naval operations in the North Atlantic. So far, he had not been able to convince Hitler, but he thought Quisling might. In two meetings with Hitler in mid-December 1939, Quisling argued for Norway's strategic significance, the necessity of a German invasion, and the NS's readiness to help.[10] Following their meetings, Hitler ordered a feasibility study, which escalated swiftly into Operation Weser (*Weserübung*), the simultaneous invasion of Denmark and Norway. It would be the first combined air, sea, and land invasion in the history of warfare.[11]

INVASION

The invasion began just before midnight on 8 April and achieved total surprise. Denmark capitulated within hours, and within a day the Wehrmacht (German armed forces) occupied the major Norwegian population centers and most strategic military sites. The only German setback was the sinking of the heavy cruiser *Blücher* as it approached Oslo with high-ranking military and Gestapo officials on board. Otherwise, Hitler's luck held. The Norwegian government had not prepared for the possibility of a German invasion, and on 8 April it had been focusing on a crisis due to British mining operations in its territorial waters, overlooking reports of a naval fleet heading north on the Kattegat. Once the invasion started, government miscommunication delayed mobilization and spread confusion in the ranks.

At 1:30 A.M., the Norwegian government convened. Three hours later, the German ambassador, Curt Bräuer, appeared and announced that Germany had invaded to forestall the Allies and demanded immediate surrender. The Norwegian government had agreed in advance that, if forced to choose, it would ally itself with the United Kingdom. It thus rejected the German ultimatum.[12] Shortly after 7 A.M., King Haakon VII, Crown Prince Olav, government ministers, representatives of the Storting, and military and civilian officials left Oslo by train for Hamar, intending to continue the war in northern Norway. On the way, the Storting stopped briefly at the small town where the Constitution had been signed in 1814. There it passed the "Elverum Authorization," granting the sitting Labor government authority to act on Norway's behalf until the Storting could reconvene. The king, prime minister, cabinet, and entourage then continued north and west to the coastal town of Molde. They were only a few miles ahead of the Germans, who advanced northwards through Gudbrandsdalen and Østerdalen into central Norway, as well as northward from Trondheim.

The Norwegians hoped to delay the Germans long enough for Allied troops to arrive. Anglo-French forces arrived between 18 and 23 April, but they arrived too late and with too little force. To make matters worse, they conducted what Churchill himself called a "ramshackle campaign" in southern Norway.[13] By 3 May the Germans controlled the entire country south of Trøndelag, the county surrounding Trondheim. In the meantime, after a harrowing trip across the central mountains, the king and government reached Molde, where they embarked on the cruiser *Glasgow* and reached Tromsø on 1 May. Military prospects looked better in the north, and on 28 May French and Norwegians forces recaptured Narvik, a strategic harbor for the export of Swedish iron ore in the winter months when the Baltic was frozen.

Hitler had kept him in the dark about every aspect of Operation Weser, but Quisling assumed that the NS was still part of German plans. On the evening of 9 April, he went into action by bluffing his way into the Norwegian Broadcasting Corporation. There he announced that the "national government has taken over governing power with Vidkun Quisling as head of government and foreign minister."[14] Proclaiming that resistance was useless and criminal, he rescinded the government's general mobilization order. Quisling had embarked on a course of ideological collaboration, charting a political course in behalf of Germany for the sake of their shared ideology and, he thought, common political goals.[15] Within Norway and without, his name became instantly synonymous with "traitor"—in several languages. His was a fateful decision, but Quisling believed in Fate.

BERGGRAV AND THE POLITICS
OF OUSTING QUISLING

Berggrav left Finland on the first plane to Stockholm, where late on 9 April he caught the night train to Oslo. In the early hours of 10 April, the train made its first stop inside the Norwegian border, where passengers bought Oslo's morning papers. Quisling's coup attempt was the topic of conversation, interspersed with the words "civil war."

Once in Oslo, Berggrav first thought his place had to be with the church. As the day progressed, however, he had a growing apprehension that the political ambiguity and "nervous unrest" in the people were leading to "chaos." The next day he changed his mind. Order, he convinced himself, belonged to the kingdom of God, and "brotherly love" compelled engagement to prevent civil war.[16]

For Berggrav, Christianity was action, and a Christianity that was not national was "just a religion, but no true Christianity."[17] Jesus' humanity and the incarnation mandated that Christians immerse themselves in the reality of what it means to be human, and to be human was to be a member of a nation. There was nothing in his temperament, faith, concept of the church, or career to suggest that he could have watched from the sidelines—or that he should have. Few national leaders still in Oslo matched his political acumen, leadership skills, international experience, knowledge of Germany, or fluency in the language of the occupiers.

His decision, however, was almost as fateful as Quisling's. In the aftermath of invasion, people are initially in shock and disorientation that soon turns to the imperative of survival. Quisling's announcement did not simply add to the shock and disorientation of the invasion, but compounded the complexity of the politics of invasion and its aftermath. Berggrav's decision was a choice for administrative collaboration. He aimed to defend his country's national interest, but he had also entered an ambiguous political space.

The ambiguity faced him almost immediately. No sooner had Berggrav made his decision for engagement than the German ambassador, Curt Bräuer, approached him for help. German Foreign Minister Joachim von Ribbentrop had ordered Bräuer to negotiate the surrender of the Norwegian government and organize the administration of the occupied territory, while Hitler had ordered Bräuer to arrange for Quisling's installation as prime minister, with King Haakon's approval. The problem was that King Haakon and Foreign Minister Halvdan Koht had already rejected German proposals to install Quisling as head of state, and a desperate Bräuer needed help to change their minds. Unfortunately for Bräuer, Berggrav was no help. Norwegians could answer to only two possible authorities, he informed the ambassador, King Haakon and the Constitution or German bayonets; Quisling was not an option. Berggrav was expressing the consensus view that was emerging among leading figures still in Oslo.

The abrupt departure of the king, the government, and the Storting had created a political vacuum that forced other tiers of society in Oslo into a political role. In the second tier was the only intact branch of government still in the capital, the Supreme Court, which normally did not function politically. A third tier consisted of high-level civil servants and national business and labor leaders. A fourth tier also emerged that historian Ole Kristian Grimnes has termed "the political Oslo milieu," a diverse group from tiers two and three as well as "active individuals" drawn into action by the crisis; from this milieu the later civil and military resistance would emerge.[18] Berggrav was both a high civil servant and one of the "active individuals."

Within the political Oslo milieu, Bräuer's consultations set in motion a series of meetings and initiatives to oust Quisling and establish an alternative administration in the occupied territories. To signify the involved individuals' conscious assumption of a political role of collaboration in order to secure the national interest, they will be referred to here as "the Oslo coalition." The coalition embarked on a strategy of collaboration with the Germans for the sake of reestablishing public order, maintaining the economy, and retaining as much Norwegian administrative control as possible. Theirs was a policy of administrative collaboration, to be distinguished from the ideological collaboration chosen by Quisling and the NS. But their decision placed them in a political grey zone, because as long as their government was at war not too far to the north, their actions were open to doubt, misinterpretation, and disagreement.

The Oslo coalition's decision was based on the premise that German military forces in the occupied zones were too powerful to justify armed resistance and that a prolonged economic standstill was not in the national interest. It also assumed that a Quisling government was unacceptable, as was one imposed by the Germans, because government administration should remain in Norwegian control. For that control to be constitutionally and politically legitimate, however, it needed the government's authorization. But the Norwegian authorities could not be reached. Faced with mounting German pressure, the coalition turned to the Supreme Court, the only branch of state still in Oslo.

With Berggrav as a central participant, the Oslo coalition agreed on a plan whereby the Supreme Court would authorize an administrative council in place of Quisling. The idea faced constitutional obstacles, but German pressure kept building, and on 12 April Chief Justice Paal Berg convened the Supreme Court to discuss how to authorize an administrative alternative. As the court met, Bräuer informed von Ribbentrop of the meeting, stressing that a solution was in sight and that Quisling remained the problem. Bräuer also insisted on a clear order from Berlin.

On Sunday 14 April, Berggrav made telephone contact with Storting

President Carl J. Hambro, who had escaped to Stockholm. It was the first direct communication between the Oslo coalition and a member of the government or the Storting since the invasion. Hambro agreed that Oslo needed "a kind of state-municipal administrative agency" under the leadership of Oslo and Akershus County's chief administrator, I. E. Christensen. This agency would have administrative authority without being a "government," and Hambro thought he could reach the king and the prime minister to speak on behalf of the proposal.[19]

The call became controversial.[20] Berggrav had failed to mention the Supreme Court's involvement in the proposal, leaving Hambro with the impression that the proposal was about a municipal or, at most, a regional administrative arrangement authorized by the government and consistent with the Constitution. With the Supreme Court's sanction, however, the proposed agency could be interpreted as a legitimate alternative government, hence the German interest in it. Not realizing that Berggrav had unintentionally misled Hambro about the scope of the Oslo coalition's proposal, the Supreme Court proceeded with the plan.[21] The Court understood that the Constitution made no provision for the crisis it faced, but Chief Justice Paal Berg argued it contained provisions that "in a way" gave the Court the right to intervene in extraordinary circumstances.[22] At a late afternoon meeting, the Supreme Court voted seven to four with two abstentions to authorize an "administrative council." Late that night, von Ribbentrop informed Bräuer that Hitler had agreed to an administrative council but insisted on an honorable exit for Quisling.

Faced with a humiliating and bitter defeat, Quisling called Berggrav twice on Monday, 15 April, urging him to stop the plan. Quisling assumed that Berggrav personally could undo it, but Berggrav refused to make any such move. From that moment, an angry Quisling held Berggrav directly responsible for his ouster and saw him as no more than a politician in clerical garb.[23] The charge was not the whole truth about Berggrav, but engaging with the Oslo coalition to oust Quisling was undeniably political.

"EVERYONE WHO ACTS RESPONSIBLY BECOMES GUILTY"

The military situation remained tense around Oslo. Quisling's ouster was still not public knowledge, and saboteurs and snipers harassed the German army. To signal the prospect of "a legal settlement of administration in the occupied territory with the understanding of the German ambassador," Bräuer asked Berggrav to broadcast an appeal for calm.[24] The legality of the proposed settlement was still in question, but Berggrav agreed to the appeal on the assumption that the consent of the king and government would be given shortly. He also assumed that the national interest in occupied territory was a quick return to normality and was, therefore, different than in territory that was still a battle zone.

Berggrav quickly regretted the broadcast. Although he substituted "with the understanding of" in place of "in cooperation with" the German ambassador, he also stated that the Norwegian government had directed authorities in Oslo to cooperate "for the protection of those who have nothing to do with the war."[25] Berggrav seems to have inferred this, because there was no such directive, and how could Norwegians have "nothing to do with the war" when their government was still battling the invader in other parts of the country? A second problem was not of his making. Following Berggrav's talk and brief statements by Chief Justice Berg and the Oslo Police Chief, Kristian Welhaven, the Germans concluded the taped addresses with a proclamation by the German army's General Nikolaus von Falkenhorst. The sequence left listeners with the impression that the broadcast was simultaneous and under German orders. To all appearances, Berggrav had moved beyond administrative collaboration to become an ideological collaborator, a "Quisling."

Unfortunately for Berggrav, he strengthened that perception in two other incidents. On Monday, 15 April, a journalist reported that German troops had surrounded demobilized soldiers north of Oslo in Nordmarka and Krokskogen, shooting them as snipers or starving them out and refusing to pardon them. Responding to anguished parents, Berggrav skied into Krokskogen with a three-man police escort to aid the young men.[26] A German officer requested a photograph of Berggrav calling to the Norwegian soldiers through a megaphone. The persistent officer promised that the photograph would be solely for private use, so Berggrav reluctantly allowed it. He continued into Krokskogen, calling at intervals until he encountered a ski patrol of six or seven soldiers, whose uniformed leader informed him of their military assignment. Berggrav returned to Oslo reassured that only regular army troops were in Krokskogen, not soldiers out of uniform or civilian snipers.

Berggrav reported on his trip to the man who had authorized it, Major General Erwin Engelbrecht, only to learn that someone had shot at German soldiers from a house in Hønefoss. Engelbrecht told him that he had decided to imprison the men of the town, shoot a hundred of them, and burn the houses. The general's words left Berggrav shaken to the bone, fearful for his country.

Concerned about useless civilian casualties, Berggrav took to the airwaves again on Tuesday, 16 April, this time to inform the public about the Hague Convention's rules of war and to warn against civilian involvement in military actions.[27] He advised civilians to refrain from bearing or hiding arms and neither to shoot German soldiers nor to engage in sabotage; such acts were the greatest violation possible against fellow citizens and could result in reprisals costing hundreds of innocent lives.

What Berggrav did not say, because he did not realize it himself, was that his interpretation of the Hague Convention applied only to occupied territories; there was nothing in the Convention that prevented a civilian from shooting soldiers in battle zones.[28] He also urged people who had fled during combat to return to their homes, act normally, and conduct themselves with dignity. Many people, he reassured listeners, could say a lot about "goodness and chivalry" among the Germans.

Berggrav's good intentions were generally understood within the occupied territory, but his words had another effect on the other side of the battle lines. Prime Minister Johan Nygaardsvold and his cabinet were listening with mounting anger until a disgusted Einar Gerhardsen turned off the radio before Berggrav had finished. Foreign Minister Halvdan Koht responded officially in a broadcast from London on 5 May, expressing his outrage at the brutality of the German invasion before directing his charges at Berggrav:

> And the German government still dares through Bishop Berggrav in Oslo to send out a request to the Norwegian people not to violate human rights rules on war in their resistance to the brutality and to encourage all peaceful citizens to feel safe. It is a sin and a shame that a senior Norwegian civil servant could allow himself to be driven to make such untruthful claims.[29]

Koht's accusation had the force of treason, and Berggrav knew he was "a suspect man."[30]

Berggrav was further compromised when the April issue of the Wehrmacht's magazine *Signal* appeared on newsstands. It contained the German officer's photograph of him in Krokskogen, with a caption stating that he was calling on Norwegian soldiers to cease their "meaningless resistance." Although Berggrav had said no such thing and had refused Major General Engelbrecht's request to do so, the *Signal* cover reinforced the impression of collaborationism. Berggrav protested to the High Command of the Wehrmacht, which apologized and confiscated remaining copies, but the damage was done.[31]

Public attacks on Berggrav continued throughout April and May. At home, many people were incensed at his words and actions while Norwegians were still fighting the Germans.[32] Abroad, the respected Swedish editor of *Göteborgs Handels- och Sjöfartstidning*, Torgny Segerstedt, declared that Berggrav's willingness "to go on errands for the Germans" would "never be forgotten." Church of England leaders charged that he was a "Quisling," and the Norwegian BBC broadcast a series of attacks. Friends and colleagues in the ecumenical movement were equally appalled.[33] Even the Germans thought he had helped their cause. Hitler was still worried about resistance behind the lines, and German reports to Berlin acknowledged the effectiveness of Berggrav's radio appeals, noting the gratitude of local German authorities. Both the Germans and their Italian allies used the incidents in their propaganda.[34]

Because of German press censorship, Berggrav could not answer his critics. The allegations hung over him for months, causing great personal distress. Berggrav had good intentions, but he could be impulsive and, with respect to the Germans, still naïve. He learned the truth of Dietrich Bonhoeffer's observation that "everyone who acts responsibly becomes guilty."[35]

TERBOVEN

On Monday, 15 April, Bräuer announced Quisling's demotion and the formation of an Administrative Council. As a solution to an immediate problem, this announcement had a calming effect on the public, and the choice of Didrik Arup Seip to direct the Ministry of Church and Education reassured the church. Seip was rector of the university, an active Christian, and Berggrav's brother-in-law, and he worked to protect church interests.[36]

The Administrative Council, however, satisfied no one. As Bräuer saw it, the Council's task was to maintain the central administration and ensure compliance with German orders. But the Administrative Council operated on the premise that the Germans were the enemy and cooperation would be limited to necessary tasks in conformity with the Hague Convention. It was a provisional administrative solution that was unavoidably politicized and could not serve German interests for long.[37]

Within a few weeks, Hitler was so dissatisfied with the Administrative Council that he fired Bräuer and reverted to an office that German governments had employed in emergencies, the Imperial Commissioner or *Reichskommissar*.[38] He would use the same office in Denmark and the Netherlands, and his choice for Norway's Reichskommissar was Josef Terboven.

Born into a Roman Catholic family on 23 May 1898, Terboven served in World War I, joined the German National Socialist Labor Party in Essen as member number 25,247, and ascended rapidly through the ranks. In 1928, Hitler appointed him District Leader of Essen. Autocratic, arrogant, and ruthless, he was also an effective party leader and administrator.[39] In 1933, he was promoted to party Assault Division (Sturmabteilung) Group Leader, and, two years later, he became First President of the Rhine Province.

Terboven had abandoned his Catholicism and was hostile to Christianity, but in the Catholic Rhineland he was forced deal discreetly with the church. In Gau Aachen and Cologne, for example, he circumspectly exploited weaknesses in the church leadership, but he became more aggressive as the local church struggle heated up. From his Rhineland experience, Terboven learned that the most resistant institution to Nazification was the church.[40]

On the day Germany invaded Poland, 1 September 1939, Terboven became Reich Defense Commissioner under Hermann Göring, his mentor and friend. He had reached the top echelons of the Nazi party and the German state. For that reason alone, he was not pleased when Hitler appointed him Reichskommissar of Norway.[41] Hitler formulated his orders in the Führer Directive of 24 April 1940, charging Terboven with protecting the interests of the Reich and granting him supreme authority in civil affairs. Terboven could rule through the Administrative Council and Norwegian authorities, but there was nothing in the wording that bound him to do so. Similarly, Norwegian law remained in force to the extent that it was compatible with occupation, but Terboven could enact laws on his own authority. Article 6 made it clear to whom he was beholden: "The Reichskommissar is my immediate subordinate and receives instructions and orders from me."[42] Norway was to become part of the future Greater Reich, and Terboven was to pave the way.

Terboven arrived in Oslo on 23 April, to the consternation of the Administrative Council. Without the king's authorization, the Council's position was uncertain, and Terboven fanned apprehensions by stating that he expected their cooperation.[43]

True to his Rhineland experience and Hitler's orders, Terboven avoided provoking the church. In Germany, the church struggle had shown Nazi leaders that "criticism of the regime possessed a greater potential force within the churches than in other sectors," and that alignment had limited success within the Roman Catholic and Protestant churches. Shortly after war broke out, therefore, Hitler directed that "no further action should be taken against the German Evangelical and Catholic Churches for the duration of the war."[44] The same policy would apply in Norway. On 1 June 1940, Terboven announced that "I am not thinking of placing any difficulties in the way of confessional or religious activity that stays free of political formulations." He also informed his staff that he wanted calm in church affairs and ordered that "everything must be avoided that would jeopardize the peace."[45] This would be Terboven's guiding principle for the duration of the occupation, and as long as the Administrative Council handled its affairs, the church did not test the limits of "political formulations."

Terboven maintained a low profile during his first months in office. Norway had not yet capitulated and his own agency, the Reichskommissariat, was not fully operational. Behind the scenes, however, he consolidated his power. He met Quisling on his first day and left convinced that he was incompetent and that the NS was in disarray. His dismissive judgment of Quisling made a political settlement more difficult, because in late April neither Hitler nor Terboven knew the way forward.[46]

Terboven also moved swiftly to concentrate political power in his office.[47] One of his first moves was to close the German embassy in Oslo and arrange for the transfer of its personnel back to Berlin. More importantly, he secured the cooperation of *Reichsführer SS* Heinrich Himmler, the man in charge of all German police and the Defense Unit (*Schutz-stafel* or S.S.), the Nazi party's "state within the state" and "army within the army."[48] In exchange for not challenging the independence of the S.S. in Norway, Terboven secured a say in appointing the top S.S. officers assigned to the country. These moves meant that within weeks of his arrival, Terboven had secured his ability to act unhindered by institutional or legal restraints in the civil sector. His only constraint was Hitler's authority and unpredictable will.

CAPITULATION

The King and the government reached Tromsø on 1 May 1940, prepared to carry on the military resistance. The government tried to mitigate Tromsø's resulting susceptibility to German attack by spreading its offices around the town. The Ministry of Church and Education settled into the bishop's quarters and appointed Bishop Wollert Krohn-Hansen to take charge of the Church Division.

The arrangement was short-lived. On 10 May, Germany invaded Belgium, the Netherlands, and France. Two weeks later, France faced collapse and the Germans were gazing across the English Channel. Needing to defend their own countries, the British and French governments withdrew military forces from northern Norway. Without Anglo-French forces, the Norwegian Army had no chance of defeating the Germans, and on Friday, 7 June 1940, the government ended its military operations in Norway and sailed for London. Three days later, the Norwegian Sixth Division capitulated. At the cost of about 1,000 Norwegian lives, Operation Weser was over.

Chapter 4

Forging a Front

———

THE DECISIVE WORD

From London, the Norwegian government would continue the war, but at home its military capitulation cleared the path for Adolf Hitler to resume demands for a political settlement with the appearance of legitimacy. The only way to his goal was to negotiate with the most "legitimate" groups left in the country—party politicians, government officials, and the Oslo political milieu. These groups now entered a process that Ole Kristian Grimnes has termed "political collaboration" in the national interest. The so-called National Council Negotiations began in June, had an interlude in July and August, and ended in September.[1]

The June negotiations were about relentless German demands and successive Norwegian concessions. Terboven's representative, Dr. Hans Delbrügge, opened on 13 June by presenting the Administrative Council with a list of demands: depose the royal family and the government-in-exile, reconvene the Storting, and form a new government. He insisted on a response by Monday, 17 June. Most of the 22 Norwegian participants—the Administrative Council, political party leaders, Chief Justice Paal Berg, Berggrav—favored concessions in order to keep the national administration under Norwegian control. Berggrav was one of four who rejected the demands unconditionally. In spite of his stand, and in part because of his German fluency, the group elected Berggrav to the nonpartisan negotiating team along with Berg and Administrative Council member Ole F. Harbek. The team's mandate was to negotiate on the condition that the king and government would not be deposed. When Delbrügge rejected the conditions, the team members pulled out.

Most Storting representatives had not left the country for London. Those who remained included the Storting's Presidium, which was now the appropriate political team to continue the next stage of negotiations. But the Presidium used its mandate to make a series of concessions. The critical day was Monday, 17 June, when news arrived that France had capitulated and was negotiating for peace. To the Norwegian negotiators, the news felt like "a world was collapsing and that it was a matter of saving what could be saved."[2] Sensing their despair, Delbrügge rejected the Presidium's latest concession and made a series of proposals in the form of demands: the Presidium was to name a national council and convene a meeting to determine its jurisdiction, and the Storting was to retract the Elverum Authorization, withdraw recognition of the government-in-exile, request the king to step down temporarily, and direct the national council to take over the functions of the king and the government. The Presidium accepted Delbrügge's conditions with one proviso: King Haakon was not to be deposed. Delbrügge rejected the condition and broke off the negotiations.

Delbrügge's decision weighed heavily on Ingolf E. Christensen, chief administrator of the county of Oslo and Akershus and chair of the Administrative Council. He had no confidence in the Norwegian people's ability to endure direct German rule. To avoid that prospect, he urged the Presidium and party leaders to take the position that King Haakon had to abdicate. Berggrav, who was also invited to the discussions, felt that the king was non-negotiable, and he pulled out of the process. Delbrügge soon pushed the Presidium and the politicians to their knees. They agreed to ask King Haakon to abdicate voluntarily; if he refused, the Presidium would initiate proceedings to depose him.[3] On 29 June, the Presidium's request reached the Norwegian government in London.

Berggrav was appalled by the developments. He was ashamed at the unwillingness of the politicians to trust the people, act on principle, or accept responsibility for their decisions; not a single politician commanded his respect.

As June turned to July, the public was also uneasy. During the occupation's first weeks, accommodation to the German invasion was surprisingly swift among some of the population. Attendance at German military band concerts was high, many women openly consorted with German soldiers, and, as invasion gave way to occupation, firms and laborers pursued lucrative contracts and high wages offered by the Wehrmacht. The public was also aware that self-appointed elites in Oslo had brought down Quisling and created the Administrative Council, but their anonymity and secrecy were disturbing. Finally, there were the rumors about Quisling lobbying in Berlin and returning to power.[4]

If the transition from accommodation and national collaboration to resistance had a precise date, it was 8 July 1940, the day King Haakon announced he would not abdicate. Before the king's stand, the Storting had appeared ready to accept a national council, even if it included NS representatives. After his stand, opinion swung against it, compelling the Germans to craft a settlement without the political or legal legitimacy they had sought. Because the king and government refused to legitimate German power and continued the war, social mobilization against Germany occurred earlier in Norway than elsewhere in occupied Europe.[5]

THE TEMPORAL AND THE ETERNAL

In the months between the invasion and a new political settlement on 25 September, there were few fixed points to guide the decisions and conduct of either leaders or the public. If the German Reich was the Norwegian future, where and how were the lines to be drawn between Norwegian and German interests? In economic life, for example, Norwegian businesses and labor were already involved with the Germans by the summer of 1940, earning high incomes for building military installations and selling supplies. Where was the line between necessary cooperation to keep the economy moving and economic collaboration to build and maintain German military power? That line was never strongly drawn.

In the Church of Norway, the only leader thinking strategically was the bishop of Oslo. To clarify the legal framework of the occupation and articulate a Christian spiritual and moral posture in the midst of the uncertainty, Berggrav conferred with the other bishops and then wrote *The Temporal and the Eternal*. Distributed in July as a pastoral letter to the entire church, the document illuminates Berggrav's thinking when the political terms of the occupation still remained unknown.[6]

Berggrav's guiding legal principle was that within occupied Norway,

German-Norwegian relations were to be conducted according to the Hague Convention of 1907, which Norway had ratified. The Convention's Article 43 specified that legislative power resided with the occupier. The Convention also stipulated that the occupier was to respect Norwegian law as far as possible, but in cases of conflict the occupier's decrees had priority over the Constitution, Norwegian law, and the decrees of the Norwegian government-in-exile. Berggrav could be naïve in dealings with the Germans, but on some occasions he only appeared to be, as in this appeal to the authority of the Hague Convention. Without believing that the Germans would hold to any promises, he assumed the authority of law in preparation for the church-state conflict that he knew was bound to come. To even pretend that the Germans would obey rules and laws, the church had to do so itself, scrupulously.[7]

Berggrav's immediate concern in *The Temporal and the Eternal* was to establish the authority of "God's Word" and of conscience in relation to the state. He drew on the traditional Lutheran parallel between the inner person and the outer body and between the eternal and temporal realms to make the case: "For the Christian and for the church, God's Word and conscience bound by God's Word stands above all human power and law if there is conflict in the innermost depths." Still, Christians remained responsible for knowing the law in order to know when an appeal to God's Word and conscience was valid. The same principle applied to the church and ecclesiastical law. The Convention allowed the occupying power to assume the authority constitutionally delegated to the government, but the Convention also stipulated that the occupier had to respect religious convictions and the free exercise of religion. Referring to Terboven's statement of 1 June that he would not "interfere in religious affairs," Berggrav assured readers that no authorities thought this should be otherwise.

This section of *The Temporal and the Eternal* was a defining statement about the church's legal status under German occupation and the principles on which its future relations would be conducted. The church would continue to function as a state church, but the relationship had legal parameters within which the church could challenge the state. The occupier had authority in the church, but it did not have authority to violate God's Word, conscience bound by God's Word, the church's identity as a Christian church, or the church's confession. Berggrav's concern at this initial stage was to prevent the occupation from diluting or fragmenting spiritual and moral life. In his mind, Christianity and the moral life that arose from it were one and indivisible. Occupation was not an excuse for avoiding moral responsibility or thinking morality and law were fluid. Situations could arise that required breaking traditional law and taking a stand that was *"fully responsible to God and human beings"* (Berggrav's italics). In sum: Christians were morally accountable to God in a situation of choice, and even occupation was a situation of choice.

The Temporal and the Eternal also aimed to establish a Christian basis for resistance. Berggrav thought of a Christian national stance—a Christian patriotism—as determined by God's Word and the Christian history of Norway. From the king and saint Olav Haraldsson to the revival preacher Hans Nielsen Hauge, Christian patriotism had entailed a sacred obligation to God. The patriotic dimension of Norwegian Christianity was acquired by growing up and living in the country, but the Christian dimension entailed cleaving to the deepest inner reality—God. The struggle for God was thus the struggle for the soul of the people. In sum, *The Temporal and the Eternal* was a Christian manifesto that articulated the legal, theological, and ethical ingredients of a Christian posture in uncertain times and established a spiritual framework for Christian resistance to a Nazi state.

BERGGRAV, HALLESBY, AND HOPE

On 25 September 1940, the Germans announced a political settlement, the political framework of their occupation. Quisling and the NS had maneuvered a return to power: the Germans would rule through a Commissarial Council (*Det Kommissariske Statsråd*) in which ten of the thirteen commissioner ministers were NS members. All ten of the NS ministers had sworn an oath of loyalty to Quisling, who presided over weekly meetings of what amounted to a shadow cabinet. Terboven was still the final authority, but it was clear that the NS now intended to Nazify Norway. This settlement and its consequences are a topic for the next chapter, but the announcement needs to be noted because it gave a new urgency to the church's persistent divisions.

Berggrav soon went into action, drawing on several lessons from the

past. The first was from 1931. Faced with the possibility of a revolutionary Labor Party forming a government, Berggrav had then explored the
idea of the Bishops' Conference forging an alliance with leaders of the mission societies.[8] From his participation in the ecumenical movement, he also
believed that the church's universality had to be maintained and expressed
in time of war. From his mentor, Archbishop Nathan Söderblom of Uppsala, Sweden, he had learned that mediation and reconciliation were the
guiding principles of Christian politics; those were the principles behind
his mediation efforts during the Phony War and his call for peace with
Hallesby in September 1939. Finally, the German Kirchenkampf and the
divisions of the German Protestants had taught him that the church had
to forge a unified front in order to effectively confront a Nazi state. It was
time to apply the lessons and put the principles into action.

Although they had broken the ice in 1939, Berggrav and Hallesby still
had not met. What drove Berggrav to Hallesby's door on 16 October
1940 was the prospect of a divided church facing a state that was already
displaying its ideological aims.[9] He put the challenge to Hallesby: Nazism
threatened the church and Christianity, and only a united Christian front
could effectively resist it. Hallesby admitted to similar thoughts, but he
could only cooperate with someone who subscribed to the Augsburg
Confession without reservations. As the discussion progressed, Hallesby
narrowed his criteria to two articles of the Apostles' Creed: the Virgin
Birth and Jesus' bodily resurrection. Berggrav assured Hallesby that
those articles did not pose a problem. Without pressing for a more precise
explanation, Hallesby took Berggrav at his word.

The next hurdle was Hallesby's ultimatum of 1937 that Berggrav
had to renounce his liberal past and subscribe without reservation to the
Lutheran confessions if he wanted the cooperation of the mission societies. Berggrav countered that his whole life was his confession; were that
not evident, he said, a few words would not put the matter to rest. After
a long discussion, Hallesby was convinced that they shared the same
faith, and, uncharacteristically, was willing "not to become hung up on
words and formalities."[10]

This meeting was a pivotal event in the history of the church. Had Berggrav not persuaded Hallesby of their shared faith, and had Hallesby not
tolerated some ambiguity in Berggrav's explanation, a unified church front
would have been doomed. It was also aided by the fact that the private

Hallesby was quite different from his severe and polemical public persona; by most accounts, the private man exuded a "warm humanity."[11]

With Hallesby on board, the example was set for other mission society leaders to follow, beginning with Ludvig Hope. Although retired, he was the spiritual leader of the Norwegian China Mission Association, which was so anticlerical that "church" was a frightening word to many members. The society had also refused to join the Council of Autonomous Organizations. Insiders even advised Berggrav against approaching the society if the front included Hallesby's pro-church Norwegian Lutheran Home Mission Society, and Hallesby himself was skeptical.[12] But Berggrav and Hope had met for the first time the year before and were surprised at how much they had in common. Hope had also welcomed Berggrav's and Hallesby's call for peace in September 1939, and the two men had similar reactions to the post-invasion developments. So when Berggrav appeared at his front door on 17 October, Hope exclaimed, "I have been waiting for you!"[13]

Presented with Berggrav's proposal, Hope quickly agreed. He was surprised by Hallesby's accommodating attitude and evidently decided that the circumstances required that he too set aside his society's prewar policy of non-cooperation with liberals, the church, and the other mission societies.[14] He agreed to join and, surprisingly, foresaw no problems from the China Mission Association. With Hope's consent in hand, Berggrav had cleared the final hurdle. As he put it himself, the names of Hallesby, Hope, and Berggrav constituted "a triangle that had contained the most typical and sharp differences in Norway's Christian world."[15] Their mere appearance on the same platform would signal a sea change—and the seriousness of the moment.

THE CASE FOR A CHURCH FRONT

Berggrav's concept of a unified church front was embodied in his proposal to establish the Christian Consultative Council (*Kristent Samråd*, hereafter the CCC). The CCC would fuse the functions of the Bishops' Conference and the Council of Autonomous Organizations and represent the church and its member organizations in all discussions with the state.

To present his case, he met with the bishops and mission society leaders on the evening of 25 October 1940. The meeting was historic, because, for the first time, bishops and leaders of the societies convened as equals.[16] The meeting was a matter of urgency: a month earlier Terboven had installed the NS Commissarial Council, and it was already Nazifying the government administration.

Berggrav argued his case with persuasive logic, drawing in his listeners with inside information on political developments after 9 April. To address the issue of why unity was necessary, his central point was that Terboven's installation of the Commissarial Council represented a shift in German policy. The Germans, said Berggrav, probably had no intention of starting a political revolution when they invaded, but they changed their minds when Quisling maneuvered behind Terboven's back to gain the support of National Socialism's chief ideologue, Alfred Rosenberg, and through him the support of Hitler. Rosenberg's support meant that the ideological battle would soon come, and the battlegrounds would be young people, schools, culture, and the church. Everyone had to see that National Socialism's ideology and practice were a satanic attack on "Jesus Christ and his gospel," and that Nazis would, as in Germany, employ "brutal Gestapo violence . . . unrestrained deceitful propaganda . . . seductive policies" and "crude threats" with grave consequences for the church. At stake was "our being or not being as a Christian people."[17]

What should be done? The German church had three weaknesses: it was "eine Pastorenkirche" ("a pastors' church") without broad support from the people, it was split into many churches, and it was riven by "unholy fragmentation and even unholier personal and group dissension." Even the Confessing Church was split by bitter resentments. Opponents could play one leader or faction against the other and use every crack to undermine the church

And the NS, Berggrav continued, would begin their attack in the cracks. The Norwegian church had its own fissures, and the NS advocates in the church were already exploiting them. But eventually they would launch a frontal attack on the "faith and the confessions" and relegate Christianity to "a catacomb existence." The result would be a society without regard for conscience, justice, or law. In short, the Germans did not install a Norwegian administration on 25 September but "an agent for the National Socialist worldview" and "the occupation of our worldview and our Christian culture." To prepare for the coming conflict, Berggrav pressed the point that the church had to create a unified front that would send a clear signal to an uncertain Christian community. Nothing they could do would be more important in creating a firm anti-Nazi Christian stance. If the church and the societies held together, the outcome in Norway could be far better than it had been in the German church.[18]

THE CHRISTIAN CONSULTATIVE COUNCIL

At the end of the meeting, the group accepted Berggrav's proposal and signed a declaration about the new body. Its 18 church and mission society leaders represented the entire Church of Norway and its affiliated organizations, but the CCC was to be purely consultative, with no authority over member mission societies.[19] The group chose 28 October 1940 and the Calmeyer Street Mission Hall in Oslo for the public announcement of its formation. The location was symbolic: from the same podium in 1920, Hallesby and the orthodox leaders had launched their attack on the liberals and precipitated the church conflict. The CCC decided not to advertise the meeting, but the news spread rapidly. By the start of the meeting, the 3,800-seat auditorium was filled almost to capacity.[20]

Hans Høeg, chair of the Oslo Diocese, opened the meeting by announcing that the CCC had been brought into being by people concerned about "a proper Christian stance" in the current circumstances. He encouraged Christians to support the CCC without reservation, because "the council wants to follow unreservedly our old proven Reformation and Haugean course on the basis of the inspired Word of God according to our church's confessions." He acknowledged that the CCC was unprecedented but hoped the unity it displayed would be carried forward.[21] Hallesby was the first speaker. "On the ninth of April God placed his mighty hand on all of us here in Norway," he proclaimed. "Everything I saw and heard made me disgusted and bitter, and I struggled with many heavy thoughts—until I caught a glimpse of God's mighty hand." Hope followed with a talk on "Our Christian Heritage," stressing the willingness to sacrifice and suffer to pass on this heritage. Berggrav closed by speaking about the confidence that comes from Christ.[22]

The CCC formally announced itself to the church in a letter of 25 October 1940. The letter spoke of the need for a closer solidarity, but made clear that this was not a body with "organizational authority." The decisive paragraph was the following:

> When we now so boldly encourage our many friends in the different camps to rally around the Christian Consultative Council, it is because the Council plainly wishes to follow our old, tried Reformation and Haugean course on the basis of God's inspired Word according to our church's Lutheran confession. We know in this great and critical time as never before that it is the old unadulterated Gospel that alone can save our people.[23]

The CCC's existence was public knowledge, but the need for confidentiality and secrecy forced it to operate as an illegal organization. It held meetings every ten days or so, but at irregular times, days, and places (usually members' homes), and no one took minutes. Berggrav usually led the meetings, but the agenda was open, deliberations were collegial, and decisions were made by consensus. The meetings would often begin with reports on a particular issue, each of the members contributing intelligence information from the sources known to them. Only the inner circles knew the identities of its members and their responsibility for the church's decisions.[24]

The CCC benefited immeasurably from Berggrav's participation in the leadership of the emerging civil resistance, jokingly referred to as "The High Council."[25] The High Council was an outgrowth of efforts to oust Quisling in April 1940, and it generally met on a weekly basis. Berggrav was thus in regular contact with leaders of other sectors of society, the most important being education and medicine. From its inception, therefore, the CCC acted in coordination with the Home Front Leadership, leaders of the professional organizations, and their respective courier services.[26]

The CCC had to maintain contact with the church under increasingly restrictive conditions. Berggrav, for example, initially held large orientation meetings with the Oslo Diocese's clergy in St. Mark's Church before resorting to contact through the church's Communication Service. The Communication Service enabled the CCC to pass information and messages to a select few of the pastors, who served as couriers and relayed the information to regional and local clergy groups. In the case of the Oslo Diocese, Berggrav divided the diocese into four groups whose leaders met weekly with the CCC.[27] From Oslo, news, messages, and directives (paroler) spread to other dioceses through people in contact with the CCC. In times of crisis, the courier service could distribute documents as often as every other day.[28]

The CCC was well received, inside and outside the church. Most observers understood what it meant—and were surprised that it had happened. The press and the public also welcomed the unity, interpreting the group's formation to mean that old theological battles had been laid to rest. It was widely recognized that the Christian community had entered a new era.[29]

THE LIMITS OF UNITY

Despite the positive reception, the CCC's theological and ecclesiological basis provoked questions and some anguish on both sides of the theological divide. The most vocal critic was the Old Testament professor at the Free Faculty of Theology, Karl Vold, who argued publicly that the CCC had no public mandate, so the church conflict was not over.[30] Vold's comments could be dismissed as those of the cantankerous old professor that he was, but he expressed what many people wondered privately. Was the conflict really over? Had the societies subordinated themselves to the church? And what did the "Haugean course" really mean?

The CCC's public announcement was vague enough for each side to have its desired interpretation, but it was open to serious questions.[31] Hallesby himself stated that unity had been achieved without compromise, so conservatives were confident that the unity had been achieved on their premises.[32] The liberals took the statement to mean that what united the two sides was now more important than what divided them. Hartvig C. Christie contradicted Hallesby in the liberal church periodical by claiming that the unity was a result of theological and ecclesiastical movement on both sides.[33]

The two perspectives led to additional questions and dismay on both sides. On the orthodox side, Hope faced harsh criticism within his organization, and liberals wondered if they were now expected to fall in behind Hallesby and his followers. The liberal New Testament professor Lyder Brun told Berggrav that the declaration represented "the greatest grief he had ever experienced," and H. C. Christie informed Berggrav that the unity was "a rotten egg."[34] Rumors flew. With the country under German censorship, misunderstanding and criticism threatened the newly forged unity.

To stem the unrest, the CCC issued a clarifying statement penned by Hope, denying insinuations of compromise and affirming the CCC's unity on biblical, Lutheran, and Haugean ground. Should anyone dare to deny fundamental Christian truths, be it by tearing apart the Bible, denying the Virgin Birth, or rejecting the bodily resurrection of Jesus, "then the CCC would certainly not stand in the way of a fight for the true faith."[35]

To reassure their constituencies in person, Hope held meetings in Ålesund and Molde and Hallesby in Trondheim. Hope's task was the more difficult, but his personal authority and assurances stilled skeptics in the West. Hallesby's difficulty was of a different order, and he addressed it with a dramatic symbolic statement. For two decades, he had refused to share a podium with theological liberals, but on 15 December 1940 he stepped up to the pulpit of Nidaros Cathedral in Trondheim with Dean Arne Fjellbu, long regarded as a liberal. The event was a sensation. Hallesby made a point of stating that the orthodox remained faithful to the truth and that the CCC was formed on "the foundation of the inspired Word of God," while Fjellbu felt compelled to declare that he had long since changed his views on the authority of the Bible and liberal theology.[36]

When questions about liberal and orthodox theology were stilled, questions remained about the "Haugean course." Hans Nielsen Hauge's inclusion in the CCC's statement was probably intended to symbolize a distinctively Norwegian Christianity and revivalist tradition linked to the mission societies. Fortunately for the church, Hauge's life and thought were sufficiently broad for both the orthodox and liberals to support the "Haugean course." This is clear in responses to the Christian newspaper *Dagen*'s questions about Hauge: Berggrav and Fjellbu emphasized his obedience to God and his example of an active Christian life; Kristian Hansson stressed his faithfulness to the church; Hope held up his approval of independent lay preaching; and the church historian Andreas Seierstad focused on his grounding in "the Lutheran pietistic doctrinal tradition" and his seriousness about life.[37] Each could see in "the Haugean course" what he wanted, and the phrase's vagueness served its unifying purpose.

Taken as a whole, however, the CCC's basis was an orthodox Lutheran theology that implicitly rejected liberal theology.[38] In the circumstances after 25 September 1940, the CCC could not have been expected to achieve a theological reconciliation before arriving at a working consensus. Furthermore, by 1940 there were relatively few liberals in the church, and it was less important to placate them than to forge a front that included the orthodox—and in many cases fundamentalist—mission societies. In short, better to risk alienating the liberals than the much larger and essential orthodox majority.[39]

EXCLUDING THE FREE CHURCHES

The free churches were also sacrificed for the sake of Lutheran unity. Their leaders welcomed the intra-Lutheran cooperation but were offended at their own exclusion from a "Christian" Consultative Council. The choice of the word "Christian," rather than "Lutheran," was intended to underline the CCC's inclusive nature and aims, but it was also symptomatic of the times that "Christian" was so readily taken as synonymous with "Lutheran." Eilert Bernhardt, for example, editor of the Methodist *Kristelig Tidende*, claimed to speak for Methodists in wishing that *"all* Christians in our land would stand together in a difficult time and be a collective testimony to the world that the Christians are *one* in Christ."[40] "Christian" unity, he thought, should include the free churches.

It did not, but free church leaders also understood the politics of Norwegian Lutheranism. They knew that if Berggrav had attempted to forge a unity that included them, the Lutheran mission societies would not have joined. Berggrav knew it too, but, unlike the rest of the CCC, he realized that excluding the free churches entirely could also be a vulnerability to be exploited by the NS and could put the Lutheran front itself at risk. To create constructive ties, in the fall of 1940 he started convening free church representatives for orientation and discussion. The meetings represented the personal—and somewhat patronizing—style of ecumenism he preferred and at which he excelled. Through them he would keep the support of free church leaders for the duration of the occupation.[41]

IN THE NICK OF TIME

The unity achieved in the CCC was the decisive development in the church's resistance to the Nazi state. It brought leaders of the church and the organizations into a common forum, created a workable basis for a Christian front, unified the clergy, and galvanized the laity. The CCC also had a unifying effect on other sectors that were being challenged by the NS. The divisions in the church were deep and particularly well publicized, but political parties, professional associations, and trade unions had their own rifts. Although forged by external pressures, the CCC's example inspired other national organizations and associations to form united fronts.[42]

The church front was created in the nick of time. By late October, the NS had emerged from the political shadows to take over administration of the country—and had given a green light to violence in the streets.

PART III

Resistance

—

Chapter 5

In Defense of a Just State

—

ASSAULT ON THE RULE OF LAW

When Hitler could not achieve his optimal political settlement, his compromise was the Commissarial Council, installed by Terboven on 25 September 1940. The Commissarial Council was not a government, because each minister answered to Terboven, but the Reichskommissar banned all other parties and declared that the NS was "the Norwegian people's only possible way to freedom and independence." As already noted, ten of the thirteen commissioner ministers were NS members, including the Commissioner Minister of Church and Education.

The NS's immediate aims were to install party members in key state offices, reorganize the bureaucracy, take control of professional and trade organizations, and recruit enough members to convince the Germans that it could form a viable government. The party made reasonable progress toward those ends. By April 1941, it controlled the state agencies, and party membership had increased from 4,202 in August 1940 to 25,914, comparable to the largest parties before the occupation.[1] In the trade and professional organizations, however, massive resistance prevented an NS takeover.

An essential feature of the "New Age" was secret police to counter political resistance. Terboven used the Gestapo to deal with military and civil resistance, and with German oversight the NS reconstituted the Norwegian State Police as a "political police." These changes were most obvious in the streets, where the NS paramilitary organization, the *Hird*, intimidated, bullied, and harassed the public. The NS-controlled police did not intervene or were inexplicably absent.[2]

The disorder in the streets was accompanied by a more fundamental assault on the rule of law in the judiciary. Hitler's directive (*Erlass*) to Terboven authorized Terboven to supersede Norwegian civil laws as needed. To make sure he had compliant courts, Terboven established the German Law Court (*Deutscher Gerichtshof*) and an NS People's Court (*Folkedomstolen*) to deal with civil resistance. In both courts, law served politics.

The Supreme Court justices had considered resigning on 25 September but decided to wait for a direct challenge to constitutional law.[3] That came in mid-November, when the Commissioner Minister of Justice, Sverre Riisnæs, replaced judges and lowered the civil service retirement age from 70 to 65. The Supreme Court considered his actions a threat to their judicial authority and independence and contrary to law, but Riisnæs dismissed their objections. Informed by Terboven that the Supreme Court had no right to judge his or commissioner ministers' decrees, the justices resigned on 21 December 1940.

CHURCH REPRIEVE

Until early 1941, the NS did not pursue an assertive church policy, largely because Ragnar Skancke (1890–1948), Commissioner Minister of Church and Education, had almost no interest in religion. Skancke had been a professor of engineering at the Norwegian Institute of Technology in Trondheim, joined the NS in 1933, and became the party leader in Trøndelag.[4] As Commissioner Minister, he left church affairs to the Director General (*ekspedisjonssjef*) of the Church Department, Søren Oftenæs, who had worked in the department since 1897 and as director general since 1927. Oftenæs was not an NS supporter, but as a senior civil servant, he could not be dismissed without cause. Declining health finally forced his retirement on 1 February 1941.

While searching for a suitable successor, Skancke announced in early October that he would not interfere in the church as long as the church did not interfere in politics.[5] Neither Terboven nor Skancke defined "politics," and only a month later, Skancke reassured Christians that the state would not repress "faith and the Christian person's freedom" but in the same breath demanded that "each one must be a willing servant" in their collective life. It was becoming clear that "politics" meant any words or actions that were not in cooperation with the Germans and the NS state.[6] But for a few months, the church was out of the spotlight.

THE CHURCH'S PRAYER OF INTERCESSION

The church also had a reprieve because Berggrav compromised on an issue that could have split the church at the outset. The Church's Prayer of Intercession (*Kirkebønnen*), a prayer for King Haakon, the royal family, the Storting, and the cabinet, was part of the liturgy. In late July, Terboven ordered Berggrav to delete the problematic political references from the prayer in radio services.[7] Berggrav replied that the Germans had the right to broadcast whatever they wished but not to alter the church's liturgy. Terboven backed down.

The day after Skancke's installation, however, Terboven ordered him to demand alterations in the prayer.[8] Realizing that NS sympathizers among the clergy could use the Church's Prayer of Intercession to pray for Quisling and the Commissarial Council, Berggrav decided that the prayer was not an issue on which to make a principled stand. Instead, he proposed striking *all* political references from the liturgy. To his surprise, Terboven approved the change.[9] The bishops announced the new wording on 30 September 1940, to shock and disappointment in the parishes. But most clergy cooperated and discovered that a meaningful pause after the petition for "our countryman far away and on the sea" fulfilled the intention of the prayer and heightened awareness of the absent king and government. To Berggrav's critics, however, it was one more example of Berggrav's willingness to accommodate the Germans and the NS.[10]

THE SANCTITY OF CONSCIENCE

The church escaped a frontal assault after 25 September, but the NS revolution forced new questions on the clergy. As civil servants, would they be forced to pledge loyalty to the new government, join the NS, or accept NS appointments to government positions? As clergy, would they be pressured to violate the secrecy of the confessional? Faced with such demands, on what grounds could they refuse? Developing answers fell largely to

Berggrav, who wrote a general guideline. In cases of conflict between normative obedience to the authorities (Romans 13) and faithfulness to God (Acts 5:29), the clergy were to obey God. The operative principle was conscience bound by scripture and the confessions.[11]

The NS did not follow through on the threats feared by the clergy, but the appeal to conscience was relevant for others, beginning with teachers. Skancke drafted a circular to be distributed on 20 November demanding that teachers submit a written pledge to "positively and actively" spread the new worldview among pupils and to oppose resistance to NS plans to transform society. Refusal meant dismissal.[12] While Skancke's letter was at the printer, an alert compositor sent it to Birger Bergersen, a professor active in the resistance, who sought advice from Berggrav. The church was embedded in the schools, which were obligated to uphold and teach Lutheran Christianity: religion classes were obligatory, functioned as confirmation classes, and were supervised by the clergy. So Berggrav quickly drafted a statement for teachers to use in response, which Berg-ersen forwarded to Justice Ferdinand Schjelderup. Schjelderup was co-leader, with Chief Justice Paal Berg, of one of the most influential circles opposing the NS's takeover of the professional organizations, a circle to which Berggrav also belonged. Having read the draft, Schjelderup sent it on to the four national teachers' organizations.[13]

Teachers thought of their profession as a calling, and Berggrav tried to formulate a statement that would draw on their positive ideals.[14] He had already appealed to conscience as the basis for the clergy's resistance, and the teachers' declaration drew on the same ideas:

> In response to the received request, I hereby declare that I shall remain faithful to my calling as a teacher and to my conscience, and on that basis I shall hereafter as heretofore follow those regulations for my work in this position that are lawfully issued by my superiors.[15]

The teachers received their standard reply forms before Skancke's circular left the printer, and, faced with mass resistance before his campaign had even started, Skancke aborted it.

Teachers used Berggrav's formulation throughout the occupation, and several other national professional organizations adopted it as well, including senior civil servants, engineers, and architects.[16] The appeal to conscience thus strengthened the moral front that Berggrav had envisioned in *The Temporal and the Eternal.*

CONFRONTING THE STATE

After the formation of the CCC, the bishops had to meet secretly. They agreed on cover names and passwords: a word to a relative or neighbor about a meeting of the coffee club at a given time and place was enough to convene a special session.[17] That was how the bishops scheduled a meeting shortly after New Year's Day 1941. The agenda was a protest against the NS's growing disregard for law and human rights. The church was to retain the initiative and go on the offensive against the NS state on the issues that were creating fear and uncertainty in the people. The bishops and cathedral deans were also prepared to follow the Supreme Court by resigning if Skancke did not provide a satisfactory response.[18]

The bishops addressed their letter to Skancke and dated it 15 January 1941. The opening paragraph was more accusatory than anything the Commissioner Ministers or the Germans had yet seen:

> According to the church's confession, the church stands in relation to a just state, insofar as the state through its agencies is presumed to uphold the God-given order of law and justice. Norway's constitution establishes that "The Evangelical Lutheran religion remains the state's public religion." It is then necessary and relevant for the church to be clear about whether the state, which also administers church affairs, accepts and feels bound by those legal and moral obligations contained in the basis of the church's faith—the Bible and the confession. This is a necessity emerging from the entire nature of the church.[19]

The letter went on to highlight specific incidents of NS violence in the streets, the NS's disregard for law and the independence of the courts, the Ministry of Church and Education's pressure on teachers to support every decision of the new order, and, most recently, the Police Department's claim of authority to the overturn the clergy's "seal of the confessional" (*taushetsplikt*). The seriousness of the letter was unmistakable.

In their letter, the bishops asked for clarification of the issues they presented, and after two weeks with no reply, on 29 January bishops

Berggrav, Støren, and Maroni confronted Skancke in person. They also handed him a memorandum dated the same day, which they proceeded to read to him.[20]

The premise of the memorandum appeared to be inspired by the ecumenical movement and the Barmen Declaration, because it was christological. Christians were committed to Jesus Christ as Lord, "completely and unconditionally," and state affairs became church affairs when they hindered obedience to the lordship of Christ. The bishops, however, did not develop the christological theme, but focused instead on the doctrine of the two realms and the orders of creation. Among God's ordinances, they wrote, were "justice, truth, and goodness as the church sees these realized in a just state," and the church was bound to protest the state's violation of them. The conditions the bishops had previously enumerated conflicted with God's law and gave the "impression of revolutionary conditions in the country," not of a lawful occupation in which laws would be upheld "to the extent they are not directly incompatible" with occupation.

The bishops continued by instructing Skancke on the nature of the church as a community of faith that owed its existence to God and his Word and was not just a state agency. Called forth by God, the church could not remain silent when God's Word was violated and violence, injustice, and the threat of coercion against conscience were allowed to flourish. "Here the church stands immovable," wrote the bishops, "and cannot by its nature be bound by any power of state." The bishops pleaded with the state "to put an end to everything that is contrary to God's holy ordinances regarding justice, truth, freedom of conscience and goodness, and to build unbreakably on God's laws of life." [21]

Skancke must have been hoping to postpone answering until after 1 February, when his new director general in the Church Department would assume his duties, because he was wholly unprepared to respond to the bishops' points. He claimed he had directed his subordinates to read the letter of 15 January, but "they had not found that there was anything to reply to."[22] The subordinate in question was probably Otto Theisen, who was in the room standing behind Skancke and whom Berggrav, at one point in the discussion, dressed down.

Skancke then pleaded ignorance of some cases, trivialized the issues, and otherwise justified the NS and its policies.[23] Outraged by his seeming indifference and incomprehension of the issues, the bishops left Skancke with the memorandum.

Berggrav thought that Skancke did not understand the implications of the bishops' memorandum, that it was signaling a new course for the church.[24] Perhaps not. Skancke replied on 1 February, first by stating that the specific cases of human rights violations referred to by the bishops would be sent to the Justice Department and Police Department for further action. On the other charges, he claimed that the new regime had "not lost sight of preserving legal protection and order," and though the seal of the confessional was never absolute, neither was the government intent on abolishing it. But then he showed that he understood more than Berggrav gave him credit for, because he concluded with a plea for understanding "in the new situation," followed by a warning of his own: actions that created public unrest could have "the most serious consequences for the church."[25]

THE PASTORAL LETTER

In light of Skancke's dismissal of their concerns and before they received his written reply, the bishops had already decided to publicize their memorandum, their correspondence with Skancke, and an account of their meeting in a document entitled *Pastoral Letter to Our Congregations from the Bishops of the Church of Norway (February 1941)*; it soon became known simply as *The Pastoral Letter* (Hyrdebrevet).[26] Berggrav sent the original to the church's printer on Monday, 3 February, with orders for a secret express run and distribution on Thursday, 6 February. He arranged for two copies each to be placed in pre-addressed envelopes and taken to distribution points, where the envelopes would be mailed to pastors and parish councils.[27]

Pastors read the letter to their congregations after the Sunday service on 9 February. Within days, the letter was widely reported in the international press. Support for the bishops came from across the Christian community: from pastors, mission societies, free churches, and individuals. One exception was parish councils, which withheld their support, perhaps out of fear, Berggrav thought; it was still early in the occupation. Nevertheless, the bishops had clearly spoken for the entire Christian community, and the support was too massive for the Gestapo or the Norwegian State Police to contemplate reprisals.[28]

Once *The Pastoral Letter* became public, the Gestapo and the NS grew apprehensive. On Wednesday, 5 February, Gestapo chief Dr. Werner Knab interrogated Berggrav for 90 minutes: Why had the bishops acted so politically? How had copies reached the Swedish papers and the London radio? What did the bishop think of doing next? Berggrav rejected Knab's contention that protesting the Hird's violence constituted "politics." He would not predict the bishops' next move, but acknowledged that resignation was a possibility.[29]

On Saturday, 8 February, Terboven began attempts to confiscate *The Pastoral Letter*. On Gestapo orders, the Norwegian police seized about 14,000 copies, but another 36,000 had already been sent and most of them had reached their destinations.[30] Protests and legal appeals against the confiscation proved futile. Despite this, Berggrav felt like the church "had actually won"—but he was also prepared to be arrested.[31] Nothing happened until Thursday, 13 February, when the Gestapo called Berggrav to Skaugum, Crown Prince Olav's residence now occupied by Terboven, for a 5:30 P.M. meeting about a "special matter." Berggrav arrived to a surprise: facing him was not only Terboven but Gestapo chief Heinrich Himmler, another man whom Berggrav took to be Himmler's adjutant, and Wilhelm Rediess and Heinrich Fehlis, the top police officials in Norway. The "special matter" was *The Pastoral Letter*.[32] The church, Terboven said, had been "reasonable and calm" since the invasion, but it looked like it was changing course and now faced a choice: bind itself to the dead letter of the law or adjust to "the law of life." If it chose the former, the consequences would be dire.

Berggrav pointed out that the situation had completely altered after 25 September. The Hague Convention gave the occupying power certain kinds of legal authority, but not the right to initiate a revolution. The "dumbest thing" the Germans had done was to support Quisling and allow the NS, backed by German arms, to "rape" the Norwegian people. The bishops, on the other hand, had "a task and an authority from the Christian congregation and from God," and the state had no right to intrude on territory determined by "God's law and by God's order." The church would not retreat. The three-and-a-half-hour meeting was revealing. Terboven neither dismissed Berggrav from office nor arrested him, and Terboven and Himmler appeared to be looking for compromise. Berggrav left the meeting with the impression that "we have a stronger standing than anyone would have thought."[33]

A FRAMEWORK FOR RESISTANCE

The Pastoral Letter was occupied Norway's first collective attack on the new order and the first articulation of a theological, ethical, and legal framework for the church's new course—resistance. It confronted the state with the church's rejection of its governing values and with the threat of future non-cooperation. As such, it had a serious impact on the Germans, the NS, the Norwegian public, the church, and the resistance. Moreover, as Bishop Skagestad observed, Terboven's attempt to confiscate it had given it "publicity out of this world" and magnified its impact.[34]

To the Germans and the NS, the bishops had served notice that the church could no longer be taken for granted, and the Germans heard the message. Wehrmacht and Gestapo intelligence reports started giving prominence to the church as a resistance front, and reports of Hird excesses declined, probably on German orders.[35]

The Pastoral Letter also changed the church. The police confiscation brought the "unjust" state into Christians' homes, striking a first blow to "the servile in the Lutheran attitude" and raising questions about the traditional interpretation of the two realms. Gestapo informant Vilhelm H. Günther registered the shift of mood and attitude, "so strong and thorough" that it strained his comprehension.[36]

The Pastoral Letter also had an impact on the wider public. Einar Molland recalled "a not particularly church-going professor reading it with tears in his eyes." In an Oslo taxi, an "I'm no church man" driver told Arne Fjellbu that nothing better had been written in Norway "in this century"; he had distributed "hundreds" of copies from his car. The most visible evidence of its public effect, however, was the rise in church attendance throughout the country, which even the Nazi-controlled press reported.[37]

This response left Berggrav "visibly relieved" and began his national rehabilitation.[38] The Norwegian government registered its "deep joy" at the church's "expression of Christian courage and Christian sense of justice." In May and June, the Norwegian government's Minister of Church and Education, Nils Hjelmtveit, traveled across America speaking about Norway, *The Pastoral Letter*, and the Church's "firm stance." Sweden's *Göteborgs Handels- och Sjöfartstidning* declared that the Norwegian bishops had "secured a place of honor in Norwegian history."[39]

The French student of European civil resistance Jacques Semelin has observed that there is a mutually reinforcing relation between popular opinion and resistance, so that "the main work of resistance is to continue convincing popular opinion of its merits." In the wake of the Supreme Court's resignation, *The Pastoral Letter* spoke with a religious and moral clarity that bolstered the public will to resist and thus helped to "guarantee the conditions" for persistent resistance.[40] Public opinion also protected the church, and Berggrav understood that the people had shielded the bishops.[41]

But *The Pastoral Letter* was only a beginning and a framework, and it contained ideas that needed more development. Minds still needed to be changed about the principles at stake and the justification for resistance. The church had signaled a new church course, but the bishops were not actually prepared to resign, because below the level of the bishops and cathedral deans the church was not ready.

RELIGION, LAW, AND THE TWO REALMS

In the midst of the tension surrounding *The Pastoral Letter*, the ceaselessly active Berggrav continued to think about religion, law, and the just state. With the Supreme Court's resignation, it was clear that the church was integrated into a state that did not recognize the authority of constitutional law, and if the church submitted to the state's instrumental view of law, it would have no legal basis for holding the state accountable. In response, Berggrav developed his central concept of "the just state" (*rettstaten*).

The English word "just" does not convey the full complexity of the Norwegian word "*rett*," which connotes "the right," "right," "rights," "just," "justice," "the law," "law," "court," and "correct," each according to context, while always retaining the full range of meanings. For Berggrav, the just state was one that upheld order, law, and justice.[42]

Berggrav developed his ideas in "Religion and Law," a talk he delivered on 5 February 1941 to the Lawyers Association. His audience must have listened intently in the aftermath of the Supreme Court's resignation, and for Berggrav the subject was very close to home. The day before, he had delivered *The Pastoral Letter* to the printer and just before the lecture had been interrogated about it by the Gestapo.

Drawing on Rudolf Otto's *The Idea of the Holy*, Berggrav made the case for the transcendence of religion and law, both of which applied to human beings but could not be remade by them. Law had to be law and religion had to be religion, and it was the transcendent in each "before which we prostrate ourselves." The transcendent was "the Holy," the objective source of religion *and* law, and it motivated a demand and an obligation.

The human faculty linking God and human action was conscience. "If the law did not transcend man," Berggrav told the lawyers, "it would be mere custom and not law," and if "religion did not transcend man it would merely be the power of emotion and not the power of conscience." Religion and law thus met in the human conscience. God's will was for the church to function in relation to a state that acknowledged and respected the sanctity of justice, law, and conscience.[43]

Berggrav had now developed a cohesive view of God, justice, state, church, and the individual. He had also articulated a theological and legal justification for resistance. But he still faced a formidable challenge in the central Lutheran doctrine: the two realms.

Church leaders had entered 1941 under heightened pressure and with a sense of responsibility to act, but on what basis could they do so? There was no precedent in all of Lutheran history for opposing the state as such, and behind that tradition was Martin Luther, the father of the Reformation, and the status Lutherans accorded to him. "In no other church in Christendom," wrote church historian Einar Molland, "does a person's authority play the kind of role that Luther plays in the Lutheran church."[44] Therein was the problem. Traditional interpretation of Luther's doctrine of the two realms separated the spiritual and temporal so sharply that the church had no theological grounds on which to confront the state. The only way out was to reinterpret the doctrine.

That, it turned out, was not as difficult as it would seem. As Berggrav himself admitted, it was "easier for the devil to read Luther with profit than to read the Bible," and if the devil could quote Luther to advantage, so could he. So in the fall of 1940 and in anticipation of the confrontation to come, Berggrav had directed a Free Faculty of Theology associate professor, Andreas Seierstad, and a parish pastor, Amund Bentzen, to search Luther's works for suitable quotations to stock his "Luther arsenal." The two men produced a 75-page collection, drawn, as Berggrav later put it, from Luther's "creative years."[45]

It was Berggrav's good fortune that his friend Bishop Gustaf Aulén was part of a lively Swedish debate reexamining the doctrine of the two realms. In a book called *Can Any Christian Demand Be Placed on State Life?*, published in 1940, Aulén argued that Luther had distinguished the two realms without separating them and that God intended both realms to live up to his "unconditional demand of impartial concern for the other." The divine imperative was a just state, that is, a state that upheld the law of love and allowed for "positive community." Were the state to claim powers above God by ceasing to be a just state, the church had the duty to call it to account and recall it to its rightful function.[46]

Berggrav read Aulén's book in January 1941, frequently remarking to his wife Kathrine as he read, "It is a long time since anything has meant so much to me."[47] The influence intensified in March 1941, when Aulén used the pretext of an official visitation to Oslo's Swedish congregation to discuss his ideas with his friend.[48] Berggrav then fleshed out his own ideas in a lecture called "When the Driver Is Out of His Mind: Luther on the Duty of Disobedience." He delivered the lecture during the spring and summer of 1941 to clerical and lay audiences "from Trøndelag to Vestfold," and the bishops arranged for the distribution of illegal copies in their dioceses.[49] Berggrav was hoping to break down "the ingrown and compact Protestant loyalty to any kind of authority whatsoever," and his lecture would change the course of Lutheran political thought.[50]

Berggrav built on Aulén's presupposition that there was only one realm, God's realm, and only one obedience in the two dimensions of that realm. The one obedience consisted in promoting love and opposing evil, violence, and unrighteousness. In the spiritual realm, the church exercised its obedience through "the Spirit," and in the temporal realm, the state exercised its obedience through "the sword." It was when the state assumed the power of God and acted "beyond the limits of the will of God" that it subverted law and became demonic and tyrannical, "like a crazed driver or a runaway horse." To be "demonic" was to "lust for power in all its forms and patterns," to exercise "power for power's sake" outside of ethical norms and outside of law. At the heart of this lust was egoism, the unwillingness "to serve love, to serve God."

The obedience of Christians to the state was thus conditional: if the state became the instrument of sin, the demonic, the church was obliged to resist. Faced with an "unlawfully constituted authority," Christians had but a single duty: "to be disobedient." To remain silent was to share in the guilt and fail God.

The duty of disobedience covered a wide range of circumstances, and for each one Berggrav could draw on a Luther quotation. Where the state ignored the law, for example, the following applied: "When your own prince is unjust, are his people obliged to follow him? No, because no one has a right to act *contrary to the law.* The law is the will of God. You are to obey God." Similarly, when the state encroached on the spiritual realm by interfering in the church, Luther wrote: "When they [rulers] want to invade the spiritual realm and take consciences captive—the realm where God alone wants to reign—then one is not to obey them at all."[51] Because the state was subject to God's law, the church was not ignoring the distinction between the two realms when it called on the state to uphold that law.

THE NEXT STEP?

The Pastoral Letter had alerted the clergy to the nature of the NS state but also surprised, stunned, and finally worried them. The letter had put the state on notice that the church's continued loyalty to the state was conditional. But what would happen if the bishops resigned or were dismissed?[52] The bishops themselves were unsure.

There were compelling reasons for the bishops to continue in office. For one thing, the bishops themselves had stated in *The Pastoral Letter* that they recognized German authority and the NS state only according to the terms of the Hague Convention, but they knew the church was neither theologically nor psychologically prepared to sever its ties to the state. Before long, therefore, a consensus grew for the bishops to stay in office.[53] Yet uncertainties remained. The bishops had raised serious questions about the legitimacy of the state's exercise of power—and issued a warning. But if an "unjust" state was insufficient reason to resign, what would be? That was the pressing question facing the CCC after *The Pastoral Letter.*[54] The answer was farther in the future than they could have imagined in February 1941, but as they wrote *The Pastoral Letter,* the man who would contribute to the answer had just assumed his new position.

Chapter 6

The NS Church System

A REORGANIZED CHURCH DEPARTMENT

Sigurd Oftenæs had been employed in the Church Department since 1897 and had been Director General of the Church Division (*Kirkeavdelingen*) of the Ministry of Church and Education since 1927, and in all that time the Church Division consisted of six "offices." Once Oftenæs decided to retire, however, Otto Theisen, who was head of one of the offices, proposed a reorganization that would transfer four offices into a new Management Division (*Forvaltningsavdelingen*).

Theisen had been at the Church Department since 1929 and had only recently joined the NS in order to save, he claimed, the church's land and property. He was a competent administrator widely disliked by fellow workers, but in early 1941 he was an effective intra-office politician. He already had influence with Skancke, who agreed to the proposed reorganization and appointed Theisen to head the new division, responsible for church finances and property.[1] The change left a reduced Church Division of two offices, the Church Office (*Kirkekontoret*) and the Auditing Office for Public Foundations (*Revisjonskontoret for offentlige stiftelser*).

According to the postwar testimony of Henry O. Østlid, Skancke initially leaned toward rural dean Ole J.B. Kvasnes as the new director general of the Church Division, but Theisen backed another rural dean named Sigmund Feyling. Østlid was the Home Front's representative in the department and shared with Theisen an office wall with a built-in cupboard. By opening the cupboard door, Østlid could hear conversations in Theisen's office. According to Østlid, in the course of Feyling's job interview, Theisen talked to him privately in his office. Theisen, it turned out, disliked Berggrav, and he told Feyling it was time to "pin Berggrav up against the wall." After Feyling returned to Egersund, Theisen followed up and persuaded Skancke to pick Feyling. Feyling had no public administration experience, so Theisen became his early mentor, and Østlid had many occasions to establish that Theisen was manipulating things behind the scenes, "pulling the strings in church matters."[2] Feyling, therefore, not only headed a reduced Church Department, he had a formidable intra-departmental equal in the person of Otto Theisen.

ENTER SIGMUND FEYLING

Sigmund Feyling, however, was an opportunist in his own right, what Americans would call a quick study. Born on 8 May 1896 in Egersund, a small town on the south coast, Feyling had a brief teaching career before studying theology at the Free Faculty of Theology.[3] After graduating in 1924, he returned to his hometown as assistant pastor (*residerende kappelan*). Hardworking and respected, in 1929 he advanced to parish pastor (*sokneprest*) in and in 1936 to rural dean (*prost*). Unusual for his generation of clergy, he was interested in Christian social ethics and thought Jesus' preaching of the kingdom of God pointed toward "a conversion of social life." He also had authoritarian inclinations. The thought of Paul Althaus appealed to him, and he was relieved that Germany had won "the race for Norway."[4]

Feyling also suffered from frustrated ambitions. He had applied to 11 positions since 1935, without success. But on 22 November 1940, he joined the NS and submitted an article to *Dagen* with the title "The Church's Yes to the Changed Times in Our Land." The article made the case for the authoritarian state on biblical, confessional, and political grounds. It was the church's hour, he declared, and it was vital for church people to commit to the NS and its cause. His bishop, Gabriel Skagestad, informed him that the article violated Terboven's order to avoid "political formulations" and advised against publication, but Feyling submitted it anyway. The paper rejected it, sparking a controversy that did not end until the article appeared in the NS national newspaper, *Fritt Folk* (Free People).[5] By the time Skancke read the article, Feyling had already sent him a letter, describing his views. His strategy worked, and, on 1 February 1941, Skancke appointed him Director General of the Church Department. The Ministry of Church and Education was the first to fill all its director general positions with NS supporters.[6]

Shortly after his appointment, Feyling went even further in his endorsement of the new order. He wrote an article on "the authoritarian state" in which he argued that God had created the state to have authority to rule, legislate, and enforce law, analogous to the role of the father in the family. To fulfill those mandates, however, the state had to be authoritarian, and the authoritarian state was necessarily totalitarian. "Nothing," he wrote, "is irrelevant (*uvedkommende*) to the state," and the church's duty was to put itself at the service of the NS state: "It is truly the church's Norwegian hour."[7]

THE GERMAN AUTHORITIES

When Feyling assumed office, the authoritarian state was already in place. At its apex were the Germans and their interests, policies, and agents, followed by the NS and theirs. It was not without tensions between the two, but it was a workable system that expected the church to be the state's religious extension.

German jurisdiction over the churches fell to the Wehrmacht, the Reichskommissariat, and the Gestapo.[8] The Wehrmacht generally stayed in the background, the Reichskommissariat was the final authority in church affairs, and Gestapo involvement grew in proportion to church resistance.

Wehrmacht policy was set by General Nikolaus von Falkenhorst, who was assigned to Norway from 9 April 1940 until December 1944. His objective was to maintain his army's freedom of operations and not to interfere in the civil sector except when military interests were at stake.[9] The Wehrmacht had little to do with the churches and mission societies outside of confiscating their facilities, but had its own espionage agency, the Abwehr, whose "Progress Reports" (*Tätigkeitsberichte*) included intelligence on developments within Norway. The church appeared only occasionally in these reports until late 1941 and early 1942, when a section on "The Church Situation" increased in scope and frequency.[10] Abwehr reports on the churches were never as extensive as those of the

Gestapo, but they indicate that the Wehrmacht took seriously the possible military implications of church resistance.

The same was true of Terboven and his agency, the Reichskommissariat. Terboven had final authority in all civil affairs and ruled through directives, the Gestapo, and courts that were instruments of his policies. He usually limited his intervention to matters that threatened his political interests and prestige, particularly his standing in Berlin.[11] Terboven probably treated the church with more caution than any other institution. That was in line with Hitler's wishes and with his own experience in Germany. He thus ordered his staff to avoid doing anything that would jeopardize peace in the church.[12] His general mode of operation was to leave church affairs to internal Norwegian jurisdiction, wanting only to be informed of general trends.

By the end of the summer of 1940, the Reichskommissariat had developed the structure and size that it would retain until the end of the occupation. It comprised four departments: administration (I), economy (II), public information and propaganda (III), and, later, technology (IV), each with several sub-departments. In 1941, the Reichskommissariat had 364 employees, not counting police, and it reached a peak of about 700 in 1943. Department IIId had responsibility for the press, propaganda, broadcasting, culture, school, church, and sports. Josef Goebbels directed much of its work from Berlin, and in Norway he had his own man in charge, Georg Wilhelm Müller.[13] The department controlled the Norwegian media through propaganda and censorship, which applied with equal force to the religious media, including newsletters, periodicals, journals, books, and preaching itself.

Although Department III had a consultant on education, there was none for religion. The reason can only be guessed at. The only official with some expertise in church affairs was the consultant on education, Dr. Alfred Huhnhäuser. His duties required interaction with Skancke and occasional dealings with the church over educational issues.[14] But the lack of a consultant on the church in Department III did not mean the Germans took the church lightly. Quite the opposite. The Germans probably did not expect any problems from teachers, based on their German experience, but they did from the church. That was the most likely reason church affairs were assigned to the Gestapo.

THE GESTAPO

The Security Police and Security Service (*Der Sicherheitspolizei und das SD*) was the Norwegian branch of Heinrich Himmler's Reich Chief Security Office in Berlin. It was not strictly part of Reichskommissariat, but it was under Terboven's personal authority and served as his extra-legal instrument of coercion, the heart of the Nazi state.[15]

The Security Police had six departments, which, in practice, overlapped. Departments I and II were administrative, and III and VI covered intelligence. Department IV was the Gestapo, which dealt with security threats, and Department V was the Criminal Police , handling ordinary crime. Church affairs were assigned to Department IV, the Gestapo.

Within Division IV, church affairs were assigned to Department IV-B, led by Captain (*Hauptsturmbahnführer*)Walter Kohlrep and his subordinate on church affairs Klaus Grossmann.[16] Kohlrep initiated the intelligence gathering operation on the churches. His chief informant on church affairs judged him to be "devoid of any religious knowledge," and he was replaced in mid-February 1941, just as the bishops were indicting the NS state for its abuse of rights.[17]

His successor, Wilhelm Artur Konstantin Wagner, did have "religious knowledge." Born in 1909 in Altenkirche, Westerwald, Wagner studied theology and philology in Koblenz before joining the National Socialist party, and on 1 May 1993 he found employment in the SS. His background and connections later commended him for a position in the Reich Security Main Office (*Reichsicherheitshauptamt*), where he gathered intelligence and reported on church affairs, Freemasons, and Jews until his assignment to Norway. Wagner arrived in Oslo on 13 February 1941 as the Gestapo's Consultant on World View Issues; his immediate superior, Helmuth Reinhardt, assumed his post at about the same time. Wagner's assignment in Division IV-B was to gather intelligence on churches, Jews, and Freemasons and to prepare reports for Wilhelm Rediess, the head of all German police agencies in Norway, and for the Reich Security Main Office in Berlin. His duties also included dealing with the political and legal infractions of groups under his jurisdiction.[18]

Wagner also served as Terboven's liaison with the Church Department. With respect to the church, Wagner performed his duties with discretion, courtesy, and a degree of sympathy.[19] He quickly surmised that Feyling rather than Skancke was "the actual church minister," and the two met regularly to discuss the church and the Church Department's goals and plans. Wagner revealed little at these meetings, but Feyling shared all significant correspondence, his monthly reports to Quisling, and his circulars to the clergy.[20] Wagner's main source of intelligence about church affairs was Feyling, but he also cultivated and paid other informants. The most effective was Vilhelm Hermann Günther, the retired pastor of the German congregation in Oslo. His wife was of Jewish descent, and he had been in a vulnerable position since 1933. Shortly after the Germans invaded, Günther agreed to report on the church on the condition that he would not reveal sources unless these wished to be known; he also omitted or rephrased dangerous statements "in a safe way."[21]

Günther's Norwegian sources were leaders of the church, including Berggrav until he was put under house arrest and thereafter Johannes Hygen, Ole Hallesby, and Johannes Ø. Dietrichson. He told informants what he was doing and to whom his reports were sent, and on that basis he asked what they wanted to convey to the Germans. Within those parameters, Günther was determined to convey the truth, and Wagner found his reports "very objective."[22]

Günther walked a tightrope between the two sides and was bound to come under suspicion. He was under German observation—as, he claimed, was Wagner—and Wagner remembered him as usually opposed to measures against the church. Günther also claimed that NS leaders viewed him with suspicion as a result of statements and events that he deliberately omitted, downplayed, or reinterpreted in his reports; that claim is plausible. On the other hand, only a handful of Norwegians knew the context of his work, and inevitably some church leaders viewed him with suspicion.[23] There is little reason, however, to doubt that Günther favored the church front, and no evidence that his reports compromised church leaders or the church's resistance.

In addition to Günther, Wagner also used NS clergy as informants. When Andreas Gjerdi and Peder Blessing-Dahle were the religious broadcast consultants, they shared with Wagner the list of clergymen who refused to cooperate. Wagner also recruited Gjerdi in the spring of 1942 to report on the mood of his parish; Gjerdi agreed but declined to provide names of his sources, and Wagner had a similar arrangement with Peder Blessing-Dahle. Some of Wagner's other NS clerical sources were true informers, citing names. On the basis of intelligence such as this, Wagner kept files on every clergyman in the country.[24]

The intelligence that Wagner and others gathered was the basis of the monthly Gestapo reports known as "Reports from Norway" (*Meldungen aus Norwegen*). These provided German authorities with a remarkably accurate picture of the Norwegian resistance and the climate of opinion during the occupation.[25] The second section, "Enemies," generally had three sub-divisions: General Resistance Movements, Communism and Marxism, and the Church. It was not the church per se but the political implications of church resistance that drew Gestapo attention. In the welter of Norwegian non-political institutions and organizations, the Gestapo viewed the church as a singular source of civil unrest and resistance.

Through Wagner's work, the Reichskommissariat maintained such accurate intelligence about religious affairs that it was rarely taken by surprise. Wagner also followed Terboven's instructions about avoiding conflict with the church, and only rarely did he intervene in church affairs. When he did, it was to prevent NS excesses.[26] But Wagner did intervene in cases of church political speech, such as in sermons, or other actions against Germany. Furthermore, when clergymen or others identified with the church distributed illegal materials, stored arms, or engaged in military resistance (*Milorg*), they were referred to the Gestapo's Department IV.[27]

THE NS GOVERNMENT

Before his formal accession to power on 1 February 1942, Quisling's role in church affairs was minimal, but thereafter he assumed authority in all political, legal, and administrative affairs, including the church. As such, he authorized all important laws and made the final administrative decisions. He could become quite engaged in church affairs during a crisis, and he occasionally intervened directly, but he left routine matters to Skancke and Feyling.[28]

Skancke was the Commissioner Minister of the Ministry of Church and Education, but he made no pretense of interest in religion or willingness to acquire competency in church matters. He thus abdicated his responsibility to his director general in the Church Department, Feyling. So complete was Skancke's abdication that Feyling always wondered if Quisling was adequately informed about church developments. One employee in the Church Department thought Quisling routinely bypassed Skancke to deal directly with Feyling, and the evidence supports that observation.[29]

Between Feyling and Skancke was a political office, the State Secretary. The first State Secretary was Nicolas Solberg, who was appointed in November 1940; he was succeeded in July 1942 by a teacher, Ole B. Pedersen. Second in command to Skancke, the State Secretary had administrative oversight of the Ministry and was the liaison to the NS. He was responsible for the "new order" being implemented in the ministry and handled the media.[30] All church matters intended for Skancke were funneled through the State Secretary, but neither Solberg nor Pedersen seemed to interfere with Feyling's access to Skancke.

Feyling was thus the architect of NS church policy and, as the church struggle intensified, the state's primary agent in the prosecution of religious resisters. To initiate proposals for new laws and regulations directed against the church, Feyling followed procedures established by Quisling and his staff. He would first consult with Skancke, presumably a perfunctory step in most cases, and then with Wagner. Once Skancke and Wagner agreed on a set of proposals, Skancke presented them to Quisling at the weekly Minister Meetings for final action. Skancke presented only the most important recommendations to Quisling for authorization as law. Once agreement was reached on proposals' final form, the decisions went to Terboven for approval before publication as laws.[31]

As the church struggle heated up, Feyling employed spies to gather intelligence on oppositional clergy and used the State Police as enforcement agents. He relied on reports from salaried Church Department spies, paid informants, NS clergy, and police investigators for information on bishops and clergy. He then consulted with colleagues in the Church Department and, after the climax of the church struggle in 1942, with the NS appointed bishops. In deciding the best course of action against opposition clergy, he claimed to give greatest weight to the opinions of the NS bishops.[32]

Though the Ministry of Church and Education was the government's administrative arm in religious affairs, the Ministry of Justice had jurisdiction over the free churches, as before the occupation. Feyling's ultimate aim, however, was complete centralization of church affairs under his jurisdiction, and on 26 March 1942, he won a prolonged bureaucratic tug-of-war and acquired jurisdiction of "the Dissenter congregations" and the Christian organizations (i.e., mission societies) as well.[33]

THE AGENTS OF ENFORCEMENT

When the Germans invaded and occupied the country, the relationship between the German police and Norwegian counterparts was tighter than in any other sector.[34] German police agencies were primarily political, however, leaving daily police work largely in the hands of Norwegian police forces.

Once the NS took over the government in 1940, it wanted a politically reliable police force. Under Jonas Lie, the State Police was established on 1 July 1941 as a political force to deal with resistance. Lie had difficulty recruiting reliable NS police officers, but by January 1942 he had built a force of 152, all but five of whom belonged to the NS. At its height in 1944, the force had 350 employees.[35] State Police headquarters were in Oslo with regional offices in Stavanger, Bergen, Trondheim, and Tromsø.

As church resistance escalated, the Church Department would turn increasingly to the State Police.[36] The police chief, Karl A. Marthinsen, worked closely with Feyling on enforcement. In the Oslo headquarters, cases involving the churches fell under Division V-A, which was also responsible for ordering and coordinating the regional police. As a rule, neither Division V-A nor the regional offices took action against the church without conferring with Feyling and receiving orders from Marthinsen.[37]

The State Police dealt with the churches in two stages: intelligence and enforcement. State Police began spying on the clergy on 1 March 1942, and agents were particularly active in times of crisis.[38] Agents were either NS members who informed on the clergy or police agents assigned to observe worship services. An NS informant's report proceeded through church channels until it reached the Church Department. If the case was serious enough, Feyling informed the State Police and advised a formal investigation.

Local State Police agents reported on church services to ensure that pastors refrained from sermons or prayers that were "political," defined by reference to current developments in church or society. Reports went up the chain of command, starting with the district State Police chief and ending up in Division V-A.[39] From there, the division chief sent copies to Feyling, Wagner, and, after 1 January 1944, to the leader of the State Police's Division III, the security police, whose officials commented and made recommendations. Through either of these two routes, intelligence reports on church opponents ended up on Marthinsen's desk. If he deemed the violations serious, he ordered a policeman to question the suspect and witnesses about the complaints, and, either before or after the investigation, would request an opinion from the Church Department. Feyling would usually respond by stating which district he wanted the bishop or pastor removed from and which one he should be sent to. Once all procedures had been followed, Marthinsen made the final decision and directed the local State Police to carry out the order. Although there were instances of the State Police behaving rudely or brusquely, officials generally conducted themselves professionally in their dealings with resistant clergy.

BETWEEN THE FRONTS

There were several "cracks" in the German and NS system of repression, beginning with a member of General von Falkenhorst's General Staff, Theodor Steltzer, and ending with the staff of the Church Department. These would ensure that the church had reliable information, permitting the church to plan with some knowledge about the opposing front.

Steltzer was a Christian from Schleswig-Holstein who became friends with Berggrav through the ecumenical movement.[40] He was drafted into the Wehrmacht and assigned to the Army General Staff in Norway as Transport Officer. He arrived in Norway on 1 August 1940 and shortly thereafter contacted Berggrav, who put him in contact with Arvid Brodersen, a sociologist at the University of Oslo, and eventually with Jens Christian Hauge, the leader of the Norwegian military resistance (*Militær Organisasjon* or Milorg).[41] Steltzer was also a member of an order in Germany called the Brotherhood of St. Michael. Founded in 1931, it comprised high-church Lutheran clergy and laity who followed a rule of spiritual practice. Several members, including Steltzer, would later found the resistance group the Kreisau Circle, which was behind the failed July 1944 plot to assassinate Hitler. Through the Brotherhood of St. Michael, Steltzer contacted a parallel Norwegian Lutheran organization called *Ordo Crucis* (Order of the Cross), formed in 1933. That group included Einar Molland and Berggrav's young clerical protégé, Alex Johnson, who would represent the church in the civilian resistance group called the Coordination Committee and in the later Home Front Leadership.

Steltzer had regular meetings with Brodersen and Berggrav, mediating between the Wehrmacht and the Norwegian civil resistance. Steltzer informed Berggrav that the Wehrmacht was subordinate to the National Socialist party's political decisions, and that General von Falkenhorst "did not have the power to make a decision contrary to the Reichskommissar." He also disabused Berggrav of any notion that Norway could maintain a state of law, but argued that a call to violent resistance would be pointless, given Germany's overwhelming military power. Berggrav should, however, call for resistance "as soon as the inner situation of the church" was threatened."[42] Steltzer did not disclose Wehrmacht secrets, but he shared information that allowed the Norwegians to have an accurate picture of the Wehrmacht, and vice versa. He also used information from Norwegian contacts to argue for a humane Wehrmacht approach, often in contrast to the Reichskommissariat. On more than one occasion, his reports altered Wehrmacht policy, and he warned of Gestapo actions that he considered wrong, such as the arrests of university students (see chapter 17).[43]

One of Steltzer's duties was to arrange transportation of Wehrmacht troops and materials through Sweden, and in that capacity he made regular trips to Stockholm, where he was in contact with the Nordic Ecumenical Institute in Sigmund. He thus became a courier of continuous information to and from the church in Norway, the Church of Sweden, and the World Council of Churches in Geneva.

The other break in the German and NS system existed within the Church Department itself. Although it was one of the first to have a completely NS leadership, the department had employees who delivered copies of Feyling's correspondence and memos to the CCC; even after the first sympathetic employees were uncovered, the CCC continued to have access to information from the department.[44]

THE CONTEXT OF RESISTANCE

Viewed solely as correspondence between the church and the Church Department, the Norwegian church struggle can have the appearance of an office war, but that would be the farthest thing from the truth. At times church leaders used bureaucratic means of resistance, but each time they resisted or opposed one of Feyling's initiatives they faced the state system of repression just outlined. The system was already operating on some levels when Feyling took office, but other levels would not fully engage until the church struggle heated up in late 1941 and early 1942. At every point in the church's resistance, however, the NS system had the potential for intimidation, coercion and repression, and at every point, church leaders felt it.

Chapter 7

Against Nazification

—

GERMANY ON THE OFFENSIVE

Between the summers of 1940 and 1941, Germany continued its military offensive in Western Europe. After defeating the Netherlands, Belgium, and France between 10 May and 22 June, Hitler ordered the bombing of the United Kingdom. When the Battle of Britain was officially over on 30 October, Germany had suffered its first setback. But the German offensive continued throughout the first half of 1941, most notably in the Blitz, a series of bombing raids on the United Kingdom that did not end until mid-May 1941.

As the bombs fell, the Norwegian government was in London, its neutrality and defense policies shattered. Determined to continue the war, it had to set up its administration from scratch, redefine policy, work out its relationship to the British government, and mobilize resources. There was then no certainty that the United Kingdom would win the war. The future looked grim.

Some positive developments, however, had emerged after the military capitulation. King Haakon VII fully supported the government and had bolstered resistance at home. The fourth largest merchant marine in the world also remained under Norwegian control, generating revenue for continuing the war and contributing significantly to the war effort.

Against this backdrop, the government made major policy decisions. In November 1940, the government abandoned neutrality for an alliance with the United Kingdom. Symbolic of the change was the government's replacement of Foreign Minister Halvdan Koht with Trygve Lie. Norwegian policy was henceforth support of the United Kingdom and the Allied war aims, the liberation of Norway, and the strengthening of civilian and military resistance at home.

At first, Norwegian interests did not necessarily coincide with those of the United Kingdom. In the spring of 1941, Prime Minister Winston Churchill was eager for signs of military success, not least to improve morale at home. In July 1940, he formed the SOE (Special Operations Executive) to direct commando operations in cooperation with military resistance groups in Europe. The British pressured the Norwegian government to sanction sabotage operations within Norway, but the Norwegians vetoed the idea for fear of German civilian reprisals out of proportion to military gains. The Norwegians finally agreed to two raids in northern Norway, and in March and April 1941 British and Norwegian commandos hit Svolvær in the Lofoton islands and Øksfjord in Finnmark. Their success boosted morale in Britain and Norway, but, as expected, Terboven retaliated by torching several houses in Lofoton and sending 63 hostages to the Grini internment camp outside Oslo.

On 28 May 1941, Norway and the United Kingdom reached a formal agreement on their military relationship and aims. Norwegians would form their own military units, to be deployed either in defense of the U.K. or the liberation of Norway. The U.K., however, retained "operational control."[1]

The difference between U.K. and Norwegian war aims within Norway would be a source of ongoing tension. The SOE continued to press for more active commando operations inside Norway, but the Norwegian government was uneasy about not having control of such operations while being held accountable for them at home. Moreover, the military resistance groups in Norway had just organized as Milorg (a contraction of *militær organisasjon*, i.e., military organization)with a central leadership called the Council (*Rådet*). The Council also viewed military operations within Norway as unrealistic until liberation was imminent. In the meantime, Milorg would organize and train in anticipation of arms deliveries just before the final battle for liberation.[2]

Although the Norwegian view generally prevailed, the Norwegian government could never rest assured that its aims and policies would not be trumped by the U.K. and, later, by the United States and the Soviet Union.

In 1941 and early 1942, for example, Prime Minister Churchill was pressing for "Operation Jupiter," a flanking operation in northern Norway that would allow the Allies to easily send provisions to the Soviet Union.[3] That idea was dropped after February 1942, but by then the United States and the Soviet Union had entered the war and were shaping Allied policy. Norway was reduced to "adjusting to policy developments determined by the great powers."[4]

The rise of Milorg highlighted another ongoing tension in the three-cornered relationship between the United Kingdom, the Norwegian government, and the Home Front Leadership: distrust. In Norway, large segments of the population remained bitter at the government's abandonment of the country. Milorg and the civil resistance leadership that was coalescing in mid-1941 were largely non-Labor, so the bitterness had political undertones. The Norwegian government felt the force of the criticism but had its own suspicions that the Home Front Leadership sought independent authority, to the point of undermining its own authority as a government. On both sides, it would take time to rebuild trust.

NS CHURCH POLICY

While the home front was evolving in 1941, the church's relationship to the state entered a new phase with Feyling's appointment as Director General of the Church Department. Feyling took office with no NS church policy in place and, of course, no implementation plan, so he had to develop both.

He announced the five principles of his policy in a radio broadcast on 20 February 1941.[5] The first was that the Church of Norway was a Norwegian church, meaning a church for the people as well as a folk church; the history of the nation was the history of the church, and there could be no breaking with that tradition. His second principle was that according to Article 16 of the Constitution the state legislated and administered all facets of the church. The third principle assumed that God had established the state, and, according to Romans 13:1, citizens and "all authorities within it" owed the state loyalty. Fourth, the Augsburg Confession established that the church was "in the state with a task from God" but not above, below, or equivalent to the state. The state also had its office and task from God and was, therefore, accountable to God—which, Feyling admitted, the church had the right and duty to declare. Finally, charges and rumors to the contrary, the state was not persecuting the church but sought peace in the church. Article 2 of the Constitution was still in effect, and the state would continue to uphold the evangelical Lutheran religion.

On a first reading, the policy appeared traditional, even familiar, because it played on strings sounded before 9 April. What Feyling did not make explicit was the new context, a Nazi state. If the church was going to be "in the state"—not above, below, or equivalent to it—then it would have to serve the NS state and its purposes. In effect, Feyling was announcing a policy for the coordination of the church with the Nazi state.

AGAINST CENSORSHIP OF THE WORD

Feyling assumed office facing one pressing issue in two venues: censorship of preaching in parishes and the National Radio Corporation. On 1 June 1940, Terboven had stated publicly that the church would have no problems as long as it avoided "political formulations," and in October Skancke advised against "disloyal formulations," a narrower proviso. The Reichskommissariat added to the pressure in early April 1941 by reminding Feyling that it wanted domestic tranquility.[6]

But with their man in the Church Department, NS members started to inform on pastors for injecting politics into sermons.[7] Church attendance was fast becoming a form of political demonstration, and for some clergy the temptation to inject a remark or two with political overtones became overwhelming. So within 11 days of taking office, Feyling informed the clergy of the problem and urged them to use "the greatest possible caution" in their preaching.[8] Informed of more serious NS charges, two months later Feyling issued a more specific warning: the clergy were to stick to "the purely inspirational and eternal aspects of the gospel," and anti-party outbursts would be taken as "hostile to the state."[9] Party and state had fused, and freedom of the pulpit was under pressure.

One reason Feyling bore down on politics in parish preaching was a conflict on the same issue in a different venue that had started months earlier and flared up again shortly after he took office. On 20 September 1940, five days before Terboven announced the new NS administration, the Germans ordered the Norwegian Radio Corporation (NRK) to schedule NS pastors instead of the designated speakers for religious broadcasts. On Sunday 29 September, Øivind Hoem used his broadcast to thank God for sending Quisling. Berggrav reprimanded him and threatened Skancke and Gulbrand Lunde, the commissioner minister in charge of broadcasting, with an all-out church conflict if they did not back down.[10]

They did for over four months, but the conflict erupted again in February 1941. On Sunday 16 February, just after Terboven confiscated *The Pastoral Letter*, Henrik Kristian Ljostveit of Larvik preached in a radio broadcast on God's struggle against "sin's destructive powers" displayed in "hate, acts of violence, and the repression of the truth." Still unsettled by *The Pastoral Letter*, Terboven responded by imposing new broadcast guidelines that excluded anti-NS speakers, banned political references, and demanded pre-broadcast manuscript reviews. He also authorized Feyling to appoint a new radio board and transferred responsibility for choosing speakers to the Church Department. Feyling appointed a board of three pastors: Peder Blessing-Dahle, an NS party member; Lars Frøyland, an NS supporter but not a member; and Ingvald B. Carlsen, who had handled the church's radio broadcasts to date. Carlsen resigned immediately in protest, to be replaced by the NS pastor Andreas Gjerdi, who was soon put in charge of the whole operation.

Church law gave pastors the right to decide whether their services would be broadcast, and in response to the new conditions many began a boycott that soon left only 58 of more than 700 pastors willing to do so. Viewed as strike breakers, the 58 were shunned by colleagues and the Christian community, the beginning of the so-called "ice front" against NS supporters and collaborators.[11] As a concession, Feyling dropped the pre-broadcast manuscript review and invited pastors to accept broadcasts of their services; in the same breath, he pointed out the seriousness of refusing.[12]

As the conflict developed in March and April, Feyling and Berggrav were walking a fine line. Terboven wanted calm in the church, yet his reorganization of religious broadcasting had provoked a boycott. For his part, Feyling wanted the church to appear supportive of the new order, but the statistics of the boycott demonstrated just the opposite. In frustration, he asked the Justice Department whether civil servants could legally refuse to broadcast services; he would later receive an affirmative answer.[13]

For his part, Berggrav knew that once the party became the state and the state became the party, the state radio network became the party's propaganda medium. He did not think that the church could participate without compromising the gospel, and he worried about pastors who would accept out of "holy opportunism."[14] A Church Department order to preach over the radio would, he believed, implicate the entire church and oblige the bishops to oppose it. By late April, Berggrav decided that the issue would merit a principled stand if the state resorted to coercion.[15] In the meantime, pastors began to approach bishops about a reckoning with the Church Department, perhaps even a separation of church and state.

In the summer of 1941, however, neither side was willing to turn conflict into a crisis. Terboven's directive for calm in the church was one reason for Feyling's reluctance to make trouble, and the Justice Department was also unwilling to support coercion of religious broadcasts.[16] The bishops were not ready to go that far either, a view they signaled in a June circular to the church cautioning against "the political in politics" while reserving the church's right to proclaim the divine standard for political and social life.[17]

The clergy's radio boycott continued until it was finally resolved by the Germans. On 2 August, the Gestapo started confiscating all radios except those belonging to NS members. Terboven did not explain the order, but the Germans recognized the BBC's role in boosting resistance to the NS, not least through its reports on *The Pastoral Letter* and its consequences. Thereafter, only NS pastors broadcast services or devotions, and only 50,000 or so NS members and their families could legally listen to them.[18]

AGAINST GERMANIC RELIGION

The Labor Party passed several school reforms in the 1930s, but a major objective of Norwegian schooling remained a "Christian upbringing." From elementary school to university curricula, Christian education classes embraced biblical instruction, church history, and Lutheran doctrine. Weekly hours devoted to religion varied from six to seven in rural areas to three to four in urban areas.[19]

The church had significant influence on the content of religious instruction. The law required the authorities to route all prospective religion texts to the bishops and theological faculties for their expert opinion before they could be authorized for use in the schools; in practice, texts were simply not authorized without the approval of the bishops. Similarly, the school authorities had to solicit the opinions of local school boards, which also had the right to select one of the authorized religion texts for use in their district.[20] Clergy of the Church of Norway were *ex officio* members of every school board and were directly responsible for supervising religious instruction in their school districts.

NS educational policy aimed to Nazify the schools from top to bottom, and the religion curriculum—so filled with "Jewish" (i.e., Old Testament) stories—was a major obstacle. Anti-Christian factions in the NS would have liked to eliminate religion, but failing that, they were willing to accept a reduction in hours. In a circular of 15 March 1941, the Education Department proposed decreasing religion hours to three to four in rural districts and two in urban schools, a reduction of 33 to 50 percent over the Labor Party government's plan of 1939.[21]

The circular took Feyling by surprise, leaving him genuinely dejected and bewildered. He could understand such a proposal coming from the Labor government, he wrote to Skancke, but he had assumed that the NS supported Christianity and would not weaken it.[22] When he recovered from the shock, Feyling responded with a counterproposal that increased religion hours by one per week. Skancke rejected the counterproposal, but he ordered that schools could use up to three hours of Norwegian language classes for Bible reading.[23]

Feyling's firsthand experience of NS hostility to Christianity did not prevent him from attempting to introduce more Germanic religion and NS ideology into the curriculum. Feyling thought of himself as an authority on religious education, and his review of religion texts left him dissatisfied with their number (32) and their dated pedagogical methods. He recommended withdrawing authorization for most them and revising the rest.[24] Feyling's ideas for revisions fell short of introducing Germanic Christianity into the religion texts, but he wanted greater emphasis on the national element of Norwegian Christianity.[25] Specifically, he wanted the "sun cross," a Germanic religious symbol that was Christianized in medieval Norway and adopted by the NS as its party symbol, to be treated as a contemporary Christian symbol. He also wanted the treatment of Norwegian Christianity to emphasize its Norwegian characteristics, not the more recent and alien Anglo-American ones. For the same reasons, he was willing to accept the swastika as a Christian symbol and treated as such in religion textbooks.[26]

Before Feyling could act on the range of his proposals, he became embroiled in a controversy that would effectively table them for good. The dispute was over his revisions of his own religion text, *Life and Doctrine*, particularly his treatment of the fourth commandment and his concluding paragraph. Feyling wanted the commandment to honor one's father and mother to extend to the country—the fatherland. Thousands of homes composed of fathers, mothers, and children were "the one big home"—Norway—and the one family of the Norwegian people. Just as father and mother had authority and were to be obeyed, so there were various authorities—school principals, police, judges, clergy, and local and national government officials—in the national home to be obeyed. "Above all," he concluded, "we owe obedience to the Fører and the state government." Opposition to either or both was opposition to God's ordinance, and incurred punishment.

Feyling's other controversial change was his injection of a Germanic religious note into his final paragraph on Christianity:

> Jesus said of himself that he was the light of the world. The Bible calls those who believe in him the children of light.
>
> Like the sun, Jesus is the great light source for all people. Read the remarkable song of praise in Psalm 18, 1–7.
>
> Also for us Norwegians, the sun from ancient times has been like a messenger from God. Which king placed the sun cross on all his army shields?
>
> Now the old sun cross symbol is once more going to gather the Norwegian people around Norway and around God.[27]

Rather than sending his revisions to the bishops and the theological faculties for review, Feyling took the authoritarian path and authorized his own text.

Reaction to Feyling's changes was swift and dismissive. The sharpest critique was from the pen of Kåre Norum, editor of *Norsk Skuleblad* (Norwegian School Magazine) and leader of the teachers' front. He was also an active Christian, and as he prepared his review he discussed the issues with Berggrav.[28] Norum had procedural and substantive disagreements. He first charged Feyling with a serious breach of tradition and law by not consulting the proper ecclesiastical and educational authorities. He then accused Feyling of introducing divisive politics into the text. His call for primary obedience to the Fører was unacceptable to Christians, because they owed primary obedience to God alone. The sun cross presented the same sort of problem, because it was at the center of a current political conflict and, therefore, divisive. The symbol that ought to be raised above all others in elementary school class was the cross, the unifying Christian symbol.

Feyling responded by claiming that the book had been reviewed by all 17 of the required specialists and was properly authorized.[29] He failed to mention, however, that his claim referred to the first edition, not the revised version with the offending passages. Skancke was equally disingenuous in his rebuttal and forced Norum to publish an opposing review by J. Eldal. Unfortunately for Skancke's case, Eldal's opening sentence declared that Feyling's was the first school textbook to bear "the clear stamp" of Nasjonal Samling's "ideology and spirit."[30]

The bishops decided to let the matter develop on its own at first, by letting Norum carry the argument to the teachers and allowing resistance to develop from school boards, parents, teachers, and others in local school districts. When it became clear in late May that Feyling's book would be sent to school districts anyway, the bishops informed the Ministry of Church and Education that Feyling's revision should have come to them for review, and had it done so they would not have approved it.[31]

The controversy developed as the bishops had hoped. As an authorized text, *Life and Doctrine* became available for adoption by school districts, but most school boards chose others. The few NS-dominated school boards that did adopt it did so over the objections of the local clergy, parish councils, and bishop.[32]

AGAINST NS CONTROL OF ORGANIZATIONS

Terboven's ban on political parties after 25 September 1940 shifted politics to trade unions and professional organizations. This increased their political influence but also led to more pressure on them from the NS. In the fall of 1940, the Church of Norway's Clergy Association was on the list of targeted organizations. Its board advised members to respond to state pressure with a statement adapted from Berggrav's formulation: "I shall—hereafter as heretofore—carry out my official duties in conformity with my conscience and ordination vow and will comply with the occupation power's decisions within the framework of international law, and I do not find myself able to make a special statement beyond this."[33] Like the declaration crafted for the teachers, this one made conscience the basis of the right to resist, supplemented by ordination and the Hague Convention.

The board's action was just in time. The next day, Albert Viljam Hagelin, Commissioner Minister of the Interior Department and aggressive Nazi, ordered county administrators to register every organization in their counties. His order required a detailed accounting of leadership, membership, and financial resources, and it included church organizations. The mission societies felt threatened, but after assurances from Feyling, they decided to comply.[34] The free churches were not affected, because they had always registered with the Justice Department under the provisions of the Dissenter Law.

Most organizations were not as yielding. Forty-three of the largest national organizations sent a protest to Terboven, indicting the Commissarial Council for decrees and decisions "explicitly opposed to international law, Norwegian law, and the general Norwegian view of law." With a combined membership of about 700,000 behind it, "The Protest of the Forty-Three," as it became known, carried enormous political weight.[35] Among the co-signers was Laurentius Koren on behalf of the Church of Norway's Clergy Association.

A furious Terboven now cast caution aside and on 18 June convened the 43 leaders to meet at the Reichskommissariat's headquarters, which was the Storting building. There he delivered a harangue that, among other things, charged them with being unrepresentative. He concluded by dismissing all 43 from their positions, arresting six on the spot, and decreeing that they must either accept NS leaders or cease functioning. The episode was a turning point in the German-Norwegian civilian relationship.

Feyling was the NS representative in charge of the clergy, and he escorted Koren out of the building to complete the formal takeover. The next day, he announced that he had appointed Oslo pastor Lars Frøyland to replace Koren and ordered the remaining board members to stay in office.[36]

The board members, however, resigned. They informed Feyling that the Association now had a political character and that continuing in office would conflict with their consciences and positions as Christian pastors.[37] Feyling promptly replaced them with NS loyalists: Johan A. Beronka, Andreas Gjerdi, Johannes Haslie, Hans Olaf Hagen, and, as substitutes, Johannes Andersen and Peder Blessing-Dahle. By the end of the year, 173 members had resigned, leaving Feyling with a shell of an organization.[38]

THE EVOLUTION OF CIVIL RESISTANCE

Berggrav had been pessimistic about the moral fiber of the people in the summer of 1940, but a year later he conceded that Norwegians had developed an inner fortitude that would endure no matter what happened. Olle Nystedt, a Swede who toured the country in the last week of May 1941, also remarked that the occupation was harsher than six months earlier but "the strength of the resistance is admirable."[39] The German/Nazi/NS constellation had incited in Norwegians an anti-German/Nazi/NS response in which religious, moral, political, and patriotic motives fused and were distinguishable only in theory.

But the stakes were rising. Terboven's arrest of the 43 organization leaders and his Nazification of the organizations ended legal politics. Resistance had to go underground, where two national leadership groups emerged, the Circle (*Kretsen*) and the Coordination Committee (*Koordinasjonskomiteen*).

The Circle held its opening meeting only two days after Terboven banned the national organizations.[40] The initiators were Tor Skjønsberg, Øystein Thommessen, and Hans Halvorsen, but among the others were Berggrav, Paal Berg, Ferdinand Schjelderup, Gunnar Jahn, and the Labor Party leader, Einar Gerhardsen. Their aim was to strengthen the Norwegian government's position at home, forge ties between the home front and the government, and seek home front representation within the government.[41] They achieved the last on 19 September 1941, when Oslo's chief financial officer, Paul Hartmann, joined the government in London.

The end of the first stage in the formation of an organized home front was followed by the second, a pause lasting until April 1942 due to the arrests or forced exile of members. Berggrav was one of six of the twelve founding members who were either arrested or fled the country before the Circle could become a functional national organization.[42] Only when preparations for the postwar era geared up in 1943 and 1944 did the church again work closely with the Circle.

The other civil resistance leadership group, the Coordination Committee, comprised leaders of the professions—physicians, teachers, pastors, engineers, and lawyers. In January 1941, the Coordination Committee had representatives from five professional organizations, including the church. As more professions sought representation, the committee expanded. Because of arrests or the necessity of fleeing the country, the average tenure of the 26 total members was 18 months.[43] The pastors' representatives were Alex Johnson, a young Oslo pastor, and Conrad Bonnevie-Svendsen. The latter's position as national pastor to the nation's deaf made him an invaluable communications coordinator for both the church and the Coordination Committee. He would have a tenure of about 36 months, making him the longest-serving member.[44] Although the group expanded after 1941, only in 1943 did it consolidate and achieve the function and form it would have until the end of the occupation.[45]

The Coordination Committee served its member organizations as a consultative and advisory forum. Depending on the context, it would initiate, inspire, influence, guide, and coordinate, but it did not direct resistance from above. Resistance came from the member organizations themselves, and through representatives on the Coordination Committee information would be shared, issues discussed, and advice sought and offered. The usual means of communication consisted of directives to provide guidelines about the most effective form of resistance and boost morale. The Coordination Committee might issue a directive, or help to reformulate one, from a member organization, but drafts of directives were cycled through the organizations and had to find acceptance there before organization leaders themselves acted on them. To fulfill its function, the Coordination Committee developed contacts throughout the country and built an efficient courier system, using both the postal service and the railroads, to distribute news and directives; the Gestapo occasionally broke up sections of it, but as a system it worked effectively throughout the occupation.

Church ties to both the Coordination Committee and the Circle were essentially through Berggrav. Several of those involved in both groups were from the circles Berggrav joined to oust Quisling in April 1940, and he kept contact with them after he dropped out of formal politics in June 1940.[46] As bishop of Oslo and the leader of the CCC, he would join the Coordination Committee as demanded by the church's situation. Furthermore, Berggrav was in constant contact with the pastors' representatives as a mentor and friend to Alex Johnson and Conrad Bonnevie-Svendsen, who ran the courier services for both the Coordination Committee and the church.

Two points are worth noting concerning the next stages in the development of the councils. The first is that resistance evolved as NS Nazification policies threatened particular sectors of society, and each sector determined the nature and form of its own resistance. Not until 1943, well after the climax of the church's conflict with the state, did the Coordination Committee and the Circle evolve into "a general national leadership."[47] And second, Berggrav was not unique in maintaining a connection to both the Coordination Committee and the Circle. The two councils evolved as distinct but closely associated groups with several members in common. Binding the two were Ferdinand Schjelderup, Tor Skjønsberg, and Berggrav.

A VULNERABLE INSTITUTION

In the summer of 1941 the church was more exposed than it had been. The Supreme Court's resignation and Terboven's dissolution of the national organizations meant that after 18 June 1941 the church was the only state or public institution outside formal NS control—and the Germans were about to change history.

Chapter 8

In Defense of the Church

——

BARBAROSSA

As summer approached in 1941, the United States and the Soviet Union were not engaged in the war. The United States was a sympathetic neutral party, but it would not be drawn into the war until the Japanese attack on Pearl Harbor on 7 December 1941. The Soviet Union was also neutral, but in a different position. Germany and the Soviet Union had signed a Non-Aggression Pact on 23 August 1939, but after Hitler's invasion of Poland the Soviet Union suddenly shared a border with Germany.

Hitler believed in the evolution of species, the distinctiveness of races, and the survival of the fittest.[1] In his view, Nazism was born in the struggle against Bolshevism and would have to eliminate it to survive. He had been open about his aims in *Mein Kampf,* and ten days before the German invasion of Poland, he told his inner circle that he intended to "crush" the Soviet Union.[2]

On 18 December 1940, Hitler made good on his threat. He issued Order No. 21, Barbarossa. "When Barbarossa begins," he told his generals, "the world will hold its breath."[3] That it did. Barbarossa commenced on 22 June 1941, and its impact on the course of the war would be profound. In Norway, the fallout began well before the invasion, and once Barbarossa commenced, its impact on the church was immediate.

BAITING THE CHURCH

In preparation for Barbarossa, Hitler redirected all available German forces to the Eastern Front and ordered all occupied territories secured against surprises. In anticipation of an Allied invasion through Norway, he took additional military measures. He extended the rail system, added bases and coastal bunkers, and augmented troop strength.[4] He also tightened the system of state terror and postponed installing a Quisling government.

Barbarossa was never about God or Christianity, but Josef Goebbels and his Ministry of Public Information and Propaganda framed it that way to elicit Christian support at home and abroad. In Norway, the media's propaganda theme was the threat posed to Christianity and the church by a Soviet victory. Graphic descriptions and photographs of Soviet religious persecution filled out the picture. German agencies also put pressure on the religious media to publish propaganda pieces. That effort, however, was effectively resisted by editors appealing to Terboven's promise of 1 June 1940 not to interfere with religious life as long as it stayed "free of political formulations." The mass media had no such recourse.

Gulbrand Lunde, Commissioner Minister of the Culture and Public Information Department, was the NS counterpart of Goebbels, and he knew the Christian community well from years as the NS leader in Stavanger. To rally the bishops and clergy to the cause, he turned to Feyling.[5] Feyling responded by drafting an "Appeal to the Norwegian People" and collecting 27 clergy signatures in support. The appeal appeared in leading newspapers on 15 July and read as follows:

> The decisive final battle against Bolshevism and the international atheistic movement has now begun. Everyone must now know what it is about. It is about the extent to which our children will continue to have a Christian upbringing and a Christian school. It is about whether we will continue to preserve Christian faith, morality, and culture in this country. The undersigned pastors encourage the Norwegian people to stand together in this fatefully grave time for our country and people. For Norway and Finland against Bolshevism.[6]

Most of the clergy found Nazism as incompatible with Christianity as Communism and refused to sign the appeal. The laity had a similar reaction. As one outraged NS clergyman, Christian Hansteen, informed Feyling, most of the faithful regarded the call "as support for an anti-Christian movement that is just as dangerous as Bolshevism!!!"[7]

The other target of NS propaganda was the bishops, above all Berggrav. Shortly after assuming his office, and no doubt with Theisen's help, Feyling decided that Berggrav was pulling all the church strings, was politically motivated, and should be dismissed.[8] The virtue of Barbarossa was that it created an occasion for attacking Berggrav.

On the day the appeal was published, the bishops were in Oslo for a Bishops' Conference. They declined to comment on Barbarossa. That was the signal for Gulbrand Lunde's propaganda office to launch an attack on Berggrav that lasted for weeks.[9] Berggrav, however, would not be baited. As long as he could not speak publicly about the un-Christian regime in Norway, he refused to condemn the Soviets.[10]

Aggravated by his initial failure, Feyling ordered the clergy to support another call, this time "For the Church and the Christian Faith Against Bolshevism."[11] An additional 21 pastors agreed to support it, bringing the total for the two appeals to 48. The second appeal was never published, however, so it was of no public consequence.[12]

The NS's attempt to mobilize the bishops and clergy for Barbarossa failed, but it forced into public view some of the clergy who supported the NS and, implicitly, those who did not. In that sense, it represented a watershed for both the church and the administration.[13] The campaign also did something more. As Arne Fjellbu noted in his diary, the assault on the bishops and pastors was so intense that it looked like preparation for "an assault on the church as soon as the illusion of the crusade against Bolshevism collapses."[14] His observation was prescient, because in the coming months Feyling engaged in a multi-pronged assault on the bishops and church order.

ASSAULT ON CHURCH ORDER

Feyling understood that an authoritarian state required an authoritarian church, but moving the church in an authoritarian direction meant that the state would have to augment its authority in the church. At issue was where the line was to be drawn between the state's temporal authority and the church's spiritual authority in church affairs. Three developments illustrate Feyling's tactics and show why they threatened the church.

The Parish Council and Parish Meetings Law of 1920 required open election of parish councils and granted the laity a role in nominating bishops. As a step in an authoritarian direction, Feyling instead proposed that the chairs and vice-chairs of parish councils be appointed by bishops and the other members by rural deans. A chair would also have the right to authorize resolutions independently of the council and establish the agenda.[15]

Berggrav advised the bishops to reject the proposal on the basis of principle rather than specifics. Were the proposal to be put into effect over their objections, he argued, a principled rebuttal would provide a basis for non-cooperation, and the bishops' refusal to appoint parish council chairs could then be justified as an unavoidable Christian and ecclesiastical duty.[16] The bishops agreed.

In an opinion in behalf of the bishops addressed to the Church Department, Berggrav thus reminded Feyling that a parish council was an advisory body and not an executive instrument for wielding power.[17] The church should not be organized along "worldly political lines" by transforming parish councils into governing rather than congregational bodies. Were that to happen, parishes would no longer regard councils as their own but as something forced upon them. Berggrav had consulted with the bishops beforehand, so all the bishops objected along the same lines. The opposition put Feyling in a bind. Having solicited their opinions, he could not proceed against a wall of episcopal opposition without risking a conflict with the church—and the consequent wrath of the Reichskommissar—so he tabled the proposals.

Two similar incidents illustrate Feyling's difficulty in attempting to politicize the church. On 18 August 1941, the county propaganda leader of the NS's Youth Corps (*Nasjonal Samlings Ungdomsfylking* or NSUF) requested use of the Oslo cathedral for a service on Youth Campaign Day, scheduled for 28 September 1941. Dean Johannes Hygen denied the request on the grounds that it conflicted with his regular service and would implicate the church in politics.[18] NSUF leaders protested Hygen's decision to the NS General Secretariat, which conferred with the Church Department. After the two parties agreed to propose a time that did not conflict with the regular service, Feyling asked Hygen to reconsider and reply through Berggrav. Once again, Hygen denied the request. Reproved the first time for not submitting the initial request to the Parish Council, Hygen submitted it this time. The result was the same: a unanimous vote against approval.[19] Berggrav's opinion supported both Hygen and the Parish Council.[20] But the second refusal did not prevent the NSUF service from taking place. Appealing to a Royal Decree of 24 October 1906, Feyling allowed the NSUF to schedule a morning devotion at a time other than the regularly scheduled service.[21]

At the same time, Hygen faced a petition from Andreas Gjerdi to allow Feyling to preach on 21 September as part of a Christian NS conference. Hygen rejected this request as well, giving as his reason that the service was political. This time Feyling admitted that the resident pastor had the right to decide on the use of the pulpit, but he pointed to the single exception to the rule: as the highest authority in church administration, Feyling claimed the right in specific cases to designate another clergyman to take over a service.[22] He informed Hygen and Berggrav that he would replace Hygen at the High Mass on 21 September. A state of emergency forced cancellation of the conference, thus preventing a crisis, but the issue did not die.[23] For the next few months, however, Feyling focused on breaking down the bishops.

ASSAULT ON THE BISHOPS

In order to crack open the solidarity of the bishops, Feyling pursued four initiatives in succession: to retire two of the bishops, to infiltrate the Bishops' Conference, to infiltrate Berggrav's staff, and to entice Bishop Støren of Nidaros Diocese into succeeding Berggrav as bishop of Oslo.

Feyling began by attempting to dismiss bishops who had reached the normal retirement age. The law stipulated that senior civil servants had to retire upon reaching the age of 70, but on 5 December 1940 the NS had reduced the mandatory retirement age to 65 in order to create openings for NS appointees on the Supreme Court. Although Berggrav and the Church Department had arranged an exemption for Støren until midsummer 1942, in early July 1941 the Church Department informed Støren, Maroni, and five rural deans that they had reached the mandatory retirement age and were dismissed from office.[24]

Unfortunately for Skancke and Feyling, the retirement notices coincided with Berggrav's meeting with Terboven on 10 July about the German requisition of church bells for recycling into armaments in the fight against Bolshevism. In the course of their discussion, Berggrav remarked that the simultaneous requisitioning of church bells and the forced retirement of two bishops would look like an attack on the whole church and have "a colossal effect" on the Norwegian people.[25]

Terboven and the Reichskommissariat were already irritated at Skancke for not implementing changes at a slower pace, and only a few weeks earlier Terboven had reiterated to his subordinates that he wanted peace in the church.[26] Surprised and angered, Terboven immediately reversed the retirement order. Still smarting from the incident a year later, Feyling complained that Terboven repeatedly blocked the Church Department's subsequent attempts to enforce the age limit. Quisling, Skancke, and Feyling were also left wondering if the Bishop of Oslo, the NS's "archenemy," had more influence on Terboven than they did.[27]

Terboven's reversal of the retirement orders should have left Skancke and Feyling wary of more precipitous action, but the specter of Berggrav still holding down the episcopal chair increased their determination to remove him from office. This time their tactic was to attack the Bishops' Conference itself, the symbol of the bishops' solidarity against the state.

Church law stipulated that the right to call Bishops' Conferences fell to the previous meeting's leader, usually the bishop of Oslo, but agenda items could be generated by any of the bishops or the Church Department.[28] On the grounds that church law granted too much control to the bishops and too little to the state, Feyling informed the bishops that the Church Department would henceforth determine meeting times, name extraordinary delegates from among pastors and the laity, and decide on the issues that outside delegates could address.[29] Feyling wanted the option not to call any meetings at all, and, if he did, to infiltrate them with NS loyalists and informants.

The ploy was easy to see through. Speaking for the bishops, Berggrav and Støren objected that the Church Department could not alter rules established by royal decree, as these had been.[30] The church's relationship to the state and its authorities depended on the right of the bishops to render their opinions on "all matters of significance" to the church, and the Church Department's proposal would create the impression that the

Bishops' Conference was no longer the mouthpiece of the church. It is difficult to assess the impact of the bishops' objections, because this issue was soon overshadowed by others, but the result was the same as in the past: Feyling backed down, unwilling to pursue that avenue against the bishops.

Feyling next tried a new tactic against the Church Department's real source of frustration, Berggrav himself. In late November, he claimed that the bishops' administrative duties were taking time away from their teaching and supervisory duties. To correct the alleged imbalance, he unilaterally transferred Berggrav's office assistant, Nils Rosef, to Hamar, with the intention of replacing him with an NS member, Olav Manders. This ploy, too, was obvious: Feyling would have a spy in the Oslo bishop's office. Berggrav responded by declining Manders's services and made his own office arrangements.

Feyling had now lost the first three rounds of his assault on the bishops, but he had not exhausted his possibilities. He decided that Bishop Støren was the weak link whom he could use to marginalize Berggrav.

On 2 December 1941, he met Støren in Trondheim and tried to persuade him to take over Berggrav's position as the presiding bishop (*preses*) and advisor to the Church Department. Such an arrangement, Feyling suggested, would "ease" Berggrav's work load.[31] Støren rejected the proposal at first, but Feyling persisted: Would Støren agree if the plan were the unanimous wish of the bishops? Støren admitted that such a wish would force him to reconsider.

Støren's account of his meeting with Feyling shocked and appalled the bishops. Skagestad was vehement: "Let it by no means happen!"[32] Providence, he said, had placed Berggrav in the Oslo bishop's chair, and everyone in the church recognized it. Skagestad reiterated his unconditional support for Berggrav and warned that weakness on that point would be the beginning of the end. Fortunately for the bishops, Støren realized his mistake, which ended the discussion.[33]

ON THE ORDER OF THE CHURCH

The Church Department's next attempts to circumvent the bishops and the church order converged on a seemingly minor issue. In August, the Church Department requested information on organists and their service in the churches, and on 4 November 1941 it followed up with a circular called "Guidelines for the Use of the Organ in Worship."[34] Both bypassed the bishops, who were supposed to be consulted on an issue within their "spiritual" jurisdiction.

The circular provoked a spirited exchange. In behalf of the bishops, Berggrav let Feyling know that "in everything affecting the service of worship it is the bishops who, in the power of their calling, represent the heart of the church."[35] Circulars affecting worship and belief, as well as everything related to the conscience and duties of ordained clergy, had to be sent through the bishops, whose opinions had to be shared with the clergy.

Feyling replied by denying Berggrav's standing as the presiding bishop: the bishop of Oslo, he wrote, was neither the first among equals nor the church's primate.[36] The Church Department had consulted him out of convenience but had the right to choose any bishop as its advisor. In addition, church law did not grant bishops any decision-making authority "alongside of or against the Church Department." As to the use of organs in the churches, the Church Department had the sole right to decide on changes to the *Prayer Book* and the right to suspend regulations about it. This jurisdiction extended to all other aspects of services as well, including the use of organs. Feyling's only concession was his willingness to solicit the bishops' opinions before making a decision.

Feyling had not exhausted this vein of argumentation. On 1 December 1941 he published his views in an article in *Aftenposten*, Oslo's leading newspaper, which carried the headline "Should the bishops be relieved of administrative duties in favor of teaching and supervisory duties?"[37] The NS media followed up by interviewing Feyling, who argued for a return to the Reformation ideal by limiting "a bit" the bishops' authority in church administration in order to allow more time for preaching and spiritual supervision.[38] The article also publicized sections of the correspondence between the department and the bishops.

The pattern of bypassing the bishops had become too cumulative to deal with case by case, so the bishops addressed the underlying principles in a pastoral letter of 15 December 1941 entitled *On the Order of the Church: The Bishops' Position on Matters of Worship.*"[39]

As Berggrav was writing it, he had a chance conversation with Wagner, the Reichskommissariat's consultant on church affairs. He told Wagner about Feyling's attempts to divide the bishops, and asserted that these attempts would fail. The bishops were too open with each other and too united for the tactic to work. Wagner was particularly interested in this point, observing that the bishops were unassailable if that was the case. The conversation strengthened Berggrav's confidence that their solidarity placed the bishops in a strong position as the confrontation intensified.[40]

On the Order of the Church made three basic points. First, the bishops established the church's right to deal with church matters by referring to historical precedent and a royal resolution of 1895 that directed the Church Department to seek the opinions of the bishops and the theological faculties before authorizing hymnals or making liturgical changes. Then they claimed that bishops derived their authority and its limits from scripture and the church through ordination, not from any other authority; the state recognized this authority but was not the source of it. The bishops' authority also had a supranational dimension, because bishops served within the holy catholic church, of which the Church of Norway was a part. The bishops' final point was that the church had allowed non-spiritual affairs and ordinances within the church to be administered and directed by state agencies, but these agencies were bound to the confessions and served in cooperation with the church. The presupposition for the normal relationship of church and state was mutuality: the church's decisions were made cooperatively by the agencies representing the church—the congregational meeting, the parish council, the Bishops' Conference, the clergy, and the bishops. When the bishops spoke, they thus spoke with the authority of the whole church.[41]

Feyling responded by claiming that he respected the spiritual authority of the bishops and wished only to strengthen it by easing their administrative burdens.[42] The striking feature of his reply, however, was his expression of "particular joy" that church and state had now established a "trusting relationship" based on mutuality. The Church Department thus accepted "with joy the outstretched hand," and saw it as a "joyous turning point" of potentially great significance for the church. Before the bishops could correct him, he turned up the pressure by publicizing their correspondence in the Oslo newspapers.[43]

Berggrav wrote to the bishops that he did not did not think it wise to reply publicly to Feyling's ploy, a course of action that seemed to be confirmed by his conversation with "a German." The man was undoubtedly

Wagner, who was appalled at a maneuver that everyone could see through. The bishops, he agreed, should not use Feyling's trap as the occasion to answer him. The Church Department, said Wagner, was actually "in full retreat."[44]

PREPARING FOR CRISIS

At the turn of the year, the editors of the orthodox *Luthersk Kirketidende* looked back on 1941 with some satisfaction.[45] Skancke and Feyling had not been able to fill pastoral positions solely with NS sympathizers. Attendance at services and meetings had risen. Sales of Bibles and demand for Christian literature were high. Theological studies continued in the seminaries. Mission work at home and abroad had a good year without notable state interference. Finally, peace reigned within the church, which the editors attributed to unification around the Word and the confession. In short, there was no reason to be pessimistic about the future.

Berggrav shared some of the optimism. He thought that he and his colleagues were experiencing events that were among the most marvelous in Norwegian church history. He would joke with Hallesby and Hope about how they would one day again be at each other's throats and would "look back on these times as the paradise we were allowed to experience on earth." He did not think that at any other time in the Protestant church there was such "harmony of heart" and such "concord among all Christians, even the so-called Dissenters."[46]

Yet, Berggrav knew that a crisis loomed. The CCC had worked well, but it was self-appointed and purely advisory. If church leaders were suddenly imprisoned or sent into exile, an alternative form of leadership with an official mandate from the church and the mission societies would be necessary. To Berggrav, that meant a new council had to be formed, consisting of the bishops and the Council of Autonomous Organizations and to be called the *Church*'s Consultative Council (*Kirkens Samråd*). The bishops approved the idea, received the CCC's approval, and in late February presented the proposal to the Council of Autonomous Organizations.

Mission society leaders were initially skeptical, unconvinced about the need and fearing a loss of their autonomy. They finally agreed because of the seriousness of the political situation, with the understanding that the Church's Consultative Council would be no more than a crisis measure whose status they would reconsider at the end of the war.[47] The Church's Consultative Council announced its formation in the two major church periodicals, and the executive committee sent a greeting to the church calling for cooperation and solidarity between all levels of the church and the societies.[48]

On paper, the church seemed to be prepared for any eventuality, but the Church's Consultative Council never became a functional leadership group. It was overtaken by the rapidity of events in the ensuing weeks, leaving the CCC to continue leading the church until it, too, would be overtaken by events.

Chapter 9

The Resignation of the Bishops

THE ACT OF STATE AT AKERSHUS

On New Year's Eve 1941, the Axis remained in control of most of Europe and eastern Asia. The Germans occupied or controlled western, central, and southern Europe and the Balkans, and on the Atlantic their submarines were devastating Allied shipping. In Asia, the Japanese controlled the Pacific Rim and the islands and had inflicted heavy losses on the British. On 7 December 1941, they attacked Pearl Harbor.

Pearl Harbor brought the United States into the war and offered grounds for Allied hope, but the United States was unprepared for war and help would not be immediate In early December on the Eastern Front, however, the Soviet Union defeated the Germans for the first time and used the Russian winter and spring of 1942 to resupply and regroup. In North Africa, the scene was different. The German offensive was so swift that by June the Allies feared defeat in the Middle East.[1] After Pearl Harbor the war became global, but the outcome was still anything but certain.

In Oslo, rumors circulated that Quisling was about to return to power. He had lobbied in Berlin throughout the fall of 1941, and his timing was good. German successes in Europe left Hitler more confident of eventual victory and receptive to giving Quisling more scope in Norway. Hitler had also become displeased with Terboven, whose unnecessary ruthlessness had stiffened resistance. Terboven himself would have liked reassignment to the continent, but, with his status questionable in

Berlin, he decided that his only choice was to negotiate with Quisling about terms for an NS government.

On Sunday, 1 February 1942, Terboven installed Quisling as Minister President. The ceremony took place at the Akershus castle overlooking the Oslo harbor. The occasion was given the high-sounding name of "The Act of State at Akershus," but for Quisling it became another occasion for humiliation.

Terboven praised the historic struggle of National Socialism and the NS, the strongest party Norway had ever seen, but instead of focusing on Quisling, he used the occasion to attack Berggrav.[2] The Gestapo had found an account of Berggrav's peace initiatives in London and Berlin when they searched author Ronald Fangen's papers in late 1940, and Terboven was furious. Berggrav, he said, had pretended to be above politics, but the Gestapo papers revealed the opposite—he was nothing more than a pro-English politician. Terboven also charged that Berggrav had made anti-Soviet remarks to Lord Halifax, yet he had refused to support Germany's invasion of the Soviet Union.

Quisling rightly interpreted Terboven's speech as a personal humiliation, but he collected himself sufficiently to express gratitude for Germany's goodwill and its support of Norway's independence and autonomy through the NS.[3] He reviewed his historic struggle from 1933 to 1942, blaming "men of the old system" for his removal from office on 15 April 1940, the day Norwegian liberty and independence was lost. Nevertheless, his "national government" was now the "only legitimate Norwegian state-bearing authority," and "the most powerful political organization Norway had ever had." More ominously for the church, he recalled the famous words of the medieval King Sverre Sigurdsson after his victory over the earls and in defiance of the pope: "One man has now taken the place of three—king, earl, and archbishop—and I am that man."

The day after the Act of State at Akershus, NS editorials reiterated Terboven's charges against Berggrav. The time was past, warned *Fritt Folk*, when "small men in great positions" would be tolerated, and the correct name for such a man was "traitor to his people and to his calling."[4]

THE NIDAROS CATHEDRAL INCIDENT

As the NS celebrated in Oslo, a confrontation unfolded in Trondheim. The source of the conflict was the NS's desire to mark Quisling's installation with a service at Nidaros Cathedral, the national shrine where St. Olav lay buried and kings were crowned.

The drama began on Monday, 26 January, when the Church Department decided that it had the authority to order an NS clergyman, Peder Blessing-Dahle, to take over the High Mass in place of Dean Arne Fjellbu.[5] Fjellbu and Støren appealed the decision, but the Church Department rejected their appeal. After consulting with Bishop Støren and the Trondheim clergy, Fjellbu postponed the regular service to 2 P.M.[6] The NS county leader was able to stop the announcement from running in one paper but not the other or the parish newsletter.

Blessing-Dahle proceeded with his 11 A.M. service on Sunday, 1 February, surrounded by NS banners and Hird divisions as he hailed the Minister President and the New Age. There were no incidents. At 12:45 P.M., people started arriving for Fjellbu's 2 P.M. service. No police officers were present, no signs indicated a cancellation, and no areas were cordoned off, but NS loyalists saw people going to the cathedral and called the police.[7] The police tried to reach Fjellbu to stop the service, but he had hidden in the cathedral architect's office, which had a secret passage into the cathedral.[8] At 1:25 P.M., the police barred the doors, informed the crowd of the cancellation, and ordered the sexton to inform the people already inside the cathedral, who by then filled the chancel and some of the west nave. As people continued to enter through the side doors, the police called in backups and closed all entrances.[9]

Reports differ on what happened next outside the cathedral. To block further entry and move the crowd, the officer in charge, Egil Lindheim, ordered the police to draw their nightsticks. A policeman struck one man and then another, three or four times.[10] Others roughed up a few people in their attempts to move the crowd of 300 to 400 away from the doors. Some police officers acted with more restraint, and Lindheim accused several officers of being unwilling to go into action.[11]

Bishop Støren arrived at 1:40 P.M. He was outraged by reports of the violence and at being prevented from entering the cathedral. After talking to Lindheim and failing to have the orders rescinded, he urged the crowd to calm down and return home. Støren succeeded where the police failed, and the crowd moved to the gates of the cathedral grounds.[12] Lindheim then permitted Støren to enter the cathedral.

In the meantime, the crowd lingering outside the cathedral gates grew to an estimated two thousand. The temperature was around -15 Celsius (5 Fahrenheit). At the suggestion of the Ivar Skjånes, the former Labor Party mayor, pastor Håkon Pharo and Methodist minister E. Anker Nilsen began singing "A Mighty Fortress is Our God."[13] They were quickly joined by the crowd as the policemen stood around "at attention." After two verses, they sang the national anthem, "Yes, We Love This Country," followed by a verse of another hymn. Then the national anthem struck up again "across the square," with increasing volume:

Norwegian men in house and cabin,
give thanks to your great God!
He willed to protect this country,
even when all looked dark.
All that our fathers have fought for,
while our mothers wept,
the Lord has quietly cleared the path for
until we won our right.

There could be no doubt about "the firmness of will behind the words," said one witness, nor of the crescendo that "roared" along adjacent street blocks with the concluding line: "And when it is demanded of us, we stand ready to defend her peace."[14] By 2:40 P.M., the crowds had dispersed.

Inside the cathedral, Støren found Fjellbu in the sacristy, in his vestments and about to begin the service. He had taken the secret route and arrived just before 2 P.M.[15] After some negotiation, the police bowed to the fact that worshippers were already inside and allowed the service to proceed.

The Nidaros Cathedral incident led to charges and counter-charges between Støren and Fjellbu, on the one hand, and the Church Department, on the other. Støren and Fjellbu argued that no one but a bishop could order a pastor to hand over his service to another celebrant.[16] The Church Department countered by pointing to a regulation of 15 August

1928 stipulating that, on special occasions, the government had "the right to arrange services of worship by someone other than the congregation's pastors." Fjellbu replied that the regulation had never been used because the Church Department later discovered it had no such right.[17]

In subsequent letters to the Church Department, Fjellbu claimed that the cathedral incident represented "the most unheard of breach of church peace that has taken place in many generations." Støren seconded that the public viewed the cathedral incident as a violation of the church's rights, and as such it concerned the whole church.[18] Støren and Fjellbu had cast the issue in terms too sharp to ignore, and on 19 February Quisling dismissed Fjellbu from office, replacing him with Einar Lothe, an NS clergyman from the Hadsel rural deanery in Vesterålen, an archipelago west of Narvik.

THE BISHOPS RESIGN

Berggrav had learned from the German church struggle that effective resistance to the Nazi authorities had to take place on a clear, dramatic, and central Christian issue that the public could easily understand.[19] Shortly after the Supreme Court resigned, Chief Justice Paal Berg had also advised the bishops to be proactive and resign before Quisling could dismiss them.[20] The cathedral incident seemed to represent the right combination of principle and drama on which to assume the initiative against the state. To discuss the next step, Berggrav convened the CCC for a meeting on 20 February, followed by a Bishops' Conference.

Before leaving Trondheim for the Bishops' Conference, Støren in his naïveté informed the Church Department that he would be traveling to Oslo in connection with Fjellbu's dismissal from office. The Church Department already nourished the hope that Støren wanted a peaceful solution, so Feyling interpreted the notification to mean that the bishop was anxious to discuss a way out of the impasse.

On Monday, 23 February 1942, the bishops met in Oslo; only Skagestad and Krohn-Hansen were absent, the first, for health reasons, and the second because Tromsø was too far away for meetings on short notice. Berggrav argued that Quisling was ready to proceed against the bishops and wanted them to maintain the initiative by resigning before they could be dismissed.[21] Recalling the advice of Paal Berg, their decision had to take the Church Department by complete surprise and preclude the possibility of retreat. As he had drafted the bishops' letter of resignation, Berggrav also recalled the distinction between state and spiritual authority formulated by general superintendent Otto Dibelius with regard to his own dismissal in 1933.[22] By the end of the meeting, the bishops agreed to resign.

At the 10 A.M. meeting the next morning, the bishops faced an unexpected problem. Støren had second thoughts. He suggested that the more Christian approach would be to negotiate first; the Christian public might lose their courage for the struggle if the bishops hurtled forward in an un-Christian manner. Støren's words sounded so "enticingly refined and thoughtful," but they left Berggrav appalled. Worse yet, it looked for a time like Maroni, Fleischer, and Hille found them persuasive.[23] Berggrav countered that Støren's path would betray the high ground they had achieved to that point, forfeit the advantage of surprise, and allow "the enemy" to undermine them. Hille was the first to agree, and, by 1 P.M., the bishops had swung to Berggrav's view.

Within the hour, Berggrav's assistant delivered the bishops' resignations to the Church Department. Krohn-Hansen and Skagestad sent theirs later.[24] The bishops then distributed their letter to the congregations and pastors, reiterating the three unprecedented violations in the cathedral incident.[25] First, the state violated church law and its duty to the church by denying the High Mass to the pastor and the congregation without consulting the bishops, and for non-ecclesiastical reasons. Second, the state magnified its violation by trying to stop the 2 P.M. service, without notifying the bishop or the cathedral dean. Finally, the Church Department's most extreme violation of duty and trust was holding the dean responsible and dismissing him from office. Instead of protecting the right of the church and congregations to worship God, the department had dismissed the pastor who had done his duty. The bishops concluded:

> The Church of Norway's bishops would be unfaithful to their calling if they continued to cooperate with an administration that in this way without a trace of ecclesiastical basis violates the congregation and even adds injustice to violence. *Therefore, I hereby announce that I am resigning from the exercise of my office.* That is to say: what the state has conferred

on me, I set aside. The spiritual work and authority that has been conferred on me through ordination at the Lord's altar remains mine by God and by right. To be the proclaimer of the Word, the supervisor of the congregation, and the spiritual counselor of pastors is and will be my calling. . . . But to continue the administrative cooperation with a state that exercises violence against the church would be to betray the most holy.[26]

The bishops had wanted to inject "tyranny" as a leading idea but decided that the authorities would interpret such wording as politics. Instead, they made the same point indirectly: "The church knows that against what Luther calls tyranny stands God himself in his Word and in the power of his spirit. Woe to us if here we did not obey God more than man."

As planned, the bishops took the NS government by surprise. The Church Department responded by denying the factual correctness of the bishops' letters, but suspended them until their "resignation requests" could be brought to the Ministers' Meeting on Thursday, 26 February.[27] In the meantime, the cathedral deans were to take over the bishops' functions.

Quisling and the Church Department could not bypass Terboven in a case of this magnitude, but Terboven had reached the end of his patience with the bishops and ordered Quisling to accept the resignations.[28] Quisling wasted no time. He dismissed Berggrav effective 26 February, suspended the rest of the bishops for an unspecified time, and, in anticipation of events, issued a law allowing any pastor of a diocese to take over as a cathedral dean.[29] The State Police also ordered the bishops to report twice daily to their local police station.[30] At the same time, the Church Department named NS pastors as replacements.[31]

Quisling was too angry to let his actions speak for themselves and followed up with an open letter to the bishops. He began with a striking sentence: "It is the people's curse that small men holding important positions, with an inadequate overview and without historical vision, destroy for the sake of imagined gain that which has been created by wise and patriotically minded men through generations of labor and cannot see the enduring damage they thereby cause.[32]" Berggrav was the small man, the "Pharisee" and "Bagler bishop," who had acted "more like a worldly politician than Christ's true servant" and drawn many "weak and dependent souls along with him." He had destroyed the country's freedom and independence and, after Terboven's revelations made his position untenable, covered up his own actions by drawing the other bishops along with him.

Quisling based the rest of his polemic on arguments used earlier by Skancke and Feyling: the Church Department had the legal right to substitute pastors, the 11 A.M. service was an "ordinary" parish service, the 2 P.M. service was a "clearly political demonstration" for which Fjellbu was responsible, and Fjellbu's earlier abuse of his office would have led to his dismissal regardless. The NS intended to protect the church from false prophets who wanted to use the church's cause "as a shield for un-national policies in the service of anti-Christian capitalism and Communism."

The next day, 27 February, Quisling called Berggrav to the palace for an interrogation about his role in the events after 9 April 1940.[33] Seated around a long table in the king's dining room were Hagelin, Fuglesang, Jonas Lie, and Sverre Riisnæs, plus two aides and two secretaries. Quisling let loose a barrage of accusations against Berggrav and former Chief Justice Paal Berg that boiled down to holding them responsible for the war in Norway and all the death and devastation in its wake—including executions of Norwegian by the Germans and the NS. By ousting Quisling's "national government" in favor of an administrative council, Berggrav had torpedoed the country's only chance for a peace agreement with Germany and brought the war and German occupation to Norway. Decapitation a hundred times over could not be punishment enough for such treason. Quisling admitted that he had fired Berggrav, but not the others. He first wanted to investigate where the others stood, particularly Støren, who was reportedly upset over the turn of events.

The Church Department urged pastors to read Quisling's letter to their congregations. Some NS pastors did; others read it in order to highlight the issues; most did not.[34] In a speech on 7 March in Skien, Quisling repeated several points he had made on 26 February in his open letter to the bishops, which newspapers reprinted.

Although the Church Department must have realized that the other bishops took the same position as Berggrav, Feyling waited for confirmation. It arrived soon enough. As expected, on 5 March 1942 the government dismissed Hille from office, followed on 12 March by Maroni, Skagestad, Fleischer, and Krohn-Hansen. That left Støren.

Støren was the oldest bishop, and in both thought and appearance he represented an earlier age. There were two sides to his nature: the one stood in solidarity with the other bishops and readily accepted Berggrav's leadership in the church struggle; the other was the conciliator, the mild-mannered bishop who disliked conflict and wished for a settlement that would avoid the unprecedented step the bishops were about to take.[35] Støren's desire for a solution caused the Church Department to treat him with more deference than the others, and at Feyling's recommendation he was honorably discharged due to reaching the mandatory retirement age of seventy. The department's action meant that he would step down from office after his colleagues had resigned, leaving him as the representative of continuity among the bishops and with the appearance of collaborating with the NS.[36]

But this time the Church Department misread Støren, who was dismayed at his special treatment. He wrote to his colleagues that it "feels as if you have received an honorable discharge, and I a dishonorable one." Too depressed to show his face in the streets of Trondheim, he wrote to the department insisting that he stood in solidarity with his colleagues, found it impossible to remain in office after their resignations, and requested immediate release from office.[37]

OCCASION AND CAUSE

In resigning their state offices, the bishops were rejecting administrative cooperation with the NS state and the Church Department but retaining rights conferred by the church to exercise their episcopal duties. Their stated reasons for resigning were twofold: as Berggrav explained, the cathedral incident was merely the occasion for the bishops' resignation; the underlying cause was a separate issue, NS attempts to indoctrinate the youth.[38] But as Torleiv Austad has pointed out, the true cause was not so much the indoctrination of the youth as the Church Department's attempts during the summer of 1941 to discharge two of the bishops in order to replace them with NS appointees—and its persistence thereafter in undermining episcopal solidarity.[39] Had the Church Department succeeded, the bishops would no longer have been able to speak or act as one, and resistance to the NS takeover of the church would have been broken.

The Church Department had not succeeded in cracking episcopal solidarity in 1941, but by mid-February 1942, three developments raised the possibility of success. The immediate problem was the Church Department's intention to replace Fjellbu with Einar Lothe, an NS supporter. Cathedral deans ranked second to bishops in the diocesan hierarchy, substituted in their absence, and worked with them on a regular basis; the relationship between bishop and dean was necessarily close. Were Lothe appointed cathedral dean under Støren, episcopal confidentiality would be undermined and with it the solidarity of the bishops. The fact that Støren had proven to be the most vacillating of the bishops meant that such an outcome was virtually inevitable.

By mid-February, Berggrav faced at least two additional considerations. He had already arranged to extend Støren's retirement date, and the extension would expire in the summer of 1942. Furthermore, both bishops Hille and Skagestad had serious health problems. Were either one compelled by illness or death to resign from office, the Church Department would have yet one more opportunity to appoint an NS replacement. In short, the bishops had no more than a few more months to lead a unified church front.

REPERCUSSIONS

Feyling discovered that the bishops' resignation letter was to be read from the nation's pulpits on Sunday, 1 March 1942. After consulting with Karl A. Marthinsen, chief of the State Police, he decided not to intervene.[40] His decision went against his instincts, but it avoided an escalation of the crisis. Had the police attempted to prevent the reading, they would have spread the confrontation directly and dramatically into every parish.

Most pastors read the letter to their congregations. Rumors had spread about something dramatic about to happen, and tension was high as people filled the churches.[41] Following the reading, each pastor declared solidarity with his bishop and announced his continued recognition of his lawful bishop. Some pastors also read declarations of solidarity by their parish councils.[42]

Following the resignation of their bishops, cathedral deans and pastors found themselves in a kind of limbo. Ecclesiastical law required cathedral deans in each diocese to take over in the absence of the bishops, but the deans denied the Church Department that option by resigning in solidarity. Pastors were in a different situation and did not resign, but they sent to the Church Department declarations of solidarity with their bishops. As news of the pastors' action spread, parish councils sent in similarly worded declarations of agreement and solidarity.

Two groups of clergy dissented from the majority. The first were NS sympathizers and members, who saw no church-state conflict. The others were pastors who wanted more decisive action. In Hålogaland, for example, three pastors resigned, leading the Church Department to suspend them before dismissing them.[43] By the end of March, 12 more pastors had unilaterally resigned.[44]

Worried that events were rapidly moving beyond their control, Skancke and Feyling ordered pastors to read Quisling's reply from their pulpits and dismissed a cathedral dean and twelve pastors.[45] But as they would soon discover, they no longer controlled the conflict.

Chapter 10

In Defense of the Young

———

THE NS YOUTH LAWS

The principles at stake in the Nidaros Cathedral incident were enough to justify the resignation of the bishops. Whether it contained enough drama to also mobilize public support is unknown, because within a week the NS launched another initiative that quickly overshadowed it.

Quisling's vision for Norway was of a corporate state: trades and professions would be organized into corporations based on the leadership principle and each corporation would have representation in the National Assembly (*Riksting*), which would replace the Storting and advise the national leader. The authority vested in the leader would guarantee that national interests governed politics, and the leadership principle meant leaders would be held accountable. Quisling set 1 May 1942 for the National Assembly's inaugural meeting.

In the meantime, he started his revolution on 5 February 1942 by issuing two laws. The National Youth Service Law (*Lov om nasjonal ungdomstjeneste*) mandated that boys and girls, "for the sake of their national upbringing and to serve their people and fatherland," were to enroll in the NS Youth Corps, effective 1 March.[1] The Youth Corps was the NS's organization for 10 to 18-year-olds, an imitation of Germany's Hitler Youth. A complementary law (*Lov om Norges Lærersamband*) established Norway's Teacher Association and authorized the Minister President to appoint its leader to serve as a liaison between teachers and state authorities. All elementary and secondary school teachers had to join the association, and the law imposed penalties for refusing. Skancke was personally keen to see teachers at the forefront of the national youth service, and once implemented he was to administer the program.[2]

Quisling staked his political future on these two laws, because he thought that their success was crucial to the rest of his agenda of a National Assembly, a peace treaty with Germany, and, with that, national independence.[3] If he could fulfill his agenda, Quisling thought he would have political legitimacy as the people's prophetic savior, the true patriotic leader who had secured Norwegian sovereignty within the new European order.

"AN ORDER OF CREATION"

On the day Quisling published the new laws, Berggrav was eluding police attention as a "patient" in Lovisenberg Hospital. Realizing that the significance of the laws far outweighed the cathedral incident, he signed out of the hospital, drafted a protest, conferred with the CCC, and sent the draft to the bishops. If the bishops agreed with the letter, they were to reply with a telegram stating: "Understood about the baptism issue."[4] On Sunday, 14 February 1942, Berggrav sent the bishops' letter to Skancke.

The bishops' opening sentence stated the premise of their argument: "The foundational relationship between parents and children is an order of creation, a God-determined relationship that endures unbreakable and sacred for all homes." For that reason, the right and responsibility of the home was "unconditional and indissoluble." To deny parents the right and responsibility to raise their own children was to violate the parents' "sacred" rights and force them into "the most extreme act of conscience." Such was the case with compulsory youth service. The bishops also asserted the right of the church and schools to protest. Parents had voluntarily baptized their children, which obligated them to raise their children in the Christian faith, and the school law's first article stated that schools were to provide children with "a Christian and moral upbringing." School and church thus stood with parents in recognition of their mutual obligation.[5]

The bishops' protest "spread like a light through the land," probably because it was the first to articulate the issues at stake and justify the right to resist. The BBC also broadcast a reading of it several times. The bishops were thus instrumental in mobilizing church, school, and parents into a united front against the National Youth Service Law.[6]

Skancke addressed his reply to Berggrav personally, as if the protest merely expressed the bishop's personal opinion.[7] He conceded that parents were responsible for raising children in cooperation with church and school, and he used Luther's explanation of the Fourth Commandment to subsume the obedience children owed parents to the obedience parents owed the state, leaving the state with primary authority over children. The state was also an order of creation, and God as Father had instituted the state so that parental responsibility would be exercised within it, not against or outside it. Skancke warned that time was running out for the church.

Berggrav could not ignore the effect Skancke's argument could have on pastors, so he solicited statements from the two theological faculties. The faculties concurred with the bishops that for Luther the home was the foundational order of creation that the state was intended to serve, not the reverse. They also agreed that the doctrine of the two realms gave the church responsibility for the spiritual and moral life of the people, and that moral education in its broadest sense was within the purview of the church.[8] The state had the more limited task of securing civil order and justice.

To be sure that parents fully understood the threat, Berggrav collected quotations from several German and Norwegian Nazi leaders showing that the aim of National Socialist and NS youth work was Nazification.[9] He attached the documentation to the bishops' letter along with Skancke's reply, supporting statements from mission societies and free churches, and the opinions of the theological faculties. For good measure, he included the bishops' letter of resignation.[10]

When the bishops resigned, the formal reason had been the cathedral incident, not the National Youth Service Law, but since then the two had become inseparable. Recognizing that compulsory national youth service was a broader issue than church autonomy, affecting teachers, parents, and the church, church leaders began to argue that the true cause for the bishops' resignation was not the cathedral incident but the far more threatening National Youth Service Law.[11]

As soon as the bishops' protest became known, private citizens, mission societies, and the free churches flooded Berggrav's office and the

Church Department with statements of support. The most critical support came from the Lutheran mission societies. Hans E. Wisløff, chairman of the Council of Autonomous Organizations, informed Berggrav that the leaders of the societies had themselves taken the initiative to support the bishops' letter.[12] All the major mission societies did the same. The Salvation Army, which was largely Lutheran in its membership, issued a separate letter of support.

The free churches had not engaged in the church's conflict with the state since *The Pastoral Letter,* but most of their children attended the school religion classes. While Berggrav drafted the resignation letter, he had been in conversation with his friend Arnold T. Øhrn, the Baptist leader of the Dissenter Parliament. Probably at Øhrn's initiative, the Dissenter Parliament sent a supporting letter on behalf of its member churches, as did the non-dissenting Evangelical Lutheran Free Church.[13]

The support of the free churches was predictable, and their solidarity in such a mass protest was not likely to incur reprisals, but the Roman Catholic Church was in a more vulnerable position. Bishop Jacob Mangers and most of his priests were foreign citizens and subject to deportation, which would have reduced their church to a "catacomb" existence. To underline the seriousness of their situation, Terboven personally warned Mangers against political involvement.[14]

But Bishop Mangers had two compelling reasons to join the protest. The first was Pope Pius XII's Christmas message of December 1941 in which he condemned laws that would separate young people from the influence of their parents, estrange them from the church, and "raise them in a spirit that is hostile to Christ by indoctrinating them in anti-Christian ideas, principles, and practices."[15] The second reason was that Mangers was a citizen of Luxembourg, but after the invasion of Norway he applied for Norwegian citizenship in order to be in solidarity with his church members. Two years later, however, his application had not been processed, and in the meantime the Germans had invaded Luxembourg and officially incorporated it into the Third Reich. By adding his support to the Lutheran bishops' letter, he risked alienating the German authorities and deportation. There was also a benefit, however, because he would be placing his office behind a protest that reached into every Norwegian family, a visible symbol of his and his church's solidarity with the Norwegian people.

Having made his decision, Mangers appeared unannounced at the front door of Berggrav's episcopal residence on the afternoon of 28 February. For years, the two bishops had worked only blocks apart, but they had never met. Shown to Berggrav's desk, Mangers wrote: "I fully support what is expressed in the bishops' statement of 14 February to Minister Skancke."[16] Mangers's declaration earned him two Gestapo interrogations, accompanied by accusations of treason and threats of deportation.[17]

Mangers was not without recourse. The universality of Christianity represented by the papacy was one reason National Socialists in Germany were particularly wary of the Roman Catholic Church. Mangers, therefore, turned to Pope Pius and persuaded him to protest the threatened deportations through the Italian legation.[18] As a result, the Gestapo dropped the matter, with only occasional reminders that it had not forgotten Mangers or his priests, also largely foreigners. Mangers's signature turned the bishops' protest against compulsory youth service into the most ecumenical document in Norwegian church history to that date and demonstrated that the entire Christian community was behind the bishops and the teachers.

THE CHURCH AND THE TEACHERS' RESISTANCE

Although secularization had complicated the relationship between teachers, Christianity, and the church, teachers came disproportionately from regions most resistant to Nazism, above all from western Norway. They were shaped by the culture of the South and the West, a culture dominated by the mission societies, the temperance movement, and the rural dialect movement. This cultural matrix prevailed in most of the teachers' colleges, whose graduates continued to be involved in the triumvirate that nourished them. For such people, teaching took the form of a calling, and in rural communities teachers were intellectual and spiritual leaders alongside the clergy.[19]

The ties between Christianity, the church, and the schools were also reflected in the national leadership of the prewar teachers' associations. The two most prominent leaders during the occupation were active Christians. Einar Høigård taught at the Oslo Cathedral School, served as executive secretary of the Education Council, and wrote the standard history of

Norwegian education. His intellect, energy, and principled opposition to Nazism propelled him to the forefront of the teachers' resistance. Said to have been the brains of the school's fight against Nazism, he could just as plausibly be described as its will.[20] He developed the "Four Cardinal Points" of the teachers' resistance: (1) refuse any demand for membership or loyalty to the NS, (2) refuse any attempt to bring NS propaganda into the schools, (3) refuse any order from an unqualified source, and (4) refuse any cooperation with the NS Youth Corps (NSUF).[21] He was the central leader of the teachers' resistance until his arrest in late 1943, when he jumped to his death to avoid informing under torture.

The other central figure among the teachers was Kåre Norum, an elementary school teacher, editor of the leading teachers' periodical *Norsk Skuleblad*, and a member of the Oslo region's executive board of the Norwegian Mission Society. As editor of the *Norsk Skuleblad*, Norum had written a sharp critique of Feyling's revised catechism. Norum was also in regular contact with Berggrav and the CCC and was one of three teachers' representatives on the Coordination Committee.

It was natural for clergy to work closely with teachers at local and regional levels, but the pattern was not uniform: some pastors cooperated closely with teachers, while others had no contact at all. Much depended on individual leadership and previously established relationships. As a rule, however, there was close cooperation between church and school in the teachers' resistance, which continued locally in 1942 and 1943.[22] For teachers who were professing Christians, school and church were but two fronts in a common cause.

While Berggrav was mobilizing the church, teachers were initially uncertain about how to respond, but they were well organized and had effective leaders. The prewar teachers' associations were organized by type of school and gender: the Norwegian Teachers' League (*Norges lærerlag*) for elementary teachers, the Norwegian Secondary School Teachers' League (*Norges lektorlag*) for secondary teachers, and the Norwegian Female Teachers Association (*Norges lærerinneforbund*) for female elementary school teachers. Their elected leaders had also established an illegal Teachers Action Committee, and from 11 to 14 February 1942 it embarked on a series of meetings with teachers in Oslo. The committee also consulted with Berggrav, the Coordination Committee, and the Circle.[23] Uncertainty prevailed until 14 February, when Olav Hoprekstad shared news about NS plans in Bergen and urged the teachers to seize the initiative and act in unison against both of the NS laws.

The Teachers' Action Committee agreed on a declaration formulated by Norum, which reflected the theme that Berggrav had suggested to the teachers in the fall of 1940: "I do not find that I can participate in the upbringing of Norway's youth according to the guidelines that have been established for the NSUF's youth service, because that conflicts with my conscience."[24] With additional objections, the teachers stated that they refused to join Norway's Teacher Association. The Action Committee sent the declaration to the nation's teachers with instructions to drop it in the mail on 20 February.

In the meantime, the bishops' protest against the National Youth Service Law had become widely known. One of its initial effects was to fortify teachers to send in their own letters of non-cooperation. How many did so is impossible to quantify, but it was certainly a significant number, particularly in the South, Southwest, and West.[25] For the Christians among the teachers, it is plausible to conclude that the bishops' protest validated resistance. In northern Norway, the Gestapo registered the "disastrous influence" of Bishop Wollert Krohn Hansen on "the attitude and decisions" of the teachers, and from Berlin Goebbels himself observed that a "greater part of the teachers have identified with the rebelling bishops."[26]

Quisling and his ministers had no contingency plans, so their only alternative was to revert to threats.[27] On 23 February, Skancke informed teachers that they had until 1 March to rescind their declarations or face dismissal. To ignore the threat was to risk loss of pensions and the likelihood of forced labor in northern Norway and elsewhere. To underline the seriousness of its intent, the government withheld February salaries in several places; in Oslo, for example, only 37 of 966 teachers received their monthly salary checks.[28]

The teachers responded with an overwhelming display of resistance to the NS Norway's Teacher Association. On the 20th and 21st of February, three to four thousand posted their declarations to the Ministry of Church and Education.[29] In the following days, another seven to eight thousand sent theirs to the headquarters of Norway's Teacher Association. The numbers grew to an estimated twelve thousand of the country's fourteen thousand teachers—an 85 percent support rate.[30]

While the teachers' declarations poured in and Skancke's deadline of 1

March approached, the government found itself at a political impasse. It had to dismiss the majority of the country's teachers or accept humiliation and retreat. Quisling found a pretext in the unusually cold winter, which, he claimed, had depleted fuel supplies. On 26 February, he declared a month's fuel holiday and closed the schools, effective the next day.

THE CHURCH AND THE PARENTAL FRONT

The fuel holiday that began on 27 February had the opposite of its intended effect. Rather than cease instruction, teachers moved classes to the homes of students. For such a plan to work, parents had to arrange schedules, transportation, and homes for the instruction of their children. Parents who had passively observed the resistance from the sidelines found themselves suddenly thrust into the center of events.

The interweaving of church and school with parents was most evident in the origins of the parents' resistance. On Sunday, 1 March 1942, high school teacher (*lektor*) Helga Stene and her sister, university English lecturer Aasta Stene, were worshiping in their local church, Nesodden, and listened as their pastor read the bishops' resignation letter.[31] The sisters were the children of missionaries, and Aasta had engaged in the secret central teachers' front and organized non-violent women's groups.[32] Following the service, the pastor informed the parishioners that officials from the sheriff's office had just visited homes and registered the names of children between the ages of 10 and 18. With anxious parents feeling something had to be done, the Stene sisters investigated how parents could support the church and the teachers.

Helga and Aasta Stene had been active in a coordinating committee for women's organizations that had been forced to operate illegally. They contacted another member of the group, Sigrid Helliesen Lund, and the three drafted a protest to the Ministry of Church and Education on behalf of parents. After trying in vain to reach Berggrav to discuss their draft, they met with a group of professors, physicians, and pastors, several of whom were members of the Home Front's Coordination Committee. Initially skeptical about a protest, the Committee was persuaded.[33] At the suggestion of Ferdinand Schjelderup, the Stene sisters and Lund amended their draft to protest on the basis of conscience rather than the illegality of the National Youth Service Law.

The women's coordination committee then wrote a circular to parents. Noting the action taken by the church and the teachers, the group stated, "We parents can neither be suspended nor discharged. Now it is our turn to strike a blow for the children." The Committee instructed parents to protest to the Ministry of Church and Education with a formulation that was simple and direct: "I do not want my child to participate in NSUF's youth service, since the guidelines that have been drawn up for this work conflict with my conscience."[34] In imitation of the teachers, the Committee directed parents to send their protest on 6 March, which gave the regime three days—until the following Monday—before threats could be published in the papers.

What followed was unprecedented. To spread the word, the women used every possible channel: friends and colleagues, clerks and students, clergy wives and physicians' wives, midwives, and teachers. Some of the channels involved a dash of innovation: secretaries produced copies that children dropped into post boxes and parents carried from door to door, while "substantial women traveled out of Oslo with several hundred mimeographed sheets under their girdles."[35]

The church—its laity, organization leaders, pastors, and bishops—contributed to the parental protest. The organizers used the church's courier network to communicate with the local leaders and spread its directives, particularly in rural districts.[36] In northern Norway, where instructions from the South were often slow to arrive, Bishop Krohn-Hansen formulated his own protest against the national youth service, which most parents from northern Norway used as a basis for their protests.[37]

Christianity itself was a rallying point in the parental resistance. The organizers formulated their instructions to parents by appealing to what they took to be shared Norwegian values—Christianity and nationalism laced with individualism. One flier, for example, warned that the NS intended to revolutionize the spirits of the young:

> Under cover of sport, play, and other lures, children are going to be raised in a spiritual direction that conflicts with Christian faith and morals, and that violates everything that we regard as great and holy in the Norwegian national view of life. . . . Each father and mother who thinks and feels Norwegian will and must know their duty and take a clear stand: When the summons comes, you must refuse to turn over your children to

the NS youth educators. . . . We Say No. Together Norway's parents are a force that no one can break.[38]

Another flier played on similar themes:

You have inherited from your home spiritual values that have meant infinitely much for you throughout life . . . a legacy of the Christian and national mentality that creates a strong personality and makes one into a good person and a right-thinking member of society. . . . From the day you turn over your child, you risk seeing it de-Christianized, emptied, a person so spiritually stripped and without personality as it must be if it is to be a passive instrument in the leader's hand. Because you will shortly be unable to resist if you don't do it while you still can.[39]

As Axel Stang, Commissioner Minister of Labor Service and Sports, worked with Skancke to organize the youth service, parents flooded the two ministries with protest letters. How many is not known, but estimates vary from 50,000 to 200,000 or more in a country with about 350,000 families with children.[40] The letters were so numerous that the departments had to collect them in clothes baskets and hire temporary staff to open them. As one participant put it, the stand of the church and teachers had "released a landslide."[41]

ANNUNCIATION DAY PROTEST

Quisling's target date for initiating the national youth service was 1 March, but the massive resistance required a change of tactics. The government had failed to mobilize teachers or parents behind the law, but it risked losing all credibility if it did not proceed. It finally decided that the youth service would be introduced selectively after the "fuel holiday," with the proviso that young people who were called up had to join.

The regime began with places where it had somewhat greater public support than elsewhere, notably Hedmark and Oppland, as well as selected rural localities and towns. In most cases, the call-ups ended in failure: only the ambivalent, the timid, and the children of NS families responded. Even where there was some initial response, opposition was so intense that the young people gradually dropped out.[42]

As February turned to March, schools remained officially closed and teachers taught in private homes. Teaching was a high-status profession in 1942, but the circumstances moved more and more teachers to view their work as a calling. Whether the calling was from God, the Norwegian people, or both depended upon the person, but teachers resisted the regime with the growing awareness that they were responsible to a higher authority than the state. As one of their leaders noted, this process was undoubtedly a parallel to the church struggle.[43]

Teachers also knew that they had the support of parents, that they were "lifted by a wave that they themselves had been part of creating." Quisling's initial threats thus had almost no effect, and by March his threats had become even less effective. When the Ministry of Church and Education, for example, warned local school boards that salary checks could only be issued to teachers with proof of membership in the NS Norway's Teacher Association, most boards disregarded the order.[44]

The mass opposition threatened Quisling's plans for a National Assembly as well as a separate peace treaty with Germany, and it created a legitimacy crisis for his regime. His options were either significant compromise or increased coercion. The first was hardly an option, because the resistance was too unified, compact, and massive, leaving coercion as the only realistic option. This took the form of a series of laws that fused the NS and the state and punished even the mildest verbal dissent.

Quisling also continued to use coercion against particularly oppositional pastors and teachers. In the case of the church, he terminated pastors once a week for the entire month of March, a total of thirteen by the end of the month (in addition to Berggrav and Fjellbu, dismissed in February, and the remaining six bishops, also dismissed in March).[45] Quisling's crackdown on teachers was harsher. He began by ordering Orvar Sæther, head of Norway's Teacher Association, to collect lists of defiant teachers.[46] On 10 March, he ordered 300 arrested and interned.[47] His response heightened public unrest, raised grave questions about the regime's legitimacy, and presented a serious challenge to the German authorities. Terboven finally decided to intervene. He and Quisling agreed on a plan, and on 20 March the Norwegian State Police arrested and interned another thirteen hundred teachers.[48]

The escalating conflict provoked a group of Oslo clergy into action. On 16 March, Johannes Ø. Dietrichson presented to the CCC a draft of a church protest against the National Youth Service Law to be delivered on the coming Sunday, Annunciation Day (*Maria budskapsdag*).[49] They also conferred with Berggrav about including a warning about clerical resignations were the church's views not respected in the future. Convinced that psychologically and tactically the timing was right, Berggrav gave his approval, as, presumably, did the CCC.[50]

The next morning, the Oslo clergy met at Frogner Chapel. Expecting his own arrest at any time, Berggrav gave a short sermon, administered the sacraments, and bid his clergy farewell. He left before the business meeting because he wanted pastors to make their decisions freely. On 13 March, the Church Department had banned public readings of any writings from the bishops or any communiqué related to their resignations. Because defying the ban involved personal risk, each pastor had to make his own decision.

On Annunciation Day, 22 March 1942, pastors read their protest.[51] Their statement reiterated that the fundamental relationship between parent and child is an order of God. The central motif was the solidarity of church, school, and home on the basis of God's commandment and conscience. Article 2 of the Constitution obliged the church to call the state to account for violating the primary relation of parent and child, just as it obliged the state to listen. The pastors ended their declaration with a warning that their continuation in office would depend on the church's views being respected.

NS REACTION

The government reacted to the pastors' protest with outward calm, but in the Church Department Feyling went to work on a number of contingency measures. He drafted proposals to prevent a mass exodus from the church, replace pastors, reorganize the administration around fewer personnel and larger districts, and transfer civil duties to lay personnel and other government agencies.[52]

Having made the necessary legal preparations, Feyling decided that an ounce of prevention was better than a pound of cure. In a widely publicized speech at the University *Aula* on 27 March, he took his case to the public.[53] Citing Article 2 of the Constitution, he declared that the church was a state agency, just like the educational, welfare, and health systems.

Feyling then followed the logic of his Fører: the highest administrative and legislative authority was the state, embodied in Quisling. He warned the "so-called" Christian front that the church's "Norwegian hour" was about to strike. A few days later, Skancke sent a circular to pastors warning against the reading of resolutions and circulars at worship services that "directly or indirectly intend to express and sow distrust of the sitting rulers of state and that contributes to creating unrest in the Norwegian population."[54] Doing so violated the state's independence and security and was punishable by up to a life sentence.

The conflict between church and state had reached an impasse. The Gestapo reported that the NS measures had created "a closed front of all the church's schools of thought and splinter groups including the sects," as well as the Roman Catholic bishop. Church circles were "unyielding."[55] Something had to give.

IMAGE GALLERY

—

Eivind Berggrav, Bishop of Oslo, 1940. Photograph: Ernest Rude/Oslo Museum

Ole Hallesby at home in Oslo, 1949. Photograph: Leif Ørnelund/Oslo Museum

The bishops of the Church of Norway at Bishop Eivind Berggrav's cottage, Asker, July 1941. From left: Johan Støren, Bishop of Nidaros; Eivind Berggrav, Bishop of Oslo; Andreas Fleischer, Bishop of Bjørgvin; Henrik Hille, Bishop of Hamar; Gabriel Skagestad, Bishop of Stavanger; James Maroni, Bishop of Agder; Wollert Krohn-Hansen, Bishop of Hålogaland. Photograph: Dag Berggrav/Norges Hjemmefrontmuseum

Vidkun Quisling holding
a press conference in the
Storting, 12 April 1940.
Photograph: Unknown
photographer/NTB
Scanpix

Reichskommisar Josef
Terboven announcing
the formation of the
Commissarial Council
in a radio broadcast,
25 September 1940.
Photograph: Unknown
photographer/NTB
Scanpix

The Christian Consultative Council (*Kristent Samråd*) in a photograph taken
just after liberation in 1945. Seated, from left: Kristian Hansson, Ole Hallesby,
Eivind Berggrav, Ludvig Hope, Ragnvald Indrebø. Standing, from left: Hans E.
Wisløff, Ingvald B. Carlsen. Photograph: Unknown photographer/Norges
Hjemmefrontmuseum

Ragnar Skancke, Commissioner Minister of Church and Education, at his desk, undated (1940–45). Photograph: Unknown photographer/NTB Scanpix

Sigmund Feyling, Director General of the Church Department, ca. 1943. Photograph: Unknown photographer/Riksarkivet

Crowd prevented from entering grounds of Nidaros Cathedral, Trondheim, 1 February 1942. Photograph: Sven Andreassen/Riksarkivet

The Provisional Church Leadership (Den midlertidigie kirkeledelse), also known as the Secret Church Leadership, 1945. Seated, from left: Alf Bastiansen, Johannes Ø. Dietrichsen, Ludwig Schübeler, Johannes Smemo. Standing, from left: Arne Fjellberg, Erling Thomle, Dagfinn Hauge, Tord Godal, Tormod Vågen, Andreas Seierstad. Photograph: Unknown photographer/ Norges Hjemmefrontmuseum

Lone worshipper at service conducted by an NS clergyman in Sæbø
Church, July 1943. Photograph: Knut Dalene/Riksarkivet

Ludvig Hope at Grini
internment camp,
19 May 1943. Drawing
by Gunnar Bratlie.
Photograph: Unknown
photographer/Norges
Hjemmefrontmuseum

The newly appointed bishop of liberated Finnmark, Arne Fjellbu, at Polmak Church, Finnmark, 18 March 1945. Photograph: Unknown photographer/Norges Hjemmefrontmuseum

Chapter 11

Easter 1942

———

CALLS FOR A DECLARATION

The Annunciation Day protest proceeded as planned, but not without signs of unrest in the ranks. Some pastors in Kristiansand and Stavanger only read summaries or did not read the protest statement at all.[1] Behind their decisions was the realization that the status quo was problematic. If the crisis justified the resignation of the bishops, why not the clergy? How could the clergy remain in office and not recognize the Quisling-appointed bishops and deans? Were the protests squandering the church's spiritual and moral capital? Should the clergy resign without a new provocation?[2] In the meantime, the government dismissed four clergy members on 5 March and a rumor spread that it was preparing preemptive action.[3] In Oslo, the clergy behind the Annunciation Day protest were pressing for a clear break before the state seized the initiative. The status quo could not hold.

After the clergy were reprimanded for recognizing the authority of the "dismissed" bishops, clergymen in Bergen sent a protest draft to the CCC.[4] Their protest was against the state's interference in the church, compulsory youth service, and the constitutional amendment barring Jews from the country. The statement concluded by offering alternatives for action: remaining in office on a purely Christian basis or resigning. They suggested Easter Sunday as a date for reading the protest.[5]

In early 1941, Bishop Gabriel Skagestad, Dean Kornelius O. Kornelius, and General Secretary Einar P. Amdahl of the Norwegian Mission

Society formed the Christian Consultative Council for the Stavanger Diocese. Olav Valen-Sendstad, a local pastor and theologian, joined the group in early March 1942. Kornelius and Amdahl had attended the first meeting of the Bergen clergy and on 18 March received the final draft of their protest. After conferring on the Bergen draft and discussing another by Valen-Sendstad, the Stavanger CCC supported the Bergen proposal and commissioned Valen-Sendstad to present it to the Oslo CCC. The Stavanger CCC had in mind a protest rather than a principled declaration of the Christian faith in relation to the state, but on the train to Oslo, Valen-Sendstad became captivated by the thought of a "kind of new Augustana" (Augsburg Confession) on church and state."[6]

Berggrav had also been thinking about a principled declaration and mentioned it to the CCC on 11 March. Five days later he proposed that the CCC draft "a confessional statement on a broad Christian basis."[7] The CCC agreed. They also agreed that only the CCC should compose the declaration and send the signal for action. By 18 March, the CCC must have arrived at a consensus that the clergy should collectively resign from their state offices.

COMPOSING A CONFESSION

On Annunciation Day, Sunday, 22 March, the CCC met for the first time with Valen-Sendstad. He shared the Bergen and Stavanger drafts and argued for a theological declaration as he shared his own. The group agreed on a broad and unified approach, and Berggrav laid out the main points that needed to be included. He was against including a statement about the Jews, as the Bergen protest did, because it would deflect attention from the church's reckoning with the state.[8] Valen-Sendstad agreed. For the next meeting, each member was to prepare points for Berggrav to use in formulating the declaration.[9]

Berggrav completed his draft on Thursday morning, 26 March, and later in the day the CCC agreed on its main points while wanting others revised. Hansson also shared ideas on ordination and the relation to the state church that found their way into the final document. The meeting concluded with Berggrav receiving Hansson's draft and the assignment to complete a final draft by the next meeting, set for 6 P.M., Saturday, 28 March.

At that meeting, the CCC reviewed Berggrav's final draft. It was the most serious and moving gathering of the CCC to date.[10] One reason was the double formulation: "We confess—We condemn." Skagestad suggested the formula, inspired by the parallelism of the Lutheran confessions. The other reason was the CCC's decision to have clergy read the declaration, now titled *The Foundation of the Church: A Confession and a Declaration* (Kirkens Grunn: En bekjennelse og en erklæring), on Easter Sunday, 5 April. The timing was tight.

The sources do not reveal much about when and where the CCC discussed the resignation statement and weighed the difference between "seek dismissal" and "lay down the office." Chief Justice Paal Berg had clarified the difference at a Bishops' Conference in January 1941. Berggrav had also informed the CCC of the precedent set by Otto Dibelius, who distinguished between his state office and "his spiritual office as preacher and counselor in accordance with the commission granted in his ordination."[11] The point was to distinguish clearly between the "spiritual" and "temporal" realms as these were institutionalized in the state and pastoral offices and to affirm the primacy of the latter, without implying that the church was separating from the state in principle.

The meeting was still in session at midnight on 28 March, because Ludvig Hope had reservations about the centrality of ordination and the pastoral office in the document. Berggrav finally asked him if he would let the words on ordination stand. In light of the situation, Hope agreed. "That was a blessed moment," Berggrav wrote later.[12]

Just before 2 A.M., with everyone in reflection, seemingly at peace, Berggrav suddenly became disquieted. He looked at Hallesby and asked, "Are you *entirely* at peace with this?"[13] Hallesby agreed that he was not; others were not either. The problem was "we condemn" at the end of each section. The words symbolized an attack, a lust for battle. Another problem was political: "we condemn" would leave clergy open to charges of rebellion and risked uniting the Germans and the NS, the very thing their strategy sought to avoid. The church's strategy had been based on non-violent resistance to the Nazification of society and the church, and the CCC did not want responsibility for the clergy being charged with outright rebellion. For that reason, their wording could not be "more politically provocative than ecclesiastically necessary."[14]

Berggrav worked on an alternative formulation for the next meeting, the afternoon of Palm Sunday. His revision replaced "We condemn" with "We confess—We declare." That satisfied everyone. They approved the text and finalized the Easter date.[15] Berggrav ended the day by meeting with Theodor Steltzer, his contact in the Wehrmacht, who agreed to warn him if the Germans or the NS discovered the plan.[16]

Berggrav knew his freedom would end on Easter Sunday. He could have escaped to Sweden or gone underground, but either option could have raised questions about motives and possibly demoralized the clergy. The CCC agreed to let Berggrav make the decision. If interrogated, they would "stand all for one and one for all" and cover for one another.[17]

Between Palm Sunday and Easter, tensions rose. Berggrav was to preach at the Cathedral on Good Friday, but Quisling learned of it and placed him under house arrest for the duration of Easter. The other bishops and dismissed clergy were placed under similar restrictions.

While Berggrav was confined to his cottage in Asker, an estimated 3,000 people filled the cathedral for the Good Friday service. A Hird battalion lined the center aisle.[18] After the opening hymn, the assistant pastor, Johannes Dietrichson, informed the congregation that the police had prevented Berggrav from leading the service. Outside the church, a crowd estimated at 10,000 sang hymns and the Fatherland Song (*Fedrelandssangen*). Contrary to Quisling's intentions, the Good Friday service became a demonstration of solidarity with the bishops.

THE FOUNDATION OF THE CHURCH

The CCC arranged for Conrad Bonnevie-Svendsen to print and distribute *The Foundation of the Church*. He was the church's representative on the Home Front's Coordination Committee and enlisted its network to help with the distribution. The system was efficient in Oslo, the region around Oslo, and in the larger cities; the farther from Oslo, the greater the difficulties. In some parishes of northern Norway, delays extended into May.[19]

The Foundation of the Church represented itself as a confession of the whole church.[20] Based on the doctrine of the two realms, the document's thesis was that the church was an autonomous spiritual institution whose legitimacy derived from God, not the state. The first section established the freedom of "God's Word" and the church's right to freely proclaim it. There could not be state instructions or restrictions on the proclamation or the proclaimer. Above all, the state had no authority to impose political conditions on servants of the church—conditions such as Feyling's circular of 10 February 1942 informing the church and mission societies that they would be free from restrictions only if they recognized the NS and the new order.

The second section declared that the church was established by God and that ordination was an "independent and integral link in a right call to service in the church." God called people into service, the church authorized their calling through ordination, and it was therefore intolerable that the state "for political-worldly considerations" could deprive an ordained man not only of his civil office but "his duty to service through Word and sacrament." When the rights and duties tied to ordination were violated, the church felt it "as a strike at the altar," and pastors owed obedience to God over human beings.

Section three delineated the church's "sacred solidarity." The church was composed not only of its official servants but of its various parts, among them Christian homes, schools, social service agencies, and voluntary organizations. Were the state to persecute any of these, the church's duty as the guardian of conscience was to stand with the persecuted. The fourth affirmation was the right and duty of parents and the church to raise children "in the church's faith into a Christian life." This was prescribed in the Bible's commandments and inscribed in Article 2 of Norway's Constitution. Through baptism, the church accepted this duty, together with home and school, and it would betray its duty if it allowed children to be handed over to those who would "revolutionize their minds" and educate them into a "view of life" foreign to Christianity.

The crucial fifth section addressed relations with the state. Based on the doctrine of the two realms and the distinction between the "spiritual church" and the "worldly state," the church was called to "administer the eternal benefits, and let the light of God's Word shine on all human conditions." The state's calling was to "protect bodies and bodily things against outright injustice and place a check on human beings in order to uphold civil justice and peace." If the state should claim to have "the highest authority and the *greatest* right over each citizen," or if the state became a demonic power and created a conflict of conscience in its citizens, then there were limits to obedience and, as Luther said, "one must not obey" such authorities.

Sixth, Norway's Constitution and laws gave state agencies an "administrative and regulative authority" in church affairs but not authority to dominate the church for reasons of state or politics. The state accepted the state church system because it wanted to serve the church and the Christian faith, and by so doing obligated itself constitutionally to scripture and the confessions. But the state was not the church, which remained "as the church of Jesus Christ sovereign in all affairs of God and spiritually free." The state, therefore, had to administer church affairs in accord with "the church's character as a confessional church."

In most places, the clergy read *The Foundation of the Church* on Easter Sunday, but in Trondheim and farther north they did so on the following Monday or later.[21] After reading *The Foundation of the Church*, the clergy announced that they were relinquishing their state offices but would continue to serve in accordance with scripture, the confessions, and the prayer book of the Church of Norway. Clergy who recognized the authority of the dismissed bishops and the CCC also signed a statement of loyalty to *The Foundation of the Church*.[22]

In many places, word got around that something was about to happen on Easter Sunday, 5 April. At Sunndal in the Nidaros Diocese, the pastor reported that most people cried and the congregation joined spontaneously and with one accord in the confession of faith and the Our Father. An old Communist who would never greet him properly before the war "cried so the tears just poured down his cheeks."[23] Most congregations were not that expressive, but churches were filled and the moment laden with emotion.

THE DECISIVE WEEK

The events of Easter Sunday took the Germans and the NS by surprise. Three days later, Quisling published a fierce rebuttal. The NS wanted the church to have complete freedom to preach and serve, he wrote. The real problem was church leaders, above all Berggrav, "this last and worst edition of Bishop Nikolas." The man who wrote so "lovingly about conscience" was a swindler and a traitor whom Quisling was forced to destroy.[24]

In the meantime, Feyling consulted the Minister of Justice, the Police Chief, and the Public Prosecutor (*Riksadvokat*), probably on 8 April. In their view, the clergy's resignation was "an act of rebellion against Norway's freedom and independence." Feyling sent a telegram on the same day warning the clergy that resigning from office was an act of rebellion.[25] Clergy who had resigned *and* been dismissed had eight days to move out of their parsonages and their districts; clergy who had resigned but had not yet been dismissed had three days to change their minds. The next day, Feyling publicly charged that the real intent of *The Foundation of the Church* was to use the church against the NS government, which was tantamount to "rebellion and war" and would be treated accordingly.[26]

The state's threats had their effect. Per Eivind Sæbø, for example, the pastor of Sirdal in southern Norway, had not yet received his copy of *The Foundation of the Church* and thus had not read it when he headed south to confer with his rural dean and other clergy in the coastal town of Flekkefjord. When he read the declaration, it made "a strong impression," he wrote later. That night he went through "a Gethsemane struggle" over the choice facing him. But the next morning he signed the standard resignation form and returned to Sirdal, expecting to move away within a few days.[27]

Around the country, clergy prepared to do the same, but the 2 P.M., Saturday, 11 April deadline came and went without repercussions. The reason was clear. Faced with 500 clergy who had resigned and had not responded to his threats, Feyling knew he could not dismiss them all without unforeseeable consequences.[28] That was why Feyling—after conferring with Quisling—informed the clergy on 11 April that it was illegal for them to resign without an official notice of "a proper dismissal." He also signaled the possibility of talks to resolve the conflict.[29]

The NS authorities were now in full retreat. As already noted, Terboven had been on an inspection trip in northern Norway and returned on the 11th. He was not happy at the turn of events and directed Quisling to embark on a "moderate course" on "the church problem."[30] To further defuse the situation, police measures against the bishops and the CCC were eased. Quisling also authorized Feyling's publication of his book called "Ecclesiastical White Book" (*Kirkelig hvitbok*), which faithfully and candidly documented the correspondence between the Church Department and the church on the issues to date.[31] Feyling hoped people would judge for themselves in the Church Department's favor. The publication was not to German liking, however, and Wilhelm Wagner confiscated it, apparently before it reached bookstores.[32]

In the meantime, resignations continued. By the end of the month, 615 of the 739 clergy who held state offices had resigned.[33] The Church Department never formally accepted most of the resignations, nor did it dismiss most of the clergy. They could not be replaced, and empty churches would only fuel charges of persecution.

THE PRICE OF LEADERSHIP

On Easter Sunday afternoon, State Police officers interrogated the CCC.[34] They wanted to know who wrote and distributed *The Foundation of the Church*. The CCC had developed common answers beforehand and replied that authorship was collaborative and they did not know about its distribution, which was the reason for turning the task over to Bonnevie-Svendsen. The State Police then sent Hans E. Wisløff, Ragnvald Indrebø, Kristian Hansson, and Ingvald B. Carlsen to Bredtvedt Prison. They were held without trial for two to three weeks before being released with moderate restrictions; Hansson remained at Bredtvedt until 11 May and was then placed under house arrest. Only Hallesby and Hope remained free, probably to avoid provoking their large constituencies.[35]

Berggrav was a special case. The police held him under house arrest until 8 April, when they transferred him to Bredtvedt Prison. Two days later he was interrogated by Sverre Riisnæs and Jonas Lie, the ministers of justice and the police. He also learned that Quisling had decided to try him before the NS's People's Court on charges of treason, insulting Hitler, false testimony, and injury to the state. Quisling wanted a quick trial, conviction, and execution.

Quisling might have had his way were it not for the intervention of three men tied to the German resistance. Anticipating Berggrav's arrest, Theodor Steltzer had sent a coded message to Helmut von Moltke, who in a few weeks would convene the Kreisau circle, a major German resistance group. He worked for the Wehrmacht's counterintelligence agency under Admiral Wilhelm Canaris, who provided official cover for the German resistance. On the order of Canaris, the Roman Catholic von Moltke and the Protestant Dietrich Bonhoeffer left for Oslo and arrived at midnight on 12 April.[36] Their assignment was to persuade von Falkenhorst and the Reichskommissariat that Berggrav's arrest could lead to public unrest, threaten Germany's military position, and encourage Norwegians in their resistance.[37] Steltzer had paved the way, so von Falkenhorst was persuaded. He dispatched Fridtjof Hammersen, another Kreisau ally on the General Staff, to discuss the situation with Paul Wegener, head of the *Einsatzstab* (task force) for dealing with the NS.[38]

At the Reichskommissariat, officials disapproved of Quisling's handling of the church crisis. Dr. Karl Ohm, the Gestapo's legal consultant, thought Berggrav's imprisonment was a "political misstep of the first order." Terboven apparently had the same reaction upon his return from his inspection trip to northern Norway on Saturday the 11th. By Monday, he must also have learned about von Moltke's and Bonhoeffer's visit, because Heinrich Himmler sent him a telegram about it. The mere fact that Berlin had dispatched investigators into the church struggle, followed by Himmler's involvement, did not reflect well on him, and Terboven canceled Berggrav's trial. He also dressed down Quisling for ordering Berggrav's arrest as well as his whole handling of the church since he became Minister President.[39]

In the meantime, von Moltke and Bonhoeffer continued to hold meetings with von Falkenhorst and his staff, and von Moltke kept Canaris informed with coded telegrams. The outcome of these developments was that on Wednesday 15 April, Martin Bormann, head of Hitler's secretariat, ordered Berggrav's release.[40] The precise chain of events leading to Bormann's order has not been traced, but a causal sequence beginning with Steltzer's initial coded telegram to von Moltke and ending with Bormann's order is probable.

Berggrav's release lasted about 90 seconds. He walked out of Bredtvedt at 4:50 P.M. on the 16th only to be whisked into a waiting State Police car and placed under house arrest at his cottage in nearby Asker for the rest of the occupation. His house arrest was probably Terboven's face-saving compromise with Quisling.[41] Because of cooperative Norwegian guards, he was able to maintain continuous contact with the Home Front and the church.[42]

THE SCOPE OF SOLIDARITY

In the course of April, declarations of solidarity with the clergy poured into the Church Department from the entire church: from the two theological faculties, who wrote their first-ever joint opinion; from clergy

employed in non-state church positions; from parish and diocesan councils; and, finally, from every mission society and other organizations in
the Church of Norway. Not a single parish council, mission society, or
church agency opposed the clergy's stand or expressed loyalty to the NS
leadership.[43]

The resignation of the clergy involved the free churches less directly
than had *The Pastoral Letter* or the protest against the indoctrination of
the young, but they understood that the events of Easter had implications
for them as well. After two years of informal meetings with Berggrav,
free church leaders felt a more personal sense of Christian solidarity with
the state church than ever before. As a consequence, the Church Department also received declarations of support from the free churches directly
or through the Dissenter Parliament.[44]

The Church of Norway's resistance was also widely reported in the
international press and in government and church publications, especially
in Sweden, the United Kingdom, and the United States.[45] Of particular
importance was Sweden. Its embassy in Oslo sent a steady stream of
church news to the Swedish government, and the Swedish press kept its
readership well informed. Steltzer and Axel Weebe, pastor of the Swedish
congregation in Oslo, also mediated church news to Swedish church
leaders and the Nordic Ecumenical Institute in Sigtuna Additionally, the
Institute served as a communications channel between the Church of
Norway and the ecumenical movement.[46] Even under house arrest, Berggrav had contact with the ecumenical movement.[47]

THE EFFECT ON QUISLING

Quisling had taken office on 1 February 1942 with ambitious plans for
Norway's political transformation, but the youth service law was the
worst decision he ever made. With the church, schools, and parents roused
into a unified front, every subsequent NS initiative became a setback.[48]
In the next months, Hitler vetoed Quisling's plans for a National Assembly, as well as his longheld desire for a formal peace treaty with Germany, and finally ordered Quisling to deal with Berlin solely through
Terboven.

The loss of Hitler's confidence left Quisling "disappointed, disillu-
sioned, and bitter."[49] He blamed Terboven for provoking the conflict

with the church, a deliberate strategy to discredit him in Berlin, and NS circles blamed the Germans for both the conflict with the church and the "striking" teachers. The party also began to turn on its own leaders and splinter into factions.[50] The church's resistance was not the sole reason for the party's declining fortunes, but it was at the center of the front that led to it.

PART IV

*Contesting
NS Legitimacy*

———

Chapter 12

Negotiations?

———

A HARSHER OCCUPATION

Just after Christmas 1941 and without the knowledge of the Norwegian government, the British carried out raids and sabotage in Måløy and Reine in the Lofoten islands of northern Norway, leaving 150 German soldiers dead and 98 taken prisoner.

The raids shocked Hitler and convinced him the Allies would invade through northern Norway. A month later he declared that Norway was the "fateful area of this war" and diverted another 150,000 soldiers to the country. On 25 March, he received a Wehrmacht report on the need to increase preparedness for an Allied invasion, and on 13 May the Wehrmacht forced 15,000 Norwegian men to begin work on military construction as Hitler continued to build Fortress Norway.

Within the country, Terboven met force with force, and April 1942 was a setback for the resistance. On Easter Sunday, he deported 54 leading Norwegians to Sachsenhausen, including Labor Party leader Einar Gerhardsen, the poet Arnulf Øverland, and the University of Oslo's president (*rektor*), Didrik Arup Seip. On the west coast, German reprisals brought the traffic of volunteers leaving Norway for the United Kingdom to a standstill. On 15 April, the coastal steamer *Skjerstad* left Trondheim for the northern town of Kirkenes with 500 teachers forcibly evacuated onboard; another 500 had been sent to the Grini internment camp.

The worst reprisal of the occupation came after 26 April, when two Norwegian commandos killed the Bergen Gestapo chief and his assistant in the fishing village of Tælavåg, just outside Bergen. Terboven personally supervised the razing of the village, deported 71 men to concentration camps in Germany, where 31 died, and interned the women and children. In the wake of Tælavåg, the Gestapo rounded up Milorg units from Bergen to Stavanger to Oslo. In this context, no one could assume that a church accused of taking a "political" stand on Easter Sunday would be exempt from harsher reprisals.

ESTABLISHING AN AUTONOMOUS CHURCH

Cutting its ties to the state launched the Church of Norway into uncharted waters. The clergy had resigned and no longer accepted state salaries, but they remained in their parishes and continued their ministries. For the rest of April, May, and June, they had no income and did not know who was leading the church. For several weeks the church seemed paralyzed.

The reason was a leadership crisis. Because of government restrictions on its members, neither the CCC nor its planned successor, the Church's Consultative Council, was able to function. In late June, however, restrictions were lifted on all the bishops but Berggrav, and the leadership could begin to reorganize. Dean Johannes Hygen of Oslo was Berggrav's representative.

Ole Hallesby was a member of both the CCC and the Church's Consultative Council, intended to be the CCC's successor but too unwieldy to work under the circumstances. Accordingly, in mid-June he took the initiative to convene the bishops and the executive committee of the Church's Consultative Council to discuss the creation of a new leadership group. The discussions culminated in the formation of the Provisional Church Leadership (PCL).[1] The PCL comprised three bishops—Berggrav (represented by Hygen), Maroni, and Hille—and three mission society representatives—Hallesby, Hope, and H. E Wisløff, chair of the Council of Autonomous Organizations. In its first phase, much of the day-to-day responsibility fell on Hallesby.[2]

On 23 July 1942, a month after its formation, the PCL sent its first message to the congregations. It claimed spiritual victory: over 90 percent of the 738 currently serving pastors had resigned, more were continuing to do so, and parish councils were rallying around their "pastors." The PCL also insisted that the church was not engaged in politics or attempting to "explode the state church." Nor was it establishing "a free folk church" or "free church." Instead, the fight was for *"the church,* for the church's inner nature and most precious right, for its God-given call to proclaim God's Word and live its distinctive life in the midst of the state." From now on, said the PCL, the work of the church would be *in the church,* serving congregations with "Word and sacrament" and not violating established church ordinances more than necessary.[3]

If the PCL's view of its mission looked restrictive, a defensive retreat to "the spiritual realm," it was. After Berggrav's house arrest, the church ceased to take a proactive stance. Even when it engaged in protest, it was reacting to events.

The NS, of course, had another view of the PCL's legitimacy. In August, the Commissioner Minister of the Interior, Eivind Blehr, informed the PCL that the Minister President was the supreme leader of state and church.[4] The state church, and the right church, was thus the one that recognized Quisling and the NS state. The PCL, therefore, was unconstitutional and in violation of the law. Accordingly, Blehr declared it dissolved, impounded its "possible" assets, and threatened it with criminal penalties. The PCL was officially illegal.

The bishops protested that there had to be some misunderstanding. It was the state that had been acting politically, forcing the church to create a provisional church leadership, but there had *"never been from our side any thought or wish to* dissolve the state church." Once tensions subsided, the PCL intended to "return to our old state church form of governance."[5] This was a message to the NS, but it was also designed for the Norwegian people and the Norwegian government in London.

ESTABLISHING THE NS CHURCH

Most of the clergy resigned, but the NS state never dismissed the majority of them from office. The reason was numerical and political: the Church Department had only a few "loyal" clergy to replace those who resigned, and a nation of empty pulpits would have given substance to charges of religious persecution. For those reasons, Quisling decided that the only way forward was to "lay a smokescreen" over the church conflict as he attempted to secure the legitimacy of the NS state church.[6]

From 5 to 16 April, Quisling began the process by issuing a series of emergency decrees. He altered the laws governing episcopal elections, lowered clerical qualifications, and abolished the Bishops' Conference. He also created a Church Advisory Conference (*Kirkelig rådsmøte*) consisting of Quisling, Skancke, Feyling, Theisen, and the NS bishops, and he expanded the number of dioceses to ten. To prevent a mass exit of members from the state church, he also amended the Dissenter Law to require the signature of the local (NS) bishop in order to withdraw membership.

The key to the NS establishing ecclesiastical legitimacy was the office of bishop, and the key to that office was ordination. Unlike the Church of Sweden and the Church of England, the Church of Norway had not retained apostolic succession at the Reformation, but ecclesiastical law stipulated that a bishop could only be ordained by another bishop selected by the king, that is, the constitutional government.[7] Because the bishops had resigned, and in any case would not have ordained an NS bishop, Feyling had to find a way to legitimately ordain NS bishops.

The first possibility was a Scandinavian or German bishop. Feyling had been thinking about the problem since the fall of 1941 in anticipation of Støren's retirement, and both he and a few other NS clergy liked the idea of reintroducing apostolic succession along with the office of archbishop, also lost at the Reformation. Sweden had retained both, and the Church of Finland also had an archbishop and claimed apostolic succession. The Swedish bishops were not a realistic possibility, however, because most of them had shown solidarity with the Norwegian bishops, but the Church of Finland looked more promising to Feyling. After Barbarossa, Finland fought with Germany against its chief threat, the Soviet Union, with the support of the church. To explore Finnish possibilities, Feyling commissioned a Finnish-Norwegian clergyman, Johan Beronka, to travel to Finland for talks with Archbishop Erkki Kaila. The Finnish archbishop, however, was unreceptive. The Church Department thought briefly about asking a German bishop, but a German bishop would not confer the legitimacy that Feyling was looking for. The only way out was to abandon the idea of ordination by an archbishop as well as apostolic succession.[8]

Like Berggrav in his quest to reinterpret the Doctrine of the Two Realms, Feyling soon found a solution in "the young" Martin Luther. In a confidential memo to Quisling titled "Reformation of the Church in the Spirit of 'the Young Luther,'" he argued that Berggrav and the bishops had actually promoted a Catholic view of ordination by claiming that they retained the "spiritual" part of their office when they resigned from their state offices. Such a view of ordination was not only theologically mistaken, Feyling wrote, but it would boost the independent authority of the bishops, and that was not in the NS state's political interest. The young Luther, in contrast, had taken the opposite course by eliminating the office of bishop altogether and replacing it with that of superintendent. Furthermore, in his "Letter to the German Nobility," Luther claimed there was no difference between the clergy and laity, and pastoral ordination need not require a bishop. It followed that ordination by a bishop conferred no more spiritual authority than ordination by a superintendent, or, in effect, an ordinary clergyman.[9]

The political solution was simpler. On 9 April 1942, Quisling repealed the laws governing the election of bishops and granted to himself the right to appoint bishops. His appointments would be at the recommendation of the Church Department, which could solicit from the church "those opinions it found desirable."[10]

With the theological and legal obstacles erased, the regime proceeded to appoint new bishops. As the new bishop of Oslo, Feyling's choice fell on Lars Andreas Frøyland. Frøyland was not a member of the NS, which disturbed some party leaders, and his family was anti-NS, but he was a respected pastor and was willing to serve.[11] As a result, on 28 June 1942, Einar Lothe, acting Bishop of Nidaros, ordained Frøyland as bishop of Oslo and Ludvig D. Zwilgmeyer as bishop of Skien, a new diocese created by the Church Department. For the time being, the other NS bishops remained "acting" bishops.

As the schism threatened to become permanent, new questions arose. At the first Church Advisory Council meeting on 30 June 1942, the NS bishops discussed the opposition clergy, parish councils, the wording of the Church's Prayer of Intercession, and theological education.[12] The Council, however, had no consensus on dealing with the opposition, and the likely reason was a surprising development in the crisis.

NEGOTIATIONS?

Perhaps nothing shows the church's reluctance to break with the state church tradition more than its willingness, only weeks after breaking with the state, to enter negotiations with the same state to resolve the crisis. From any angle, this was a puzzling move. Why would a church that had so dramatically repudiated the state decide within a few weeks to enter negotiations with it? And why would a state that had just provoked the church into schism and charged its leaders with rebellion extend such an invitation? The church risked the spiritual and moral capital it had accumulated since *The Pastoral Letter*, and the state risked another demonstration of its political impotence. The stakes were high on both sides.

Despite the risks to its reputation, the state had little to lose. After Easter, the NS state had imprisoned church leaders and intimidated and threatened pastors, without changing minds. It had no highly respected candidates to ordain as bishops, few loyal pastors for vacant offices, and not enough lay followers to muster a majority in a single parish. Furthermore, Quisling's provocations since 1 February had raised the "fighting spirit of the Norwegians" to such a level that "today it will hardly be understood by people outside Norway."[13] Merely easing tensions would not be enough. The longer the stalemate continued, the less likely the state would be able to turn it to advantage. That was why Feyling informed the State Police that the government had "found it necessary to bring about the greatest possible easing of tension in the church situation."[14] For the same reason, Feyling invited the clergy to name a delegation to negotiate with the Church Department.

Hallesby and Hygen accepted with the condition that only their bishops, as leaders of the church, would negotiate in behalf of the church.[15] Feyling rejected the condition, but he nevertheless invited Hallesby and Hygen to an open-ended conference on 22 June.

Although Feyling had just rejected their condition for talks, and the purpose of the conference was unclear, Hallesby and Hygen accepted his invitation. Moreover, they had been participating in the formation of the PCL, which was announced the next day and was supposed to create and lead an autonomous church. Under the circumstances, why would they consider one more talk with Feyling?

A FREE FOLK CHURCH?

After the war, the CCC members were silent about their motives for accepting the state's invitation, but the reason must have been a "manifesto" from the Stavanger Christian Consultative Council. This was the same group that had sent Olav Valen-Sendstad to Oslo about a declaration on church and state.

The driving force behind the manifesto, however, was Einar Amdahl, executive secretary of the Norwegian Mission Society, but the document had the support of the entire Stavanger CCC. Three clergymen in Hauge-sund had also seen and approved it.[16] Dated 13 June, it reached Oslo just before Hallesby and Hygen agreed to see Feyling and the announcement of the PCL.

The Stavanger manifesto was prompted by three concerns. The first was the sense that the interim situation had become untenable. The church could not continue to commit itself to resuming the church-state relationship while the state was establishing an NS state church. That problem was illustrated by the second consideration, which was the state's plan to ordain Lars Frøyland as Bishop of Oslo, characterized as "an act of violence against the church." Finally, just as the clergy's status had been untenable after the resignation of their bishops, so was the status of the parish councils after the clergy resigned. How could they continue when their bishop and clergy had resigned? Logic dictated that parish councils also should resign from their state duties and reorganize as free parish councils.[17]

The Stavanger manifesto thus called for each congregation to declare itself "the true congregation" of the "Free Norwegian Lutheran Folk Church" in its locality. From the moment of that declaration, state church members living within the parish were to be viewed as members of the "Free Norwegian Lutheran Folk Church," and they would charge their local parish councils to call pastors to serve their congregations.[18] The manifesto was to be read and accepted at congregational meetings. The proposal envisioned the establishment of an entirely free church based on a radical decentralization of ecclesiastical authority, essentially a congregational church. The Stavanger CCC was aware that its proposal for mass withdrawal and formal separation from the state church would raise questions and, possibly, cause divisions, but, as things stood, they thought an air of illegality and illegitimacy hung over the whole church.[19] By deliberating and carrying out their tasks freely, congregations would experience a "liberation of conscience."

The Stavanger CCC was not intimidated by the thought of being a free church. In the mission societies of the West and Southwest, the widespread assumption was that the state church was unbiblical, and some societies had almost a century of success as voluntary organizations. The moment looked propitious for their vision of the church.

In Oslo, however, the manifesto was deeply troubling, and on the very day that the PCL announced its existence, Hallesby and Hygen answered Amdahl with three objections. The first was that the Germans would view a change of polity as church *politics* rather than church *work*, leading to a direct conflict. The prudent thing was to continue limiting the church's policy to strictly church matters: "And just that," wrote Hallesby and Hygen to Amdahl, "is the strength of our position: We show in our actions that we do not want anything more than to serve our congregations with Word and sacrament, pastoral care, visits to the sick, confirmation instruction, burial, etc."[20] The second was that the NS would use wholesale changes in polity to discredit the church's claim to be acting on conscience when the clergy resigned from their state offices. The NS could charge that church leaders had really wanted all along to separate from the state and institute long-desired church reforms or were simply power hungry. Finally, there was the probability that the Stavanger proposal would split the church front into those who wanted a "free folk church," those who wanted a "free church," and those who simply wanted a freer state church on the model of Sweden and Finland. It was best to leave well enough alone.

Behind the Hallesby's and Hygen's formal objections there must have been other concerns as well. The first was that in a censored society, the church could not openly discuss a topic as complex as reorganization. The transformation from a state to a free church had ramifications that were too wide-ranging and unforeseeable to enact under the circumstances, and it also involved the Norwegian government, the other partner in the equation. This analysis had added weight in the context of the wider war, which looked like it would soon end in Allied victory.

Other concerns must have been brought to the surface by the mere appearance of the Stavanger proposals. The PCL had just released its first message, taking great pains to show that it had not separated from the state as such. Having severed its ties to the state, however, had the church launched itself on a logical trajectory to a free church? What were the consequences of institutionalizing an autonomous church for an undetermined period until liberation? Would an indefinite period as a free folk church make reconstituting the state church in the postwar era more difficult? Behind such questions was the weight of a nearly thousand year state church tradition, from which the Oslo leadership did not wish to separate more than absolutely necessary. It did not want even the hint of "a free church" attached to it.

If the free church threat posed by the Stavanger proposal was not behind the church's interest in reconciling with the state that it had repudiated only weeks before, it is impossible to explain why its leaders would risk so much.

PRELIMINARY TALKS

The state's decision to negotiate began with the NS acting bishop of Stavanger, Ole J. B. Kvasnes, who sent Feyling a proposal for peace in the church.[21] Perhaps he had found out about the Stavanger manifesto, which he would have disliked. Kvasnes's proposal initiated preliminary talks that lasted until September. Their duration reveals the depth of the desire for resolution, and their substance clarifies the issues.

The state negotiators were Skancke and Feyling, aided by the unlikely intervention of a precentor from Lindås, L. Lothe. Representing the church were Hallesby and Hygen in consultation with the bishops (several of whom, including Berggrav, were under house arrest) and the PCL. In the first round, the negotiators agreed on four conditions for further talks: Skancke and Feyling would represent the state, the bishops would represent the church, Berggrav would be freed in order to participate, and there would be no preconditions.[22] Signed and dated 15 August, the agreement was to be presented to authorities on both sides before talks resumed.

Quisling naturally had doubts about liberating Berggrav, who had already refused to recognize the legality of the Commissarial Council. Moreover, negotiations could end with the bishops refusing to recognize the NS government, and Quisling was not about to be humiliated one more time. As a result, when talks started again on 21 August, Skancke demanded that the church recognize the legality of the NS government as a precondition of negotiations. Hallesby and Hygen however, rejected the condition; only the bishops had authority to speak for the church and confer such recognition.[23]

Hallesby and Hygen were treading a fine line and did not want their position to imply opposition to the Germans so they drafted a new statement for review by the bishops. It stated that the Church of Norway would adhere to "its Lutheran confession and keep the church out of politics." The crucial sentences followed:

> It recognizes and cooperates with any form of state that recognizes the church's right to live its life and fulfill its task according to God's Word and the church's confession and that recognizes the church's right to be the conscience of the state by protecting the people's freedom of conscience and legal rights. Our church, therefore, will also recognize our present state ruler to the extent that it will recognize the just mentioned God-given rights of the church.[24]

To be sure that the Germans understood their intentions, Hallesby and Hygen asked Günther to pass this statement on to the Gestapo church affairs officer, Wilhelm Wagner.

After Quisling reviewed the statement, he amended most of the third paragraph to read:

> It [the church] recognizes and cooperates with any form of state that recognizes the church's right to live its life and fulfill its task according to God's Word and the church's confession. Therefore, we also recognize our current state government because it has expressed its recognition for precisely the named God-given right. Cf. the Minister President's circular of 26 February this year to all clergy in the Church of Norway where it states: "It is my and the national government's intention in accordance with the Constitution to protect the evangelical Lutheran religion, so that the church will have the freedom to preach God's Word to our people and carry out its social work."[25]

In the ensuing discussions, Skancke permitted the bishops to convene in Oslo and, along with Hallesby and Hygen, to confer with Berggrav at his cottage in Asker, but Feyling added the proviso that Quisling's amended statement would be the only document under discussion. To the bishops and the PCL, Feyling's proviso was an ultimatum, and the bishops rejected it as contrary to the agreement of 15 August. Free negotiations were impossible, they declared, on the basis of the new conditions.[26]

In spite of all that had happened to that point, the bishops were still willing to proceed on the basis of the terms agreed to on 15 August and enter into a third round of negotiations. Skancke, however, continued to insist on recognition of the government, and the bishops continued to insist that Berggrav had to be freed before negotiations could begin.[27] As they waited for Skancke's reply, the PCL drafted a position paper for the anticipated negotiations, but it was a wasted effort. Skancke and Feyling had already decided to break off talks, probably at Quisling's order, and directed the police to reinstate the punitive measures against the clergy, including eviction from their parishes.[28]

A NEW CONTEXT

With the end to any hope of a negotiated settlement, the schism that began on Easter Sunday formed the new context of religious life. From 5 April 1942 until the end of the occupation, the Church of Norway was divided between a small minority who recognized the legitimacy of the NS state and the NS state church and an overwhelming majority who did not recognize the legitimacy of either one.[29]

From now on, therefore, the conflict would not so much be a church-state conflict as a church-church conflict. And the question contested was fundamentally simple: Which church was the right church, the legitimate Church of Norway?

Chapter 13

The Autonomous Church

―

FROM RESISTANCE TO OPPOSITION

This chapter is about the formation of an autonomous church organization to serve its members with "Word and sacrament"; the next chapter is the story of the NS's attempt to rebuild the state church. Both chapters are also about each side's strategy to contain the other, to deny the other legitimacy.

At first glance, building an organization may seem peripheral to the story of the church's resistance to Nazism, a diversion from the important issues, but that is not so. The clergy's mass resignation on Easter 1942 made it central. Deprived of the economic and institutional support of the state, and in order to fulfill its stated mission of serving the people with Word and sacrament, the church had to create an alternative institutional structure. Doing so was necessary to maintain its interpretation of Christianity, but it was also necessary in order to contest the legitimacy of the NS church and, indirectly, the NS state.[1]

THE GUIDELINES OF NON-COOPERATION

The Church of Norway was so entangled with the state that the PCL's first order of business was developing policies for its disentanglement. In its first message to clergy, parish councils, and congregations, the PCL issued specific guidelines, which were supplemented over time and became known as "the ten commandments."[2] The underlying principles were continuation of ministry and systematic non-cooperation with the state along clearly defined lines. The purpose was to delegitimize the NS church and, indirectly, the state that supported it.

The clergy were thus directed to continue their ministry without regard for the Church Department's dismissals or appointments. This meant dealing solely with legitimate bishops, deans, and parish councils; continuing to live in parsonages; using parish churches and their facilities; and, with modifications, maintaining birth, baptism, marriage, and other records. Clergy were to have no dealings whatever with the Church Department, the NS bishops, deans, clergy, or parish councils. Salary checks and correspondence were to be returned unopened, and the same applied to income due from local governments.

Similarly, councils were to communicate to parishioners that they remained the legitimate councils and to cooperate solely with "pastors" who had resigned from their state offices. Only these were to be recognized as legitimate pastors of the parish, to have automatic membership on the parish councils, and to have use of the church, its facilities, and manse. When a parish pastorate became vacant, councils were to request replacements from their rightly appointed bishops. The elected parish councils were to decline nomination to appointed NS councils, refuse to prepare budgets for municipalities, and assert their right to oversee church property and determine its use. If an NS clergyman was appointed to the parish, they were not to inform him about meetings or to deliberate with him. A parish council dismissed by the NS Church Department was to continue as if it had not been dismissed, precisely as the clergy were doing. Overall, pastors and councils were to ignore, shun, and boycott the "Nazi Church," ignore state and local government authorities, and resist both if they interfered with their legitimate duties.[3]

ADMINISTRATION

For practical reasons, PCL members were full-time clergy who lived in Oslo. Erling Thomle related that the group usually met on Mondays, unless circumstances required greater frequency. Meetings would begin with prayer, a news update, and then discussions that often lasted from 11 A.M. to 3 or 4 P.M., because decisions were made by consensus. Initially, they met at an office on St. Olavs Street until a police raid on 9 November

1942 forced them to move to the sacristy of the Church for the Deaf and, later, a small room in Oslo's Frogner Church. The Frogner room had poor ventilation, which, Thomle noted, was hard on non-smokers because "the smoke was often thick and the tobacco not of the best." Thereafter, they would also meet occasionally in the apartment of Lilly Schübeler, a sister of one of the PCL members, Ludwig Schübeler. They stored records in specially built cupboards and hiding places in the Frogner Church, in a suitcase Thomle buried in his back yard, or in boxes hidden at the homes of Lilly Schübeler, Johannes Dietrichson, or Thomle.[4]

PCL members were surprised they were not caught, and they had reason to be. The group was in constant contact with the bishops, of whom all but Berggrav continued to administer their dioceses even under police restrictions. They were also in regular contact with the Home Front, notably the Coordination Committee and the teachers. Finally, they kept the Oslo clergy up to date through weekly meetings. The PCL had a large institution to administer. In March 1943, the PCL counted 858 ordained pastors in the church, mission societies, and other positions. Of those, 797 (93 percent) had pledged loyalty to *The Foundation of the Church* and 61 (7 percent) remained in the NS state church.[5]

The PCL's first administrative task was filling the nation's pulpits with pastors loyal to *The Foundation of the Church*. Parishes became vacant for all the usual reasons—illness, retirement, and death—to which were added the government's dismissal of clergymen, usually accompanied by expulsion from their parishes and dioceses. The PCL had responsibility for finding and assigning pastors to the vacant positions, a task that was essential for the autonomous church to fulfill its spiritual mission and preempt the NS state church. The church had not ordained new pastors since the occupation, but the PCL's task was eased by a prewar surplus of theological graduates and the willingness of mission societies to reassign their clergy as needed. Pastors expelled from one district were sometimes reassigned to parishes vacated by other expelled clergymen, although the PCL proceeded cautiously in such cases.[6]

COMMUNICATION

There could be no administration without a communication network. This service was the most demanding and dangerous aspect of the church administration, and it was led by Conrad Bonnevie-Svendsen, pastor to the nation's hearing-impaired and deaf.[7] He had permission to travel throughout the country, which enabled him to oversee the national network and to serve as a courier himself. He also was the church's representative on the Coordinating Committee, where he played a leading role.[8] In spite of holding two sensitive positions, he was not found out until March 1945, when he escaped to Sweden to avoid arrest.

Other members of the PCL also held offices that offered similar opportunities. Tormod Vågen, for example, was the secretary general of the China Mission Association, and Ludwig Schübeler served as chairman of the Diakonhjemmet Hospital executive committee. Both traveled frequently and doubled as couriers. Most of the couriers, however, were clergymen, aided by theological students. When these failed, Bonnevie-Svendsen could usually draw on the Home Front's courier network.[9]

As early as September 1942, the church also built diocesan communication networks. Before his arrest, Berggrav had instituted a system in Oslo Diocese whereby four pastors each had responsibility for maintaining contact with a quarter of the other pastors, and the PCL adopted a version of that system. Each diocese had a "responsibility center," usually consisting of about a dozen clergymen representing rural deaneries, each responsible for relaying information to and from the parishes.[10] In Oslo, the PCL held weekly meetings with the clergy, while in other dioceses meetings were on a monthly or quarterly basis. These helped to maintain clergy morale, trust, and solidarity.[11]

Couriers became even more important as the Germans clamped down on the press. They had censored the press from the outset, but in late 1942 and early 1943 they rationed paper severely and church periodicals and parish newsletters had to cease publication as well. The PCL filled the vacuum with two newspapers. One was directed at the clergy and went by several names, such as "Greetings Between Clergy Brothers" (*Hilsen mellom prestebrødre*). It was generally inspirational in character but also contained material on the church's aims and current situation.[12] The main source of hard news, however, was "The Church Today" (*Kirken i Dag*), which was, strictly speaking, an illegal newsletter, since it began publication in March 1944, after the state declared the PCL illegal.[13] It included PCL directives as well as the latest reports on the Church Department, the NS church, and police measures against the bishops and

clergy. It was edited by PCL member Andreas Seierstad, aided by a journalist, Hans Høivik (Høeg), and a student from the Free Faculty of Theology, Nils Bloch-Hoell.[14]

The illegal newsletters and the courier network worked effectively
until the end of the occupation. Even while under house arrest, Berggrav
received regular outside information and communicated his counsel.[15]
The contact helped to maintain the trust and solidarity essential to a
secret leadership and its constituency.

FINANCING THE CHURCH

As state civil servants, the clergy were paid by the state. In 1939, they
received a base salary plus additional income for every three years of
service, income from the parish lands or the equivalent, and income from
other fees.[16] After 5 April 1942, the clergy returned state letters unopened,
including salary checks from the state and municipalities. That left the
clergy in a vulnerable position, and there was a possibility that their
resolve would waver. Voluntary giving for clergy salaries was unknown
territory and there was no way of knowing how congregants would
respond. Far-sighted clergymen had started saving as early as 1940, and
parishes had rallied round their clergymen in the chaotic days of April
1942, but the clergy needed a more secure arrangement.[17]

In early 1942—before the resignation of the clergy—a finance committee connected to the Church of Norway's Clergy Association had
been established in Oslo.[18] It consisted of Sam Knutzen, a businessman,
Leif Eriksen, a lawyer, and Hans Sande, the secretary general of Norway's Christian Youth Association, a merger of the YMCA and YWCA.
But the first sign that raising the necessary funds for clergy salaries was
possible came from shipping magnate Arnt Mørland in Arendal. He
headed the Agder Diocesan Council and after Easter 1942 organized a
diocesan collection for resigned clergy that exceeded expectations. In
Arendal, for example, Gjerulf Fløystad, an insurance executive working under Mørland, quickly collected 10,000 kroner more than he had
requested. Afraid that the church struggle would rapidly become a fiasco
if salary arrangements were not made promptly, the PCL arranged for
Mørland to meet with Hallesby, Hope, and Knutzen in Oslo.[19] Following the meeting, Mørland returned to the Agder Diocese and within a week

created a revenue collection organization before moving on to do the same in Stavanger and Bergen.

The new financial arrangements were noticed in the NS Church Department, and Quisling passed a law prohibiting collections for the resigned clergy, or for anyone involved in anti-state activities.[20] An obvious alternate avenue for collecting funds would have been the mission societies, which had fund-raising systems in place. But in May 1942, the Norwegian Mission Society rejected the idea, because it did not want to give the state cause to investigate it for misuse of funds.[21] Other societies took the same stand. Collections would have to take place through the autonomous church.

In Oslo, Knutzen became chairman of the Secret Finance Leadership, which was founded in April 1942 and operated until May 1945. The organization used distinctive fictional code names to hide their identities: as national leader, Knutzen was known as "L.L.," for Lauritz Larsen; each diocese had a leader who went by "B.L.," for Birger Larsen; and each district had a "D.L.," or David Larsen, to organize collections from the congregations in the district. The system ultimately depended on these local organizers, usually parish treasurers, who arranged for collections from congregations.[22] Leaders also developed other means of collecting funds, such as monthly pledges. The whole organization was directed and run by laymen who, with few exceptions, avoided police detection for the three years of its operation. If caught, they faced six years in prison for aiding a terminated civil servant.[23]

If every parish had been able to support its pastor, a national finance leadership might not have been needed, but for a variety of reasons, some parishes could not collect funds. Sagene Church in Oslo, for example, ceased collections after the first month because the police discovered the names of contributors; not only were parishioners fearful of reprisals, the identity of the local organizer was at risk, leading to the possibility of further exposures.[24] The finance leadership thus redirected excess funds from some congregations to others.

Although most clergy received lower salaries than they had as state employees, contributions were generous. An exceptional example was the parish of Åseral in the Agder Diocese, a rural mountain parish that collected the equivalent of their pastor's salary in two days.[25] The generosity was facilitated by high German wages and a scarcity of consumer goods;

people had money to give.[26] As one clergyman, Rasmus Håskoll of Askvoll put it, the clergy lived "in a golden age of love from our people."[27] That might be so. Supporters also must have realized, however, that without a system of financial support, the church's resistance would have been compromised.

CLAIMING THE PARISHES

The experience of parishes during the occupation was so varied that no generalization is adequate. Some parishes hardly noticed the occupation. Their clergy reported that they had never seen German troops in their parishes, none were stationed close by, the Gestapo never appeared at their door, there were few NS members in their communities, and they never had to deal with NS pastors, even those appointed to their parishes. In other parishes, the picture was entirely different. In northern Norway, for example, several had such high concentrations of German troops that soldiers outnumbered inhabitants, altering the whole tenor of communities, including the parishes. The majority were in between, where the war, the Wehrmacht, the Gestapo, the NS state, and the NS church intruded on parish life to a greater or lesser degree. Whether local church struggles erupted after 5 April depended on whether an NS pastor was appointed to the parish and how many NS parishioners in the parish were willing to support him actively. Because NS clergy and supporters were so few, the clergy generally worked without significant competition or opposition. In parishes with no NS clergy and few NS members, serving the church became, if anything, more fulfilling.[28]

Non-cooperation did not mean passivity. Parish leaders organized boycotts of NS church services, some going as far as to stand at the doors to the churches, note pads in hand, recording the names of those who attended; this form of intimidation discouraged all but the most zealous or courageous of NS Christians.[29] With baptisms, confirmations, weddings, and funerals, as well as weekly services, parishioners boycotted NS clergymen and sought out the clergy of the autonomous church. In parishes with NS clergymen, parishioners usually worshipped and underwent the rites of passage in adjacent parishes. In some cases, truckloads of confirmands were driven to other parishes for confirmation instruction. This was the "ice front" of social non-cooperation.

Parishioners also rallied around the church and their local pastors by attending services at a much higher rate than before the occupation and by contributing to pastors' financial support. No detailed national study of parish attendance exists, but church leaders reported that they had not experienced such high attendance rates for a generation, and an abundance of anecdotal and statistical evidence from many parishes supports this observation.[30] In May 1943, for example, Bishop Andreas Fleischer reported that in 62 out of 92 parishes in the Bjørgvin Diocese church attendance had risen. In the city of Bergen, the number had jumped from 20 to 28 percent of the population; figures for the whole diocese showed a 30 percent increase in communicants, with some rural parishes reporting 100 percent attendance.[31] Compared to prewar levels, such numbers were astonishing, and the rise in communicants seemed to indicate that church attendance was now on a "different plane" than sensation-seeking.[32]

The times were heady for pastors, and it was easy for them to be carried on the wave of popular support. Some could not resist injecting provocative political opinions into their sermons, it and it was always possible to preach about the present by pointed reference to events two thousand years earlier. Both satisfied a need to express political dissidence in a censored society.

The PCL and the clergy saw signs of spiritual renewal in the increased church attendance, but there is every reason to think that patriotism explains most of it.[33] For one thing, according to accounts from both sides of the conflict, sermons were no more scintillating or relevant during the occupation than before. An expelled clergyman who used his freedom to attend the services of many colleagues reported that the preaching might as well have been delivered in 1895.[34] NS local leaders and church spies were similarly unimpressed. The NS leader in Saltdal complained to the Justice Department that a local pastor who had preached to "just about an empty church" was suddenly attracting a "a huge crowd," including "true blue old Communists and atheists."[35] Sympathetic outside observers made the same point. An unidentified Englishwoman who reported on the church for British intelligence thought the church was "hidebound by its orthodox rigidity" and the rise in church attendance was "mainly due to a desire to make a political demonstration and to support the priests in their patriotic stand."[36]

The patriotism, however, may also have had a genuinely spiritual and religious dimension. In a homogenous country with a thousand-year state church tradition, religious and national identity were inseparable. The wartime attendance may thus have been an expression of a religious patriotism that activated the middle and outer circle of believers who were normally passive church members.

In some areas of church life, conditions actually led to a decline in church participation. The public boycott of NS clergy meant infants were not baptized, children were not confirmed, and couples did not seek the church's blessing after civil weddings. The fall-off was probably greatest in northern Norway, which had a high concentration of German troops and long distances between communities. Bishop Krohn-Hansen of the thinly populated northern Hålogaland Diocese reported that in 46 of his 72 parishes there were 2,143 church weddings in 1941 but only 656 in 1942.[37] He thought that the schism was one reason; people who boycotted the NS church had to be married by a judge and then arrange for a church blessing of their union. Conditions also occasionally forced bishops to authorize emergency measures. Krohn-Hansen was cut off from many of the Bishops' Conference meetings because it took days to reach Oslo, and in many ways he had to lead his own church resistance from Tromsø. He cited these extraordinary conditions as his reason for authorizing unordained people to administer the sacraments.[38]

THE SUPPORT OF MISSION SOCIETIES

Except at the beginning and end of the occupation, the Lutheran domestic and foreign mission organizations were able to work without major interruption or interference during the five years of occupation.[39] In 1940, from the invasion on 9 April to the capitulation on 7 June, they lost facilities in battle zones and financial contributions slowed. The Norwegian Lutheran Home Mission Society reported 12 bombed chapels, most of them in regions where the fighting had been heaviest: Narvik, Bodø, Namsos, Steinkjer, Kristiansund, and Elverum. The same organization had 107 chapels requisitioned by the Germans.[40] Within a few weeks of the capitulation, however, normal activities resumed in most places. At the Council of Autonomous Organizations meeting in January 1941, leaders reported that local chapters were functioning normally: meetings were held on a regular schedule, and contributions held steady or had increased.[41] In 1941 and 1942, chapel attendance steadily rose, and societies reported several local revivals; the Western Home Mission Association reported more revivals than in any year since 1905, the year of Norway's independence. Mission society leaders also reported a new seriousness about religion among the people who sought out their chapels.[42]

Mission society leaders continued to serve in the PCL, ensuring the ongoing cooperation of the societies with the autonomous church. Ludwig Schübeler, a member of the PCL in the last two years of the occupation, was right: the church front had the societies to thank for becoming a people's front, and the PCL realized that it could not have functioned without them.[43] Although the societies did not use their own fund-raising system for pastoral salaries, they supplied their clergy—pastors who had been educated at the two theological faculties and ordained in the church—to prevent the NS Church Department from taking advantage of prolonged vacancies.

The solidarity of the societies also bolstered the church front in a more fundamental way, because among Norwegian popular movements the mission societies and the free churches were the most resistant to Nazism. Studies have also shown that the most NS resistant regions were those where the mission societies had their greatest numerical strength.[44] These were the areas that traditionally voted for the Liberal Party and resisted the Labor Party: southern, southwestern, and western Norway, along the coast and its hinterlands from Kristiansand to Trondheim.[45] The NS barely gained a toehold in those regions, and the same was true of the NS state church.

These are significant statistical facts. If religion involves world building, that is, maintaining the plausibility of a symbolic universe or worldview, then the mission societies were bulwarks of an orthodox, confessional, Lutheran worldview. The characteristics that made them militant sources of hyper-orthodoxy, anti-liberal theology, and anti-secularism in times of peace also made them impervious to Nazi ideology in times of occupation.

POLITICS?

From the first week of the occupation, when Quisling accused Berggrav of responsibility for his downfall, the NS accused the church of engaging in politics. Church leaders just as routinely denied the charge, countering that theirs was a spiritual resistance. Both charges were true.

The church's resistance was "spiritual" insofar as it was non-violent and engaged the state on issues of justice, freedom of speech, freedom of conscience, human rights, and freedom of religion. These were moral and religious issues. Nevertheless, the NS was also correct in charging the church with politics. From the moment Berggrav convinced the future CCC members that Nazism was a demonic ideology, and the church had to oppose it, the church committed itself to politics.

There was also no way around politics. In any state church system, political leaders try to check the power of the church, and church resistance to that check can lead to charges of politics. Under a Nazi state, however, church resistance on theological, moral, or ecclesiastical grounds was inevitably political. A Nazi state was by definition ideologically and structurally totalitarian, seeking to align every individual and institution with itself. From that perspective, resistance in any form was "politics," including religious resistance. It was particularly political to recognize as an authority anything outside the Nazi state, be it God, "the Word," morality, church, or reason. The charge that the church was playing "politics" was, therefore, as correct as it was unavoidable.

Chapter 14

The NS Church

———

A PARTY CHURCH?

The segment of the Church of Norway that recognized the state after 5 April 1942 has been known by different names: the "Nazi church," the "Quisling church," and the "NS church." For its supporters, it was simply the Church of Norway. It had adhered to Lutheranism's traditional interpretations of obedience to the state and the doctrine of the two realms and it did not matter that the state was an NS or Nazi state. The state was not accountable to the church, the church had no right to be a "power factor" in the state, and no action of the state was relevant to the church.[1] In recognition of its loyalty and submission to the NS state and party, the "NS church" is an appropriate name.

MEMBERSHIP PROFILE

Who were the NS Christians, and why did they remain in an NS state church? There is no simple answer. They did not necessarily think of themselves as "Nazis," for example, and, like other NS members, their motives were probably complex.

There are no statistical studies of NS Christians, but postwar studies of the motivations of NS members showed 26 reasons for joining the party.[2] The most commonly cited was to "avoid German influence in Norwegian civil administration" (17 percent), and only one person (0.2 percent) mentioned "attitudes towards Jews." Motivations were so varied that only one generalization applies, which is that the NS "became a vehicle for structuring the world into which all kinds of needs and aspirations were projected."[3]

Although the NS represented all ages, regions, and strata of Norwegian society, some characteristics stand out: leaders came from high-status ranks and members from the lower; most recruits were young and urban; white-collar groups were over-represented; the majority (64.4 percent) were from eastern and eastern inland Norway; recruitment was lowest in the South and West.

The demographic profile of NS Christians probably mirrored the party as a whole. This is indicated by the NS church's lay support organization, Christian Union (*Kristen Samling*). It formed in 1941 in Skien to overcome the isolation of NS Christians in their communities.[4] Christian Union established local chapters in only a few places, but their concentration in eastern Norway corresponds to the general party distribution.[5] Like the party, Christian Union had strong urban representation and was weak in the South and West, where the mission societies helped to create a culture that was "immune" to the NS.[6]

The number of active NS church supporters is a matter of conjecture. Christian Union members met in local, regional, and national conventions, and the annual conventions were well-publicized events of 300 to 500. The organization also published a paper with about 2,000 subscribers. Because NS support was often concentrated in families, the periodical could have been read by twice as many people.[7] Allowing for supporters who did not subscribe, a generous estimate would be 4,000 to 5,000.[8]

Data on the NS clergy are more detailed and reliable. The first tier consisted of 54 who were ordained before Easter 1942 and remained loyal to the NS state church; the second tier consisted of the 32 recruits ordained after Easter 1942.[9] Combined, there were 70 pastors who remained loyal to the NS state church. About half were NS members; their average age was 50, seven years older than the average of all clergy; they were generally orthodox Lutherans with culturally conservative and "national church" tendencies; theological liberals were underrepresented, but two-thirds were graduates of the Theological Faculty. Finally, their service had been in rural eastern and northern Norway, where socioeconomic divisions and class conflict before the war had been sharper than elsewhere.[10] Those who were ordained after 5 April 1942 were from a variety of backgrounds, including the mission societies and free churches. Which of these factors actually caused them to become NS clergy is uncertain, because many more clergy who remained loyal to *The Foundation of the Church* shared the same characteristics.[11]

CORE IDEAS

The NS church did not produce a new creed or confession, but its clerical adherents issued three collective statements and intended a fourth.[12] These statements are instructive because they represent the only collective declarations by NS clergy and thus provide a clue to the weight that should be given to their motivations.

Their primary conviction was that opposition to existing authority was opposition to the ordinance of God, based on Romans 13:2.[13] They thought that the only basis for opposing the state was if authorities prohibited the preaching of the gospel, which they judged had not occurred. The church opposition, therefore, had simply acted politically to topple the government.

Their state loyalty was related to their second core conviction, that the NS church preached "the same gospel of the cross" and recognized the same theological and ecclesiastical authorities as its opponents: the Bible, the creeds, Martin Luther, the Lutheran confessions, Hans Nielsen Hauge, Paul Althaus, and Ole Hallesby.[14] They were genuinely puzzled that anyone would think otherwise.

Finally, the NS Christians viewed Communism as the overwhelming threat to Christianity, particularly the "Bolshevism" of the Soviet Union.[15] Feyling's 1941 appeal to the clergy to support the Germans against Bolshevism attracted 27 clerical signatures, and another planned appeal garnered an additional 21 signatures, for a total of 48. This was the most signatures on any of the NS collective declarations, and most of the signees remained NS clergy after Easter 1942.[16] The lay Christian Union periodical also included numerous articles and letters articulating a fear of Communism.

It could be argued that anti-Semitism was a fourth core conviction, but not without qualification. There was a range of opinion among NS church leaders about Jews, anti-Semitism, and the deportation of the Jews, and anti-Semitism did not have the power to mobilize NS Christians as anti-Communism did, although Feyling tried (see Chapter 15). Nevertheless, there were serious anti-Semitic currents within the NS church: anti-Semitic comments appeared in NS sermons and articles; anti-Semitism was not censored in NS Christian circles and publications; the NS church did not repudiate anti-Semitism as contradictory to Christianity; its most prominent figure, Feyling, was openly anti-Semitic; and finally, NS Christians remained loyal to an openly anti-Semitic state.[17]

It would seem to follow from NS anti-Semitism that "Aryan" Christianity would also be a core idea, but that is not the case. The NS Christians were not the German Christians of Norway. There were articles on the desirability of a more Germanic or Norwegian Christianity, but most of them did not turn Jesus into an Aryan Christ or eliminate the Jewishness of the Bible.

When this did occur in the wake of a provocative article, the NS Christian reaction is instructive. Ernst A. Schirmer was a member of a National Socialist faction of the party that proclaimed Aryan racial superiority and neo-pagan religion. In March 1943, he published an article under the pseudonym "Ivar Aker" called "Northerndom and Easterndom." The article attacked Christianity as a "Jewish swindle" in the name of Germanic "politically realistic race religion." NS Christians were appalled and sent a "flood of protests" to NS authorities.[18] Feyling forwarded the protests to the Ministry of Culture and Public Information, reiterating the complaints and noting that the article contradicted the Fører's wish to avoid all unnecessary conflict within religious circles.[19] The minister, Rolf Fuglesang, let the publication's editor know that the article had only worsened the "church conflict" and created division in the ranks, and Skancke notified the clergy that the party had intervened to prevent further incidents. Although several anti-Christian articles were published after this incident, none provoked a comparable reaction.[20]

The NS Christians were thus very much like their fellow Christians, which makes it difficult to assess the reasons for their choices. The reasons probably cannot be reduced to a single cause, but a constellation of convictions add up to a cast of mind that could be reconciled with Nazism: authoritarianism, theological state loyalty, church nationalism, anti-Communism, and, in many cases, anti-Semitism. Perhaps the safest generalization is that a prewar fear of Soviet Communism, particularly its anti-religious ideology and record of church persecution, combined with a theological tradition of state loyalty, persuaded a minority of Christians to support the NS state, whether or not they shared NS ideology or became NS members.

CONTAINING THE AUTONOMOUS CHURCH

From the moment he became Minister President on 1 February 1942, Quisling assumed that he was the highest spiritual and temporal authority in the Church of Norway and replaced the Bishops' Conference with a Church Advisory Conference. Composed of Quisling himself, Skancke, Feyling, Theisen, and the NS bishops, the Church Advisory Conference met three times from June 1942 to December 1943.

Their first meeting was held on 30 June 1942 to consider the NS church's response to the crisis of Easter 1942. In his opening speech, Quisling directed the church to stay out of party politics and focus on aligning the church with the party and the state.[21] Although it was discussed extensively, a strategy for dealing with the schism and church opposition eluded the attendees.

The same problem was the main agenda item at the second Church Advisory Conference on 27 January 1943.[22] The participants narrowed the alternatives to a proposal by Ludvig D. Zwilgmeyer to make significant concessions and renew negotiations and Feyling's proposal to contain the opposition while building the state church. All the NS bishops favored negotiations, but they could not agree on a way forward. For lack of a consensus, Feyling's proposal became policy.

Feyling's strategy assumed that the political divisions in the country cut through the church and could not be ignored. It also assumed that the state could not dismiss 93 percent of the nation's pastors without exposing the weakness of the state church, closing churches, and provoking charges of anti-Christian persecution.[23] Nevertheless, the autonomous church had to be contained, which meant using the coercive powers of state against the worst clerical offenders.

Dismissal from office was the first option. The legal basis was a German ordinance of 4 October 1940 authorizing the state to dismiss and expel civil servants; on 16 April 1942, Quisling added a supplemental clause that such action could be taken without regard to the Constitution.[24] The specific grounds for action against the clergy were usually provided by local NS party leaders, paid and unpaid informants, NS pastors, deans, and bishops, and the police. Feyling prepared the formal charges, which Quisling signed off on, usually with immediate effect.

Between the bishops' resignations in late February and 16 April 1942, resignation from office was usually a sufficient cause for dismissal, though it was never used on most of the clergy. There were, however, degrees of dismissal. The most lenient was dismissal from office with retention of all ministerial rights; the most severe was dismissal with loss of the right to wear clerical garb, which meant the loss both of state office and of the right to continue in ministry. With the escalation of the conflict after Easter 1942, expulsion from parishes, deaneries, and dioceses increasingly accompanied dismissal from office; for persistently oppositional clergy, it became the preferred punishment. The place of exile could be just "outside the district," but it could also be a remote location, often in northern Norway.[25]

The ecclesiastical causes for dismissal were usually related to the autonomous church's policy of non-cooperation, such as denying an NS bishop, dean, or clergyman access to the church for services or refusing to allow an NS bishop to carry out a visitation or office inspection. Cause could also involve ignoring state restrictions, such as persistently speaking in churches while under a public speaking ban.

Many of the clergy were well known opponents of the NS, and the reasons for their dismissal could cover several pages. Alf Bastiansen, for example, became an oppositional figure in his inner city parish of Kampen, Oslo. His notification of dismissal was three pages long and included alleged Marxist views, boycott of radio worship services, withdrawal of his membership from the Clergy Association, and hostile articles in the parish newsletter. It also charged that he belonged to an "inner circle of the clergy" that used the church as a "political battle front."[26]

When the preliminary talks to end the schism broke down in late 1942, Feyling realized he could not continue to dismiss clergy without appointing NS loyalists in their place. He had already dismissed more than 40 clergy, with no "loyal" replacements for most of the parishes. As a result, he proposed to the party that it would benefit the state to overlook the oppositional activity of most pastors and deal only with the most provocative cases. There were 35 of those by the end of 1942 and more in 1943.[27]

Feyling used the State Police to intimidate the clergy and enforce his orders. Police informants reported on worship services and other religious functions. The State Police forcibly opened church offices for NS bishops, confiscated liturgical vestments (church law required the appropriate vestments in order to conduct services), and shut down leading periodicals, such as the liberal *Norsk Kirkeblad*, for taking a "disloyal stand." The state's policy was thus to intimidate, harass, isolate, and silence the autonomous church.[28]

In some cases, the Germans stepped in. Arne Fjellbu was expelled to Hvitsten, only to become a local resistance leader. When Wagner received reports suggesting that Fjellbu had ongoing connections and held closed-door meetings with the "illegal" church leadership, he banished Fjellbu to Andenes, a village on an island just west of Tromsø.[29]

BUILDING THE NS STATE CHURCH

The NS vision was an authoritarian church within the authoritarian state, and at the heart of this vision was the "leadership principle." Because Feyling made a written record of his plans for church reorganization, we know what such a church would look like.[30]

At the most basic level, the church's polity would retain its traditional form, from bishops to parish councils, and the state would continue to govern, legislate, and administer for the church. The difference was that the entire structure would have an authoritarian emphasis.

At the top, all power would be concentrated in the Fører, namely Quisling. He would have the formal authority to govern, legislate, and administer. As Fører, he would be advised by a Church Parliament (*Kirketing*), composed of 60 persons appointed by Quisling but representing all levels of the church. The Church Parliament would meet every third year, and when it was not in session, the Minister President and the Minister of the Church Department would be advised by a smaller group of 11 Church Parliament members to be called the Church Council (*Kirkerådet*). The Church Department would carry out the Fører's orders and would be responsible solely to him.

The church hierarchy would also be reorganized from the top. The bishop of Nidaros would become an archbishop.[31] This was not a new idea, but Feyling liked the thought of tying the church to the Middle Ages, Norway's "era of greatness"; this was an aspect of his ecclesiastical nationalism. The archbishop would be the highest church authority, presiding over nine other bishops, as per Feyling's reconfiguration of the dioceses. At the diocesan and parish levels, the respective councils would be retained but also reconfigured around state control and the leadership principle.

These plans remained almost entirely in the visionary stage, because the NS had too small a following, the opposition was too effective, and the war ended too soon for their enactment. The only functional part of the NS church was the Church Department, but, as its foremost student has noted, it was "a department without a church."[32]

The NS church problem boiled down to arithmetic. From 1942 to the end of the war, the NS church had 54 ordained clergy who remained at their posts after Easter 1942, another 32 who were ordained thereafter, and ten clergy in other categories, such as mission society or seaman's mission pastors. The total of 96 "loyal pastors" was not enough to fill vacancies created in the same period by the 135 clergy who were dismissed, resigned for other reasons, or retired.[33]

Given the numbers, Feyling adopted the only logical policy: fill the vacancies at the top of the hierarchy, work down, and appoint one man to fill several positions. Thus bishops were also cathedral deans, rural deans combined multiple deaneries and were also parish clergy, and pastors served more than one parish.

The best of the NS clergy were appointed bishops, but only four were actually ordained. Frøyland and Zwilgmeyer were joined on 5 December 1942 by Ole J.B. Kvasnes as Bishop of Stavanger and Jørgen Sivertsen as Bishop of Trondenes. The rest remained "acting" bishops, much to their dissatisfaction and perplexity, most likely because all but one were Freemasons.[34]

Farther down the hierarchy, however, Feyling had more difficulty filling appointments. By the end of 1943, he had replaced the cathedral deans with NS loyalists, but he could not do the same with rural deaneries. There were too many of them. Only in the Hamar Diocese did he fill every deanery, and that was only by appointing three deans to serve eight deaneries.[35]

At the parish level, Feyling's strategy was to appointed loyal clergy-men to "strategically important places" first and keep the most important institutions functioning.[36] Multiple appointments were common. In the state church system, however, multiple appointments meant that NS clergy were more occupied by office work than ministry. To address the need for clergy, the Church Department authorized the ordination of lay persons, with disappointing results. The candidates were neither of sufficient quantity or quality.

NS LIFE IN THE PARISHES

Being an NS clergyman or lay member was not for the faint of heart, because the social isolation was unsparing. Ever since late 1940, when NS Christians began to make themselves known in public, they complained about being "frozen out" of parish life, worship services, and the mission societies, and after Easter 1942 the "ice front" was even more oppressive.[37] At the Christian Union convention in the summer of 1942, five hundred participants issued a public appeal for an end to the "coldness" and "hate" directed at "thousands of professing Christians" because of their political opinions, and they pleaded for toleration and cooperation "for the sake of God's kingdom."[38] Their appeal fell on deaf ears. Christian charity could not cross the patriotic and political divide without serious consequences to the one extending it.

At the Church Advisory Conference in January 1943, Otto Theisen of the Church Management Division painted a particularly dark picture. He reported that 86 of 726 pastors accepted their state salary checks and the number was declining. Then he described the working conditions of NS pastors:

> Those pastors who lean toward NS are virtually unable to fulfill their official duties, cannot get on speaking terms with congregations, preach to practically empty churches (listeners usually vary from 1 to 30, when services aren't canceled), are not asked to visit the sick and are boycotted for confirmation instruction, weddings, and congregational events. Inspectors are placed at the doors who take note of church attendees and influence them to stay away, and terror is inflicted in many other ways. It

is understandable that the loyal pastors leave and that our own approximately 50 NS pastors are by and large dead tired.[39]

Such was the fate of the NS clergy, and Theisen's summary is supported by the monthly reports of every NS bishop.[40]

In their despair, the clergy looked to Feyling for state intervention, but there was little he could do. In 1943, for example, Harald Fosse served the rural parish of Kopervik, one of three NS clergymen in the Stavanger Diocese. In February he complained that the "terror front here seems to be immovable" and made for "unbearable conditions."[41] He appealed to the Church Department for help, but Feyling's only solution would have been a transfer with no replacement. If Fosse could not make it in Kopervik, Feyling reasoned, a new man would not either. Feyling dealt with many such requests, but transferring clergymen merely shifted the problem.[42]

Feyling tried to break through the ice front with new laws. Ecclesiastical law gave clergymen the right to their pulpits, effectively barring the access of NS clergy, deans, and bishops to churches served by autonomous church clergy. Feyling responded by permitting a clergyman to conduct services in any church in his parish, a dean in any church in his deanery, and a bishop in any church in his diocese.[43] The NS hierarchy could then legally take over any church "outside the regular worship services and church rites" in order to serve their constituencies in a given congregation or parish.[44] The measure enabled NS clergymen to serve their NS constituencies in neighboring congregations and parishes, but it also tended to exacerbate conflicts.

Feyling also tried to gain control of the parishes by passing a law that suspended existing elected councils in favor of new appointed ones. The law reduced parish councils to the clergyman and two "advisers," one appointed by the bishop and other by the local mayor, all NS members. This was an example of the leadership principle at the parish level.

In late 1942, Feyling claimed that the new parish councils were operating more or less throughout the country, but, in reality, most were paper councils.[45] Skien Diocese is illustrative. While Feyling was reporting that parish councils were active around the country, NS bishop Zwilgmeyer was complaining that the new parish councils were so persecuted and harassed that "lots of members" had already requested to step down, entire councils had asked to be relieved, and in some parishes conditions precluded NS councils from forming.[46]

A "NAZI CHURCH"?

In the newsletters produced by the autonomous church, the NS church was often referred to as "the Nazi church." Such a label was knowingly pejorative, and it was natural in the polarized circumstances, but was it fair?

NS Christians did not think so, because with respect to Christianity and the church they saw no difference between themselves and their opponents: they claimed that they shared the same scripture, Gospel, theology, and moral code as their opponents, and no one has proven otherwise. As individuals, therefore, many were probably right in claiming not to be "Nazis."

Nevertheless, the NS church deserves to be called "the Nazi Church" for one reason: it was a church that recognized the absolute authority of a Nazi state, and NS Christians chose to be loyal to it. Like any organization or institution, a church is more than the sum of its parts. It has its own collective identity, above and beyond what individual members think about it, and after Easter 1942 it was clear that the NS church was a Nazi party church within a Nazi state. Because the vast majority of the population took a stand against Nazism and the NS state, no NS Christians could—or did—claim that they were coerced; they made a choice. The fact that the choice could be so socially isolating underlines its seriousnes. As with their Christian opponents, their choice was spiritual and it was "politics."

The NS Christians could rationalize their choice because they and their leaders understood Christianity in "spiritual" terms, reducing it to an otherworldly gospel and cultic observance. Feyling was explicit on this point: what the Germans and the NS state did outside the "spiritual," such as indoctrinating the youth, was of no consequence to the church, and when he called for a more "socially accented" Christianity, he meant a "National Socialistic Christianity."[47] If NS Christians were still naïve about Nazism after Easter 1942, their naïveté would be strained when Hitler moved to solve "the Jewish problem."

PART V

Final Protests

—

Chapter 15

In Defense of Jews

***

FIRST SIGNS

Terboven's Reichskommissariat and the German Security Service included staff specialists on "the Jewish question." As the invasion settled into occupation, their first task was to gather reliable information about Norwegian Jews, and a month after Operation Weser they ordered the confiscation of all radios belonging to Jews, a crude means of conducting a survey. Berggrav learned about the confiscation two days later, but he decided to let the matter rest as a *fait accompli*.[1] The Administrative Council, formed right after the invasion to safeguard Norwegian administration and interests, took the same approach.

Within weeks of the invasion, however, clergy reported that the Germans had forced Jewish businesses in Sarpsborg to display yellow "Jewish business" signs, and they urged Berggrav to intervene. Berggrav was hesitant, reasoning that the Germans should not be stopped from "committing stupidities" until their "true intentions" became clear; the war had not yet ended in northern Norway, and Norwegians in the occupied areas had just started to deal with German civil authorities.[2] Insistent pleas from Jews and his clergy soon changed his mind. He privately approached officials in the Reichskommissariat and urged them to remove the anti-Semitic placards, which by then had appeared in several towns. During these talks, Assistant Department Head (*Ministerialrat*) Georg W. Müller, head of the Public Information and Propaganda Branch, observed that Norway did not have a "Jewish problem" and the few Jews in the country had no special influence. The remarks etched themselves on Berggrav's mind and perhaps helps to explain his subsequent decisions.[3]

The Germans removed the signs on 1 June 1940, the day Terboven broadcast his promise not to interfere in the exercise of religion that was free of politics. Many Jews took his speech as a sign that it would be safe to remain in Norway, and others returned from Sweden after having fled in the first days of the invasion.[4]

THE NEW AGE FOR JEWS

That time of illusions continued a while longer. The NS began to publish anti-Semitic propaganda in the press, the Hird harassed Jews in public places, and NS bureaucrats intimidated Jews in professional associations and trade unions—but still, a certain ambiguity remained. Anti-Semitic propaganda, for example, was directed at world Jewry, not Norwegian Jews.[5] Jews were occasionally harassed on the streets, but so were many other Norwegians. Berggrav continued to protest privately, but he did not draw public attention to the distinctive situation of Jews.

In March 1941, NS intentions became clearer. At a Nazi rally in Frankfurt am Main, Germany, Quisling described the "fateful influence" of Jews in Norwegian history. To solve the "Jewish problem," he advocated termination of Jewish civil rights through legislation on a European scale.[6] He also singled out Christian groups as problematically pro-Jewish. After Quisling's speech, NS anti-Semitic propaganda intensified. Christian churches were not targeted, but they were affected episodically. Locally, church protests could moderate or reverse German decisions.[7]

Early in the summer of 1941, Wilhelm A. K. Wagner, Gestapo consultant on Jews and the churches, received orders from Berlin to proceed against Norwegian Jews as had been done in Germany.[8] The order must have been related to Operation Barbarossa, the German invasion of the Soviet Union on 22 June 1941; on 18 June the Germans arrested all Jews in northern Norway, and on the day of the invasion they detained stateless Jews throughout the country. Most were released after two or three weeks, but propaganda continued to emphasize alleged Jewish links to Bolshevism.

At this point, the church had the influence to reverse anti-Semitic measures, as two cases illustrate. On 13 June 1941, Skancke drafted a proposal to prohibit Norwegian citizens from marrying anyone of Jewish or Sami (Lapp) extraction up to the third generation.[9] Following standard procedure, he sent it to Berggrav, who replied for the bishops in early September. The bishops declared that the Christian view of marriage was based on the fundamental unity of humanity, which meant that people of all races had the same human worth. The church, therefore, protested "making Norwegian citizens with some Jewish blood in their veins pariahs as inferior human beings."[10] Faced with the bishops' protest, Skancke tabled the proposal.

The harsher political climate soon affected the Mission to Israel, a mission society directed toward the conversion of Jews in Hungary and Romania. The German invasion of the Soviet Union was underway, and on 15 July, the Press Directorate prohibited mention of the society and its work in articles or advertisements. Several mission societies protested, so Feyling requested a statement from the society about its mission and how it could carry on without conflicting with "the ongoing solution to the Jewish problem in a number of countries."[11] Christian Ihlen, Professor of Systematic Theology at the Theological Faculty and chair of the Mission to Israel's board, replied on behalf of the society. He insisted on the unity of humanity in Jesus Christ, pointing out that the society's views on Jewish policy were very different from those of Germany. But he also conceded the possibility of "certain restrictions" as long as they avoided personal abuse and violence.[12] Ihlen's tortured reasoning satisfied the NS and the Germans temporarily. Funds continued to flow to the society's work in Europe until the end of the war, and the Mission's periodical continued publication until 11 February 1942, when an article in memory of a martyred Jewish-Christian colleague in Romania crossed the line, and it was shut down.

These incidents were minor affairs for the Germans and the NS, but more sweeping measures were coming. In October 1941, the Commissioner Minister of Justice, Sverre Riisnæs, ordered all county commissioners to discreetly register Jewish property. Riisnæs next prepared a law mandating that a "J" be stamped on Jewish identity cards, effective 10 January 1942. Finally, on 12 March Quisling reinserted the section of the Constitution's Article 2 excluding Jews from the country.

STRATEGIC OMISSION

By March 1942, no one could doubt German and NS intentions, yet the anti-Semitic legislation was decreed without protest from any quarter. Even the Church of Norway, which in February 1941 had stepped forward as the moral guardian of society, kept its own counsel. Why was that the case? There is no easy explanation. Perhaps the reason was simply the anti-pluralism of a still very homogeneous society, which tolerated prejudice and relegated minorities to its margins—and indifference.

It is more possible to explain why Berggrav did not rally the church in March 1942. As the CCC discussed and prepared the drafts of *The Foundation of the Church*, members studied a draft resignation statement written by the pastors of Bergen who, on the basis of conscience, protested the NS reinstating in the Constitution the clause excluding Jews from the country. The Bergen pastors viewed the clause's repeal in 1851 as a victory for Christian thinking: there was no Jew or Greek in Christ, and since Christ had not rejected his people, no one else was entitled to either. The Stavanger clergy echoed those convictions in a draft by Olav Valen-Sendstad.[13]

Berggrav, however, opposed any reference to Jews in the final draft of the document that became *The Foundation of the Church*. He wanted a confessional statement of principles, not a list of cases, and he wanted the statement to encourage and liberate the clergy. Five years after the event, Berggrav recalled how he reached this conclusion:

> Moreover I thought the point about *the Jews* should be omitted. This last was for a particular strategic reason. I had reason to believe the Germans themselves were not too happy about the brutality and aggressiveness that Quisling and the NS had shown in their actions against the church. It was important for us not to taunt the Germans at the wrong time and give the Germans a pretext for taking over Quisling's actions or for engaging themselves actively in support of them. Now they certainly let Quisling carry on, but the Germans kept themselves more in the background. To my mind, it was not necessary *now* for us to drag the extremely explosive Jewish aspect into the Norwegian church's reckoning with the Nazi state, because it would only mean that our own lines became less simple and less clear and that—as I said—the Germans thereby would have grounds

to make common cause with the NS. We ought now to stick to the direct challenges to our own church.[14]

Berggrav's arguments carried the day: Valen-Sendstad changed his mind, and the members of the CCC concurred.

Berggrav reasoned as Karl Barth had in the Barmen Declaration: it was better to omit reference to the Jews in a confessional document. Barth later admitted he was wrong; Berggrav did not.[15] Despite overwhelming evidence of Jewish vulnerability since the first days of the occupation, the church did not issue a protest when it could have influenced public opinion and changed German and NS conduct.[16] In March 1942, however, Hitler's plan to kill all Jews had just gone into effect and was not widely known.

ARRESTS

Between June 1941 and January 1942, Hitler's Jewish policy on the continent moved from forced resettlement, to mass killing of Jews in Eastern Europe and the Baltic countries, and then to the "Final Solution," an explicit plan developed in September and October for the elimination of all Jews.[17] By mid-1942, the Germans had collected the necessary data, and between midsummer and 24 October, Gestapo headquarters in Berlin sent orders to Heinrich Fehlis, Gestapo chief in Norway, instructing him to expel Jews in cooperation "with the wishes of the Norwegian government."[18]

An important opportunity was missed during this period. German resistance leader Helmuth von Moltke visited Oslo in mid-September and met his Kreisau Circle contact in the German army, Theodor Steltzer, and members of the Norwegian Home Front.[19] Von Moltke warned his contacts that plans were afoot for action against Norwegian Jews, but he did not know the nature or timing of the proposed actions. The Home Front leaders could have acted on von Moltke's warning by alerting Jews immediately and aiding their escape to Sweden, but in the uncertainty no one did.

The sequence of events that led to Auschwitz began in earnest in early October 1942, after the Norwegian resistance sabotaged German installations at Majavatn, north of Trondheim. Terboven retaliated on 6 October by declaring a state of emergency and, as atonement for the German victims of Majavatn and other incidents, ordered the execution of ten well known Norwegians, followed a few days later by 24 others, among them one Jew.[20] The next day, all male Jews in the Trøndelag region over the age of 14 were arrested and imprisoned. Three were executed. In the Jewish community of Oslo, the news from the north heightened apprehensions that were already high following the arrests of several Jews in August and September.

Some resistance leaders sensed that the arrests were the prelude to something worse and warned Jews to flee. Some decided to do so; others stayed put. On 12 October, Quisling ordered the death penalty for anyone caught helping Jews to escape. Among the many who helped hide Jews and secretly guided them to the border were pastors and theological students like Hans C. Mamen, who was responsible for guiding 25 Jews in eight groups to Sweden. The Deaconess Home Hospital also hid 25 to 30 Jews as "patients" before helping them to the border.[21]

Nationwide, mass arrests began after a policeman was killed in an incident involving Jews trying to escape to Sweden. Quisling responded on 24 October with an order for the arrest of all male Jews over the age of 15, followed two days later with another confiscating all Jewish property. All Jewish women were also ordered to report daily to the local police. The Norwegian State Police were to begin the arrests on the 26th, holding their victims at camps near Oslo and Trondheim. On the night of the 25th, police contacts warned resistance leaders that the mass arrests would begin early the next morning. Not all Jews could be reached in the few hours before the arrests began, but a number were located and warned. Some made their way to Sweden, mostly through the resistance escape network. The most recent estimate is that about 60 percent of Jews living in Norway—1,260 people—fled to Sweden between 26 October and 26 November 1942.[22]

CHURCH PROTEST

The mass arrests were soon known throughout the country, and the Gestapo reported that in church circles they had "an exceedingly strong" effect.[23] The first public protest, however, came from an unexpected source. At the conclusion of a sermon broadcast over the radio on 1

November, Lars Frøyland, the NS-appointed bishop of Oslo, said that the actions against the Jews were sad and dishonored the Norwegian people. Was it right, he asked, to put everyone in the same basket, the guilty with the innocent? Then he exclaimed with genuine outrage: "We are after all Norwegians! We are after all Christians!"[24] Frøyland was not a member of the NS, and the rest of his family were patriots throughout the war and actively aided Jews. Frøyland himself helped Jewish friends of the family in November 1942.[25]

In the meantime, Arnold Øhrn, the Baptist chair of the Dissenter Parliament, took the initiative to urge the Provisional Church Leadership (PCL) to protest the arrests.[26] Why the PCL should have needed prompting from a "Dissenter" is an interesting question, but Hallesby saw the point and wrote the first draft of a protest statement. This statement was revised and approved by the PCL on 30 October and then sent to the Lutheran mission societies and the free churches for supporting signatures. Jacob Mangers, the Roman Catholic bishop, was also approached, but he declined to sign because he was appealing to exclude some baptized Jews from the ordinances and did not wish to jeopardize their chances. The PCL sent the letter to Quisling on 10 November.

The PCL's protest charged that the measures against the Jews were contrary to the Christian commandment of brotherly love and the most elementary demands of justice. The failure to recognize the human worth of Jews was "in direct contradiction to God's Word that from cover to cover proclaims all peoples are of one blood, see in particular Acts 17:26." The next point approached the heart of Christianity itself: "And above all else: When God through the incarnation became man he allowed himself to be born in a Jewish home of a Jewish mother." This formulation fell short of making the obvious point that Jesus was a Jew, but the letter did make the case that "according to God's Word, all human beings have in principle the same human worth and thereby the same human rights."

The protest continued by affirming that the church was bound by "the deepest pangs of conscience" to protest against "this legalized injustice against Jews." Anything less would have made the church "responsible for and complicit in this injustice." The appeal was not to be dismissed as church interference in politics. Christians were called to obey God more than man (Acts 5:29) and Luther himself rejected the charge of interference in temporal affairs when the church exhorted the authorities "to be obedient to the highest authority, which is God." The final section reads as follows:

> In the power of this our calling we admonish, therefore, the temporal authority and say in the name of Jesus Christ: Stop the persecution of Jews and stop the racial hatred that is spread by the press throughout our land. . . . The Minister President has on several occasions emphasized that the NS according to its platform wants to protect Christianity's fundamental values. Now a Christian value is in danger. If it is to be protected it must be protected immediately.[27]

Pastors read the letter from their pulpits between 15 November and 13 December, and many services included a prayer for the Jews.[28] The church's underground distribution network spread the protest widely, the illegal press copied or summarized it, and the BBC broadcast it in Norway. The two theological faculties, 19 mission societies and associations, five free churches, and a free church organization added letters of support. Some parishes sent their own protests as well.[29] Outside the country, the Allied press publicized the letter, the Swedish bishops wrote a pastoral letter calling for prayer for the Jews, and the German Foreign Office received several reports on the matter.[30]

THE NS CHURCH RESPONSE

The NS media responded by publicizing the anti-Semitic venom of the father of the Reformation.[31] While the Nazi press called upon the authority of Martin Luther, Quisling sent the protest to Feyling, who forwarded copies to the NS bishops in preparation for a formal reply. Frøyland drafted the reply on 26 November, observing that the mass arrests of that very day made any response "of purely theoretical interest" and of no consequence for the fate of the Jews.[32] Although he found the church's protest one-sided, he agreed with its basic position. He knew firsthand that the radical nature of the measures had shocked many people, and many who might have supported the party would be scared away forever. The measures were wrong and unwise.

O.J.B. Kvasnes of Stavanger also agreed with the fundamental position of the protest but found the tone "unnecessarily provocative." He did not think Norwegians really understood the problem that Jews posed in other countries, and he was sure that Hitler would treat the Jewish question justly so that Jews could live from their own labor in their own homeland, rather than "as parasites on the bodies of other peoples." Nevertheless, Kvasnes encouraged the government to treat the Jews completely fairly and respectfully, "so we can stand at the judgment seat of future history with a clean slate."[33] Ludvig Daae Zwilgmeyer thought Jewish capital might have been behind the damaging activities of movements like the church front, and he could understand why the authorities would want to control Jews and their property.[34] In Zwilgmeyer's opinion, Jews were really "naturalized foreigners" who could "never become real Norwegians." The authorities would have to do what they thought best for the nation, recognizing that they, too, were accountable to their consciences, their people, and God. Finally, Georg Falck-Hansen, a rabid anti-Semite, thought Jews were "plague germs" and found internment entirely in order.[35]

Feyling drafted a six-page reply that showed he had evolved into the complete Nazi.[36] The Jewish problem had to be solved on a European scale, he declared, because ten million of the world's nearly seventeen million Jews lived on that continent. Anti-Semitism was not the result of artificial propaganda but existed wherever Jews lived, including Norway. The reasons for anti-Semitism were a number of "entirely immoral" Talmudic regulations and the failure of the dispersed Jews to either assimilate or establish their own state. The "Jewish problem," he went on, began after the American and French revolutions. Jews began to assimilate in order to compete with the "host people" in all fields while never ceasing to be Jews or to think of themselves as anything else. Intellectual Jews denied the relevance of the race question, but the Jews' "racial consciousness" was the secret to their surviving in the midst of other peoples throughout the world.

In Feyling's view, anti-Semitic legislation in Germany was justified and Norway could not help but be affected by "the European solution to the Jewish question." The law confiscating Jewish assets was the opening step in Norway's cooperation in the solution, and the detention of male Jews was just a temporary preventive measure and not "a rejection of the Jews' human value." Feyling also thought that the religious side of the issue could be disposed of by reference to Martin Luther's little piece of 1543 on "The Chosen People." The measures Luther advocated would not be taken in this case, he wrote, but current policy was in complete accord with Luther's admonition to prohibit Jewish "usury" and deprive Jews of their assets and gold, "because they have stolen everything from us." Christians could be assured that since Luther finally turned to the state authorities and asked them to "exercise a stern compassion" toward the Jewish people, "then the regard for compassion will also be considered in the further treatment of the Jewish question." Feyling's treatise remained a draft. He wrote it in November, but the NS bishops were still sending in protests in December. By then, the first deportation already had taken place. Feyling must have sensed that his words were already empty, although he was probably unaware that Norwegian Jews were destined for an extermination camp.[37]

AFTERMATH

The Jewish community had no time to hope anything would come of the churches' protest. On 25 November, Wagner ordered Norwegian police chief Karl A. Marthinsen to arrest all remaining Jews, mostly women and children. The State Police arrested 562 Jews, 532 of whom were transported by sea on the *S/S Donau aus Bremen* to Stettin, where trains took them to Auschwitz. Having already confiscated Jewish private property, the Nazi authorities went on to confiscate synagogues and their assets for NS use. Ever the bureaucrat, Feyling had no objection because "as far as anyone knows" the synagogue leaders and their members had left the country.[38]

Two Christian communities sent belated protests to the NS Church Department. First, three representatives of the Society of Friends in Stavanger wrote on the last day of 1942 about their "profound sorrow" at Norway's deportation of Jews and their certainty that the Ministry of Church and Education would "do everything to change the step taken by the national leadership."[39] The second letter was from a representative of the Pentecostal Assemblies, which had no central organization. On 19 January 1943, Oswald Orlien, pastor of the Philadelphia Church, Pentecostalism's mother church in Oslo, sent a belated letter of support for the PCL's protest.[40] Although the letters were late, they arrived before the final deportations. Most Jews from Trondheim and northward were not transported to Oslo in time to make the November departure of the *S/S Donau*, so they were interned—and treated brutally—outside of Oslo until another vessel was available. On 24 February 1943, the *S/S Gothenland* left Oslo with 158 Jews, the majority from the Trondheim congregation. About 120 went directly to Auschwitz.

Norway's prewar Jewish population was 2,100, and of these, 771 were deported, mostly to Auschwitz; only 34 survived. Most of those who were not deported escaped to Sweden in late October, with the aid of the Home Front, a few days before the mass arrest of Jews.[41]

Chapter 16

Against Compulsory Labor Service

———

THE MOMENTUM OF WAR

Between the fall of 1942 and the spring of 1943, the war in Europe shifted in favor of the Allies. Churchill hesitated about claiming too much, but he thought that November 1942 was "the end of the beginning."[1] That seemed to be the Norwegian view as well; the Gestapo's November report emphasized the new confidence of "the Norwegian population" in an Allied victory, and reports from all over the country noted expressions of "joy" from "Jøssings," the NS name for their opponents.[2]

In the early fall, German armies had been advancing on all fronts: in Russia, they closed in on Stalingrad, and in North Africa they were moving toward Cairo. Then the momentum shifted. On the Western Front, the British defeated the Germans at El Alamein, Egypt, on 2 November 1942 and began moving westward across the North African desert as Anglo-American forces moved eastward from Morocco and Algeria. But World War II was won on the Eastern Front, and the decisive battle was the Soviet victory at Stalingrad (Volgograd), "the fiercest battle ever contested," fought "on a scale never before seen in the annals of warfare." It left 1.1 million people dead; the German army alone lost twenty divisions.[3] The Soviets accepted the surrender of the German Sixth Army on 31 January 1943 and began the slow re-conquest of their own country.

Stalingrad changed German policies and the pattern of resistance in occupied Europe. In May 1943, Hitler called on his people to mobilize for total war. He directed all available forces to the Eastern Front and all the resources of the occupied territories toward the defense of the Reich.[4] In Nazi propaganda, Germany and the Soviet Union were in the war of the ages, Aryans against Asians, civilization against barbarism, Christianity against atheism. Stalingrad was also a turning point for the European resistance.[5] After Stalingrad, resistance shifted from self-preservation to liberation, from civil resistance to military action. As the Allies forced German forces into a defensive posture, military resistance organizations in occupied Europe emerged to harass them from within. This was the dynamic that unfolded in Norway.

The Norwegian government in London made several breakthroughs in 1943. After a good deal of mutual recrimination and distrust, followed by fairly sharp disagreements about operations within occupied Norway, the British decided in February 1943 to stop building a separate organization outside of the Norwegian military resistance, Milorg. Future operations and sabotage would be planned with Norwegian authorities and arms would be shipped directly to Milorg. In May, Milorg leaders met with the Norwegian government's Defense High Command in Sweden to plan for their roles in the liberation, beginning with an accelerated arms buildup.

The Norwegian government's relations with the home front also improved. In 1943, three home front leadership groups had emerged with three distinct functions.[6] As the end of the war approached, however, Milorg worked so closely with the two civil resistance groups, the Circle and the Coordination Committee, that they sometimes acted as one, called the Home Front Leadership. The group was overwhelmingly non-Socialist, but it recognized that it had to cooperate with the Labor government in London in planning for liberation. It also informed the government that events at home had created a new political reality that would require a national coalition government from the moment of liberation until new elections could be held. On 8 February 1943, the government agreed, leading to growing trust between the two.

THE NEW REALISM

The church's negotiations with the state in the summer of 1942 had an unreality about them, as if the PCL still did not understand the nature of the NS state. That changed in early 1943. The best evidence is the PCL's

New Year's message in January 1943.[7] The lengthy greeting to the church represented the end of illusions, a recognition that the NS state would not rectify its injustices. The PCL cited three issues: the church, the Jews, and the youth service campaign.[8] The PCL began with the state's repeated violations of church order in its attempts to control the church and gave several examples of state coercion against the clergy and the parishes. The second issue was the state's internment and deportation of Jews, a clear instance of the state ignoring God's Word about human value and love. The church had protested, but Quisling had ignored it. Finally, the PCL drew attention to the government's renewed campaign in selected towns and districts coerce children into the national youth service. Police had taken children from their homes and imprisoned resistant parents, and the PCL urged parents "not to deviate from the right path and not to compromise their conscience" at any price.[9]

The PCL summed up the situation by charging that the state's treatment of the clergy and others was persecution, and that it was now useless to turn to the authorities for help. Instead, congregations were to remain alert and faithful to conscience. Pastors read the message from most of the nation's pulpits on Sunday, 17 January, accompanied by a prayer that church, home, and parents would receive power to stand firm.[10]

In the atmosphere of state terror that prevailed in the fall and winter of 1942–1943, the PCL's message was provocative. The police interrogated Hallesby and Hope, as well as several pastors who had read the message to their congregations. The police also registered the property of Hallesby, Hope, Hygen, Maroni, and H.W. Wisløff and froze their accounts; Hille had already suffered the same fate.[11] The PCL was under a new level of surveillance.

QUISLING'S INTERPRETATION OF HISTORY

As the first anniversary of Quisling's rise to power approached, rumors circulated that Quisling would soon receive new powers from the Germans, reach a formal peace accord, and draft young men for the struggle against Bolshevism.[12] On 1 February 1943, his followers expected to celebrate with fanfare the first anniversary of the Act of State at Akershus.

Instead, they heard a somber assessment of where the party stood within the sweep of world history. The nation, said Quisling, had reached a turning point. Having fought from 1930 to 1940 against "the old leaders" who "betrayed our country," the country was on its way to independence. Unfortunately, until Germany won the war it could not achieve its full freedom and greatness. Groups in the service of Moscow and London, chief among them the teachers and the pastors, were jeopardizing these great aims. The pastors were led by a minority clique of 60 to 70, who "terrorized" the rest by claiming that the NS threatened Christianity and the church. Their allegations, however, were legends, distortions, or outright fraud manufactured for political ends. All the government wanted from church leaders was a return to the truth and an end to their hatred and schism.[13]

Quisling also showed his displeasure at the Swedish press for creating a hero out of Berggrav and a villain of him. Ever since 9 April 1940, Quisling charged, the Swedish press had "systematically" slandered him, his party, and his government. In contrast, Swedish journalists had turned Berggrav into a "Nordic spiritual hero." The real danger to the church, however, was not the NS but Bolshevism. Quoting the Dean of Monmouth, who had defined Communism as human society organized against God, Quisling urged church supporters to open their eyes. It was not the "paganism" in National Socialism that threatened them; it was Bolshevism.

Quisling gave his speech on 1 February, perhaps knowing that the German Sixth Army had capitulated the day before at Stalingrad. The Germans did not report the news in Norway until 4 February, but they warned that Germany was not going to spill its blood for the rest of Europe without help. Rumors about the forced labor mobilization of Norwegian young men were suddenly plausible.

THE NATIONAL LABOR SERVICE LAW

After Stalingrad, Germany needed all the human and material resources within reach, and on 22 February 1943 Terboven and Quisling proclaimed the National Labor Service Law. Newspaper headlines read, "Total Norwegian Labor Contribution in the Fight Against Bolshevism."[14] Every Norwegian male between 18 and 55 and every female between 21 and 40 was called on to contribute labor to the nation. Quisling emphasized that the law was intended to increase Norway's capacity to supply itself and strengthen its defenses, and Terboven pointed out that the initiative had come from the Norwegian government, but added that behind the law was the authority of the German Reich.[15]

Two facts put this law in perspective. From the beginning of the occupation, economic exploitation was second only to Germany's military aims in Norway. As a result, there has never been a five-year period in which the Norwegian economy has undergone "greater and more wide-ranging change."[16] The other salient economic fact is that Norwegian businesses and labor willingly contracted with and worked for the Wehrmacht throughout the occupation. Whether this was simply economic collaboration or collaborationism has been widely debated, but from 1942 to 1944 about 100,000 Norwegians had steady work at high wages constructing German military installations, and as many as 147,000 worked for Germans in some capacity. This "German work," as it was called, was so widespread that it hardly featured in later treason trials.[17]

The new law, however, was based on forced labor service, and recruitment began with university students. On the day of the announcement, the Nazi leader of the Norwegian Student Association staged a meeting that gave the appearance of student compliance with the new law, a maneuver that shocked the majority of the students. Some sought advice from Home Front leaders and the university faculty's action group leader, Harald Schjelderup. He and another Home Front leader, lawyer Ferdinand Schjelderup, discussed the issue with Hallesby. Although Free Faculty of Theology students were not part of the university, Hallesby represented those who wanted to support the movement against the NS Norwegian Student Association.[18]

Home Front leaders concluded that the best response would be individual protests and formulated a statement that rejected the Norwegian Student Association's claim to represent students. Within a few days, student leaders collected 2,563 protests from a total of 2,745 students, all of which they sent to the university, where the police confiscated them.[19]

CONFUSION IN THE HOME FRONT

The Circle and the Coordination Committee had evolved parallel to one another as distinct but closely associated groups. The Circle formed during the spring and summer of 1941 in order to mediate between the Home

Front and the Norwegian government. It represented an alliance across party lines, and in early 1943 the government recognized the Circle as its official representative at home and granted it civil jurisdiction. The Circle, in turn, secured the Labor government's civil legitimacy.[20] With jurisdiction over the transition to peace, the Circle's closest relations were with Milorg. The church's initial relationship to the Circle was through Berggrav, but after his imprisonment the church had almost no representation in the group.[21] Only as preparations began for the postwar era did the church again work actively through the Circle.

The church's relationship to the Coordination Committee was more consistent. In January 1941, the Coordination Committee included representatives from five professional groups. The church's representatives were Alex Johnson and Conrad Bonnevie-Svendsen, who coordinated communications for both the Coordination Committee and PCL. The Coordination Committee expanded its representation after 1941, but not until 1943 did it consolidate and achieve the form it would have until the end of the occupation.[22]

The mass mobilization of early 1942 was no longer possible only a year later. After September 1942, Terboven had used brutal measures against Jews and all forms of resistance, and the NS had generally refrained from pressing provocative policies.[23] The notable exception was the National Labor Service Law.

Initially, the Home Front Leadership was unsure about how to respond. In key discussions of the Coordination Committee, Tor Skjønsberg called for immediate and resolute mass resistance on the assumption that the law's hidden agenda was to mobilize Norwegian labor in support of Germany's military aims.[24] The other members were not persuaded. Most members, including Alex Johnson, did not think that Norwegian workers would be used for Germany's war aims or that Norwegians would be deported to Germany. The Committee had intelligence from NS offices to support this argument, and lawyers on the Committee noted that international law sanctioned an occupier's right to order work within the country, even on military installations.[25] The Coordination Committee finally agreed to recommend that Norwegians should complete the Labor Service's registration forms but postpone other actions. Pastors were the sole exception. The Coordination Committee advised them not to respond to the call-up at all.[26]

The PCL stayed in close contact with the Coordination Committee, and in the course of February and March the two had discussions about the National Labor Service Law. Perhaps because of Alex Johnson, the PCL shared the Coordination Committee's majority opinion about the intent of the law and its status in international law.[27] The PCL was thus predisposed to adopt the Coordination Committee's cautious approach. The PCL had just protested the internment of Jews, and its members felt it was "a bit of a miracle" that the Germans had not arrested Hallesby and Hope.[28]

TARGETING PASTORS

On the day after Quisling issued the new labor law, Ansgar N. Høyer, pastor of the Sandsvær parish, charged that Christian Sandberg, a former colleague, was one of the more dangerous Jøssings—the NS name for its opponents. Høyer suggested that Sandberg should be put to work in accordance with the new law.[29] Feyling liked the idea and consulted with Skancke, who brought it to the attention of Quisling.

Somewhere in the discussions, one of the three, probably Feyling, saw the possibilities of using the National Labor Service Law against the entire church front. Quisling was ready to listen. Apparently at his suggestion, Skancke sent orders to the labor employment office to apply the law to opposition pastors. Two lists of names accompanied the order. List A comprised 200 names of theological graduates and ordained clergy without current permanent positions in the church. According to Skancke, these men had ignored the Church Department's offer of employment in the state church or had responded with a declaration of loyalty to the resigned pastors. List B consisted of 75 pastors whom the Church Department had dismissed from office.[30] Some had been expelled from their parishes, and others were young pastors who had resigned their state offices, rejected their salaries, and refused to discharge their duties. The Minister President himself had decided they should do labor service, and Skancke gave away the government's intentions by stating that if the listed clergy did not respond to the summons, they were to be sent to the remotest location possible.[31]

Anti-NS employees in the Church Department copied most significant documents and sent them to the PCL. Someone in the PCL forwarded

Skancke's document to Sweden, and through Swedish newspapers, news of the plans reached the Allied press. That was how Reichskommissariat officials learned of Skancke's threat. Not to be humiliated, the Reichskommissariat forced Skancke to rescind his order. As a result, the clergy were never called to national labor service. The few who were summoned ignored the order, with no consequences.[32]

FROM CAUTION TO DECISIVENESS

In March 1943, the Gestapo reported that most people were "worried, uncertain, and anxiously expectant," particularly at the prospect of being sent to Germany or eastern Europe and at the thought that the labor law was "a prelude" for a military mobilization.[33] The *London News* observed that complete bewilderment prevailed; a resistance leader from Ålesund made the same point. One reason for this anxiety was that the Home Front Leadership had not developed specific guidelines for resistance, and in the course of March 1943 there were complaints from several quarters about the lack of clear directives. Other local leaders, however, agreed with the Coordination Committee's cautious stance, and the guidelines continued to omit specific instructions about resistance.[34]

The turning point occurred in early April, when reports reached the Coordination Committee that the chauffeurs' school at Svelvik was requiring participants to wear German uniforms. The Coordination Committee discussed the report on 12 April, but some members still did not think the report warranted mass defiance of the law.[35] Tor Skjønsberg had thought from the start that the real purpose of the law was to mobilize youths for German military service, and he argued once more for firmly opposing it. His view did not prevail, but some members were sufficiently uneasy that another meeting was called for the following night. One was pastor Alex Johnson, who wrote later that it was the information about Svelvik that first made the Coordination Committee realize that the labor mobilization was for purely military purposes.[36]

Tor Skjønsberg remembered the pivotal meeting well, and his account of the meeting revealed the tension:

> I was intensely engaged and used the arguments mentioned earlier. I remember that one of those present said he did not feel competent to make

such a serious decision, and that he had not asked to be put in the position he found himself in, to which I replied that no one had asked about any position or responsibility but that we, and we alone, were in the actual position to give the necessary orders. Twice before during the war the Norwegian people had been weakened by those who had authority without using it—the first time by the government in April 1940 and the second time in the summer by the Storting Presidency. It must not happen again that the Norwegian people are weakened by those who had authority but failed to use it. The room where the meeting was held was filled with tension and the anxieties were great.[37]

Skjønsberg was persuasive. The committee decided to issue instructions for unqualified non-cooperation. It was the clear directive that many had been looking for. A Communist resistance group underscored the seriousness of the directive by sabotaging the registration office in Oslo; the authorities caught two of the five saboteurs soon after and executed them.[38]

THE CHURCH PROTESTS

Once the Home Front arrived at a consensus for a firm resistance to the National Labor Service Law, the other resistance organizations, including the church, rallied in support. The PCL held several meetings on the matter, and after significant debate finally agreed on a public protest. Since the law was proclaimed in Quisling's name, the PCL addressed the protest to him. The date was 8 May 1943.[39]

The PCL charged that the National Youth Service Law forced Norwegians to contribute labor for the military aims of a state their country was at war with. This both contravened the law's alleged intent and violated the Hague Convention. The law created a conflict of conscience, and the church could not remain silent:

It [the church] would then betray both its Lord and the congregations and individual people it is to serve and protect. As Christians we must look upon our country as a gift of the Lord that is entrusted to our people by God. For each Norwegian citizen—as for the citizens of every country— it is, therefore, an indissoluble duty of conscience to be faithful and to do right by that country and that people God has placed him in. This duty is sacred, because it has its source in God's order and is corroborated in God's Word.[40]

The PCL justified its position theologically by referring to God's call to the church to be "the guardian of conscience," a concept used in earlier protests to deflect charges of interfering in temporal affairs. The leadership decided that the two members most known to the public, Hallesby and Hope, would sign the letter. In the atmosphere of terror and reprisals, the PCL knew the letter would not go unpunished and wanted to protect itself against decimation.[41]

ARRESTS

The PCL gave up any hope that the co-signers might go free by sending copies of its protest to London, where it was read over the air on 12 May, and to Swedish newspapers, which published it the same day. The next day, Wagner called Hallesby and Hope in for a meeting at his Gestapo office. Wagner took them to the Storting building to meet with Terboven.[42] Terboven lined up six officers, including Wagner, behind him, facing Hallesby and Hope on the other side of the large desk. Hallesby spoke passable German, so the conversation was largely between him and Terboven.

Hallesby knew that the sources he cited in the protest were reliable, but to protect their identity he could not name them. Terboven, however, was not concerned about leaks. He was angered that the protest was directed at Quisling when he, Terboven, had issued the law. Terboven curtly informed Hallesby of his mistake, but did not accept Hallesby's apology.

Terboven then wanted to know why the church had not protested violations of international law by the English, as when commando groups had kidnapped Norwegians—including NS civilians—on the coast and forced them back to England. Hallesby replied that there was no violation of international law until it could be shown that they had been forced to join the British army; only at that point would there be a violation of international law that corresponded to German violations in Norway. Terboven was not used to being addressed so directly. Having exhausted his store of arguments, he dressed Hallesby down. Hallesby later recalled that he had "never before been so reprimanded, either in Norwegian or in German."[43]

These exchanges turned out to be preliminary to Terboven's real concerns, and Hallesby described what followed:

> After that he moved on to the real charge, in that he charged me directly with high treason. I had, he said, made contacts with foreign powers in order to harm the occupying power in general and the Wehrmacht in particular. "I have followed you closely," he said, "and know precisely how impudently you have acted against our cause under a church and Christian cover. In my great patience and generosity of spirit I have put up with it up to now, but now it has gone so far that I have to put a quick stop to your further activity.[44]

When Hallesby informed Terboven that he had had nothing to do with sending the letter out of the country, Terboven did not believe him. Hallesby and Hope were both old men, he said, but had to accept the consequences of their actions, which was deportation to Germany. He arrested them on the spot and sent to them to the Grini internment camp to await deportation.

AFTERMATH

The PCL's protest was publicized through the illegal press, the Swedish press, and the BBC. In the atmosphere of the day, it bolstered the Coordination Committee's call for non-cooperation. But the protest against the National Labor Service would be the church's last. Despite the risks to its leaders, the PCL had believed that public protests were worthwhile. At the very least, they maintained the appearance of meaningful public discourse. Like the others, however, this last protest was actually made without any realistic hope that the government would change its policies. Its real aim was bolstering the will to resist.

PART VI

Holding Out

—

Chapter 17

Between the Times

AT A CROSSROADS

Between 20 June 1942, when the PCL announced its formation, and 13 May 1943, when Hope and Hallesby were arrested, the PCL had led the church through historic changes: it had established an autonomous church, disentangled the church from the state, built an effective administration, undermined the NS state church, and protested the deportation of Jews and compulsory labor service; it had also lost its best known leaders.

At the same time, its reputation abroad had never been higher: in a radio address to Nazi Germany on 1 June 1943, the German Lutheran theologian Paul Tillich observed that among churches in occupied Europe it "is particularly the Norwegian church that has offered, and is still offering, resistance."[1] But the church was at a crossroads, facing decisions that were related to the larger course of the war.

AFTER STALINGRAD

After Stalingrad, in the first half of 1943, the Soviets went on the offensive, but on the Western Front the tide did not turn until the second half of the year. In July, British and American troops landed in Sicily, and in September they invaded the Italian mainland and fought their way northward. From British airfields, Allied bombers penetrated deep into Germany, destroying factories and razing cities. Confident of victory, the

Allies entered into agreements on postwar cooperation, but not until the early summer of 1944 were they ready to open a western front. When they did, it was Germany's turn to be taken by surprise.

On the morning of 6 June 1944, Major Werner Pluskat peered through the narrow slits of his bunker overlooking Omaha Beach in Normandy, France. Facing him on the seas of the English Channel were hundreds upon hundreds of ships, as far as his eye could see, moving directly toward him. At that moment, he had a single thought: "This is the end for Germany."[2] Without Germany's knowledge, the Allies had mobilized the largest invasion fleet in history.

Final victory, however, was not as swift as the Allies expected. Germany had nine million men in uniform, the Allied advance was slow, and the German army had its own surprise in store. On 16 December 1944, the Wehrmacht counterattacked in the Ardennes, a forested region covering parts of France, Belgium, and Luxembourg, catching the Allies off guard. The Battle of the Bulge ended in late January, delaying the Allied crossing of the Rhine until March 1945, much later than the Allied Supreme Command originally thought.

In Norway, uncertainty about the outcome of the war turned in early 1943 to confidence in Allied victory, and by the fall Quisling himself accepted that Germany would be defeated.[3] In May 1944, he warned the public that Germany's downfall meant a "new and worse" Bolshevik occupation, the end of Norway.[4] Many in his own party had also ceased to believe and joined the so-called "rowing club" out of the party. Those who remained split into nationalist and pan-Germanic factions. The NS was fragmenting.

As Germany weakened in late 1943, the British began to bomb selected targets in Norway, including the heavy water production plant in Rjukan, and the British Special Operations Executive expanded sabotage operations against shipping, industry, and railroads. Despite severe setbacks, Milorg increased its recruitment and training, built up arms caches, and carried out selective acts of sabotage.[5]

THE "SECRET CHURCH LEADERSHIP"

The beginning of the end of the church struggle may be dated to 13 May 1943, when Terboven arrested Hallesby and Hope. The most profound impact of the arrests may have been on the their large following in the church and the mission societies. In his report to the Gestapo, Vilhelm H. Günther observed that the Christian community interpreted their arrests as outright persecution of Christianity.[6]

The arrest of its leaders forced the PCL to reconstitute itself as a secret organization. Leadership fell to Johannes Ø. Dietrichson, an Oslo assistant pastor and chair of the Council of Autonomous Organizations. Anticipating the possibility of arrest, Hallesby and Hope had recommended two replacements cut from their own cloth: Andreas Seierstad, an associate professor of church history at the Free Faculty of Theology, and Tormod Vågen, Secretary General of the China Mission Association. Rounding out the group were Ragnvald Indrebø, assistant pastor of the Jacob Church in Oslo; Ludwig Schübeler, assistant pastor of Frogner Church in Oslo; Johannes Smemo, Principal of the Free Faculty of Theology's Seminary for Applied Theology; Alf Bastiansen, parish pastor of the Kampen Church in Oslo; Arne Fjelberg, parish pastor at the Frogner Church; and Dagfinn Hauge, so-called "small church" pastor.[7] Erling Thomle was the secretary until his arrest in January 1945, when he was replaced by Tord Godal. The reorganized PCL was known informally as the Secret Church Leadership.

The reorganized PCL developed its policy on the assumption that the war would soon be over, an assumption that most Norwegians shared.[8] The PCL therefore defined the church's task as holding out and positioning itself for the postwar era. Institutional self-interest began to reassert itself; the battle for the church and democracy had been won, and the PCL was convinced it could not afford more losses as a result of confronting the state directly. There would also be no more public protests, as long as the state did not interfere with the church's spiritual work. If forced to go public, however, Dietrichson and Smemo were to step forward as cover for the others.[9]

INTERNMENT AS NS CHURCH POLICY

At its Church Advisory Conference in January 1943, the NS church conceded that it had lost the church struggle and adjusted its policy accordingly—to the dissatisfaction of many NS political and church leaders. They viewed the clergy's continued provocations as political and expected the Church Department to take more severe punishment, but there was no agreement on this or any other plan of action.[10] Because the Reichskommissar did not want to provoke the church, and because Feyling could not dismiss and expel many more clergy than he already had, he began to refine his strategy.[11] In the late summer of 1943, he gained Wagner's approval for a three-point policy of avoiding any measures that could be construed as persecution, overlooking smaller infractions, and only prosecuting serious violations.[12]

Feyling thought that party interference in church affairs was detrimental to the NS church and needlessly provoked opposition, so he also negotiated a mutual non-interference agreement with the party leadership. The agreement stipulated that the party would not mention the church conflict in public meetings or the media, and the NS church would not interfere in party matters, including the political indoctrination of the young.[13] Additionally, party officials would refer serious charges to legal and police authorities, not the Church Department.

By September 1943, Feyling had to admit that the expulsion policy spread resistance rather than stopping it.[14] In October, Bishop Ole J. B. Kvasnes suggested solving the problem by resurrecting an earlier proposal by NS pastor Falck-Hansen: confine 60 to 70 of church's leaders in one place.[15] Feyling took to the idea, worked with the State Police, and decided on Lillehammer. This plan had the advantage of containing clerical resistance, while avoiding charges of persecution, and it began in early 1944.

Had pastors been confined to a remote and inaccessible location, they might have felt more deprived, but Lillehammer was mild punishment for the 62 bishops and pastors eventually sent there. They moved freely about the town, participated in religious life, and created a congenial "clergy colony." The courier service also functioned without difficulty, so bishops and clergy continued to carry out their duties.

Not surprisingly, Lillehammer proved unacceptably porous to the outside world, so on 8 December 1944 Feyling moved the colony to Helgøya, an island in Lake Mjøsa, facing Hamar. For the authorities, Helgøya's advantage was that it was more remote, but for the church it had most of the same benefits as Lillehammer: internees formed an even closer community, with ample time for fellowship, worship, study, lectures, discussion, and planning. Four of the bishops (Hille, Maroni, Skagestad, and

Krohn-Hansen) were among them and held regular planning sessions on the postwar church.[16] Unfortunately for the Church Department, lax enforcement made Helgøya almost as porous as Lillehammer. Courier, postal, and telegraphic services operated more or less unhindered. Even Bishop Wollert Krohn-Hansen, who had been confined there since May 1943, was easily able to administer his distant northern diocese. On 2 July 1944, he also ordained 18 pastoral candidates, the first ordinations since the German invasion.[17]

The number of pastors expelled to remote locations or Lillehammer and Helgøya rose from 60 at the end of 1943 to 100 at the end of 1944, and to 128 by the war's end.[18] From the government's point of view, the policy worked because 128 bishops and clergy were not spreading unrest around the country.

CLOSING THE THEOLOGICAL FACULTIES

Both the university's Theological Faculty and the Free Faculty of Theology experienced a brief disruption following the German invasion but quickly resumed instruction. At crucial points in the church's confrontation with the NS state, they gave theological opinions supporting the church's stand.

The university was a self-governing institution under the jurisdiction of the Ministry of Church and Education, but resistance there was slow in forming. Although the university faculty had close ties to German universities, published most of their work in German, and, in some cases, had closely observed the rise of Nazism in Germany, they did not grasp the depth of the Nazi revolution's impact on German universities, nor had they developed a strategy against the probable Nazification of their own institution.[19] When the NS tried to take control of it shortly after assuming power on 25 September 1940, the Theological Faculty initially escaped direct pressure, partly because it was exempted from the university's new political admissions standards and partly for lack of NS supporters among the faculty and students. But among the faculty who would become leaders in the resistance that emerged in 1941 and 1942 and had ties to the church leadership were Einar Molland, professor of church history at the Theological Faculty, and Einar Høigård, who had a fellowship in educational research and was the teacher's resistance leader.[20]

The Theological Faculty's first serious conflict did not erupt until the summer of 1943. Its Seminary for Practical Theology, which trained students in the everyday aspects of pastoral ministry, had a board composed of its own professors, the rector of the seminary, and the bishop of Oslo. When the Church Department appointed Lars Frøyland to replace Berggrav, the board followed the PCL's guidelines and refused to recognize Frøyland or inform him of meetings. Skancke and Feyling then dismissed the board and reconstituted it with Frøyland, the NS rector of the university, Adolf Hoel, and the seminary rector, Peter E. Marstrander. But Marstrander resigned in protest, students boycotted classes, and the seminary ceased operation. After pledging themselves to *The Foundation of the Church*, students completed their requirements at the Free Faculty of Theology's seminary instead.[21]

In late August 1943, a series of conflicts in the university culminated with the government proposing admission requirements that gave Hoel authority to choose new students and consider non-academic factors in admissions. The faculty protested, but Quisling insisted on implementing the new rules, and just before dawn on 15 October 1943, the State Police arrested ten faculty members and fifty to sixty students. Still unwilling to submit to the new rules, the students were sentenced to six months of preventive detention. The issue remained unresolved on 28 November, when an independent resistance group set fire to the university *Aula*, the large hall used for ceremonial events. In response, Terboven was prepared to execute every tenth student, but decided to deport them to Germany instead. He set 29 November as the date for their mass arrests.

Theodor Steltzer heard about this secret plan from General von Falkenhorst and warned his contact in the Home Front, Arvid Brodersen, a research fellow at the university.[22] Brodersen informed Home Front leaders, and their warning enabled 2,000 students to escape. A hospital chaplain, Peder Olson, passed the warning on to Nils Bloch-Hoell, a Free Faculty of Theology student, who warned his fellow students to abandon the school. Bloch-Hoell also warned Theological Faculty students, but they were skeptical. As a result, all of the Free Faculty of Theology students escaped arrest, but Theological Faculty students were among the 1,200 students the Wehrmacht rounded up. About 700 university students were deported to concentration camps in Germany, and on 30 November 1943 Terboven closed the university.[23] The deportation was a violation of human rights, but the PCL decided to adhere to its policy against further protests.[24]

Having escaped arrest, students at the Free Faculty of Theology showed their solidarity with the Theological Faculty students by boycotting classes for the spring semester, but the Free Faculty of Theology's Seminary for Practical Theology continued to operate—for a short time.[25] When very few among the pool of 350 recent theological graduates were willing to fill vacancies in the NS church, the Church Department gave up recruiting them. Rather than moving against them, Skancke closed the Free Faculty of Theology on 28 February, followed two weeks later by its Seminary for Practical Theology.[26]

The closing of the two theological faculties ended the church's theological education in Norway, but a seminary-in-exile continued in Sweden. Some of the university faculty—most conspicuously Einar Molland—escaped to Sweden, where they established themselves at the University of Uppsala. Until the end of the war, they taught Norwegian theological students who had also fled to Sweden. Swedish bishop Gustaf Aulén did his part by ordaining one candidate just before Christmas 1943 and six more in 1944.[27]

When the theological faculties closed, Kvasnes proposed establishing an NS-friendly theological "college" (*høgskole*) and, as a temporary measure, a brief theological course of study.[28] Under the leadership of Karl Malde, a former opera singer and theology graduate, the course began in September 1944 with five or six students, too little and too late to make a difference.[29]

THE NS TAKEOVER OF THE
NORWEGIAN MISSION SOCIETY

An exception to the NS's pattern of repression was its takeover of the Norwegian Mission Society (NMS) in 1944. Feyling was aware of the support that the mission societies had given to the church, and he had looked into ways of gaining control of them, including state financial audits.[30] The roots of the NMS takeover, however, were in Stavanger. The instigator was the most aggressive of the NS bishops, Ole J.B. Kvasnes, who was eager to control the NMS. To that end, in April 1944 he recommended that the Church Department appoint liaisons to the boards of all the large mission societies.[31] Feyling was not willing to provoke all the societies, but he agreed to appoint Kvasnes as the department's liaison to the NMS, and then Feyling and Kvasnes began to apply pressure.

At the instigation of Kvasnes, on 19 May 1944 the State Police searched the homes of several NMS board members and employees, interrogated several people, and confiscated suspicious-looking papers.[32] Included in society leader Einar Amdahl's confiscated papers was a Communist memo of 30 September 1941 that he had picked up as a curiosity, two drafts of a manifesto urging parish councils to resign from their state functions and declare themselves the Free Norwegian Lutheran Folk Church, and papers that the police viewed as support for enemies of the state.[33] The investigation was a prelude to more serious intervention. On Saturday, 3 June, the State Police once again interrogated the board members and three employees. After two hours, all but Amdahl were allowed to return to their homes. Amdahl, however, was arrested, interrogated, jailed, and condemned to four years of imprisonment at the Berg internment camp near Tønsberg.[34]

In the meantime, Feyling was intent on further action. On 6 June, he recommended to the State Police that they rescind travel passes for the Society's clergy and employees.[35] The next day, he informed Quisling that the NMS board had spent the previous two years advancing "the Berggrav coalition's home front tasks in the interests of the emigrant government" and should be replaced. Two days later, he advised the Associations Office (*Foreningskontoret*) of the Interior Department that a recent police raid had produced proof of the Society's political activity.[36] The Rogaland NS leader, Per Gjerstad, bolstered the argument by informing the NS General Secretariat in Oslo that the case had implications for the entire church struggle.[37] The buildup culminated on 5 July with the Church Department charging the NMS board with violating its own statutes by supporting resistance to the country's authorities in order to create chaos and lawlessness. Feyling dismissed the Society's board and named Kvasnes as the new chairman and Adolf Thunem, the Society's treasurer, as the new general secretary.[38] The next day, the NS national newspaper, *Fritt Folk*, announced the news and charged the NMS with longstanding subversive Communist activity.[39]

Hundreds of NMS leaders, employees, chapters, and members responded by sending Feyling, Kvasnes, and Thunem declarations of non-recognition and non-cooperation. All but two of the employees in the Stavanger headquarters also resigned, depriving Kvasnes of any hope of running the Society. In the meantime, John Nome led the Society's board in establishing a secret Provisional Mission Administration to lead the Society's "mission front." The Provisional Mission Administration (*Det midlertidige misjonsstyret*) rapidly won the approval of the local societies, arranged financing, established a courier system, and operated a distribution center out of Oslo.

Kvasnes was depressed by events, but in late July he threatened the Society's employees and missionaries with penalties for violating their contracts and resigning illegally. When his threat had no effect, the State Police detained several NMS employees at the Stavanger headquarters before sending the men to six months of hard labor and the women to three months of labor at a German laundry.[40] Kvasnes believed, with Martin Luther, that the state should intervene when Christians resisted it, so when he was unable to obtain the 1944 district financial reports, he called in the State Police. The police investigations began in April 1945, and they had not concluded when the Germans capitulated. The resistance of the NMS thus held Feyling and Kvasnes at bay long enough to prevent a complete takeover.[41]

THE STATISTICS OF REPRESSION

The PCL's policies did not win universal assent within the church, but, given the situation, dissent was precarious. Nevertheless, some clergy circles regretted the change from the offensive policy prior to Hallesby's and Hope's arrest to the "passive" resistance policy followed thereafter.[42] The PCL justified the policy as necessary for maintaining church unity, fearing, no doubt, the Stavanger proposal for a free folk church. But for some, the policy was dispiriting, and they argued that a return to the active policy of the first years would be more unifying. They also connected the "cautious" policy to what they described as the "ruthlessness" of the state's internment of bishops and clergy at Lillehammer and Helgøya, as well as the takeover of the NMS. The dissenting views were no doubt discussed, but the PCL did not change course.

As the war drew to a close, trivial acts of dissidence could have grave consequences. Expressing anti-German or NS sentiments in a shop could lead to an internment camp, and against Milorg the Gestapo imposed the death penalty with increasing frequency.[43] The Germans executed 37 Norwegians in 1940 and 1941, which escalated to 121 in 1942, 110 in 1943, 105 in 1944, and 44 in the first four months of 1945.[44] No clergymen were executed, but two theological students who had joined a Milorg unit, Cay Børre Kristiansen and Tomas Per Trægde, were executed on 4 July 1944 for "actions in behalf of an enemy state."[45]

The autonomous church's bishops and clergy were also caught in the net of Gestapo interrogations, searches, and arrests, and many were imprisoned. Most sentences related to their church activity, but some were for other forms of resistance. Between 1942 and 1945, 81 church leaders were imprisoned—four in 1942, 23 in 1943, 42 in 1944, and 12 in 1945.[46] Thirty spent time in one of the internment camps—Grini (Oslo), Falstad (Levanger), or Berg (Tønsberg)—six were deported to German concentration camps, and two died in prison. Ingolf Boge (1900–1944) of Fjell Parish, just west of Bergen, died on 1 April of double pneumonia at a German concentration camp. Arne Thu (1891–1944), who had objected to the altered version of the Church's Prayer of Intercession and persisted in using the traditional version, died on 27 June 1944 after a five-hour penal exercise at Grini internment camp, apparently of heart failure.[47]

THE EFFECT OF REPRESSION

The intensified repression in 1943 and 1944 took its toll on the church. In its 1944 Easter message, the PCL noted that most parishes were able to continue their work, but the authorities had turned progressively to police action, leaving many parishes without pastors.[48] The PCL's tabulations demonstrated the trend: before 31 December 1943, about 26 bishops and members of the clergy were in prison or under house arrest, and after that the figure rose to about 55.[49] There are no similar statistics on the chronology of the 127 expelled from their parishes, but the increase was in roughly the same proportions. Another 19 to 24 pastors escaped to Sweden, including Arne Fjellbu and Conrad Bonnevie-Svendsen.[50]

At the end of the occupation, the PCL tabulated a statistical summary of state action against the bishops and clergy:[51]

Total of ordained clergy loyal to the church: 815

Prevented from exercising their duties in whole or in part: 222
(27 percent)

Dismissed from office: 91 (11 percent)

Expelled from parishes: 127 (16 percent)

Imprisoned: 92 (11 percent)

Fled the country, mostly to Sweden: 19 (2.3 percent)

Prohibited from speaking in public: 15, of whom 6 were bishops
(1.8 percent)

Deaths in internment or concentration camps: 2

PREPARING FOR THE POSTWAR FUTURE

In 1943, the PCL began discussing the postwar church, and it focused on three issues: the reckoning with the NS, the basis of the church's unity, and the future of the state church. Only on the first did it make headway during the war.

Discussion about the postwar treatment of NS supporters and church employees began in the spring of 1943 and led in the fall to the PCL issuing a memorandum as an initial attempt to influence public opinion. It had two themes: justice and forgiveness.[52] The NS and other war criminals had violated the norms and laws of Norwegian society, and justice would not be satisfied if society returned to normal as if nothing had happened; without accountability before the law, the Nazis would have won. The PCL followed up in its Pentecost message of 1944 on the necessity of love and forgiveness. "God is always wholly just *and* wholly loving," they wrote, and love meant "reconciliation and forgiveness" of enemies, at home and abroad. "If we cannot forgive our countrymen who have committed an offense, but who are repentant and serve their penalty, we shall move into the future with an open wound in the life of the people." In short: "Complete forgiveness belongs to a complete reckoning."[53]

By the end of 1944, the PCL had also decided on the criteria for dealing with NS church employees and had begun field testing them in the dioceses.[54] NS clergy would be divided into four categories based on Norwegian law supplemented by broad criteria that church law did not anticipate or address. Only clergy in the first category would be dismissed outright; this included those appointed by the Church Department after

5 April 1942, those appointed between 25 September 1940 and 5 April 1942 whose appointments were ecclesiastically indefensible, and those who were illegally ordained. The other three categories took into account ameliorating circumstances and required less severe action, such as suspension and reinstatement.

While the PCL was drawing the lines between church loyalty and collaboration, it was also framing the basis of church unity. Orthodox members interpreted the unity achieved in the CCC and PCL as the surrender of theological liberalism to confessional Lutheranism, a conclusion liberals had to reject. There was no opportunity to resolve the conflict during the war, but a revealing incident showed how the PCL dealt with the issue in practice. When Johannes Smemo had to escape to Sweden in late 1944, Andreas Seierstad and at least two other members blocked the candidacy of liberal professor Hans Ording to replace him on the PCL. Seierstad was a hardline neo-Pietist confessionalist, for whom the formation of the CCC represented "a verdict on liberal views of scripture and the confessions" as well as "other fundamental deviations from the Reformation line."[55] He turned his opposition into a matter of conscience, and because the PCL made decisions by consensus, his stand blocked Ording's appointment. In effect, orthodox members held the PCL hostage to their demand for theological conformity.

Krohn-Hansen had pressed for the discussion about the treatment of NS pastors after the war, and he had also wanted a discussion on the future relationship of church and state.[56] Thinking, no doubt, about the Stavanger proposals of early 1942, he was afraid that liberation would arrive with demands for separating church and state. He himself thought a state church had proven to be a blessing, largely because it had given the church a legal right and duty to call the state to account. That discussion, however, had to wait until after liberation.

Chapter 18

The Reckoning

Had Colonel Claus von Stauffenberg succeeded in assassinating Hitler on 20 July 1944, the war might have ended earlier and differently, but Hitler survived. Key military conspirators refused to act, and the conspiracy fell apart. Among those implicated were men with connections to the Norwegian church struggle: Helmut von Moltke was tried and hanged on 23 January 1945; Theodor Steltzer was condemned to death but released two weeks before Germany capitulated; in prison since 6 April 1943 on other charges, Dietrich Bonhoeffer was hanged on 9 April 1945.[1] Admiral W. W. Canaris suffered the same fate on the same day at the same place.

Hitler also paid a price. His paranoia intensified, and he slowly lost touch with his people, his subordinates, and military reality. To the end, he thought that the Allies would invade Germany through Norway. As teenagers defended Berlin in May 1945, Germany had 340,000 soldiers defending Fortress Norway.

With Germany in retreat, the global war returned to Norway. In May 1944, the Norwegian government signed agreements with the United States, the United Kingdom, and the Soviet Union about their respective jurisdictions during the liberation. Per agreement, the Soviet army crossed the Pasvik River in Finnmark on 23 October 1944. Five days later, Hitler ordered the evacuation of Finnmark and North Troms. As the 20th German Army retreated, it burned farms, villages, and towns. On 10 November, the first Norwegian troops entered Kirkenes.

In May 1943, the former cathedral dean in Trondheim, Arne Fjellbu, had been banished to Andøya, a small village in northern Norway, and at the end of 1944 he escaped to Sweden. The Norwegian government appointed him bishop of the liberated areas, and on 12 January 1945 he arrived at Kirkenes to begin his duties.[2] His jurisdiction extended from west of Kirkenes to the Tana valley, where the Soviets stopped their advance in November. The Germans halted around Alta and Repparfjord and stayed until their capitulation.

In central and southern Norway, the question was when and how the occupation would end.[3] General Franz Böhme, von Falkenhorst's successor as the Wehrmacht's Commander-in-Chief, had about 340,000 soldiers positioned for battle, but the British, in charge of Allied operations in Norway, had no intention of diverting a comparable number of troops from the continent.[4] Both sides wondered if the end would come as a military conflagration or an orderly transition.

Hitler's suicide changed the dynamics of the capitulation. Before he shot himself on 30 April, Hitler designated Great Admiral Karl Dönitz as his successor. Dönitz hoped to negotiate, but the Allies demanded unconditional surrender. At 2:41 A.M. on 7 May 1945, in Rheims, France, the Allied supreme commander, General Dwight D. Eisenhower, accepted Germany's surrender, effective at the end of the next day, 8 May— Victory in Europe Day (VE-Day). In the Pacific, the war would not end until 2 September.

The human cost of death and suffering during World War II was beyond comprehension. A conservative estimate is that fifty million people died across the globe as a result of war. Soviet losses alone were 27 million, of whom two million died fighting the Germans just between D-Day on 6 June 1944 and V-E Day almost a year later, three times the combined losses of the U.K., Americans, Canadians, and French in the same period. German military losses were also high: 2.4 million soldiers killed on the Eastern Front from Barbarossa to the end of 1944, and 202,000 in the same period on the Western Front, almost equivalent to Norway's 2.8 million population in 1938.[5] Against such losses, Norway's loss of life bears no comparison: 10,000 total casualties, of whom 2,000 died in military combat, 1,400 in the armed resistance (Milorg), and 4,200 in the merchant marine. Within the total were over 700 Jews and almost 800 volunteers recruited by NS to fight on the Eastern

Front. Per capita, Norway's losses were among the lowest in occupied Europe.[6]

LIBERATION

In the fall and winter, the Norwegian government and the Home Front agreed to unify the civilian and military resistance under the Home Front Leadership. They also reached an agreement on the transition to peace, and Norway's liberation went better than anyone had a right to hope. On 5 May 1945, Prime Minister Nygaardsvold authorized the Home Front Leadership to assume responsibility for public order and civil administration until the government's return. The Allies counted on the Wehrmacht to maintain its command structure and internal discipline, a plan that, in the end, coincided with German wishes. Reichskommissariat officials tried to escape by blending into the demobilized Wehrmacht, others committed suicide, and yet others were identified and faced their fate. Wilhelm Rediess, the head of the SS, shot himself on 8 May, and a few hours later Terboven blew himself up. Five days later, Gestapo chief Heinrich Fehlis followed suit.

For the NS, all was lost. Their leaders spent their final days burning incriminating documents, Feyling among them.[7] Quisling delivered his last radio broadcast, a defense of his regime, on 5 May, and early on 9 May he and most of his ministers surrendered to the police. A few hours later, Chief Justice Paal Berg announced that Norway was once again a constitutional state.[8]

The first delegation of the Norwegian government arrived in Oslo on 13 May, and the next day the Home Front Leadership transferred authority to the government. Prime Minister Nygaardsvold and his cabinet returned at the end of May, and King Haakon followed on 7 June. His return officially ended Allied military authority. The Nygaardsvold government remained in office until 25 June, when Einar Gerhardsen formed a national coalition government. He named Conrad Bonnevie-Svendsen as Minister of Church and Education, and Kristian Hansson assumed Feyling's position as Director General of the Church Department. On 14 June, the Storting reconvened and set new elections for 8 October. The election returned the Labor Party to power under Gerhardsen. The transition to peace was complete.

RECONSTITUTING THE CHURCH

After his escape to Sweden in February 1945, the church's representative in the Home Front Leadership, Conrad Bonnevie-Svendsen, traveled to London to present the PCL's views on the transition to Nils Hjelmtveit, Minister of Church and Education. Throughout the war, the Ministry of Church and Education had functioned with minimal staff to maintain funding for the seamen's churches, global missions, education for children of exiles, and the Norwegian Broadcasting Corporation.[9] There had been no direct contact between church leaders and the Ministry, but Bonnevie-Svendsen and Hjelmtveit smoothed the way for agreement on the PCL's provisional advisory authority and its plan for the purge of NS church personnel. As of 18 May 1945, the Norwegian government recognized the PCL as an official advisory body in place until April 1946.[10]

For imprisoned church leaders, personal liberation preceded national liberation. Due to his advanced age, Hope had been set free on 30 August 1943 and retired to private life. Berggrav escaped from his cottage on 16 April 1945 and went into hiding in an Oslo apartment. On 5 May, the Home Front escorted Hallesby out of the Grini internment camp and drove him the short distance to his home.

On 7 May, Berggrav resumed his role as national church leader. He had lost none of his decisiveness. Within two hours of resuming office, he had arranged for the clergy to ring church bells from 3 to 4 P.M. the next day, sent telegrams to convene a Bishops' Conference, and directed the clergy to reinstate the traditional version of the Church's Prayer of Intercession.[11]

The Bishops' Conference convened on 9 May to reconstitute the church. The first order of business was reinstating the resigned pastors and informing them of their status. Then they turned to the NS clergy. Following the PCL's National Plan, they charged all NS bishops and clergy with aiding the enemy and violating the Constitution and the human rights of Norwegian citizens. At the end of the first day's work, they had suspended 63 pastors and 13 other illegally ordained clergy, and they ordered another 31 who had been ordained by NS bishops to step down at once.[12] The bishops also authorized members of parish councils elected in 1937 and loyal to *The Foundation of the Church* to resume their positions until the next election.[13]

In his first broadcast to the Norwegian people, the new Minister of Church and Education, Conrad Bonnevie-Svendsen, counted the material costs of the occupation: 26 churches and all 15 parsonages destroyed in Finnmark; seven churches burned and destroyed in Troms and Nordland counties; six churches damaged farther south; a large number of parish centers and chapels razed. The free churches had similar losses.[14]

THE TREASON LAWS

More difficult than restoring buildings or repairing relations with sister churches was the reckoning with the NS, otherwise known as the "settlement." Two sections of the Penal Code formed the legal foundation of the trials.[15] Section 86 applied to citizens who bore arms illegally against Norway or offered aid to the enemy; Section 98 applied to anyone who cooperated in illegally altering the constitutional basis of the state.

The war produced additional laws, notably a decree on war crimes to supplement the Penal Code, particularly with regard to individual membership in the NS as aid to the enemy and, therefore, an act of treason, and the reintroduction of the death penalty. These and other laws were replaced by the Treason Decree of 15 December 1944, followed on 4 May 1945 by a law directed at foreign war criminals. The first was intended to make lesser violators accountable, and the last was applied to Germans implicated in crimes against Norwegians. Cases involving imprisonment of more than three years were usually tried under the Penal Code, while the Treason Decree applied to lesser cases.

THE TREASON DEBATE

Public debate about treason and the treason trials began as soon as the celebrations were over. Berggrav published a stern judgment of the NS in his journal, *For Church and Culture*, and distributed offprints throughout the country.[16] His central and most controversial point was that NS members had incurred guilt simply by joining the party. The NS was a double conspiracy, he wrote, first between NS members and then between them and the nation's enemies, and it was based on threats, violence, and death. All NS party members should receive a basic sentence, because even passive members were "the guarantors" of the violence carried out in the name of the party. Berggrav's judgment probably articulated the way most people felt at the time, and more than any single piece of writing it established the base line for a stern judgment.[17]

At the end of his article, however, Berggrav expressed a view that ran counter to majority opinion. "Each death sentence," he wrote, "will be a detriment to the people's case"[18] So soon after liberation, Berggrav's stand against the death penalty was so provocative that it seriously eroded the goodwill that the church had gained during the occupation.[19] But he was not alone among church leaders. Two weeks after liberation, the Society of Friends protested to the Storting that the death penalty violated "the humane legal principles that ought to remain in force in every country that calls itself Christian," and in August, the Methodist Church's Annual Conference stated that the death penalty was contrary to "our people's fundamental Christian view of life" and urged the government to pardon generously.[20]

Berggrav himself came under scrutiny for his conduct. Several Oslo newspapers, particularly the Communist *Friheten*, the Labor *Arbeiderbladet*, and the liberal *Dagbladet*, criticized him severely for his words and actions during the first weeks of the invasion, and the Storting's Investigative Commission, of which Hallesby was a member, included him and other members of the Oslo coalition in their official investigation. The Commission raised questions about Berggrav's part in Quisling's removal, the establishment of the Administrative Council, and the "June negotiations." He defended himself through letters to the Commission and his book, *When the Struggle Began* (Da kampen kom). Although the Commission basically exonerated him and the coalition he worked with, charges of collaborationism continued and still appear in histories of the occupation.[21] The public scrutiny and steady stream of criticism, which could be very personal, began to affect his health, and in 1946 his doctor blamed overwork and stress for his weakened heart muscles and edema.[22] He took a four-month sick leave and to relieve his workload briefly considered a transfer to the Hamar Diocese.

"THE TRIAL OF THE CENTURY"

Quisling's trial began on 20 August 1945 in *Eidsivating lagmannsrett*, a district court of appeals, with a full complement of Norwegian reporters and 200 foreign journalists in attendance. In the words of an American journalist, the trial proceeded with "the quiet decorum of a Lutheran Church service."[23] The state based its nine charges on alleged violations of both the military and civil penal codes. The most serious were the first three, in which the state accused Quisling of directly aiding the German invasion of Norway, conspiring with the Germans to occupy the country, and providing military support to the Germans that was damaging to Norway and her allies.

The state's charges regarding the church related to the fourth of the major charges, which was attempting to change the constitutional state by illegal means, but they were a minor aspect of the trial and did not affect the court's verdict. The most serious of them was that Quisling planned to try Berggrav in a people's court and execute him. Important testimony against Quisling came from Fridtjof Hammersen, a major in the Luftwaffe assigned to General von Falkenhorst's staff as an interpreter and orderly and also a member of the Kreisau Circle and a friend of Theodor Steltzer.[24] Hammersen testified on the authority of *Gauleiter* Paul Wegener, the German political liaison to the NS, that Berlin prevented Quisling from trying Berggrav. Quisling, however, placed the blame on the State Police for wanting the trial and execution.

On 10 September 1945, the court found Quisling guilty on all major charges and sentenced him to death. Count 4, which included his measures against the church, found him guilty of illegally altering the Constitution by establishing and extending a Nazi form of government. The court also found that he sanctioned state expropriation of church properties and knowingly accepted the illegal transfer of the Fyresdal parsonage and lands to his private ownership.[25]

In his last weeks, Quisling sought the counsel of hospital chaplain Peder Olsen, with whom he discussed religion and philosophy, read the Bible, prayed, sang hymns, and shared the Eucharist. Olsen also gave him books, including Hallesby's *From the World of Prayer*, which he particularly liked. Perhaps this reversion to his childhood spirituality gave him comfort, but right to the end he continued to develop his philosophical Universism.[26] Olsen was left with the impression that Quisling was "an idealist without realism," a man who lived in a world of illusion and paranoia, and not for a moment did he think he had done anything wrong or had reason to feel guilty.[27] In his own final reflections, Quisling was still the prophet of a new vision of life that would ultimately triumph. He would die a martyr, like Jesus and St. Olav, and upon death he would enter life eternal. "We are not just ripples of a wave on the sea of eternity," he wrote to his wife, "but an eternal part of the eternal God."[28] Death came by firing squad at 2:40 A.M., 24 October 1945.

THE TRIAL OF RAGNAR SKANCKE

Skancke was tried in May 1946. The state's general charge was that he aided the Germans, promoted Nazification, and used coercion against the resistance.[29] Specifically, he staffed the Ministry of Church and Education with NS supporters, instituted Nazi laws, and made "persistent and malicious attacks on the church and its men in order to enact the appointment and leadership principle and otherwise subordinate and exploit the church for political aims." He was charged with doing the same with the schools and the university. Under Section 86 of the criminal code, the state charged him with 31 counts of violating the church. The charges ran the gamut of the church struggle, from his attempt to Nazify the church to his appointment of bishops on political grounds. Other charges covered his use of coercion against church leaders, including using the State Police and the German Security Police to enforce his church policies.

The court upheld all but three major charges and condemned him to death. Skancke appealed, but the judge found insufficient grounds for commutation to a life sentence. The sentence was controversial, and among those who pleaded for commutation to a life sentence were 668 of the clergy.[30] He was executed on 28 August 1948, one of two commissioner ministers to receive the death penalty.

THE TRIAL OF SIGMUND FEYLING

Feyling's trial began late, on 7 June 1949. The state prosecutor indicted him on 107 counts of violating various sections of the penal code. The grounds for most of the charges were his actions as head of the Church Department. The state accused Feyling of being Skancke's "closest co-worker and advisor." He "took a leading role in the work of advancing the enemy's plans against Norway and Norwegians" and was one of "the driving forces in the Nazis' infringements on the church and the congregations."[31] The charges also claimed that he initiated Nazi church legislation, promoted Nazification of the school curriculum, the church, and the Church Department, and in other ways exploited the church for political ends, in tandem with Reichskommissariat, the German Secret Police, and the Norwegian State Police. He was the Nazis' handpicked man in its struggle against the church and its clergy.[32]

Feyling defended himself by claiming that he had acted solely to help his church, people, and country. He also claimed that he was not aware Norway was at war with Germany, a legal finesse based on the Storting's not having participated in the declaration of war.[33] He appealed to the traditional Lutheran interpretation of obedience to the state (Romans 13:1). Berggrav's decision to strike the reference to the King in the Church's Prayer of Intercession, he said, was a recognition of "the way things were" and had influenced him to join the NS. He could not understand how his NS membership aided the enemy.

Feyling also accused Quisling, Skancke, and radical elements in the party of being responsible for state coercion against the church, and asserted that he had been a force for moderation. Quisling had wanted to dismiss all the clergy who resigned from office, but Feyling persuaded Skancke to give up the idea. At several other stages of the church struggle, Feyling had advised Quisling against pursuing a hard line against the clergy. Feyling also held Skancke responsible for legislative and administrative decisions and argued that he himself had simply given them written form.

Feyling added that Skancke had wanted the best for the church and was not responsible for the use of force against it. When Feyling had used the State Police in clergy cases, it was because Quisling, Skancke, and he were under pressure from radical elements in the party. Radical NS pressure for action against the church was also the reason Quisling and Skancke had ordered Feyling to handle more and more church cases through the State Police. As Director General of the Church Department, Feyling was not responsible for everything that happened in his name.

He admitted to doubts. The ideology that German advisors forced on the Hird and the youth service was "partly anti-Christian," and after 8 May 1945 he had seen that he underestimated "the less attractive features" of National Socialist ideology.[34] He did not elaborate.

The verdict fell on 8 July 1949. The judge sentenced Feyling to fifteen years of forced labor with credit for time served, the loss of civil rights for ten years, and permanent loss of clerical rights. It was the harshest sentence meted out to a member of the NS clergy. He was released on 21 December 1951 and died in 1980 at the age of 85.

TRIALS OF THE NS BISHOPS

Indictments against bishops were more extensive than those against the clergy because of the greater authority and responsibility of their offices. The NS bishops were charged and found guilty under the Penal Code's Section 86, aiding the enemy, Section 98, altering the state's Constitution, and Section 222, using threats to coerce others. Parts of the Treason Decree were also used. Of the twelve who at some point functioned as "bishops," only two were not NS party members—Frøyland and Kvasnes.[35]

The general charge was that they had actively participated in instituting "the new order" in the church. The charges began with their membership in the NS, appointment as bishops in the NS church, and illegal exercise of the episcopal office. The specific charges included dismissing and expelling clergy, informing on clergy, forcibly gaining access to parish offices, and preventing clergy from carrying out their prescribed duties. They also encompassed preaching or writing in support of the Quisling government and signing the anti-Bolshevist appeal of 1941, a serious charge of supporting the enemy against a Norwegian ally. Charges under Section 98, altering the state's Constitution, included implementing the Parish Council Law of 30 July 1942, which had nullified the Parish Council Law of 1920.

The NS bishops were sentenced to imprisonment and forced labor with loss of civil and clerical rights. Four were given sentences of three to four years and the rest from seven to ten years. Einar Lothe, as bishop of Nidaros, received ten years, and Lars Frøyland, the bishop of Oslo, was sentenced to seven. For both bishops and clergy, the later the case came to trial, the milder the sentence, and most who received longer sentences were released early.

Of all treason trial cases, only those who had informed on, tortured, or murdered people—fewer than 200—were still in prison by 1951. Even those who received the most severe sentences served a quarter to a third of their time.[36]

THE TRIALS OF THE NS CLERGY

The NS clergy were tried after the more serious treason cases, and the last clergy trial was not until 1952. The Bishops' Conference and the PCL slated 58 clergy members, 35 of whom belonged to the NS, for immediate suspension and referral to state prosecutors. Of the 58, 48 went to trial, 21 were sentenced 60 days to seven years in prison, and the remainder received milder forms of punishment.[37]

Two features of the clergy trials stand out. One was the appeal to the absolute authority of the state based on Romans 13:1. Most of the NS bishops and clergy used the doctrine in a more or less pro forma manner; others made it a central argument. They claimed that they had no theological or ecclesiological differences with their opponents, so they were not "Nazi Christians," and by remaining loyal to the state they were following Lutheran tradition, unlike their church opponents.[38] Furthermore, *The Foundation of the Church* itself was a political document created by power hungry bishops. Forced to choose between anti-Christian Bolshevism and pro-Christian Nazism, they chose the latter. They appealed to the thought of Sigurd Odland, whose case had led to the establishment of the Free Faculty of Theology and who had argued that even a state that achieved power illegally should be obeyed. Above all, they appealed to Ole Hallesby, who in his book of 1928 on Christian ethics had made a strong argument for an authoritarian state and obedience to the state.[39]

The second feature of note is the NS pastors' interpretation of the bishops' recognition of the state after 25 September 1940. Their argument was, first, that the NS had been a legal party before 1940, and they did not understand why the Norwegian government should label it "illegal" after the invasion. Second, they assumed that Norway was no longer at war after its forces capitulated, and the Hague Convention gave Germans the right to intervene in the country and to appoint a Norwegian administration.

Finally, they argued that Berggrav himself had condoned their joining the NS after 9 April 1940. In *The Temporal and the Eternal* in July 1940, and later on 23 October 1940, he had recognized the Germans and the NS government. In the second message, written after the Germans had established the Commissarial Council, Berggrav advised the clergy that each person had to "follow his own conscience and conviction."[40] Finally, by altering the Church's Prayer of Intercession, Berggrav had implicitly acknowledged the new government. Therefore, the pastors argued, the NS government and NS party membership were perfectly legal and worthy of loyalty. Because they also thought the NS government had not interfered in the church's preaching, order, or life, they saw no reason to resign on Easter Sunday 1942.

THE JEWISH QUESTION

The case against NS leaders in the deportation of Jews in late 1942 is not strictly an aspect of the church's resistance to Nazism, but NS church leaders shared the party's anti-Semitism and, insofar as they acted on it, were held accountable. The PCL's protest against the deportation of Jews also entered into the trials.

Charges of anti-Semitism could be prosecuted severely, a precedent established with the fifth count against Quisling: violation of the Penal Code's Section 233, which made murder punishable by a minimum of six years to life. This was the count under which the prosecution charged Quisling with encouraging anti-Semitism, issuing the law on registration of Jews, and allowing the Norwegian police to aid in the arrest of Jews deported to Poland. The state also charged that Quisling knew his actions would cost many Jews their lives. Furthermore, the "deportation from the country was arranged by Germans on the basis of Quisling's express wish to have the Jewish question solved in this manner as quickly as possible."[41] The court found Quisling guilty on all counts.

Skancke's part in the deportation of Jews, count 25 in his trial, found him guilty under paragraph 86 of the Penal Code of agreeing to the dissolution of the Mosaic Society and the Jewish congregation, confiscating Jewish property after the deportations, and agreeing to the transfer of Jewish property to the NS Relief Fund. He was also found guilty of working for the enactment of a law that would have prohibited Jewish intermarriage with non-Jews.

Feyling's duplicity was most evident when the court considered his role in the deportation of the Jews. The state brought two charges against him, to which he pleaded innocent. Under the Penal Code and the Treason Decree, the court found him guilty of drafting laws prohibiting marriage between citizens of "Norwegian descent" and citizens of Sami or Jewish descent up to three generations. He was also found guilty of cooperating in the dissolution of the Jewish synagogue and the distribution of its assets to the NS, as well as of writing a circular to the NS bishops and clergy in order to solicit their opinions on the Jewish question. He pleaded innocent on both counts.

THE FINAL RECKONING

The final figures for Norwegians charged with treason were double the Norwegian government's wartime projections: 92,805 cases. After the treason trials, 25 were executed, about 20,000 were imprisoned, and 77 received life sentences; 37,150 cases were dismissed because of the legal shortcomings of the evidence.[42]

The statistics mask the rapid softening of public opinion and the courts as the war receded. After serving their sentences, only a few NS pastors requested reinstatement. Their appeals led to lengthy debate in the Bishops' Conference, and the issue was not resolved until 1955, when the government decreed that clergy who had served their sentences could be reinstalled in a special ceremony created for the purpose. The church eventually reinstated ten former NS pastors.[43]

Epilogue

Legacies

The Church of Norway's resistance to Nazism and subsequent break with the NS state had repercussions as well as historical significance. This epilogue considers a few of its repercussions in postwar Norway and the global church, compares and contrasts it with the German Kirchenkampf, returns to the question of why it was different from its German counterpart, and, finally, assesses its significance within Norwegian church history, general church history, the history of World War II, and movements of non-violent resistance.

NATION, CHURCH, AND SOCIETY

Viewed politically, Norway's postwar era may be considered as the period of Labor dominance under Einar Gerhardsen from 1945 to 1965 an era marked by a heightened sense of national unity.[1] The common war against the occupation brought people together across class and political lines and was symbolized by the first coalition government's "Common Platform": constitutional democracy, the right to work, and the preservation of freedom and independence.

After winning the first postwar election, the Labor Party continued as a social democratic party that dominated politics and directed and coordinated the growing economy while guaranteeing higher social security and economic equality. As the virtues of the party's social democratic ideology took hold, opposing political ideologies lost their force within a broad segment of the population.[2]

Internationally, Norway joined with other governments intent on avoiding another global tragedy and promoting new thinking about preserving peace through non-violent change and conflict resolution. In the first rank of institutions dedicated to such ends was the United Nations, founded in 1945. Norway was a founding member of the United Nations, and Trygve Lie, Norway's foreign minister for most of the war, became the United Nation's first Secretary General. Militarily, Norway became a founding member of the North Atlantic Treaty Organization (NATO), formed in 1949 to secure the peace in Europe and North America.

Ecclesiastically, Norway's postwar era was briefer—1945 to 1953. The era proved to be in marked contrast to the church's experience during the occupation. The Church of Norway entered the era with high expectations of spiritual and cultural renewal under its aegis. Signs of spiritual renewal during the occupation raised church hopes of a postwar religious revival and church renewal, and the moral capital it had accumulated fueled hopes for a "re-Christianization" of culture.

The church was disappointed on both counts. Almost immediately after liberation, church attendance dropped to prewar levels, and the same was true in the mission societies. Three years after the war, Hallesby confessed that there had been "few people, no revival, tiredness, dispiritedness, and criticism."[3]

Why were church hopes so quickly crushed? One reason was that church leaders misread the signs. The increased church attendance during the war was more patriotic rather than religious, a venue for demonstrating dissidence when others were closed.[4] Another reason was war weariness. After five years of occupation and material deprivations, people were intent on rebuilding their personal lives and careers. The church was not the only institution they neglected. Participation in all cultural and political organizations, including the labor movement, experienced similar declines. The deepest and most long term reason, however, was probably secularization. In Christian circles, secularization was identified as our "great opposition," but unlike Nazism it could not be resisted with protests.[5]

The church's plans to capitalize on its new wartime reputation included a broad renewal of Christian culture. Stephan Tschudi expressed the vision with the slogan, "Everything concerns the church." Church and people belonged together, he thought, and the church had to go on a broad offensive to create a national Christian cultural awakening.[6] To that end, church leaders launched new initiatives. Tschudi, Alex Johnson, and Kåre Eide formed *Land og Kirke* (Land and Church), a publishing house that aimed to publish more broadly and on more contemporary issues than existing Christian publishers.[7] A second venture was *Vårt Land* (Our Land), a Christian daily newspaper in Oslo intended to "bring forth the Christian spirit and Christian view of life in all sectors of the people"; its first issue appeared on 31 August 1945.[8]

The names of these ventures are telling about Christian hopes, because they spoke of the union of Christianity, church, and country against what the church interpreted as the causes of the war. The church interpreted the war as a consequence of modern secularization and a judgment on the secular values of "materialism, modern morality, and human self-sufficiency"; as such, the war was a consequence of global trends in the prewar era.[9] From that perspective, the National Socialist state was "a demonic symptom of a general tendency within the development of the modern state." The good society—including a more economically and socially egalitarian one—would only emerge through the "spiritual and moral conversion" of individuals, and the church struggle seemed to confirm church hopes that Christianity would continue to be the source of the country's values and its sense of community.

But hopes for a national Christian cultural renewal were crushed almost as quickly as hopes for a spiritual revival. As early as 1946, Bishop Arne Fjellbu observed that "the church's status was already not what it was a year earlier."[10] Part of the problem was that in the euphoria of the church's role in the resistance, leaders like Fjellbu advocated Christianity and Christian culture as the sole basis on which a postwar society should be built. Not only did this overstate the church's role in the resistance, it ignored other powerful interests.[11]

The Labor government, in particular, had another interpretation of the occupation and its own vision of postwar national unity. In Labor's view, the prewar "crisis" was a reflection of capitalistic economics, the non-Socialist parties' indifference to economic injustice, and the divisions that their indifference had created. The war was thus a judgment on the prewar political and economic order, and the national unity achieved during the occupation was a step toward a postwar welfare state. National unity and a sense of community would be created by a state that became "a safe and good home for all." A nation at one and at peace would be built by commitment to common secular values, by allowing science to guide politics and defining the good life as a higher standard of living.

This view was symbolized in 1946 by the state's takeover of the Home Mission Society's teachers' college in Oslo. Education was to be an entirely state-run enterprise, serving the common good as the party defined the good. In postwar Labor ideology, the state was to be a unitary state, not least in education, and religion was a private matter. A bitterly disappointed Hallesby charged that the Labor government was engaging in state dictatorship; it was unnecessary to add that it was acting like the NS.[12] In this case, however, the state was acting not only constitutionally but on values shared by the electorate, including Christians. Unlike in the 1930s, therefore, Hallesby could not mobilize his supporters to reverse the decision. Christians, apparently, had become more invested in social democracy than in preserving a distinctively Christian culture through the education of teachers.[13]

One Christian initiative did establish an enduring presence on the national scene. Christians became more politically conscious and engaged as a result of the prewar crisis and the war. The Christian Democratic Party that had elected two representatives in the 1936 Storting elections added six more in 1945 and reached fourteen by 1953. The numbers did not make for a mass movement, because Christians remained divided about a "Christian" party and the meaning of "Christian" politics, but the party was a political voice for Christianity's place in "the public square."

CHURCH AND STATE

In the wake of the church struggle, there was a widespread feeling in the church that the postwar state had to recognize that there really were *two* realms, state *and* church, and that the only basis for cooperation was greater church autonomy in its own affairs.[14] No one had greater hopes than Berggrav. He had used his house arrest to propose a new church order that was supported by the Provisional Church Leadership and published in 1945 as *The Church's Organization in Norway: Retrospect and Prospect.*[15]

The cause looked promising. Prime Minister Einar Gerhardsen's Labor government of 1945 appointed a Church Order Commission to explore the need for greater church authority and the forms it might take.[16] The commission comprised familiar figures, including Berggrav, Hallesby, Molland, and Nils Hjelmtveit, the Labor Government's Minister of Church and Education before and during the war. The Commission's central proposal, announced in 1948, was a national church synod that would be the church's "spiritual authority on matters of church principle," a visible manifestation of the church's spiritual freedom.[17] The proposal had the broad support of church officials, church agencies, and the Labor Government's Church Department.

Timing is everything in politics. The Storting delayed consideration of the Church Order Commission's proposal until 1953. By then the occupation was becoming a distant memory and the Labor Party was creating the unitary, egalitarian, welfare state. The radical wing of the party's Storting delegation argued that the proposal was contrary to Labor's egalitarian agenda because it would grant the church more autonomy than other state institutions. In the course of debate, that argument became increasingly persuasive, and the Storting finally voted down the proposal. The Church of Norway "was put in its place as a state church in a secular state."[18]

Behind the decision was growing dissatisfaction in the Labor Party with church criticism of the welfare state. Led by Berggrav, church leaders were particularly afraid of the secularizing and totalitarian potential of a centralized welfare state. To opponents, however, it looked like Berggrav and the church were simply seeking more state power for church ends, which would undermine national community as Labor envisioned it.[19] The Norwegian Church Order Law that the Storting did pass in 1953 simply perpetuated the tradition of state primacy.

CHURCH UNITY AND THEOLOGY

The unity forged between the orthodox and the liberals during the occupation represented a historic breakthrough, but world peace did not necessarily mean peace in the church. The church struggle had raised Lutheran confessional consciousness, and in 1945 Hallesby warned that the church conflict of the 1920s would resume at the first sign of compromise with liberal theology.[20] In his understanding of the church, there was no room for anything but confessional Lutheranism.

Calm prevailed until 25 January 1953, when Hallesby himself shattered it without meaning to. In a radio sermon, he concluded by warning his listeners: "You know that if you dropped dead to the floor at this moment, you would drop straight into Hell." The secular Oslo press was outraged. So was the former radical theologian Kristian Schjelderup, who had undergone a conversion during the war and was now Bishop of Hamar. "Teaching about eternal punishment in Hell does not belong in the religion of love," he replied, and with that the "Hell Controversy" was on. It did not end until February 1954, when the Ministry of Church and Education ruled that Schjelderup's opinion did not place him outside the church's confession.[21] The ruling was yet another sign that the confessional state was weakening.

The "Hell Controversy" also showed that history of the orthodox-liberal church conflict was still being written. In the CCC and PCL, church leaders had overcome differences for the sake of a unified front against a Nazi state, but this did not—and could not—resolve the deep theological divisions created within Christianity by modernity itself.

CREEDAL CONSEQUENCES

Loyalty to *The Foundation of the Church* had been the clergy's basis for resigning from their state offices, the church's united front during the occupation, and the condition for service in the postwar church. Although it has never had the renown of the *Barmen Declaration,* it ranks as an enduring confessional statement from the Nazi era. The postwar question was: how enduring?

Any debate about its status was irrelevant as long as the state did not recognize *The Foundation of the Church*, and the state pointedly ignored it. All three governments of 1945 viewed it as an emergency measure whose validity would cease the moment the constitutionally elected government of Norway resumed its duties.

In the church's postwar debate, three points of view emerged: 1. it was a "church political document" and not a true church confession; 2. it was a "temporary confessional writing" limited to the years 1942–45; and 3. it was a "fully valid church confession" for the Church of Norway.[22]

The matter was never formally resolved, but in his authoritative study published in 1974, Torleiv Austad summed up its status:

It may be characterized as a particular confession insofar as it only takes a position on the theological and ecclesiastical questions at issue in the church struggle. *The Foundation of the Church* is therefore not a compendium of central articles of the Christian faith. Moreover, the document has such a national ecclesiastical dimension that only with difficulty could it be appropriated by another church.[23]

The Foundation of the Church was thus a temporary confession from 5 April 1942 to 8 May 1945, and thereafter had no claim of validity as "a binding doctrinal norm" in the church.[24] Austad's conclusion has been so widely accepted that the question of the document's status has been laid to rest, although its ideas reverberate.

REHABILITATING LUTHER AND LUTHERANISM

During and after the war, Martin Luther and his political ethics came in for severe criticism in the Anglo-American world. From the perspective of what Nazism had wrought, National Socialism was discredited and its pedigree came under judgment. Lutheranism could not emerge from the ruins without taking responsibility, but it was so rooted in the thought of Martin Luther that he, too, was held responsible.

Even before the war, Scandinavian Lutherans had started to think that German Lutheranism had proved so bankrupt that they had to step up to represent genuine Lutheranism. From that perspective, the Norwegian church struggle was a usable counter-narrative, an alternative interpretation of Luther and Lutheran political ethics. Lutheranism could take a new path, and the Church of Norway seemed to point the way.

Berggrav was keen to rehabilitate Luther. In his Burge Memorial Lecture, delivered on 30 April 1946 in London, Berggrav claimed that "Luther became our great exemplar" and "the best arms in our struggle with the power of German Nazism." Moreover, "we—to an unparalleled degree—felt our confession to be our best armor."

There was truth in these claims, but he went too far when he told his English audience that Lutheran confessional consciousness was not "felt as a burdensome duty," as it had been in the past.[25] What Berggrav should have admitted was that he and his church were, in fact, highly burdened by the traditional Lutheran interpretation of state authority, the doctrine of the two realms, and state servility. He wrestled long and hard with these doctrines before he came up with the interpretation that enabled him to use them against the state. Once he found the solution, he spent the spring and summer of 1941 trying to persuade the clergy that his interpretation was the "genuine" Lutheran position. What he told his English audience was the truth about Luther and the confession *after* he had found an innovative interpretation that supported resistance, not before.

In resisting the NS state, the Church of Norway had thus diverged decisively from the Luther and the Lutheran theological tradition that it had accepted since 1536. Viewed through the tradition up until 1940, it was un-Lutheran for the church to apply ethical norms to public life, un-Lutheran for the church to call the state to account, un-Lutheran for the church to withhold cooperation from the state, and, above all, un-Lutheran to claim that the church had an independent spiritual foundation and status.[26] The Lutheran significance of the Norwegian church struggle was that the Church of Norway acted against type, and had to "rediscover" a long-hidden "subversive" Luther in order to reset the tradition.

What Berggrav also could have told his English audience was how fortunate he had been to be able to appeal *against* Lutheran tradition to a Luther who was as "genuine" as the Luther of tradition. The German Evangelical Church's response to the National Socialist state had demonstrated the bankruptcy of Lutheranism's canonical doctrine of unconditional obedience. Berggrav's interpretation showed a way to understand obedience as conditional and the doctrine of the two realms as an effective instrument for holding the state accountable—and still be Lutheran. As a consequence, it stimulated new studies of Luther's views in Sweden and Germany and influenced a rethinking of the issues throughout postwar Lutheranism.[27] If the only religions that do not change are dead ones, Berggrav's reinterpretation was a sign of a living tradition.

AN ECUMENICAL IDENTITY

Berggrav's approach to the occupation drew on ideas from the ecumenical church, from his national and international ecumenical leadership before the war, from his initiative to maintain solidarity with the Protestant free churches, and from the Roman Catholic Bishop Mangers's signing of the youth service protest. This created the beginnings of an ecumenical identity in the Church of Norway that went beyond the "confessional ecumenism" of the anti-ecumenical orthodox.

Signs of the change appeared in the PCL's Pentecost message of 1944, which acknowledged an ecumenical reframing of the Church of Norway's identity [italics are mine]: "Recently, Christ's church—and our Norwegian church as a part of it—has appeared to us in a *new way* as our spiritual home. . . . To work and fight so that our Norwegian church in our own time can assert itself as Christ's church, a living branch of the great church body—that is our task as pastors."[28] Berggrav struck a similar tone in an ecumenical service at the Cathedral of St. Peter in Geneva, Switzerland, in early 1946. "Strangely enough," he said, "it was precisely in our isolation, when all legal communication with the outside world was strictly forbidden that we in Norway *really learned for the first time the meaning of "ecumenical"* [italics are mine], which is the living, inner fellowship of Christians in the world."[29]

Einar Molland, was more specific. He claimed that the Norwegian church struggle "must be seen in an ecumenical perspective to be rightly understood" and acknowledged the ecumenical debt in specific terms. If Paul Althaus could declare that it was Lutheran not to exercise "judgment in the name of Jesus" on political developments, he wrote, "then our bishops have been marvelously un-Lutheran."[30] He continued:

> Precisely because they have exercised "judgment in the name of Jesus," passed judgment in the name of the gospel on political developments, asserted God's relevance in all areas of life, the Norwegian churchmen have shown that they are related not only to Luther and the Lutheran church fathers, but also to Boniface VIII and Calvin. We are not separated by any insuperable cleft from the Roman teaching about the church's *potestas indirecta* in temporal affairs, or from the Reformation teaching about the church's right and duty to exercise supervision in all areas of life, also the political. In this respect, the church struggle has undoubtedly had ecumenical significance.[31]

The outstanding question was how deeply an ecumenical self-understanding had penetrated the Church of Norway, beginning with its relation to the free churches.

DOMESTIC ECUMENICAL CONSEQUENCES

The church's leadership acknowledged the ecumenical context of the church struggle as long as Berggrav led the resistance, but once Terboven placed him under house arrest, the church stopped going on the offensive, and the PCL excluded the free churches from further orientation and consultation.[32] After the war, the question was whether the Church of Norway's relations with the free churches would be determined by the spirit of Berggrav or Hallesby.

The answer turned out to be both. In the first year of liberation, the Lutheran mission societies retreated into confessional isolation, which Hallesby and others justified as ecumenism on a confessional basis. The Bible as distilled in the Lutheran confessions was the sum of truth, so unity on any other basis was in principle a betrayal of truth.[33] That view was also the reality on the ground. Hallesby advised the mission societies against any cooperation with free churches, which the societies turned into policy. Their leaders rejected free church participation in the new newspaper, *Vårt Land*, and in January 1946 the Council of Autonomous Organizations voted to exclude the free churches from the National Convention of Friends (*Landsvennestevner*), which had been held annually since 1919 with free church participation. The free churches learned of the decision through the newspapers, with no reasons given.[34]

To the obvious surprise of the mission societies, however, their decision was criticized by leading Lutherans such as Ronald Fangen, as well as by *Dagen*'s editor, Johannes Lavik, who objected that the decision "was interpreted in wide circles as a principled break with the ecumenical view."[35] The decision stood, however, but attendance at the conventions declined for other reasons until the event was suspended in 1951 and never resumed.

There were a few ecumenical voices in the church. In the latter half of 1946, Egil Brekke called for closer relations with the free churches and for the formation of a Norwegian council of churches to actively promote ecumenism at home. Berggrav endorsed the idea, and this time the Council of Autonomous Organizations did as well, claiming it had not intended to cut off all relations with the free churches.[36] For several years, the proposal had no traction, until Berggrav took the next step. In 1950, with the approval of the Bishops' Conference, Berggrav formed the Contact

Circle for Church Communions (*Kontakt Kretsen for Kirkesamfund*). Grateful to the free churches for their "unreserved support in the spiritual struggle," he thought that the mutual fellowship of the occupation years was worth preserving. The Contact Circle was to be a voluntary meeting twice a year "in a brotherly and free fashion."[37]

Even this informal gesture was too much for the mission societies, who boycotted the Contact Circle and in other ways worked to exclude free churches.[38] It is a measure of the persistent strength of Lutheran confessionalism that this modest endeavor, no more than an ecumenical coffee hour, ranked as the most important forum for the discussion of ecumenical issues in the postwar Norway.[39] Nevertheless, this modest outcome should not deflect attention from the ecumenical watershed that had occurred. As Lars Østnor notes in his study of interwar Norwegian ecumenism, the experience of the churches during the occupation "created the basis for a new situation between Christians and between Christian churches in this country."[40] Building on that basis would take time.

INTERNATIONAL ECUMENICAL CONSEQUENCES

Before the war, the churches of Scandinavia had their closest ecclesiastical relations among themselves, but their differing wartime experience strained their former unity.

Germany occupied Denmark on the day it invaded Norway, 9 April 1940, but unlike Norway the Danish government remained in place until August 1943, and even thereafter the Church of Denmark was not under direct German control. For that reason, the Church of Denmark did not protest or resist the government's concessions to the Germans, and there was no church struggle.[41] The church, however, did protest the deportation of Jews in late September 1943, as well as the German murder of the well-known pastor and author Kaj Munk, and the church was generally understood to be on the side of resistance.[42]

The Church of Finland was in a different situation. Finland's government and church policy were dominated by fear of the Soviet Union, and, forced to choose, patriotism dictated allying itself with Germany. Finland thus lost the 1939–40 Winter War against the Soviet Union, and from Barbarossa until late 1944 joined Germany in its war against the Soviet Union. There is scholarly disagreement about the Church of Finland's posture toward Nazism and Nazi Germany, but a fair generalization is that for the sake of patriotic loyalty neither Finland nor the Church of Finland spoke out against Nazism or Germany. It is also fair to say that the Church of Finland retained its ties and cooperated more than it needed to with the official German Evangelical Church rather than the Confessing Church [43]

The same may be said of the Church of Sweden. Sweden was a neutral that escaped the war altogether, tilting toward Germany until 1943 and the Allies thereafter. Public opinion was generally anti-German, anti-Nazi, and in solidarity with their Norwegian neighbors, and there were outstanding church figures opposed to Nazism, notably theologian Anders Nygren and theologian and bishop Gustaf Aulén. However, a large segment of the Church of Sweden's clergy and some of its bishops were pro-German, and under the cautious leadership of Archbishop Erling Eidem of Uppsala, the Church of Sweden's policy toward Nazi Germany mirrored that of the government. Eidem took his cue from Sweden's Foreign Office and did not take a strong public stance against Nazism or German policy. An exception in the church was the Nordic Ecumenical Institute under Harry Johanson, who maintained close ties to the World Council of Churches in Geneva, had a clear anti-Nazi position throughout the war, and informed the Swedish church about conditions in neighboring countries.[44]

At the first Scandinavian bishops' conference, held in late August 1945 in Copenhagen, Berggrav was the one who wanted a full and open discussion about the problems that emerged from the war. He did not withhold his outrage at Sweden for allowing German military transport through its territory into Norway. Nor did he withhold his criticism of the Church of Sweden, particularly Bishop Carl Block, for not defending him or his church from the pen of Ivar Rhedin, the pro-German clergy editor of the *Gothenburg Diocese Times* (Göteborgs Stiftstidning). He also had harsh words for Finland, for its military alliance with Germany from 1941 to 1944 and for the Church of Finland's cooperation with the official German Evangelical Church. Neither the Swedish nor the Finnish bishops had good answers to his charges, but the discussions aired the differences and began the process of reconciliation.[45]

The reorientation of the Scandinavians was symbolized by their participation in two new organizations, the Lutheran World Federation formed in 1947 and the World Council of Church formed in 1948. In the first, the discussion about reconciliation, the rehabilitation of Lutheranism, and the coordination of Lutheran interests would have a Lutheran platform, but the most important ecumenical institution to emerge was the World Council of Churches. It brought together the Life and Work and the Faith and Order branches of the ecumenical movement, and in the postwar era it, too, dealt with delicate issues surrounding the German church's role before and during World War II and how to reach reconciliation among the churches. Because of his ties to Germany, his fluency in German, and his stature within Lutheranism, ecumenical leaders chose Berggrav to repair relations with the discredited German Evangelical Church.

The Church of Norway's recognition of a new ecumenical context was its decision of 1946 to join the World Council of Churches. In announcing its decision, the Bishops' Conference noted that the church had adopted a "reserved attitude" toward the formation of a World Council of Churches before the war, but that it had now discovered it was "not right" to remain in isolation. The bishops stressed that it was not a matter of giving up Lutheran confessional identity; it was just that ecumenism could no longer be ignored, especially since the other Nordic churches had already joined. The reluctant endorsement notwithstanding, a new ecumenical era had begun.[46] Leading the ecumenical re-orientation was Berggrav, who was engaged in all things ecumenical and became the most important ecumenical figure in postwar Norway.[47] His ecumenical stature received a boost from the elevation of the Church of Norway's international reputation during the war and from his emergence as an authentic Christian hero of the Nazi era, among the ranks of Niemöller, Barth, and Bonhoeffer. He became the personification of the church's resistance, symbolized by *Time* magazine choosing him for its 1944 Christmas cover story.[48] After the war, he was in high demand abroad as a speaker and church leader. In Great Britain alone, he lectured in 1946 on the Church of Norway's resistance, received the Lambeth Cross, and was awarded an honorary doctorate from St. Andrew's University.

Berggrav played a variety of ecumenical roles. The Dutch general secretary of the World Council, Willem Visser 't Hooft, sought his help in turning the World Council of Churches into "a living" organ and voice of a reunited Church.[49] As a result, Berggrav became one of the presidents of the WCC and a leading ecumenical figure until the Evanston Assembly in 1954.

CASE STUDY IN CIVIL RESISTANCE

The wartime publicity about the Church of Norway's resistance was a natural expression of Allied solidarity, but the memory of it gradually faded in the English-speaking world. In studies of non-violent resistance, however, the church's resistance is regularly cited as a case study. This dimension accounts for much of its ongoing relevance outside the church itself.[50]

But was the Church of Norway deserving of its reputation as an exemplar of non-violent resistance? The answer is "Yes," with qualifications. The Church of Norway was a state church and a national church, and it was loyal to the necessities of national defense. Few Church of Norway clergymen and academicians were pacifists, and far fewer were after the German invasion.[51] Nevertheless, the church's resistance was non-violent in principle. Its weapons were "the sword of the Spirit" and the "willingness to suffer." This was true of protests limited to church issues, but also of protests against violations of law and human rights. The church as church did not endorse or engage in violent resistance.

After an initially accommodating posture, *The Pastoral Letter* established the church as the moral voice of the people, the defender of human rights, the right to free speech, and the church's rights. From 1942 to the end of the occupation, it continued its non-violent institutional opposition, sabotaging the NS's claims to legitimacy in both church and state. It was an impressive case of non-violent, institutional, mass resistance.

But too much can be made of the church's resistance, for three reasons. First, the Church of Norway was resisting within the context of a national resistance, not against its own people. Second, its resistance was to a widely unpopular collaborationist government, not its own constitutional government. Third, the church was protected by the German fear of church unrest, and it was treated with more moderation than, for example, the teachers. Finally, Germany did not treat "Aryan" Norwegians with the brutality with which they treated Eastern Europeans; had they done so, there is no telling if the church would have, or could have, resisted.

THE GERMAN AND NORWEGIAN
CHURCH STRUGGLES COMPARED

In an article published in 1943, the renowned Swiss Reformed theologian Karl Barth asserted that the church struggles in the Netherlands and Norway were more significant than the German Kirchenkampf because the Dutch and Norwegian churches went on the offensive:

> This issue is not merely the rights of the church but also the restoration of the general state of civil law destroyed by the German invasion; not faith alone is at stake, but the belief in the validity of God's commandments; it is not just a question of the Jewish Christians, but of the Jews in general. Even in the eyes of the individual who is only superficially, if at all, interested in Christian affairs, this struggle is now an important part of the general battle against National Socialism.[52]

Barth was right. In studies of religious resistance, the Dutch and Norwegian cases should have received more attention in gauging the Christian church's response to Nazism, but especially in judging the response of "Lutheranism."

That said, understanding the Norwegian church struggle without reference to the German Kirchenkampf is impossible, because the Kirchenkampf preceded the Norwegian "kirkekamp" and Berggrav drew several lessons from it: the need to overcome state servility by reinterpreting obedience to the state and the doctrine of the two realms; the importance of uniting principle with drama to communicate the nature of the issues to the public; the necessity of internal unity; and finally, from Bishop Otto Dibelius, the distinction between the state and the pastoral office.[53]

Finally, the German Confessing Church's resistance impressed upon Adolf Hitler and Josef Terboven that churches were the most resistant institutions to a totalitarian state, and that church criticism of the Nazi regime possessed "a greater potential force" than criticism from any other sector.[54] Not only does this reality highlight the lost possibilities of all German churches in preventing the rise of Nazism, it helps to account for German moderation in the Norwegian church struggle. The Norwegian churches thus had the German Kirchenkampf to thank for Terboven's policy of relative restraint in the church struggle.

A comparison and contrast of the Church of Norway and the Confessing Church's resistance is worthy of an independent investigation.[55] The comparisons are obvious: both were Lutheran or largely Lutheran churches; both faced Nazi states; both articulated the singularity of their identities against Nazi attempts to neutralize and redefine them.

The contrasts, however, overwhelm the comparisons, beginning with context. The German church confronted its own popularly supported, elected, and legal government, whereas the Church of Norway confronted an unwelcome foreign occupant and its minimally supported collaborationist government; to resist the one was to risk charges of treason, but to resist the other was a patriotic duty. Furthermore, the Church of Norway was one of many institutions in a common front against the NS state and part of a larger resistance movement that extended to almost the entire population, while the German Confessing Church had the support of a minority within the church and after 1933 stood alone among German institutions in resistance to the state.

There were other important contrasts. First, uniting a Norwegian church that embraced 96.5 percent of the people was simpler than uniting 28 multi-confessional German regional churches. NS Christians also posed little or no theological threat to the integrity of the Christian faith or the church, whereas the German Christians undermined both. Third, the Church of Norway's initial act of resistance was offensive, directed against the injustice of the Nazi state and its assault on the rule of law, and thereafter it sought to maintain the initiative at each point of the crisis. The German church, however, remained silent about far more serious state violations of human rights and disdain for the rule of law, and for the most part limited itself to a defensive resistance in behalf of the church alone.

A DIFFERENTLY CONFIGURED LUTHERANISM

Norwegian Lutheranism exhibited three traits necessary for resistance to Nazism, traits that the German Lutherans lacked.

The first was the assumption that Christianity and Nazism were incompatible. From the moment Norwegian Christians encountered Nazism in Germany and at home, they denounced its racism and anti-Semitism as incompatible with Christianity. A fundamental Christian doctrine is that all human beings are one, which in Norway raised a doctrinal wall between Christians and support for the NS. This was unlike German Protestantism's normal and pervasive racism and anti-Semitism, even within the Confessing Church, and the German Christian movement's consequent denial of human universality. It is difficult to overstate this point: if Christians accepted that anti-Semitism was compatible with Christianity, the path to Nazism was open; if Christians rejected anti-Semitism, the road to Nazism was blocked.

Second, the course of Nazism in Germany had shown Norwegian church leaders, most notably Berggrav, that Nazism was not only incompatible with Christianity but was anti-Christian and demonic. That is the argument Berggrav used to persuade the bishops and leaders of the mission societies to form the CCC. With the irreconcilability of Christianity and Nazism as common ground, he convinced Norwegian church leaders that a confrontation with the NS state was inevitable, that the NS state had to be resisted, and that it ultimately had to be defeated. The future of Christianity was at stake.

Third, most of the clergy in the Church of Norway were politically and theologically conservative and infected, as Berggrav put it, with Lutheranism's traditional state servility—but, unlike German Lutheranism, the rest of the church was not. The church was not a "Pastors' Church" or a "Listeners' Church." The so-called "Christian people" (*kristenfolket*) came from a tradition of activism in church and society harking back to Hans Nielsen Hauge and his "friends." They were behind the rise of the democratizing and liberalizing Liberal Party (*Venstre*) in the nineteenth century, the grassroots activists for prohibition in the late nineteenth and early twentieth century, and the orthodox agenda of re-Christianization in the inter-war era. They had also judged Marxism incompatible with Christianity, and by 1940 they had two decades of experience in resisting it as a hostile ideology. They were loyal citizens, but state servility was not in their makeup. The same, of course, could not be said of the clergy.

Finally, there is no way to explain the effectiveness of the Church of Norway's resistance without the exceptional leadership of Eivind Berggrav. The Church of Norway may have resisted Nazism and the NS state without him, but the resistance would most certainly have emerged far later, taken a very different form, and been far less effective. No one among the bishops or in the CCC had his intellect, flexibility of mind, force of personality, persuasive power, ecumenical exposure, political acumen, rhetorical flair, foresight, capacity for work, strategic thinking, or tactical brilliance. He was not the whole of the church's resistance, but he was the essential ingredient who brought the parts together in effective resistance.

A HISTORIC EVENT

The Church of Norway's resistance to Nazism was a historic event in Norwegian church history, but it also had a significance within general church history and the history of resistance to Nazism during World War II.

In the history of Christianity in Norway, only three events were of greater consequence: the introduction of Christianity in 1030, the Lutheran Reformation of 1536, and the Dissenter Law of 1845. The first established Roman Catholicism as the state religion for over five hundred years, the second instituted Lutheranism as the state religion into the twenty-first century, and the third introduced religious toleration that led to religious pluralism, freedom of religion, and, in 2012, the disestablishment of the Church of Norway. Each of these had more long-term effects than the Church of Norway's resistance to Nazism.

Nevertheless, the mass resignation of the clergy on Easter Sunday 1942 has a strong claim to be fourth on the list. It was without doubt the most important event in twentieth-century Norwegian church history, and it had two dimensions the others lacked: it was an act of the church, not the state, and it had international repercussions and relevance.[56]

The Norwegian church struggle had a medieval feel to it, harking back to the great conflicts between popes and emperors, and as such it takes its place in the two thousand year history of church-state relations. There are no analogous events in the history of state church Lutheranism, but there is at least one in the history of state churches in the Reformed tradition. It is known as the Disruption.[57]

On 18 May 1843 at the General Assembly of the Presbyterian state Church of Scotland, held at St. Andrew's Church in Edinburgh, retiring Moderator David Welsh read a protest before walking out of the church. Following him were 123 pastors and 70 elders. This initiated the Disruption, the result of a conflict that began in the 1780s and had intensified in the previous decade. Within a short time, 454 of 1,195 clergy resigned their offices, forfeiting their state salaries and manses. The Disruption was "the most momentous event" in the history of nineteenth-century Scotland, the climax of a struggle between Evangelicals and Moderates for "the soul of Presbyterianism."[58] But it was also about the relationship of church and state: did the church have "independent spiritual jurisdiction," or did it not? Those who left to form the Free Church of Scotland claimed it did, and they also claimed that after 1838 the church faced a state that no longer protected the church but "gave a new interpretation of the law and encroached upon the rights and priviliges of the Church." The 454 pastors who left the Church of Scotland no more wished to break with state church tradition than their Norwegian counterparts a century later, but the principle was the same.[59]

Finally, the Church of Norway's resistance has significance within the history of the Christian churches during World War II. Generalizations are hazardous, but a safe one is that the Church of Norway's resistance was the sole example of Lutheran *state church* resistance in German occupied Europe. The other is that it shares with the Reformed churches of the Netherlands the distinction of being the outstanding example of Protestant resistance.

The resistance of the Reformed churches in the Netherlands was very different and far more ecumenical. The Netherlands was 47.8 percent Reformed (Calvinist) Protestant and 36.4 percent Catholic during World War II, and the churches were not state churches.[60] The split between the Catholics and Protestants was profound, reaching into every corner of life, and the Reformed churches were further split among themselves.

Nevertheless, resistance brought the churches together in their common struggle. They first created an ideological front within their churches. In 1941, they followed up by denouncing government laws and actions, becoming "the conscience of the community," and engaging in proactive resistance to anti-Semitism and anti-Semitic laws. In the end, some churches became resistance organizations in all but name. For their resistance, the Dutch churches also paid a far higher price than their Norwegian counterparts: 43 Protestant ministers and 49 Catholic priests lost their lives.[61] In sum, the Netherlands and Norway were the outstanding cases of effective Protestant resistance to Nazism and Nazification in occupied Europe.[62]

THE CHURCH'S "FINEST HOUR"

Bruce Lincoln has argued that "religions of the status quo" generally disseminate an ideology that furthers the interests of established power, whereas "religions of resistance" advocate values that challenge this power.[63] Before 9 April 1940, the Church of Norway was the religion of the status quo. As the political status quo turned upside down in the name of a totalitarian state that denied citizens' freedom, violated human rights, attempted to reduce Christianity to cultic and private life, and persecuted Jews, the church became a religion of resistance. It then did what a religion of resistance must to succeed, which is to "defend itself against the ideological domination" of the new political and religious order.[64] In doing so, the Church of Norway had its "finest hour"—and among the finest of twentieth-century Christianity.

Abbreviations

BA   Bundesarchiv [Federal Archives], Koblenz, Federal Republic of Germany
CCC   Christian Consultative Council [Kristent Samråd]
EZ   Evangelisches Zentralarchiv [Evangelical Central Archives], Berlin, Federal Republic of Germany
HI   Hoover Institution, Palo Alto, California, U.S.A.
KKS   Kirkekampens sentralarkiv [The Church Struggle's Central Archive], Nasjonalbiblioteket [National Library], Oslo, Norway
KM   *Kirkelig motstand* [Church Resistance] by Torleiv Austad (see bibliography)
LA   Landsarkivet [County Archives], Uppsala, Sweden
NA   National Archives, Washington D.C., U.S.A.
NB   Nasjonalbiblioteket [National Library], Oslo, Norway
NEI   Nordiska Ekumeniska Institut [Nordic Ecumenical Institute], Uppsala, Sweden
NHM   Norges Hjemmefrontmuseum [Norway's Home Front Museum], Oslo, Norway
NKR   Norges Kristne Råd [Norway's Christian Council], Oslo, Norway
NMS   Det Norske Misjonsselskap Archives [The Norwegian Mission Society Archvies], Stavanger, Norway
NS   Nasjonal Samling [National Union Party]
NSUF   Nasjonal Samlings Ungdomsfylking [NS Youth Corps]
PCL   Provisional Church Leadership [Den midlertidige kirkeledelse]
PRO   Public Record Office, London, United Kingdom
RA   Riksarkivet [National Archives], Oslo, Norway
RAS   Riksarkivet [National Archives], Stockholm, Sweden
SAH   Statsarkivet [State Archives], Hamar, Norway

SAK	Statsarkivet [State Archives], Kristiansand, Norway
SAS	Statsarkivet [State Archives], Stavanger, Norway
UBL	Universitetsbiblioteket [University Library], Lund, Sweden
UBT	Universitetsbiblioteket [University Library], Trondheim, Norway
WCC	World Council of Church Archives, Geneva, Switzerland

Notes

1 Karl Barth, "The Protestant Churches in Europe," 269. For studies of non-violent protest and civil resistance that cite the church struggle in Norway, see William R. Miller, *Nonviolence: A Christian Interpretation*; Adam Roberts, ed., *Civilian Resistance as a National Defense: Nonviolent Action against Aggression*; Joan V. Bondurant, ed., *Conflict: Violence and Non-Violence*; Gene Sharp, *The Politics of Non-Violent Action*; and April Carter, "The Literature on Civil Resistance."

2 Jacques Semelin, *Unarmed Against Hitler: Civilian Resistance in Europe 1939–1943*, 65–67, 97.

3 Eivind Berggrav, *Da kampen kom: Noen blad fra startåret* [When the Struggle Began: Some Pages from the First Year] and *Front—fangenskap—flukt 1942–1945* [Front—Imprisonment—Escape, 1942–1945]; Ludwig Schübeler, *Kirkekampen slik jeg så den* [The Church Struggle As I Saw It]; and Wollert Krohn-Hansen, *Den brente jord: Dagboksoptegnelser fra krigen og kirkekampen i Nord-Norge* [The Scorched Earth: Journal Entries from the War and the Church Struggle in Northern Norway].

4 Oddvar Høidal, *Quisling: En studie i landssvik* [Quisling: A Study in Treason]; Hans Fredrick Dahl, *Vidkun Quisling* (1991–1992); Gunnar Heiene, *Eivind Berggrav: En biografi* [Eivind Berggrav: A Biography]; Berit Nøkleby, *Josef Terboven: Hitlers mann i Norge* [Josef Terboven: Hitler's Man in Norway]; Robert Bohn, *Reichskommissariat Norwegen: "National-sozialistische Neuordnung" und Kriegswirtschaft* [Reichskommissariat Norway: "National Socialist New Order" and War Economy].

5 Austad, *Kirkens Grunn*, 60–62.

6 Arnd Heling, *Die Theologie Eivind Berggravs im norwegischen Kirchenkampf: Ein Beitrag zur politischen Theologie im Luthertum*, [The Theology of Eivind

279

Berggrav in the Norwegian Church Struggle: A Contribution to Political Theology in Lutheranism], 98–102.

7 Aud V. Tønnessen, *"…et trygt og godt hjem for alle"? Kirkelederes kritikk av velferdsstaten etter 1945* ["…a safe and good home for all"? Church Leaders' Critique of the Welfare State After 1945].

ACKNOWLEDGMENTS

1 Review of Kristian Hansson's *Stat og Kirke* [State and Church], *Dagen*, 13 February 1946.

2 The companion volume is *Kirkelig motstand: Dokumenter fra den norske kirke-kamp under okkupasjonen 1940–45 med innledninger og kommentarer* [Church Resistance: Documents from the Norwegian Church Struggle During the Occupation with Introductions and Commentary]. Because it appears frequently in the notes, I have abbreviated it to *KM*.

I. GERMAN PRELUDE

1 Keller, *Church and State,* 347.

2 My account deals only with the Protestant church struggle, because it was the focus of Norwegian church observers; the Roman Catholic Church struggle was equally important in Germany, perhaps more so, but not to Norwegian Lutherans.

3 Statement of the newly formed Protestant Church Confederation, 1921; Scholder, *Preliminary History,* 37–40.

4 Ibid., 49.

5 Paul Althaus used the phrase "unity of blood"; qtd. in Scholder, 112.

6 Ibid., 75.

7 Ibid., 113.

8 In ecumenical debates of the 1930s, Althaus argued for the legitimacy of a totalitarian state in service to God; see Tønnessen, "trygt og godt hjem," 54.

9 On the constellation of attitudes that led to Protestant Nazi support, and later rendered Protestants unable to engage in political resistance, see Bracher, *German Dictatorship,* 382.

10 Mann, *Fascists,* 186–89.

11 Hitler, qtd. in Barnett, *Soul of the People,* 30, 32.

12 Scholder, *Year of Disillusionment,* 22.

13 Scholder, *Preliminary History,* 88.

14 Quotations from the Barmen Declaration are from Cochrane, *Church's Confession,* 237–42.

15 Helmut Gollwitzer, qtd. in Barnett, *Soul of the People,* 55.

16 Keller, *Church and State,* 348.

17 Scholder, *Year of Disillusionment,* 263.

18 On the Confessing Church's reluctance to act as a political resistance movement,

see Niemöller's disclaimer in Boyens, *Kirchenkampf und Ökumene 1933–1939*, 171; see also Bracher, *German Dictatorship*, 382.

19 Conway, *Nazi Persecution*, 162.

20 Ibid., 163.

21 Ericksen, *Complicity in the Holocaust*, 121–22.

22 "A Painful Declaration," *Swiss Evangelical Press Service*, June 1939, box 12, Ehrenström Papers, WCC.

23 Ibid.

24 Nils Ehrenström to Erling Eidem, 11 July 1939, box 12, Ehrenström Papers, WCC.

25 Helmreich, *German Churches*, 335–36.

26 Kershaw, *Hitler 1936–1945: Nemesis*, 40, 130, 424, 428; Hitler, February 1942, qtd. in Bullock, *Hitler*, 389. See also Scholder, *Requiem for Hitler*, 116, and Bracher, *German Dictatorship*, 389–90.

27 Perhaps the most influential of such early explanations in American scholarship was McGovern's *Luther to Hitler*.

28 Scholder, *Requiem for Hitler*, 51.

29 Ibid., 52.

30 Ibid., 49–50.

31 McGovern, *Luther to Hitler*, 31. McGovern uses the term "etatism"; 14–15.

32 Ibid., 33; Shirer, *Rise and Fall*, 236.

33 Mann, *Fascists*, 186–88.

34 Ehrenström, *Christian Faith and Modern State*, 99; Sanders, *Protestant Concepts*, 30–31.

35 For more on the primacy of family, *Volk*, and state among the orders of creation, see Hockenos, *Church Divided*, 25.

36 Scholder, *Requiem for Hitler*, 51.

37 On the organic metaphor used by Lutheran theologians who justified accommodation to Nazism, notably Althaus, Gogarten, and Hirsch, see Forell, "State as Order," 40.

38 This summary draws on Bergen, *Twisted Cross*, 156, 158, 174.

39 Rasmussen, "Det indre og det ytre," 21.

40 Forell, "State as Order," 38–39.

41 Ehrenström, *Christian Faith and Modern State*, 171.

42 Conway, *Nazi Persecution*, 335; Rudolf Weckerling, qtd. in Barnett, *Soul of the People*, 12; Forell, "State as Order," 39; Sanders, *Protestant Concepts*, 55.

43 Berggrav, "Stat og kirke i dag," 452.

44 Conway, *Nazi Persecution*, 335.

45 Pierard, "Why did Protestants Welcome Hitler?" 12.

46 Kolb and Wengert, *Book of Concord*, 92.

47 Ibid., 92–93.

48 Shirer saw Luther at the heart of German anti-Semitism; *Rise and Fall*, 236. And recently MacCulloch has claimed that Luther's 1543 polemic against the Jews "is a blueprint for the Nazis' *Kristallnacht* of 1938"; *The Reformation*, 666. Oberman,

on the other hand, argues that "the 'brown' (National Socialist) Luther is dead and gone"; *The Reformation*, 53.

49 My use of the term "betrayal" of the Jews comes from the title of Ericksen and Heschel, *Betrayal*. On the anti-Semitism of German Protestantism and the Confessing Church, see Gerlach, *Witnesses*.

50 Goldhagen, *Willing Executioners*, 112–13.

51 Keller, *Church and State*, 169, 172–73. For a Norwegian confirmation of Keller's point, see Molland, "Den norske kirke – en luthersk folkekirke," 9.

52 This was a point made by Thorleif Boman in "Luthers kamp på fire fronter," *Dagen*, 13 January 1934, where he also attempted to show that Luther himself was not at fault.

2. NORWEGIAN PRELUDES

1 Smemo, "Norsk kristendom," 288–89.

2 For the church statistics in this section, see Lundby, "Norge," 168.

3 The others were: Johan N. Støren (1871–1956), Bishop of Nidaros since 1928; James Maroni (1873–1957), Bishop of Agder from 1930; Andreas Fleischer (1878–1957), Bishop of Bjørgvin from 1932; Henrik Hille (1881–1946), Bishop of Hamar from 1934; Gabriel Skagestad (1879–1952), Bishop of Stavanger from 1940; and Wollert Krohn-Hansen (1889–1973), Bishop of Hålogaland from 1940.

4 Aarflot, *Bisperåd*, 78–79; Ellingsen, *Kirkestyre*, 43.

5 Det teologiske Menighetsfakultet is currently known in English translation as the Norwegian School of Theology. Though still essentially Lutheran, it has developed into an ecumenical institution. In the 1940s, however, the usual translation was Free Faculty of Theology, which I am retaining to be true to the time, but also because it better signifies the faculty's freedom from the state and ties to the congregations and mission societies.

6 Repstad, *Kristian Schjelderup*, 241.

7 Lundby, "Norge," 162–63.

8 A social scientific poll in 1957 yielded the 75 percent figure for passive members; Rokkan, "Geografi, religion, og samfunnsklasse," 173. This number may have been marginally lower in 1940. On "anonymous" Christianity, see Berggrav, "Beretning fra Oslo bispedømme 1939," 165; Kjeldstadli, *Splittet samfunn*, 147; and Smemo, "Norsk kristendom," 301. For statistics on Agder and the other dioceses in 1939, see Bishops of the Church of Norway, "Beretninger om Den norske kirke i 1939," 150–204; on the empty pews, see "De tomme kirkebenkers problem," *Dagen*, 4 April 1940. For religion as the "sacred canopy," see Berger, *The Sacred Canopy*.

9 Lundby, "Norge," 164, 181.

10 Wisløff, *Norsk kirkehistorie*, 221; Lavik, *Spenningen*, 184–85. On the basis of a national survey taken in 1957, Stein Rokkan claimed that in the South and West about a quarter of adults were religiously active largely through lay mission soci-

eties, not the official church; see "Geografi, religion og samfunnsklasse," 173–74. Percentages may have been slightly higher in 1940, and in the rest of the country rates of engagement were probably lower.

11 Welle, "Den norske folkekirke," 9.

12 I refer to these mission societies by the names in use from 1940 to 1945, but, for clarification, note that in 2001 the Norwegian Lutheran Home Mission Society and the Norwegian Santal Mission joined to form Normission, and the Norwegian Lutheran China Mission Association is now the Norwegian Lutheran Mission Federation.

13 In the 1930s and 1940s, free church leaders expressed their resentment at the term with some regularity; see Arnold T. Øhrn's article, "Kirke og sekt," *Dagen*, 7, 9, 11 April 1934, originally given as a speech to the Dissenter Parliament. See also Eilert Bernhardt's editorial of 22 February 1940 on Bishop James Maroni's use of the term in *Kristelig Tidende* 69 (1940): 120–21, and Zander Bratland, "Uviljen mot kristne minoriteter," *Dagen*, 3 October 1940.

14 Ingunn Folkestad Breistein has documented both the discrimination and the struggle of the free churches for religious freedom in *"Har staten bedre borgere?"* On their disproportionate influence, see Boman, "Kirken og dissenterne," 566, and Berggrav, *Norwegian Church in Its International Setting*, 15. Lundby fuses the census figures of 1930 and 1946 to arrive at the 2.7 percent figure for 1938 in "Norge," 178, 181.

15 Eidsvig, "Den katolske kirke," 47, 385.

16 For the economic situation and statistics see Bull, *Klassekamp og felleskap*, 15, 18–19; Furre includes a concise summary in *Norsk historie 1914–2000*, 38–39.

17 Lavik, *Spenningen*, 91.

18 Qtd. in Molland, *Fra Hans Nielsen Hauge*, 97.

19 Johan M. Wisløff used "not Christianity" in his opening speech to the convention; Wisløff and Rudvin, *Sokneprest Joh. M. Wisløff*, 282; Molland, *Fra Hans Nielsen Hauge*, 98; Wisløff, *Norsk kirkedebatt*, 42. Hallesby and the orthodox crusaders against liberal theology and secular culture meet all the criteria of fundamentalism established by the comparative study of fundamentalist movements; see Marty and Appleby, *The Glory and the Power*, chapter 1.

20 For the harsh view each took of the other, see Hallesby's remarks on liberal theology, "Teologisk forvirring," *Dagen*, 26 March 1938, and Hestvold's description of the liberal reaction had Berggrav's protégé, Alex Johnson, reciprocated Hallesby's interest in him; Hestvold, *Alex Johnson*, 160. There are many other examples. On the "peaceful" and "featureless" characterizations of the decade, see Molland, *Fra Hans Nielsen Hauge*, 102, and Lavik, *Spenningen i norsk kirkeliv*, 165.

21 Lavik, *Spenningen*, 160; Tønnessen, *". . . et trygt og godt hjem"?*, 48.

22 Lavik, *Spenningen*, 91.

23 Original translation published in 1814 by the Norwegian government in Andenæs, *Constitution*, 47.

24 Translations of titles follow the usage of the 2012 Norwegian government as fol-

lows: *Storting* is Parliament; *minister* is the political head of a government ministry; *departement* is a ministry (in U.S. terms, a government department), and
ekspedisjonssjef is director general. For detailed descriptions of the Ministry of
Church and Education just before and during the German occupation, see Kolsrud, *En splintret stat*, 263–70, and Norrman, *Quislingkyrkan*, 41–43.

25 Oftestad, *Statsreligion*, 43, 98; Lundby, "Norge," 166.

26 Austad, *KM*, 13, and "Der Widerstand der Kirche," 84.

27 Lavik, *Spenningen*, 135.

28 Oftestad, *Statsreligion*, 176.

29 For Hope's justification of the church-state status quo, see *Kyrkja og guds folk*,
94.

30 Tønnessen, "*. . . et trygt og godt hjem"?*, 358; Smemo, "Norsk kristendom," 291.

31 Wisløff, *Norsk kirkehistorie*, 281.

32 Furre, *Norsk historie*, 72; Dahl, *Norge mellom krigene*, 66.

33 Agøy, *Kirken og arbeiderbevegelsen*, 555–68; Pryser, *Klassen og nasjonen*, 74–78,
181.

34 Agøy, *Kirken og arbeiderbevegelsen*, 576.

35 Hjelmtveit was on good terms with the church throughout his tenure as Minister
of Church and Education; Hjelmtveit, *Vekstår*, 58.

36 Bull, *Klassekamp og felleskap*, 318; Lønning, "Arven fra Luther," 44–48.

37 Danbolt, "Ronald Fangens kamp mot nazismen i 1930-årene," 233–36; Oftestad,
Kristentro, 237.

38 Fagerland, "*Dagen* og fascismen," 101–3. Giverholt's full name was Ragnar Arne
Giverholt and he went by the name of "Rag." in his columns; however, his editor,
Johannes Lavik, referred to him as Arne Giverholt in *Spenningen i norsk kristen-
liv*, 176.

39 Arne Giverholt ("Rag"), "Fra folkekirke til nazistisk sekt," *Dagen*, 11 September
1933; Ivar Welle, "Intrykk fra Tyskland," *Luthersk Kirketidende* 70 (1933): 465.

40 Berggrav to Molland, n.p., 27 March 1934, box 28, Berggrav Papers, RA.

41 For the latest statistics, I have used "Deportasjonen av de norsk jødene" [Depor-
tation of the Norwegian Jews], website of Senter for studier av Holocaust og
livssynsminoriteter [Center for Studies of the Holocaust and Religious Minori-
ties], Oslo, www.hlsenteret.no. Accessed 20 September 2012.

42 Johansen, *Oss selv nærmest*, 93; Mendelsohn, *Jødenes historie*, 662–63; Christie,
Den norske kirke, 266; Carlsen, *Kirkefronten*, 140.

43 Mendelsohn, *Jødenes historie*, 563–64, 582, 613–38.

44 On xenophobia and its relation to the restrictive refugee policy, see Eriksen, Har-
ket, and Lorenz, *Jødehat*, 402, 408, 460–61, 467.

45 Ibid., 419, and, on the "Jewish problem," 460–68.

46 Austad, "Sviktet kirken?," 18, 48.

47 *Mendelsohn, Jødenes historie*, 556–83, 613–63.

48 Definitions of Fascism generally include National Socialism as a German variant
distinguished by its racist anti-Semitic themes, among others; see Carsten, *Rise*

of Fascism, 31; Bracher, *Age of Ideologies*, 106. For a dissenting view, see Neocleous, "Racism, Fascism and Nationalism," 356.

49 Bruknapp, "Ideene splitter partiet," 11–12, 14–15, 19–39.

50 Austad, *KM*, 271–72.

51 Conference at Oxford on Church, Community, and State, *Churches Survey*, 57–63, 67–86, 188–274.

52 Ibid., 84–85.

53 On the scope of ecumenical engagement, see Østnor, *Kirkens enhet*; on Berggrav's role in mediating ecumenical ideas, see Austad, *Kirkens Grunn*, 60–62; on the ideas of the ecumenical conferences, see Karlström, "Movements for International Friendship and Life and Work, 1910–1925," 509–42; Ehrenström, "Movements for International Friendship and Life and Work, 1925–1948," 545–96; Sundkler, *Söderblom*, 198–205; and Heling, *Theologie*, 100.

3. WESERÜBUNG

1 Conference at Oxford on Church, Community, and State, *Churches Survey*, 68–75.

2 Kullerud, *Hallesby*, 310.

3 Molland, *Fra Hans Nielsen Hauge*, 104.

4 Austad, *KM*, 26.

5 Berggrav, *Forgjeves for fred*, 153. My presentation of Berggrav's peace initiative is based on Berggrav's account in this book.

6 Ibid., 158.

7 Bull, *Klassekamp og fellesskap*, 338–39; Christensen, *Okkupasjonsår*, 127–36; Lange, *Samling om felles mål*, 69–70.

8 To my knowledge, Hans–Dietrich Loock was the first to point out the importance of Universism in understanding Quisling; my own view is that Quisling ceases to be "a riddle" once his Universism is understood; Loock, *Quisling, Rosenberg und Terboven*. On his Universism, see Braw, "Quislings tro," 1–18; Norderval, "Quisling, kirken og kristendommen," 91, 215–31; Barth, *Gud, det er meg*.

9 On Quisling identifying himself as the Christ of the new age, see Braw, "Quislings tro," 11–13.

10 For Quisling's meetings with Hitler, see Høidal, *Quisling*, 265–67, and Dahl, *Fører for fall*, 42–45.

11 Moulton, *Norwegian Campaign*, 11.

12 Grimnes, *Overfall*, 99–100.

13 Churchill, *Gathering Storm*, 608.

14 Quisling, *Quisling har sagt* (1940), 118–19.

15 I am drawing on the categories of Grimnes in "Kollaborasjon og oppgjør," 46–55, and Semelin, *Unarmed*, 37–40, 47–50.

16 Berggrav, *Da kampen kom*, 8–9, 11.

17 Heiene, *Berggrav*, 416.

18 Grimnes, *Hjemmefrontens ledelse*, 41. Grimnes's book is the standard work on the Home Front leadership.

19 Berggrav, *Da kampen kom*, 20.

20 Investigative Commission of 1945, *Innstilling fra Undersøkelses-kommisjonen av 1945*, 148–52. For a contemporary critique of Berggrav's actions, see Fjørtoft, *Ulvetiden*, 179.

21 Investigative Commission of 1945, *Innstilling*, 151–52.

22 The Investigative Commission of 1945 concluded that the Supreme Court knew it did not have a basis in "the written word" to authorize the Administrative Council. It nevertheless took the initiative because of the "extraordinary circumstances" and trusted that the King would support its action and without the majority of the court thinking the King's prior approval was actually necessary. See Investigative Commission of 1945, *Innstilling*, 305.

23 Berggrav, *Da kampen kom*, 26–27. On the Quisling–Berggrav relationship, see Dahl, "Brand til Quisling," 3–9; for the NS view of Berggrav as a politician in the guise of a church leader, see Melsom, *Kirke- og kulturkampen*, 10, 53.

24 Berggrav, *Da kampen kom*, 24

25 Ibid., 193.

26 Berggrav, *Da kampen kom*, 27–33; Heiene, *Berggrav*, 297–303.

27 Berggrav, *Da kampen kom*, 196–97.

28 Heiene, *Berggrav*, 303.

29 The original text is reproduced in Berggrav, *Da kampen kom*, 202.

30 Berggrav, "Etterpå-Dagbok 1940–42," box 15, Berggrav Papers, RA.

31 Berggrav, *Da kampen kom*, 51–54, 201.

32 Berggrav to Søren Oftenæs, Oslo, 23 December 1940, box 13, Berggrav Papers, RA.

33 Berggrav, *Da kampen kom*, 53; William Paton to the Dean of St. Paul's (W. R. Mathews), 16 October 1940, box labeled "Bishop Berggrav's Peace Action and the Meetings in Zilven, 1940," William Paton Papers, WCC. On the BBC broadcasts, see collection summarized by Berggrav in introduction to "Dagbok" (Uken 9.–16. April 1940), box 19, Berggrav Papers, RA. On the ecumenical community's response, see Boyens, *Kirchenkampf und Ökumene 1939–1945*, 159–60.

34 On Hitler's thinking, see "Unterredung des Führers mit dem Norwegischen Gesandten Scheel am 13. April 1940 bei Anwesenheit des Reichsaussenministers und U.St.S. Habicht und VLR. Hewel," German Auswärtiges Amt, Microfilm frame 22410, box 30 II, HI. On German reports from Oslo, see V. H. Günther to Bishop Theodor Heckel, 21 May 1940, Kleine Erwerbungen 298–2, V. H. Günther Papers, BA; telegram 578, Hans J. (von) Neuhaus to Auswärtiges Amt, Oslo, 16 April 1940, German Auswärtiges Amt, Microfilm frame 148599, box 220 I, HI; telegram 584, (von) Neuhaus to Auswärtiges Amt, Oslo, 17 April 1940, German Auswärtiges Amt, Microfilm frames 578567–9, box 2969, HI; telegram 584, (von) Neuhaus to Auswärtiges Amt, Oslo, 17 April 1940, German Auswärtiges Amt, Microfilm frame 148616–8, box 220 I, HI. The general secretary of the World

Council of Churches, Wilhelm A. Visser 't Hooft, referred to the need for reliable information on Berggrav to counter the German and Italian propaganda that had "been making use of his name"; W.A. Visser 't Hooft to Bishop of Chichester, Geneva, 25 April 1940, General Secretariat Correspondence, box 9, WCC.

35 Bonhoeffer, *Ethics*, 275.

36 Berggrav "Etterpå-Dagbok 1940–42," box 15, Berggrav Papers, RA.

37 Seip, *Hjemme*, 32; Debes, *1940–45*, 59–60.

38 Skodvin, *Striden*, 173, 176–88.

39 Bohn, *Reichskommissariat*, 32.

40 Nøkleby, *Terboven*, 48–50.

41 Nøkleby, *Terboven*, 73.

42 Skodvin, *Striden*, 197.

43 Loock, *Quisling, Rosenberg und Terboven*, 370.

44 Bracher, *German Dictatorship*, 389–90; Conway, *Nazi Persecution*, 303–4.

45 "Reichskommissar Terboven talte lørdag for første gang offentlig om norske forhold og de kommende opgaver," *Fritt Folk*, 3 June 1940; deposition by Alfred Huhnhäuser, July 1945, Oslo, personal collection of Magne Skodvin.

46 Loock, *Quisling, Rosenberg, und Terboven*, 367–69.

47 Ibid., 358–60.

48 Wheal, Pope, and Taylor, *Dictionary*, 447.

4. FORGING A FRONT

1 Grimnes, "Kollaborasjon," 48. My account is based on Berggrav's notes in "Etterpå-Dagbok 1940–42," box 15, Berggrav Papers, RA, and Steen, "Riksrådsforhandlingene," 129–283.

2 Steen, "Riksrådsforhandlingene," 199. The Storting's Presidium comprised six representatives elected to coordinate legislation: the presidents and vice-presidents of the Storting as a whole and two representatives of each of its two houses.

3 Ibid., 233.

4 Fjellbu, *Minner*, 46.

5 Semelin, *Unarmed*, 53. See also Schjelderup, *Norges kamp*, 136, and Grimnes, *Hjemmefrontens ledelse*, 40.

6 Bishop of Oslo to clergy and parish councils, "Det midlertidige og det evige" (The Temporal and the Eternal), Oslo, July 1940, Austad, *KM*, 30–33. A good indication that only Berggrav was thinking strategically were the platitudes offered by the church and mission societies in response to a series run by *Dagen* in July 1940 about how the church should "meet the new age—spiritually and practically."

7 Berggrav, *Da kampen kom*, 80. I do not think that Berggrav was engaging in post-facto rationalization when he cited the legal rights of the occupying power, because there are other indications that this was a conscious strategy.

8 Ibid., 114.

9 Unless otherwise noted, this account of the events leading up to the formation of

the CCC is based on Handeland, *Kristent samråd*, certified for accuracy by Berggrav, Hallesby, and Hope.

10 Ibid., 21.

11 Solum, *Kryssende spor,* 87; Norborg, *Vekkeren*, 205.

12 Berggrav, *Da kampen kom,* 106.

13 Handeland, *Kristent samråd*, 23–24; Berggrav to Hallesby, Oslo, 17 October 1940, box 29, Berggrav Papers, RA; Berggrav, *Da kampen kom*, 106.

14 Handeland, *Kristent samråd*, 25.

15 Berggrav, *Da kampen kom*, 106.

16 Handeland, *Kristent samråd*, 26. In addition to the bishops, Hallesby, and Hope, those present were Einar Amdahl, general secretary of the Norwegian Mission Society; Johan M. Wisløff, executive secretary of the Norwegian Lutheran Home Mission Society; Tormod Vågen, general secretary of the China Mission Association; Ingvald B. Carlsen, assistant pastor and consultant for religious broadcasting; Kristian Hansson, director general in the Justice Department; Hans Høeg, school principal and representative of the Santal Mission and Oslo Diocese; Ragnvald Indrebø, assistant pastor and chairman of the Council of Autonomous Organizations; attorney Wilhelm Beck; and Einar Smebye, mission pastor representing the foreign mission fields.

17 Berggrav, *Da kampen kom*, 107–15.

18 Ibid.

19 Austad, *KM*, 44–45; Handeland, *Kristent samråd*, 32; Carlsen, *Kirkefronten*, 26. In addition to Berggrav, Hallesby, and Hope, the CCC consisted of Kristian Hansson, director general in the Justice Department, as legal consultant; Ragnvald Indrebø, assistant pastor in the Jacob Church representing the Council of Autonomous Organizations; Hans Høeg, school principal of the Christian Gymnasium and chairperson of the Oslo Diocese, Ingvald B. Carlsen, assistant pastor at the Old Aker Church and church programming consultant for the Norwegian Broadcasting Service; and Einar Smebye, who represented the Norwegian Mission Society. Poor health soon forced Høeg to resign, and he was replaced by H.E. Wisløff, assistant pastor at Trinity Church and chairman of the Santal Mission. Smebye died in 1941 but was not replaced. All of these members were orthodox men, by virtue of heading major mission societies, and apart from Berggrav, no liberals or women were ever represented. As with the free churches, their inclusion would have met with orthodox theological objections and rendered the CCC impossible. See Tønnessen, *trygt og godt hjem*, 105.

20 Carlsen, *Kirkefronten*, 28.

21 "Kristent samråd i Norge," *Kristen Gemenskap* 13 (1940): 199–200.

22 The speeches were published in *Kirke og Kultur* 47 (1940) and *Dagen*, 31 October and 11, 12, and 14 November 1940, and in a booklet by Berggrav, Hallesby, Hope, and Støren called *Under Guds veldige hånd*.

23 Austad, *KM*, 45.

24 Berggrav, *Da kampen kom*, 115; Handeland, *Kristent samråd*, 33–35.

25 Others in the "High Council" were Paul Berg, Gunnar Jahn, Ferdinand Schjelderup, Johan Scharffenberg, and the labor leaders Einar Gerhardsen, Birger Bergersen, and Olaf Helsen; Christensen, *Okkupasjonsår*, 325–26.

26 Berggrav, *Da kampen kom*, 116.

27 Schübeler, *Kirkekampen*, 32–33, 37–38.

28 Berggrav, *Da kampen kom*, 116..

29 *Aftenposten* published an announcement of the CCC, "Kristen enhet: En erklæring på kirkelig fellesmøte," on 30 October 1940 and a statement from the CCC, "Kristen Samråd," on 4 November 1940. For observers' reactions, see Christensen, *Okkupasjonsår*, 271. For press proclamations of a new era of Christian cooperation, see editorials in *Morgenbladet*, 30 October 1940, and *Dagen*, *Utsyn*, *For Fattig og Rik*, and *Norsk Kirkeblad*, compiled in *Kristen Gemenskap* 13 (1940): 200–4.

30 "Hvad skal dette bety?," *Morgenbladet*, 31 October 1940.

31 For some views, see "Den haugianske linje," listed in the bibliography.

32 Editorial, *For Fattig og Rik*, cited in *Kristen Gemenskap* 13 (1940): 202.

33 Editorial, *Norsk Kirkeblad* 37 (1940): 526–27.

34 Løsnesløkken and Hjemdal, *På ditt ord*, 137; Christie, qtd. in Austad, *Kirkens Grunn*, 72.

35 "Tilleggserklæring fra Kristent Samråd," 23 November 1940, in Austad, *KM*, 45–46.

36 "Stort enhetsmøte i Trondheims domkirke," *Dagen*, 20 December 1940.

37 Austad, *Kirkens Grunn*, 75. See responses from Berggrav, Fjellbu, Hope, Kristian Hansson, and Andreas Seierstad in "Den haugianske linje: En Enquête i Norsk Kirkeblad," *Dagen*, 23 December 1940.

38 Austad, *Kirkens Grunn*, 76.

39 Ibid., 76.

40 Editorial, *Kristelig Tidende* 69 (1940): 528.

41 Editorial, *Banneret*, 16 June 1945; on Berggrav's general relationship to the free churches, see Engelsen, "Økumenen på hjemmeplan."

42 Schjelderup, *Fra Norges kamp*, 201; Wyller, *Nyordning*, 19–20.

5. IN DEFENSE OF A JUST STATE

1 Larsen, "Social Foundations," 599–601; Skodvin, *Krig og okkupasjon*, 123.

2 Bohn, *Reichskommissariat*, 79. The term "political police" was used in an internal memo of 6 August 1941, cited by Aukrust in "Ellers intet illegalt å bemerke," 193. See Ringdal, *Mellom barken*, 93, for German oversight of the State Police, and 43–52 for the police and the Hird in 1940 and early 1941.

3 In Norwegian terms, they waited for a challenge to the constitutional state (*rettsstaten*); see Nøkleby, *Nyordning*, 60.

4 The Norwegian Institute of Technology in Trondheim is now the Norwegian University of Science and Technology; for a biographical sketch of Skancke, see Devik, "Skancke, Ragnar," 442–47.

5 "Kirken skal ha full arbeidsro, *Dagen*," 11 October 1940; "Det nye styre garanterer kirken full arbeidsro," *Fritt Folk*, 12 October 1940.

6 "Kirkestatsråden taler," *Dagen*, 7 November 1940; Grimnes, *Hjemmefrontens ledelse*, 45–46.

7 For Berggrav's account of the case, see *Da kampen kom*, 78–85.

8 Berggrav to clergy of Oslo Diocese, 26 September 1940, box 29, Berggrav Papers, RA.

9 Berggrav to Wollert Krohn-Hansen, 3 October 1940, box 29, Berggrav Papers, RA.

10 Berggrav, *Da kampen kom*, 84; Christie, *Kirke i kamp*, 39; Olav Valen-Sendstad, "Eivind Berggrav," *Dagen*, 2 January 1946. See a copy of the revised prayer in Austad, *KM*, 40–41 and, for an example of the initial clergy reaction, see Olav Valen-Sendstad, *Dagen*, 2 January 1946. Particularly critical of Berggrav's alteration of the prayer was Herman E. Jørgensen, editor of *Lutheraneren*, the official periodical of the Norwegian Lutheran Church of America; "Kongens navn i den norske kirkebønn," 13 November 1940, and "Norges reviderte kirkebønn," 8 January 1941. The Norwegian government also criticized Berggrav's decision in a BBC broadcast on 20 November 1940, which Berggrav thought actually helped to insulate him from NS attacks; "Til dagbok," 20 November 1940, box 35, Berggrav Papers, RA.

11 Berggrav to clergy of Oslo Diocese, 23 October 1940, Austad, *KM*, 34.

12 Skancke to teachers, 20 November 1940, box 14, Berggrav Papers, RA; "Erklæring," box 14, Berggrav Papers, RA; Aartun and Aartun, *Motstandskampen*, 40.

13 Apparently, Schjelderup made no change to Berggrav's formulation; Schjelderup, *Bred front*, 40.

14 My thanks to the late Magne Skodvin for bringing to my attention the centrality of teaching as a "calling" for that generation of teachers.

15 Schjelderup, *På bred front*, 40.

16 Jensen, "Kampen om skolen," 77; Wyller, *Nyordning*, 15 and 325n10.

17 Berggrav, *Da kampen kom*, 133.

18 Fjellbu, *Minner*, 77–78.

19 The letter is included in *The Pastoral Letter*; Austad, *KM*, 51–53.

20 For the bishops' record of the meetings, see Berggrav, *Da kampen kom*, 134–45.

21 Berggrav, *Da kampen kom*, 133. The central section of the memorandum is included in "Hyrdebrev til våre menigheter fra Den norske kirkes biskoper (februar 1941)," Austad, *KM*, 51–53.

22 Ibid., 135.

23 Berggrav, *Da kampen kom*, 134–45.

24 Berggrav, *Da kampen kom*, 33.

25 Skancke's letter is included in "Hyrdebrev til våre menigheter fra Den norske kirkes biskoper (februar 1941)," Austad, *KM*, 53–54.

26 Ibid., 50–59.

27 Berggrav, *Da kampen kom*, 157.

28 Ibid., 164; Norrman, *Quislingkyrkan*, 64.

29 Berggrav, *Da kampen kom*, 147–52.

30 Christie, *Kirke i kamp*, 59. On Terboven as the source of the order, see Berggrav, *Da kampen kom*, 175.

31 Berggrav, Støren, and Maroni to Skancke, Oslo, 11 February 1941, box 484, KUD A Kontoret, RA; Berggrav, Støren, and Maroni to Feyling, "Bispeskrivet av 15 Jan. 1941," Oslo, 12 February 1941," box 4, Feyling Papers, RA; Henning Bødtker to Police Chief in Oslo og Aker, Oslo, 11 February 1941, box 484, KUD A Kontoret, RA; Berggrav, *Da kampen kom*, 165.

32 Berggrav, *Da kampen kom*, 166–80, for an account of the meeting.

33 Ibid., 180.

34 Wyller, *Nyordning*, 20; Christensen, *Okkupasjonsår*, 273; Gabriel Skagestad to Berggrav, Stavanger, 12 February 1941, box 29, Berggrav Papers, RA.

35 For the Gestapo, see V. H. Günther's report,"Norwegische Kirche. Übersicht über das 1. Vierteljahr 1941," Kleine Erwerberungen 298–4, Günther Papers, BA. On the effect of *The Pastoral Letter* in checking the Hird, see, for example, Amdahl, "Misjonsselskapet i krigsårene, 1940–1945," p. 36, Amdahl Papers, NMS.

36 Berggrav, *Da kampen kom*, 160–61. On Christian views of the NS and the Germans, see V. H. Günther, "Norwegische Kirche. Übersicht über das 1. Vierteljahr 1941," p. 3–5, Kleine Erwerberungen 298–4, and "Kirchlicher Stimmungsbericht. 12. Mai 1941," p. 92–93, Kleine Erwerberungen 298–6, Günther Papers, BA.

37 Handeland, *Kristent samråd*, 38; Molland, "Kirkekampens historie," 113–30; Fjellbu, "Dagbok," 17 March 1941, UBT. For Nazi press coverage, see "Stigende søkning til Oslokirkene," *Aftenposten*, 27 February 1941.

38 Fjellbu, "Dagbok," 12 February 1941, UBT.

39 *Norsk Tidend*, 7 February 1941; the newspaper printed *The Pastoral Letter* in its entirety in the 18 February 1941 issue; Hjelmtveit, *Vekstår*, 243–55. The reaction from *Göteborgs Handels- och Sjöfartstidning* is quoted in *Norsk Tidend*, 18 March 1941.

40 Semelin, *Unarmed*, 105.

41 Berggrav, *Da kampen kom*, 164.

42 Austad, *Kirkens Grunn*, 106–7.

43 Reprinted in Berggrav, *Staten og mennesket*, 209–18, and Austad, *KM*, 66–71. English quotations are from the translation by George Aus in Berggrav, *Man and State*, 287–99.

44 Molland, *Konfesjonskunnskap*, 188.

45 Berggrav, "Da Kirkens Grunn ble til," p. 14, KKS; Heling, *Theologie*, 253; Berggrav, *The Norwegian Church*, 17. Berggrav pointed out the usefulness of flexible interpretations of Luther's writings in a postwar foreword to an English book on Luther; see "Bidrag til en engelsk bok om Luther—Forord—Utgitt 1946," p. 1, box 18, Berggrav Papers, RA.

46 Aulén, *Kan något kristet krav?*, 46, 65, 68–69; Austad, *Kirkens Grunn*, 105–6.

47 Postcard from Kathrine Berggrav to Gustaf and Titti Aulén, Oslo, 14 January 1941, box 13, Aulén Papers, UBL. See also Austad, *Kirkens Grunn*, 106.

48 Austad, *Kirkens Grunn*, 106; see also 106n172 for the correct date of Aulén's visit.

49 Berggrav, *Staten*, 219. For the lecture in Norwegian, see Berggrav, *Staten og mennesket*, Austad, *KM*, and an English translation in Berggrav, *Man and State*, 300–19, from which my quotations are drawn. For more on Berggrav's efforts to counteract clerical state servility, see Hassing, "Core Ideas," 12–13. On changing Lutheran political thought, see Heiene, *Berggrav*, 336. There is a discrepancy in Berggrav's dating of this lecture. In *Staten og mennesket*, p. 200, he writes that he delivered the lectures "at various places in Norway during the spring and summer of 1940," but on p. 219 he states that it was delivered in "the spring of 1941." His biographer, Gunnar Heiene, writes that he wrote it after *The Pastoral Letter* and delivered it in "the winter of 1941," i.e., no earlier than February 1941; Heiene, *Berggrav*, 336. The correct dating must be the late winter, spring, and summer of 1941.

50 Heiene, *Berggrav*, 336.

51 For the references to Luther's works, see Berggrav, *Staten og mennesket*, 232, and, in English, Berggrav, *Man and State*, 319.

52 Fleischer described the clergy as initially "somewhat hysterical"; Andreas Fleischer to Berggrav, Bergen, 13 February 1941, box 29, Berggrav Papers, RA; E. Solum, "Rapport om reise til Oslo den 9. febr. 1941 for Sambandsutvalget i Nidaros ved pastor E. Solum," included in Arne Fjellbu's "Dagbok," UBT.

53 Andreas Fleischer to Berggrav, Bergen, 13 February 1941, box 29, Berggrav Papers, RA; E. Solum, "Rapport om reise til Oslo den 9. febr. 1941 for Sambandsutvalget i Nidaros ved pastor E. Solum," included in Arne Fjellbu's "Dagbok," UBT.

54 Berggrav, *Da kampen kom*, 192.

6. THE NS CHURCH SYSTEM

1 On Theisen, see Kolsrud, *En splintret stat*, 263–71.

2 Østlid's signed police statement to the Treason Division of the Oslo Police in the Feyling treason case, Oslo, 20 January 1947, document 17 in folder "Feyling. Dok. 1–43," Feyling Treason Trial Records, RA. Østlid could observe Feyling on a daily basis, and there is no reason to disbelieve his testimony; it fits with other witness accounts. For the record, however, Østlid was the Home Front representative (i.e., spy) in the department from 1941 to 1943, and was one of the employees smuggling reports and correspondence to the CCC.

3 For a biographical sketch, see Berglyd, "Presten som ble landsforræder," and Norrman, *Quislingkyrkan*, 49–53.

4 Feyling, "Vår tids sosiale krise i lys av Den annen bønn," *Dagen*, 16 April 1934; Feyling, "Hvorfor jeg er medlem av NS," *Fritt Folk*, 5 February 1944.

5 Johannes Lavik to Gabriel Skagestad, 5 December 1940, box 29, Berggrav Papers, RA; "Kirkens ja til tidsskiftet i vårt land," *Fritt Folk*, 29 November 1940, reprinted in Feyling, *Stat og kirke*, 9–12.

6 Feyling refers to his attempt to reach out to Skancke in Feyling to Gulbrand Lunde, 29 November 1940, and Skancke to Feyling, 13 December 1940, in "Utdrag av dokumenter i Mappe I i offentlig straffesak ved Eidsivating lagmannsrett," Feyling Treason Trial Records, RA.

7 Feyling, "Kirkens Ja til tidsskiftet i vårt land" and "Den autoritære stat," in Feyling, *Stat og kirke*, 9–12, 25–40.

8 The best study of German and Norwegian intelligence is Pryser, *Hitlers hemmelige agenter*, to which I am indebted for the general background of this section.

9 Steltzer, *Sechzig jahre*, 131–32.

10 Abwehr reports on the church are available on microfilm in the National Archives, Washington, D.C.

11 Steltzer, *Sechzig jahre*, 131–32; report by Wilhelm Wagner to the British Security Service about a conference with Hallesby, Akershus, 30 September 1945, Wagner War Crimes Trial Records, RA.

12 Testimony of Huhnhäuser, Oslo, July 1945, private collection of Magne Skodvin.

13 Bohn, *Reichskommissariat*, 59, 63–65.

14 Huhnhäuser's statement after the war provides valuable insight into the inner workings of the Reichskommissariat in church affairs as well as education; see his statement of July 1945, personal collection of Magne Skodvin. His memoirs have been deposited at the Institut für Zeitgeschichte, Munich, but I have not seen them. For a profile and analysis of his work in Norway, see Fure, *Universitetet*, 107–10.

15 Nøkleby, *Terboven*, 116.

16 Deposition of Wilhelm Artur Konstantin Wagner taken by Torger Leirud, Oslo, 25 July 1945, O. Pk. V J. sak 11210/45, Wagner War Crimes Trial Records, RA. Hereafter, Wagner deposition.

17 V. H. Günther, "Mitt forhold under okkupasjonen," Kleine Erwerbungen 298–10, Günther Papers, BA.

18 See Wagner's statements of 9 September 1945 in O. Pk. V J. sak 11210, Wagner War Crimes Trial Records, RA, and of 2 April 1947 in O. Pk. V J. 463 46–47, "Feyling Dok. 1–43," Feyling Treason Trial Records, RA. For Wagner's autobiography and conditions of employment, see Wagner deposition.

19 See depositions of Skancke, Feyling, Berggrav, and Hallesby taken by Torgeir Leirud, "Rapport til Oslo Politikammer (Landssvikavdelingen)," O. Pk. V 11210/45, Wagner Case, Treason Trial Records, RA.

20 Wagner deposition; deposition of Feyling, 18 January 1946, Wagner War Crimes Trial Records, RA.

21 Günther, "Mitt forhold under okkupasjonen," p. 4, Kleine Erwerbungen 298–10, Günther Papers, BA. Unless otherwise noted, information on Günther's role in the occupation is drawn from this postwar account.

22 Wagner deposition; I concur with Wagner's judgment about Günther's objectivity.

23 Günther, "Mitt forhold," pp. 8–9; report by Wilhelm Wagner to Deputy Chief of Police Kjelstrup, Akershus, 9 September 1945, O.Pk.V 11210/45, Wagner War Crimes Trial Records, RA; Schübeler, *Kirkekampen*, 203.

24 Wagner deposition.

25 Berggrav was impressed by their accuracy; qtd. in Dyrhaug, *Norge okkupert*, 11. The reports have been published in three volumes; Larsen, Sandberg, and Dahm, eds., *Meldungen aus Norwegen 1940–1945*.

26 On Wagner's desire to avoid a church struggle, see deposition of Feyling taken by Odd Kvalvik, 15 September 1946, Oslo, 16 September 1946, Feyling Treason Trial Records, RA.

27 Report by Wilhelm Wagner to Deputy Chief of Police Kjelstrup, Akershus, 9 September 1945, Wagner War Crimes Trial Records, RA.

28 On Quisling's occasional intervention, see deposition of Feyling taken by Odd Kvalvik, Oslo, 14 September 1946, Feyling Treason Trial Records, RA.

29 On Feyling's bypassing of Skancke, see Henry Oscar Østlid's deposition, Oslo, 20 January 1947, Feyling Treason Trial Records, RA. On Feyling's concern about orienting Skancke, see Feyling to Lundesgaard, Oslo, 24 February 1944, copy in "Utdrag av dokumenter i Mappe I i offentlig straffesak ved Eidsivating lagmannsrett," Feyling Treason Trial Records, RA

30 Kolsrud, *Splintret stat*, 264, 268; Norrman, *Quislingkyrkan*, 41.

31 Testimony beginning "Ordningen fra 25/9/40 var følgende med hensyn til den tekniske ordning av lovgivningsarbeide," p. 2, Sverre Riisnæs Treason Trial Records, RA. For more on the NS system of governance, see documents on administrative procedures in file marked "Diverse dok. om regjering og departement," box "Statsrådsekretariatet NS Administrasjonen," RA.

32 Feyling's later accounts probably exaggerated the degree to which he consulted the NS bishops in order to avoid responsibility for police actions; see "Rapport av politikonstabel Hans Kr. Halvorsen til Herr Politimesteren i Telemark angående vitneforklaringen om L. D. Zwilgmeyer," L. D. Zwilgmeyer Treason Trial Records, RA.

33 Skancke, co-signed by Feyling, to Justice Department, Oslo, 26 November 1941, Ministry of Church and Education, "Kopibok 1941: 4 kvartal," RA. For more on Feyling's struggle to centralize church affairs, see Hassing, "Ecumemical Aspects," 27–29.

34 Ringdal, *Mellom barken*, 94.

35 On the State Police's establishment and statistics, see Ringdal, *Mellom barken*, 94, 197–98. The term "political police" was used in an internal memo of 6 August 1941 cited by Aukrust, "'Ellers intet illegalt,'" 193 and 197, citing Per Ole Johansen.

36 "Statspolitiets Hovedkontors virksomhet i 1942 i forbindelse med kirkestriden," in "Utdrag i sak for Eidsivating lagmannsrett nr. 148/1946," vol. 3, p. 315, Skancke Treason Trial Records, RA.

37 For example, Division V directed the State Police to report on services in Bergen, which resulted in State Police Chief Marthinsen ordering tighter enforcement of the restrictions on Bishop Andreas Fleischer; see Andreas Gjøsund to Marthinsen, Bergen, and K. O. Marthinsen, co-signed by O. Landerud, Oslo, 15 September 1943, box 4, Feyling Papers, RA; "Statspolitiets Hovedkontors virksomhet," vol. 2, p. 315, Skancke Treason Trial Records, RA.

38 For details on the state police's intelligence gathering at church services, see Aukrust, "'Ellers intet illegal,'" 193–213; the dates are noted on p. 197.

39 Ibid., 205. For a firsthand account of how Division VA functioned, see Thorbjørn Frøberg's deposition, Ole Landerud Treason Trial Records, RA.

40 Unless otherwise noted, my account of Steltzer is based on his autobiography, *Sechzig Jahre Zeitgenosse*, 120–48.

41 Hestvold, *Alex Johnson*, 170.

42 Ibid.; Steltzer, *Sechzig Jahre*, 131.

43 Steltzer, *Sechzig Jahre*, 132; Hauge, *Rapport*, 221.

44 Proof that the CCC had access to Church Department files is the collection that comprises much of the KKS; see also Schübeler, *Kirkekampen*, 202.

7. AGAINST NAZIFICATION

1 Riste, *Norway's Foreign Relations*, 159.

2 This section is based on Riste, *1940–1942*, 17–130.

3 Riste, *1940–1942*, 203–4.

4 Riste, *Norway's Foreign Relations*, 170.

5 Feyling, "Den norske kirke og det norske folk," 19–24.

6 Terboven, "Reichskommissar Terboven talte lørdag for første gang offentlig om norske forhold og de kommende opgaver," *Aftenposten*, 3 June 1940; Skancke, interview, 12 October 1940, in "Kirken 1940–42," KKS; (Feyling) to Huhnhäuser, 1 April 1941, box 1, Feyling Papers, RA.

7 Skancke, co-signed by Feyling, 11 February 1941, in Feyling, ed., *KH*, 25.

8 Ibid. This circular implied that Skancke and, therefore, Feyling, knew about Terboven's wishes for peace in the church and warned against future actions hostile to the state.

9 Skancke, co-signed by Feyling, to clergy and parish councils, Oslo, 5 April 1941, in Feyling, ed., *KH*, 45–48.

10 Referred to in [Berggrav] to [bishops], 2 October 1940, in "Kirken 1940–42," KKS.

11 The figure of 58 pastors broadcasting their services is listed in "Fortegnelese over prester som har gitt sitt samtykke til å la sine gudstjenester kringkaste og til å holde andakter i kringkastingen, " box 1, Feyling Papers, RA.

12 Skancke, co-signed by Feyling, to clergy and parish councils, Oslo, 5 April 1941, in Feyling, ed., *KH*, 46.

13 Terboven claimed his orders to maintain calm in the church were based on the

final battle with Great Britain, but the planned invasion of the Soviet Union was the more likely reason; Feyling to Andreas M. Olay, Oslo, 18 April 1941, copy in Austad Collection; for statistics on the clergy boycott see lists of May 1941 and [Feyling] to Riisnes, 19 May 1941, box 1, Feyling Papers, RA.

14 Berggrav to "Friend," Oslo, 20 March 1941, box 29, Berggrav Papers, RA.

15 See Berggrav to Henrik [Hille], Oslo, 27 April 1941, box 13, Berggrav Papers, RA.

16 The Justice Department had holdovers who continued to apply Norwegian law as much as they could.

17 Berggrav, "Til overveielse," March 1941, p. 1, box 29, Berggrav Papers, RA; Feyling, ed., *KH*, 56–59.

18 Dahl, *Dette er London*, 309, 315.

19 Dale, "Kirken på vikende front," 83.

20 Hansson, *Norsk kirkerett*, 147–48.

21 Feyling to Cabinet Minister [Skancke], 22 March 1941, box 1, Feyling Papers, RA.

22 Draft, [Feyling] to Cabinet Minister [Skancke], 22 March 1941, box 1, Feyling Papers, RA.

23 Skancke [Bakke] to school principals, 8 April 1941, copy in Berggrav to clergy, 25 April 1941, Austad Collection.

24 [Feyling] to Herr Statsråden [Skancke], 25 March 1941, box 1, Feyling Papers, RA; "Forslag til innskrenkning av antall lærebøker i kristenlære (katekisme)," 1 April 1941, box 1, Feyling Papers, RA. In this case, Feyling was actually taking up a theme that the bishops had on the agenda for their 1940 episcopal meeting.

25 Feyling, review of "Kristendomskunnskap II (Kirkehistorie) av Marthinussen og Ribsskog," 14 March 1941; Feyling, review of "Ragnar Aasland: Religionshistorie," 21 April 1941; Feyling, "Forslag til innskrenkning av antall lærebøker i bibelhistorie," 8 May 1941, box 1, Feyling Papers, RA.

26 See Feyling's review of "Kristendomskunnskap II (Kirkehistorie) av Marthinussen og Ribsskog," 14 Mars 1941, box 1, Feyling Papers, RA.

27 Feyling, *Liv og lære*, 52–53.

28 Kåre Norum, review of "Sigmund Feyling: Liv og lære; Kristendomslære med øvinger," *Norsk Skuleblad*, 24 May 1941, in Feyling, ed., *KH*, 63–68. Norum's contact with Berggrav is mentioned in Berggrav to bishops, 29 May 1941, box 29, Berggrav Papers, RA. Norum told the story of his work, with a brief mention of his Christian view of life, in an interview with Ragnar Ulstein, 25 August 1970, NHM.

29 Berggrav to bishops, 29 May 1941, box 29, Berggrav Papers; Berggrav's account in "Kirken 1940–42," KKS.

30 J. Eldal, "Sigmund Feyling: Liv og lære," *Norsk Skuleblad* 23 (1942), Feyling, ed., *KH*, 69.

31 Gabriel Skagestad to Berggrav, 13 March 1941, and Berggrav to bishops, 29 May 1941, box 29, Berggrav Papers, RA; Feyling, ed., *KH*, 78.

32 Christie, *Kirke i kamp*, 83. On one case of *Life and Doctrine*'s adoption over community objections, in South Frøn, see Henrik Hille to School Superintendent, Hamar, 29 September 1941, box 15, Berggrav Papers, RA.

33 Austad, *KM*, 34–35.

34 Feyling, ed., *KH*, 41–42.

35 Skodvin, "Det store fremstøtt," 648, 651; Wyller, *Fra okkupasjonsårenes maktkamp*, 33.

36 Feyling to Central Board, Oslo, 19 June 1941, in "Kirken 1940–42," KKS. Berggrav was officially *preses*, i.e., presiding bishop.

37 Svendsen, *Presteforening*, 70; Johannes Smemo, Eivind Berggrav, Gabriel Skagestad, Peter Marstrander, Jon Mannsåker, and Hartvig C. Christie to Herr Kommisaren for Den Norske Kirkes Presteforening, 28 June 1941, box 15, Berggrav Papers, RA. [Central Board of the Church of Norway Clergy Association] to the Commissioner for the Church of Norway Clergy Association, Oslo, 28 June 1941, in "Kirken 1940–42," KKS.

38 "Utmeldelser av Den norske kirkes presteforening," box 1, Feyling Papers, RA.

39 Berggrav's remarks are quoted in the confidential report of Olle Nystedt to Archbishop Erling Eidem and the Ecumenical Institute in Sigtuna, Sweden, Göteborg, 4 June 1941, "Inkommande Information E V: 2 1941–1942," NEI. See also V. H. Günther, "II. Die Einstellung der christlichen Kreise zu der deutschen Besetzung und zu Deutschland," in "Kirchlicher Stimmungsbericht. 12./26. Mai 1941," Bestand 5/200, EZ.

40 Grimnes, *Hjemmefrontens ledelse*, 122, 125.

41 Ibid, 122, 153–54.

42 Ibid., 154.

43 Ibid., 106.

44 Ibid., 96, 106. For Bonnevie-Svendsen's account of his work, see Ragnar Ulstein's interview of 12 October 1972, NHM.

45 Grimnes, *Hjemmefrontens ledelse*, 79.

46 Ibid., 154. Berggrav, for example, was in regular contact with a central figure in both the Coordination Committee and the Circle, justice Ferdinand Schjelderup; Schjelderup, *På bred front*, 27.

47 Grimnes, *Hjemmefrontens ledelse*, 66–68.

8. IN DEFENSE OF THE CHURCH

1 On Hitler's world view, see Jäckel, *Hitler's World View*.

2 Qtd. in Clark, *Barbarossa, 1941–45*, 25.

3 Qtd. in Clark, *Barbarossa*, opposite title page.

4 Kjeldstadli, *Hjemmestyrkene*, 49.

5 Norrman, *Quislingkyrkan*, 95.

6 "Opprop til det norske folk," *Aftenposten*, 15 July 1941. The 27 clergy members who signed the appeal were Johannes Andersen, Johan Beronka, Peder Blessing-

Dahle, Georg Falck-Hansen, Sigmund Feyling, Lars Frøyland, Knut Geelmuyden, Andreas Gjerdi, Marcus Gjessing, Sigurd Haga, Hans Olaf Hagen, Christian Fr. Hansteen, Øyvind Johan Hoem, Haakon Hovdin, Ansgar Høyer, C. J. Ingier, R. S. Kreutz, Aksel Kvam, O. J. B. Kvasnes, Einar Lothe, O. J. Modvar, A. M. Olay, J. E. Sivertsen, Peder Ulleland, Reidulf Wormdal, Dagfinn Zwilgmeyer, and Ludvig Daae Zwilgmeyer.

7   Christian F. S. Hansteen to Feyling, Herefoss, 27 July 1941, box 7, Feyling Papers, RA.

8   Feyling to Reichskommissar, Oslo, 27 May 1941, box 4, Feyling Papers, RA.

9   For examples of the campaign against Berggrav, see editorial, *Fritt Folk*, 25 July 1941; Marcus Gjessing, "Åpent Brev," *Fritt Folk* and *Aftenposten*, 2 August 1941; Torgeir Audunson, "Du kirkens mann—gi svar!" [poem], *Fritt Folk*, 4 August 1941; Kristen Gundelach, "Geistlig smørgås," *Fritt Folk*, 18 August 1941; Supreme Court Justice Andreas Mohr, "Åpent brev til biskop Berggrav," *Fritt Folk*, 26 August 1941; "Hvem tjener kristendommens sak," *Fritt Folk*, 5 September 1941; Feyling, "Skal kirken være nøitral?," *Fritt Folk*, 24 September 1941; Sigurd Haga, "Den norske kirkes sammenbrudd eller nyordning," *Fritt Folk*, 17 October 1941; and editorials, *Fritt Folk*, 13 and 17 October 1941.

10 Claes Westring to Brother (Söderblom), Oslo, 14 October 1941, Utrikesdepartementet HP 177, RAS.

11 Feyling, ed., *KH*, 129–30.

12 Norrman, *Quislingkyrkan*, 96; Rostrup, "Legionæroppropet," 12–13. Rostrup counts 47 clergy supporters.

13 Norrman, *Quislingkyrkan*, 97.

14 Fjellbu, "Dagbok," 16 August 1941, BT.

15 Feyling, ed., *KH*, 107.

16 Berggrav to bishops, 2 September 1941, box 1, Hille Papers, SAH.

17 Feyling, ed., *KH*, 111–12.

18 Ibid., 101–2.

19 Ibid., 102–3.

20 Ibid., 104.

21 Ibid.

22 Feyling to Bishop of Oslo, Oslo, 8 September 1941, K.D.J. 3941 A. 1941, Ministry of Church and Education, "Kopibok 1941. 16. aug.–30. sept.," RA.

23 [Skancke] to Dean of Oslo Cathedral, Oslo, 12 September 1941, K.D. J. 4020 A. 1941, Ministry of Church and Education "Kopibok 1941. 16. aug.–30. sept.," RA.

24 The five dismissed rural deans were Ivar Welle, Conrad Megrund, Tycho Castberg, Christian Erichsen, and Brage Høyem, all between the ages of 66 and 69; "Kirken 1940–42" KKS.

25 "Biskop Berggrav's samtale med Reichskommissar 10/11 juli/41," in "Kirken 1940–42," KKS. Berggrav, the Bishops' Conference, the clergy, and the Church Depart-

ment resisted the confiscation order to the point that the Germans decided not to act. A registration and research project was launched that was deliberately prolonged until 1945, saving the church bells; see Norrman, *Quislingkyrkan*, 92–94.

26 Deposition of Alfred Huhnhäuser, private collection of the late Magne Skodvin.

27 Feyling, "De to biskoper og de fem prester som fikk avskjed i henhold til oppnådd aldersgrense den 5. juli 1941," 24 July 1942, box 10, Feyling Papers, RA. For Quisling's view, see the secret memorandum of Wegener to Herr Reichskommissar, Oslo, 1 September 1941, Quisling Treason Trial Records, RA.

28 Hansson, *Norsk kirkerett*, 42.

29 Feyling to bishops, 23 October 1941, referred to in Berggrav and Støren to Church Department, Oslo, 10 November 1941, box 3, Feyling Papers, RA.

30 Berggrav and Støren to Church Department, Oslo, 10 November 1941, box 3, Feyling Papers, RA.

31 Støren to bishops, Trondheim, 2 December 1941, box 1, Hille Papers 1942–45, SAH.

32 Skagestad to Støren, Stavanger, 6 December 1941, box 29, Berggrav Papers, RA.

33 Støren to Feyling, Trondheim, 3 December 1941, box 1, Hille Papers, SAH.

34 Feyling, ed., *KH*, 133–35.

35 Ibid., 136–37.

36 Ibid., 137–39.

37 Feyling, "Bør biskopene avlastes administrative gjøremål til fordel for lære-og tilsynshvervet?" *Aftenposten*, 1 December 1941.

38 "Bispeembetet i den norske kirke skal fornyes i reformasjonens ånd," *Aftenposten*, 6 December 1941, in Feyling, ed., *KH*, 147–49.

39 Bishops to Church Department, "Om 'Kirkens orden.' Biskopenes of kirkens stilling i gudstjenestlige saker," 15 December 1941, Austad, *KM*, 103–5.

40 Berggrav to Hille, Oslo, 17 December 1941, box 1, Hille Papers, SAH.

41 Austad, *KM*, 102–5.

42 Ibid., 105–6.

43 Feyling, "Gledelig vendepunkt i forholdet mellom kirke of stat," *Fritt Folk*, 27 December 1941; Feyling, "Biskopene finner tiden inne til å etablere et tillitsforhold overfor det statsbærende parti, konstaterer Kirkedepartementet og tar med glede mot den fremstrakte hånd," *Aftenposten*, 27 December 1941.

44 Berggrav to bishops, Oslo, 29 December 1941, box 1, Hille Papers, SAH.

45 Editorial, *Luthersk Kirketidende* 79 (1942): 3–5.

46 Berggrav to Jens Nørregaard, Oslo, 7 January 1942, box 29, Berggrav Papers, RA.

47 H. E. Wisløff to Andreas Seierstad, Bodø, 14 April 1966, KKS korr. om Kirkens Samråd, KKS; Ragnvald Indrebø to Andreas Seierstad, Dvergsdalen, 12 June 1966, KKS korr. om Kirkens Samråd, KKS. See also the Church's Consultative Council, "Protokoll," Ms. Fol 2646, Special Collections, NB.

48 From the Church's Consultative Council, January 1942, in Austad, *KM*, 110–11.

9. THE RESIGNATION OF THE BISHOPS

1 Fischer, *Nazi Germany*, 477.

2 Terboven, "Der Herr Reichskommissars tale," *Aftenposten*, 2 February 1942, and other major newpspapers.

3 Quisling, "Quislings tale," *Aftenposten*, 2 February 1942, and other major newspapers.

4 Editorial, *Aftenposten*, 3 February 1942; editorial, *Fritt Folk*, 6 February 1942.

5 Feyling, ed., *KH*, 189.

6 Fjellbu, *Minner*, 130–31; Feyling, ed., *KH*, 189–91.

7 Lauritz Bang-Hansen, "Trondheim 1. februar 1942," box 29, Berggrav Papers, RA.

8 Fjellbu, *Minner*, 134–35.

9 The two primary accounts of this incident are compatible: Egil Lindheim, "Rapport til politimesteren i Trondheim," 1 February 1942, box 10, Feyling Papers, RA, and Lauritz Bang-Hansen, "Trondheim 1 februar 1942," box 29, Berggrav Papers, RA. Bang-Hansen estimated the number of police at ten; Lindheim did not mention a number.

10 Bang-Hansen, "Trondheim 1 februar 1942," box 29, Berggrav Papers, RA; Fjellbu, *Minner*, 135; Christian Gierløff, Karl Johan Tangen, Hugo Nilsen, and Anna Holand, signed testimonies to Fjellbu, 7 February 1942, KKS.

11 Lindheim, "Rapport," box 10, Feyling Papers, RA.

12 Feyling, ed., *KH*, 192–95; Bang-Hansen, "Trondheim 1 februar 1942," box 29, Berggrav Papers, RA; Lindheim, "Rapport," box 10, Feyling Papers, RA.

13 Einar Anker Nilsen, "Episoder fra krigstiden," private collection of Peder Borgen.

14 Anonymous eyewitness account, "Trondheim 1. februar 1942," box 29, Berggrav Papers, RA.

15 Fjellbu, *Minner*, 135.

16 Feyling, ed., *KH*, 189–201.

17 Hansson, *Norsk kirkerett*, 184; Fjellbu, *Minner*, 131.

18 Feyling, ed., *KH*, 198.

19 Berggrav, "Arresterte prester," 193–206.

20 Berggrav, "Notat på hytta våren 1945," box 13, Berggrav Papers, RA; Berggrav, *Front*, 19.

21 Berggrav, *Front*, 19.

22 Ibid., 20.

23 Berggrav does not mention Støren by name; ibid.

24 Ibid., 21.

25 Austad, *KM*, 128–30.

26 Ibid., 130.

27 Feyling, ed., *KH*, 226–27; Director General for Church Division (Sigmund Feyling) to Bishops of Oslo, Hamar, Agder, Bjørgvin, and Nidaros, Oslo, 25 February 1942, K. D. J. 793 A. 1942, A Kontoret KD, Kopibok. 1 kvartal 1942, RA.

28 Finn Støren qtd. in Melsom, *Fra kirke- og kulturkampen*, 71–72; Høidal, *Quisling*, 429.

29 See Sakliste, "Til behandling i regjeringsmøte hos Ministerpresidenten den 26. februar 1942," box "Statsrådsekretariatet, NS—administrasjon. Foredrag 1942 5/2–16/4," RA; Feyling to Huhnhäuser, 2 March 1942, box 5, Feyling Papers, RA.

30 Two weeks later, the order was cut back to once daily and ceased altogether just before Berggrav was imprisoned; Berggrav, *Front*, 28; K. A. Marthinsen to Berggrav, Oslo, 25 February 1942, KKS; Christie, *Kirke i kamp*, 133.

31 Telegram, Church Department to Hagen, Wormdal, Kvasnes, Zwilgmeyer, Berg-Rolness, Falck-Hansen, 27 February 1942, KD A Kontoret, "Kopibok. 1 kvartal 1942," RA.

32 Austad, *KM*, 130–34.

33 For Berggrav's account, see Berggrav, *Front*, 30–36.

34 Christie, *Kirke i kamp*, 136.

35 Støren to Berggrav, 3 March 1942, box 29, Berggrav Papers, RA.

36 Christie, *Kirke i kamp*, 141, and published in leading newspapers 13 March 1942.

37 Støren to Hille, Trondheim, 13 March 1942, box 1, Henrik Hille Papers, SAH.

38 Austad, *Kirkens Grunn*, 91.

39 Ibid, 92.

40 Feyling to Huhnhäuser, 2 March 1942, box 5, Feyling Papers, RA.

41 Berggrav, *Front*, 36–37. For example, an NS report on Vestfold churches showed that of the 23 churches reported on, the letter was read in 15; N. Schinning Olsen to Richard S. Kreutz, Tønsberg, 3 March 1942, box 5, Feyling Papers, RA.

42 Austad, *KM*, 135.

43 The pastors who resigned were Odd Lothe, Kaare Berg-Hansen, and Erling Haugen; Christie, *Kirke i kamp*, 134.

44 Austad, *KM*, 136.

45 Christie, *Kirke i kamp*, 142; Austad, *KM*, 135.

10. IN DEFENSE OF THE YOUNG

1 Nøkleby, *Nyordning*, 41.

2 Deposition of Feyling, 26 August 1945, in the trial of Ragnar Skancke, Feyling Treason Trial Records, RA.

3 Jensen, "Kampen om skolen," 83.

4 Berggrav, *Front,* 14.

5 Austad, *KM*, 116–17.

6 Hoprekstad, *Frå lærarstriden*, 35; Aartun and Aartun, *Motstandskampen i skolen*, 60; Christie, *Kirke i kamp*, 47; Dietrichson, "Trekk fra kampen mot ungdomstjenesten," 11.

7 Austad, *KM*, 117–18.

8 Austad, *KM*, 118–22.

9 "Barna våre og den nye livsanskuelse. En dokumentasjon februar 1942," KKS.

10 Berggrav, *Front*, 16.

11 Berggrav, *Front*, 13–14.

12 H. E. Wisløff to Berggrav, Oslo, 27 February 1942, Fjellbu, "Dagbok," pp. 214–15, UBT. The letter contains the list of organizations that declared their support, as well as statements from the Evangelical Lutheran Free Church and the Dissenter Parliament.

13 Copies of the supporting letters, KKS.

14 Rieber-Mohn, "Vi var med," 86, 84.

15 Pope Pius XII, "Pavens julebudskap," *St. Olav* 54 (1942): 4.

16 Berggrav, *The Norwegian Church*, 21, and *Front*, 16–17.

17 Deposition of Wilhelm Wagner, 9 September 1945, Wagner War Crimes Trial Records, RA.

18 Rieber-Mohn, "Vi var med," 93.

19 Gram, *Norske tilstande*, 106; Bull, *Klassekamp*, 250; Myklebust and Hagtveit, "Regional Contrasts," 637, citing the work of Stein Rokkan.

20 Jensen, "Kampen om skolen," 80; Nøkleby, *Nyordning*, 77; Helland, "Einar Høigård," 8–12.

21 Jensen, "Kampen om skolen," 80; Aartun and Aartun, *Motstandskampen*, 87–88.

22 For an overview of clergy resistance in the parishes and the clergy's relationship to local teachers' resistance, see the clergy's answers to the church's postwar questionnaire about their wartime activities, KKS. The questionnaire was commissioned after the war by the church to document the clergy's resistance in the parishes, their response to directives from the CCC and its successor, the Provisional Church Leadership (Den midlertidige kirkeledelse), and their relationship to other fronts, such as the teachers. On the local struggle, see the teachers' front directive titled "Nytt skoleår," September 1943, box 15, Berggrav Papers, RA.

23 Gjelsvik, *Hjemmefronten*, 69; Schjelderup, *På bred front*, 137; Hoprekstad, *Frå lærarstriden*, 31; Jensen, "Kampen om skolen," 84.

24 Qtd. in Hoprekstad, *Frå lærarstriden*, 33.

25 Ibid., 36.

26 Larsen, Sandberg, and Volker, eds., *Meldungen*, vol. 2, 577; Goebbels, *Goebbels Diaries* (4 March 1942), 111.

27 Høidal, *Quisling*, 427.

28 Nøkleby, *Holdningskamp*, 83.

29 Jensen, "Kampen om skolen," 85.

30 Nøkleby, *Holdningskamp*, 78.

31 Ibid., 123.

32 Aartun and Aartun, *Motstandskampen*, 89.

33 Austad, "Pacifists," 405. Lund was also active in rescuing Jews and was honored as one of the "righteous" among the nations at Yad Vashem, Jerusalem; Abrahamsen, *Norway's Response*, 21.

34 Nøkleby, *Holdningskamp,* 123–26.

35 Ibid., 127.

36 Christie, *Kirke i kamp,* 157.

37 Krohn-Hansen, *Brente jord,* 110.

38 "Norsk Foreldre" (mimeographed flier), KKS.

39 "Mor og far!" (flier), KKS.

40 Voksø, *Krigens dagbok,* 218.

41 Jensen, "Kampen om skolen," 86.

42 Dietrichson, "Trekk fra kampen," 120–22, citing *Fritt Folk,* 4 March 1942. There is much research to do on this, and it is possible that there was more compliance than postwar accounts indicate.

43 Jensen, "Kampen om skolen," 96.

44 Ibid., 87.

45 Norrman, *Quislingkyrkan,* 200.

46 Høidal, *Quisling,* 432.

47 Christie, *Kirke i kamp,*154.

48 Høidal, *Quisling,* 432.

49 Kristian Hansson, "Arbeidet i Kristent Samråd med 'Kirkens Grunn,'" box 13, Berggrav Papers, RA.

50 Berggrav, "Da Kirkens Grunn ble til (mars 1942)," pp. 10–11, KKS, and Kristian Hansson, "Arbeidet i Kristent Samråd med 'Kirkens Grunn,'" box 13, Berggrav Papers, RA.

51 Austad, *KM,* 140–41.

52 See S. F. [Feyling], "Innstilling, Midlertidig lov om opphævelse av adgangen til å melde seg ut av Statskirken," 5 April 1942, box 4, Feyling Papers, RA; Feyling, "Forslag til forholdsregler i tilfelle av at prester i større utstrekning nedlegger sine embeter," 23 March 1942, box 5, Feyling Papers, RA.

53 Feyling, ed., *KH,* 255–62.

54 Ragnar Skancke and Sigmund Feyling to clergy, Oslo, 30 March 1942, in Austad, *KM,* 141.

55 Larsen, Sandberg, and Dahm, eds., *Meldungen,* vol. 2, 575.

11. EASTER 1942

1 Statement by Carl F. Wisløff, 7 January 1948, KKS.

2 Reservations and considerations of some of the clergy in Stavanger are documented in Olav Valen-Sendstad, "Hvordan 'Kirkens Grunn' ble til," *Dagen,* 20 January 1948; Gabriel Skagestad, Kornelius O. Kornelius, and Einar Amdahl to CCC, March 1942, KKS; Kristian Hansson, "Arbeidet i Kristent Samråd med 'Kirkens Grunn,'" KKS; Berggrav, "Da Kirkens Grunn ble til (mars 1942)," pp. 15–16, KKS. According to Carl F. Wisløff there was also unrest in Kristiansand; see his statement of 7 January 1942 in connection with Valen-Sendstad and the events leading up to the writing of *The Foundation of the Church,* KKS.

3 Hansson, "Arbeidet i Kristent Samråd med 'Kirkens Grunn,'" box 13, Berggrav Papers, RA.

4 Austad, *KM*, 135. On developments in Bergen, see Amdahl, "Misjonsselskapet i krigsårene 1940–45," 63–64, Amdahl Papers, NMS.

5 [Andreas Fleischer] to [Eivind Berggrav], Bergen, 19 March 1942, box 13, Berggrav Papers, RA.

6 Valen-Sendstad's inspiration became a matter of controversy beginning in late 1947, when he claimed primary authorship of *The Foundation of the Church*; see his interview, "Mennesker og interesser 215: Residerende kapellan Olav Valen-Sendstad," *Stavangeren*, 20 January 1948. The other members of the Stavanger CCC denied that Valen-Sendstad had a mandate to draft a confession; Gabriel Skagestad, Kornelius O. Kornelius, and Einar Amdahl to members of the CCC in March 1942, Stavanger, 2 January 1948, KKS.

7 On the evolution of his thinking and on his proposal see Berggrav, "Da Kirkens Grunn ble til (mars 1942)," pp. 8–15, KKS.

8 Ibid., 17.

9 Hansson, "Arbeidet i Kristent Samråd med 'Kirkens Grunn,'" box 13, Berggrav Papers, RA.

10 Ibid.

11 Berggrav, "Innledning til en trykt norsk utgave av *Kirkens Grunn*," pp. 6–7, box 13, Berggrav Papers, RA.

12 Berggrav, "Da Kirkens Grunn ble til (mars 1942)," p. 24, KKS.

13 Berggrav, "Da Kirkens Grunn ble til (mars 1942)" p. 25, KKS; Hansson, "Arbeidet i Kristent Samråd med 'Kirkens Grunn,'" box 13, Berggrav Papers, RA.

14 Berggrav, "Da Kirkens Grunn ble til," 25.

15 Berggrav, "Innledning til en trykt norsk utgave av Kirkens Grunn," p. 9, box 13, Berggrav Papers, RA.

16 Berggrav, "Da Kirkens Grunn ble til (mars 1942)," p. 27, KKS.

17 Ibid.

18 "Memorandum: Events in the Norwegian Church Strife Leading Up to the Arrest and the Subsequent Release of Bishop Eivind Berggrav," p. 5, in enclosure 1 to dispatch 611, Herschel V. Johnson to the Secretary of State, Stockholm, 30 April 1942, file 857.404, sub. 21, Department of State Files, Diplomatic Branch, NA. Christie placed the number in attendance at 3,000 in *Kirke i kamp*, 162; Berggrav cited other estimates of 10,000 in *Front*, 65.

19 Christie does not mention use of the Coordination Committee's courier network in Christie, *Den norske kirke*, but such is the claim of Nøkleby, *Holdningskamp*, 58. The best sources for the dates are in the clergy's answers to a postwar questionnaire, KKS.

20 The definitive analysis of the history, theology, and consequences of *The Foundation of the Church* is Austad, *Kirkens Grunn*. For a briefer analysis, see Austad, *KM*, 143–49.

21 Krohn-Hansen, *Brente jord*, 125–26.

22 For the formulaic declarations, see Feyling, ed., *KH*, 272–73.

23 Sigurd Opdahl, "Opplysninger om kilder til kirkekampens historie avgitt av sokneprest Sigurd Opdahl," Sunndalsøra, KKS.

24 Austad, *KM*, 153–56. Bishop Nikolas Arnesson (ca. 1150–1225) led the Bagler party in the civil war against King Sverre Sigurdsson and his Birkebeiner. King Sverre ruled from 1177 to 1202 and opposed the Catholic hierarchy and the papacy over control of local churches and priestly appointments, traditionally in the hands of local farmers. For his stand, King Sverre was excommunicated by Archbishop Eirik Ivarsson, as were the bishops loyal to him, by no less than Pope Innocent III.

25 Quisling drafted the telegram with Sverre Riisnæs, but it was sent over the signature of Skancke, co-signed by Feyling; Austad, *KM*, 156–57.

26 Feyling, "Kirkens Grunn," *Fritt Folk*, 9 April 1942, in Austad, *KM*, 157–58.

27 Per Eivind Sæbø, "Opplysninger som svar på spyrjeskjema frå Kyrkjekampens Sentralarkiv av 8. jan. 1946," Sirdal, 9 May 1946, KKS.

28 Church Department to Minister President, 27 April 1942, "Utdrag av dokumenter i Mappe I i offentlig straffesak ved Eidsivating lagmannsrett . . . mot Sigmund Feyling," Feyling Treason Trial Records, RA.

29 Feyling, ed., *KH*, 292–93.

30 Church Department to Minister President, 27 April 1942, "Utdrag av dokumenter," Feyling Treason Trial Records, RA.

31 Feyling, ed., *KH*.

32 Norrman, *Quislingkyrkan*, 177.

33 For the statistics used in this section, see the folder titled "Embets-nedlegginga 1942," KKS. The figures in these documents do not always add up, particularly the percentages.

34 Depositions of Hans E. Wisløff, Kristian Hansson, Ingvald B. Carlsen, Ole Hallesby, Ragnvald Indrebø, Eivind Berggrav, and Ludvig Hope to E. Dønnum, Oslo, 5 April 1942, box 4, Feyling Papers, RA.

35 Feyling may also have thought he could play on lay anti-clericalism by focusing charges on the bishops and clergy of the CCC, a point made in Christie, *Kirke i kamp*, 171. I have no direct evidence to support this supposition, but it is plausible.

36 Helmut von Moltke wrote in some detail about his and Bonhoeffer's movements in his letter of 17 April 1942 to his wife, published in *Briefe an Freya*, 364–66.

37 Van Roon, *German Resistance*, 182.

38 Brodersen, *Mellom frontene*, 64–65.

39 Nøkleby, *Terboven*, 210–11.

40 Heiene, *Berggrav*, 356.

41 Ibid.

42 Ibid., 360.

43 Austad, *KM*, 167–170. For originals and copies, see KKS; boxes 13 and 15, Berggrav Papers, RA; and "Kirkeordningen," 95, 96, KUD A Kontoret for Kirke og

Geistlighet 1819–1950, RA. If there was any opposition to the clergy's stand, I have not seen any record of it.

44 Declarations were sent by the Evangelical Lutheran Free Church, the Dissenter Parliament, and the Pentecostal Churches of Oslo; KKS.

45 For Sweden, see Norrman, "Sverige och norska kyrkokampen – en översikt," and Aulén, *Den norska kyrkostriden.* For the Norwegian government in the United Kingdom and the United States, see Fen, *Nazis in Norway,* and Ager and Høye, *Fight of the Norwegian Church.* The British government established a Ministry of Morale that published *The Spiritual Issues of the War,* with many articles on the Norwegian church, and Bishop George A. K. Bell edited Berggrav's writings and church struggle documents; Berggrav, *With God in the Darkness.* The Norwegian church struggle featured in English works on the churches in Europe as well; see Martin, Newton, Waddams, and Williams, *Christian Counter-Attack,* 55–71, and Williams, "The Church in Norway and the Pastorals," in *No Other Gospel,* 43–51. For the U.S.A., see the Norwegian Lutheran Church of America's periodical, *Lutheraneren,* and books such as Singer, ed., *White Book of the Church of Norway,* and Van Dusen, *What IS the Church Doing?*

46 Glenthøj, "Det Nordiske Økumeniske Instituts betydning," 71–76.

47 Heiene, *Berggrav,* 414.

48 Høidal, *Quisling,* 435.

49 Sørensen, *Hitler eller Quisling,* 205.

50 Larsen, Sandberg, and Dahm, eds., *Meldungen,* vol. 2, 607, 609, 611, 651, 682.

12. NEGOTIATIONS?

1 O. Hallesby, Henrik Hille, Ludvig Hope, Johs. Hygen, J. Maroni, and H. E. Wisløff to clergy, parish councils and congregations, Oslo, July 1942, KKS; for the timing of the announcement, see Christie, *Kirke i kamp,*191.

2 Handeland, *Kristent samråd,* 45.

3 Austad, *KM,* 185.

4 Ibid., 186.

5 Ibid., 186–87.

6 Feyling, "Rapport utarbeidet for Førertinget," 13 June 1942, "Utdrag av dokumenter i Mappe I i offentlig straffesak ved Eidsivating lagmannsrett . . . mot Sigmund Feyling," Feyling Treason Trial Records, RA.

7 Hanson, *Norsk kirkerett,* 37.

8 Norrman, *Quislingkyrkan,* 228–31.

9 Skancke, co-signed by Feyling, to Quisling, "Reformasjon av kirken i 'den unge Luthers ånd,'" Oslo, 26 May 1942, box 5, Feyling Papers, RA; Norrman, *Quislingkyrkan,* 230.

10 Qtd. in Norrman, *Quislingkyrkan,* 173.

11 On Frøyland, see Øybekk, "Lars Andreas Frøyland."

12 Minutes, "Kirkelig Rådsmøte 30. juni 1942," box 3, Feyling Papers, RA.

13 "Situation in Norway," intelligence items from the Norwegian embassy in Stockholm to the Norwegian government in London, translated and extracted by Gathorne-Hardy for the Political Intelligence Department of the British Foreign Office, 13 May 1942, Registry N 261/40/30, FO 381/32823, PRO.

14 [Feyling] to State Police, Oslo, 4 May 1942, J. 3781 A. 1942, p. 1723, "KUD A Kontoret: Kopibok 1942: 2 kvartal 1285–2503," RA.

15 Hallesby and Hygen to Church Department, Oslo, 19 June 1942, KKS.

16 The Haugesund pastors were Haugsnes, Samsonsen, and Telhaug; Amdahl to Skagestad, 13 June 1942, Thunem-Feyling Case Papers, NMS.

17 Einar Amdahl to Gabriel Skagestad, Stavanger, 13 June 1942, Thunem-Feyling Case Records, NMS. In addition to Einar Amdahl, the Stavanger manifesto was the work of Kornelius O. Kornelius, Martin Blindheim, and Olav Valen-Sendstad.

18 "Til brødrene," Stavanger, 1 June 1942, Thunem-Feyling Case Records, NMS.

19 "Et motiverende anhang til punkt 4–5," appendix to "Til brødrene," box 9, Feyling Papers, RA.

20 Hallesby and Hygen to Amdahl, Oslo, 23 June 1942, Thunem-Feyling Case Records, NMS.

21 Kvasnes to Feyling, Stavanger, 23 June 1942, KKS.

22 Untitled agreement signed by Ragnar Skancke, Ole Hallesby, Johannes Hygen, Einar Lothe, and Sigmund Feyling, Oslo, 15 August 1942, KKS.

23 Unless otherwise noted, my presentation of the preliminary talks is based on Church Department, "Forsøk på forhandlinger i 'kirkestriden,'" KKS, and Bishops and CCC to clergy and parish councils, "Forsøk på forhandlinger i kirkestriden," Oslo, 14 September 1942, KKS.

24 Hallesby and Hygen statement, 25 August 1942, "Oversikt over prof Hallesbys og domprost Hygens forhandlinger med Kirkedept.," appendix 9b, KKS.

25 Unsigned draft, Oslo, August 1942, "Oversikt over prof Hallesbys og domprost Hygens forhandlinger med kirkedept.," appendix 10, KKS.

26 [PCL] to Church Department, Oslo, 4 September 1942, "Oversikt over prof Hallesbys og domprost Hygens forhandlinger med Kirkedept.," appendix 12, KKS.

27 [James Maroni, Andreas Fleischer, Gabriel Skagestad, Henrik Hille, and Wollert Krohn-Hansen] to Church Department, Oslo, 5 September 1942, in "Oversikt over prof Hallesbys og domprost Hygens forhandlinger med Kirkedept.," appendix 15, KKS.

28 PCL, "Dagbok over de videre forhandlinger," 10 September 1942, KKS.

29 The break off of negotiations was not quite definitive, because both sides continued to want a resolution and as late as early 1943 engaged in a brief exchange about the possibility. This attempt foundered on the same issues, as well as on a new church condition that participation in the youth service be voluntary until the end of the war. See "Uopgivelige forhåndskrav fra Kirken før eventuelle forhandlinger kan finne sted," February 1943, in "Utdrag i sak for Eidsivating lagmannsrett nr. 148/1946," Skancke Treason Trial Records, RA.

13. THE AUTONOMOUS CHURCH

1   On the link between world views and their social bases, see Berger, *Sacred Canopy*, chapters 1 and 2.

2   "En redegjørelse fra 'Den midlertidige kirkeledelse,' til landets prester, menighetsråd og menigheter," 23 July 1942, and the "ten commandments," in Austad, *KM*, 176–77, 182–86.

3   PCL circular, Oslo, 22 September 1942, KKS.

4   Schübeler, *Kirkekampen*, 203–4; Thomle, "Innberetning fra hjelpeprest i Vålerengen, Oslo, Erling August Thomle," [1945], Oslo, KKS.

5   "Oversikt over presteskapet pr. 1. mars 1943," KKS. These figures are generally but not entirely accurate. Bishop Krohn-Hansen, for example, later supplemented them with new information from his diocese; Wollert Krohn-Hansen to the Provisional Church Leadership (DMK), Tromsø, 13 April 1943, KKS.

6   PCL to Bishop Fleischer, Oslo, 24 October 1942, KKS.

7   Christie, *Kirke i kamp*, 201. The only scholarly historical article about the church's information system is Nils Bloch-Hoell, "Den norske kirke," 5–25. Bloch-Hoell was also on the editorial team and served as a courier while a student at the Free Faculty of Theology.

8   Grimnes, *Hjemmefrontens ledelse*, 411.

9   Schübeler, *Kirkekampen*, 203, 239.

10 Ibid., 202; Christie, *Kirke i kamp*, 201.

11 Schübeler, *Kirkekampen*, 202; Christie, *Kirke i kamp*, 314.

12 See, for example, Christmas message of 1943, "Hilsen mellom prestebrødre," KKS, which summarized details of the state's persecution of the Church and encouraged readers to rededicate themselves to continue the struggle along the "same *pure lines* and with the same *unbreakable concord*."

13 On "Kirken i Dag" as the church's only illegal paper, see Bloch-Hoell, "Den norske kirke," 20.

14 Bloch-Hoell, "Den norske kirke," 20–21.

15 Schübeler, *Kirkekampen,* 239

16 Norrman, "Prästerna," 191.

17 Ibid., 197.

18 For a detailed study, see Norrman, "Prästerna," 173–209.

19 Ibid., 197.

20 For Feyling's role, see "Offringer i kirken," 27 May 1942, and Feyling, draft to the clergy, 1 June 1942, box 10, Feyling Papers, RA.

21 Amdahl, "Misjonsselskapet i krigsårene 1940–1945," p. 70, Amdahl Papers, NMS.

22 Norrman, "Prästerna," 197–98.

23 Christie, *Kirke i kamp*, 208.

24 Norrman, "Prästerna," 198.

25 Nøkleby, *Holdningskamp*, 67.

26 Norrman, "Prästerna," 198–99.

27 Qtd. in Norrman, "Prästerna," 198.

28 Postwar clergy reports, KKS. Some clergy, however, reported no attendance increases and, apparently, no effect of the occupation on their parishes; see reports by Sigvald Krohn (Biri), Kristian Olaf Syvertsen (Ringsaker), and Mikael Gladhaug (Vang).

29 Intimidation of NS worshippers occurred, for example, in Karmøy; Kvasnes to Church Department, Stavanger, 24 November 1942, box 19, Feyling Papers, RA.

30 Postwar clergy reports, KKS. For examples and statistics on increased attendance in specific parishes, see the reports of Carsten Baekken (Askim), Salmund Djuvik (Nes in Hallingdal), P.T. Lund (Lesja), Henrik Tveit (Borge), S.J. Vigar (Fridalen, Bergen), Ivar Glette (Gjerstad), and K. Varman (Tysford). On not seeing such figures in a generation, see the PCL's statement of 23 July 1942, Austad, *KM*, 182, and Christie, *Den norske kirke*, 197.

31 Andreas Fleischer to Ole Hallesby, Bergen, 11 May 1943, KKS.

32 Molland, "Den norske kirkekamps status," 174.

33 Austad, *KM*, 182.

34 Qtd. in Schübeler, *Kirkekampen*, 284. Berggrav also had a low regard for the clergy's preaching .

35 Samuel Giæver to Sverre Riisnes, Saltdal, 3 March 1943, KKS.

36 Press Reading Bureau, Stockholm, to Political Intelligence Department, Stockholm, 18 May 1944, "The Church Struggle in Norway," N 3215/110/30, FO371/43225 XC/A/044111, PRO.

37 Wollert Krohn-Hansen to clergy in Hålogaland, Tromsø, 6 April 1943, KKS.

38 Krohn-Hansen, "Beskikkelse av... nadverdforvalter," 30 March 1943, KKS.

39 Løsneløkken and Hjemdal, *På ditt ord*, 142–43; Rudvin, *Indremisjonsselskap*, vol. 2, 379; Handeland and Thorvaldsen, *Herrens Tjeneste*, 45; Eide, *Vestlandske Indremisjonsforbund*, 306–8.

40 Rudvin, *Indremisjonsselskap*, 352.

41 "De frivillige kristelige organisasjoner har hatt et godt arbeidsår," *Aftenposten*, 21 January 1941. This article was published under German censorship but is consistent with postwar reports.

42 Rudvin, *Indremisjonsselskap*, 355; Eide, *Vestlandske Indremisjonsforbund*, 307–8; Det norske lutherske Kinamisjons forbund, *Årbok 1941*, 19–20.

43 Schübeler, *Kirkekampen*, 298.

44 Bull, *Klassekamp og fellesskap*, 389–90; Myklebust and Hagtvet, "Regional Contrasts," 633, Table 1a.

45 Compare the voting maps in Stein Rokkan, "Geografi, religion og samfunnsklasse," 150–51, 154–55.

14. THE NS CHURCH

1 Feyling, "Rapport utarbeidet for Førertinget," 13 June 1942, Feyling Treason Trial Records, RA.

2 Larsen, "Social Foundations," 614. For data on NS membership, see Larsen, "Social Foundations," and Myklebust and Hagtvet, "Regional Contrasts."

3 Larsen, "Social Foundations," 615; Myklebust and Hagtvet, "Regional Contrasts," 626. These were postwar studies, so allowance has to be made for postwar rationalizations.

4 On Christian Union, see Ivar Torgersen von Mehren, "Kristen Samling—et fenomen," 43–63, and Stridsklev, "Kristen Samlings historie," 23–41.

5 Stridsklev, "Kristen Samlings historie," 28.

6 Myklebust and Hagtvet, "Regional Contrasts," 626.

7 Stridsklev uses the family argument to arrive at 4,000 for the number of Christian Union supporters; "Kristen Samlings historie," 28. Larsen and Dahl support the claim that once family members were socially isolated, entire families joined the NS; Larsen, "Social Foundations," 606, and Dahl, Hagtvet, and Hjeltnes, *Den norske nasjonalsosialisme*, 156.

8 Stridsklev estimates 4,000 in "Kristen Samlings historie," 28.

9 Norrman, *Quislingkyrkan*, 243. For a list of those ordained by the NS church, see Carlsen, *Kirkefronten*, 170–71; see also the list of persons illegally ordained by Lars Frøyland, deposition to Kriminalkonstabel Assmundsen, Oslo, 31 August 1945, Frøyland Treason Trial Records.

10 Karsrud, "Prestene," 53.

11 Ibid., 54.

12 For a more extended treatment of this section, see Hassing, "Core Ideas."

13 Frøyland et al., "Opprop til vår kirkes prester og menigheter," Oslo, 30 June 1942, published in leading Norwegian newspapers. For other statements regarding obedience to the authorities, see Ludvig Daae Zwilgmeyer, "Luther og nutiden," *Fritt Folk*, 2 May 1941; O. J. B. Kvasnes, "Kirkens Grunn," *Kristen Samling* 2, no. 16, 1 September 1942, and reprinted, KKS; Lars Erlandsen, "Kirken og øvrigheten," *Fritt Folk*, 25 and 26 February 1943, and published as a brochure in 1943; Trygve Tomter, "Mitt syn på de kristnes forhold til de rådende øvrigheter," *Kristen Samling*, 15 January and 1 February 1944.

14 Lars Frøyland et al. to the Church of Norway's Congregations, Oslo, 3 December 1943, in Austad *KM*, 238–39.

15 "Opprop til det norske folk," *Aftenposten*, 15 July 1941.

16 Norrman, *Quislingkyrkan*, 94–96.

17 Anti-Semitism was more widespread, I think, than Stridsklev judges it to be in "Kristen Samlings historie," 33–35.

18 "Ivar Aker" [Ernst Schirmer], "Nordendom og Austendom," *Ragnarok* 9 (1943): 19–26; the quotation is from page 20. For the NS church reaction, see Emberland, *Religion og rase*, 385–87.

19 [Feyling] to Culture Department, n.p., n.d., KKS.

20 Fuglesang quoted in Emberland, *Religion og rase*, 386–87; Skancke, co-signed by Feyling, to clergy and parish councils, Oslo, 12 June 1943, box 15, Berggrav Papers, RA; Norrman, *Quislingkyrkan*, 237.

21 On the three meetings, see Norrman, *Quislingkyrkan*, 233–39.

22 For the minutes, see "Referat av Kirkelig Rådsmøtes rådslagning på Slottet onsdag 27. januar 1943 kl. 12," box 3, Feyling Papers, RA.

23 Skancke, co-signed by Feyling, to NS representatives, Oslo, 5 March 1943, box 5, Feyling Papers, RA. Feyling also sent a virtually identical circular to the clergy and parish councils; Feyling to clergy and parish councils, Oslo, 17 March 1943, KKS; Church Department to bishops, Oslo, 15 December 1942, box 5, Feyling Papers, RA.

24 Norrman, *Quislingkyrkan*, 201, 204.

25 Ibid., 209, 215.

26 Ibid., 202.

27 Ibid., 205; H.C. Christie, "Forviste prester," *Aftenposten*, 15 August 1945.

28 Skancke (actually Feyling) articulated the policy of intimidation in a letter to the Chief of the State Police; Skancke, co-signed by Feyling, to Marthinsen, Oslo, 9 October 1943, box 19, Feyling Papers, RA. For a survey of the evictions, see H.C. Christie's "Forviste prester," *Aftenposten*, 15 and 17 August 1945.

29 Wagner to Feyling, Oslo, 20 May 1943, box 13, Feyling Papers, RA.

30 Feyling, "Utkast til organisasjon av Den norske kirke," 25 November 1944, box 15, Berggrav Papers, RA. For a detailed description, see Norrman, *Quislingkyrkan*, 360–62.

31 Norrman, *Quislingkyrkan*, 355–60.

32 Ibid., 159.

33 Ibid., 243.

34 Ibid., 228, 233. Norrman points out that segments of the party opposed the Freemasons, regarded as the product of a Jewish conspiracy, and their ordination would create too many political problems for Quisling.

35 Ibid., 208.

36 [Feyling] to Skien Bishop (Ludvig D. Zwilgmeyer), Oslo, 11 October 1943, J. nr. 2731 A 1943, in A. Kirke-Departementet, "Kopibok 1943, 4. kvartal 2294–2876," RA; Feyling to bishops, Oslo, 4 January 1944, J. nr. 34 A 1944, A. Kirkedepartementet, "Kopibok 1944, 1. Kvartal, 1–769," RA.

37 The term "ice front" is quoted by Feyling in a circular from the Ministry of Church and Education to clergy and parish councils, Oslo, 5 April 1941, Austad, *KM*, 83.

38 *Kristen Samling* 2, no. 11 (15 June 1942): 3.

39 Otto Theisen to Quisling, "P.M angående kirkestriden," Oslo, 11 January 1943, "Kirkelig rådsmøte 27. Jan 1943," "Kirkelig Rådsmøte 25–27 jan 1943," box 3, Feyling Papers, RA.

40 Monthly reports of NS bishops are in KKS; Norrman also quotes extensively from 105 extant reports in *Quislingkyrkan*, 251–91.

41 Harald Fosse to O.J.B. Kvasnes, Kopervik, 2 February 1943, "Bispearkivet IX: Inngående korrespondanse 1939–1945," SAS.

42 Sigmund Feyling to O.J.B. Kvasnes, Oslo, 21 September 1943, "Privatbrever,"

Kvasnes Treason Trial Records, RA. For more examples of issues with clergy transfers, see Georg Falck-Hansen to Church Department, 20 April 1943, KKS; B. Nøding-Bentzen to Church Department, 29 April 1943, KKS.

43 "Instilling. Ministerpresidentens beslutning om å gi prostene rett til å bruke kirkene innen prostiet," box 7, Feyling Papers, RA.

44 Skancke, co-signed by Feyling, to clergy and parish councils, Oslo, 11 June 1943, Journal Nr. 1779 A. 1943, copy entered as Journal Nr. 1625, Bishop in Skien, "Journal 1943," Skien bispedømme, SAK.

45 Feyling to Minister President, Oslo, 7 November 1942, box 2, Feyling Papers, RA; Feyling, "Kirkesituasjonen," Oslo, 10 January 1943, copy in "Journal 1943," Skien bispedømme, Statsarkivet i Kristiansand, RA.

46 For NS reports, see Ludvig D. Zwilgmeyer to Church Department, Skien, 15 December 1942, L.D. Zwilgmeyer Treason Trials Records, RA; Georg Falck-Hansen's report for May 1943, Bjørgvin Diocese, KKS.

47 Feyling to Minister President (Quisling), "Reformasjon av kirken i 'den unge Luthers ånd," Oslo, 26 May 1942, KKS.

15. IN DEFENSE OF JEWS

1 Berggrav, "Til dagbok," 16 May 1940, box 35, Berggrav Papers, RA; Berggrav, *Kampen*, 54–55.

2 Berggrav, *Da kampen kom*, 54–55. Similar reports of Jewish persecution arrived from nearby Fredrikstad as well; Fjellbu, *Minner*, 27.

3 Berggrav, diary entries, 31 May and 1 June 1940, "Etterpå-Dagbok 1940–42," box 15, Berggrav Papers, RA; Fjellbu, *Minner*, 27.

4 Harry Koritzinsky is quoted by Abrahamsen to the effect that Terboven's speech of 25 September reassured Jews about remaining in Norway. That speech, however, made no reference to Jews or religion, and it is difficult to understand how anything else in it could be interpreted as reassuring. Koritzinsky probably meant Terboven's speech of 1 June; Abrahamsen, "Holocaust in Norway," 125.

5 [Harry Koritzinsky], "Jødene i Norge 1940–42," file D II cb: 4 "Handlingar rörande Norge 1942–46," Erling Eidem Papers, LA; newspaper clippings, Wagner War Crimes Trial Records, RA.

6 Quisling, *For Norges frihet*, 103–120.

7 Fjellbu, *Minner*, 106, 109.

8 "Rapport til Oslo Politikammer," 25 July 1945, Wagner War Crimes Trial Records, RA.

9 Skancke, co-signed by Feyling, to Bishop of Oslo, 13 June 1941, J. 2772 A. 1941, "Kopibok 1941 juni," Ministry of Church and Education Archives, RA.

10 Feyling, ed., *KH*, 123–25, and Austad, *KM*, 221–22.

11 Feyling to Christian Ihlen, 20 August 1941, box 1, Feyling Papers, RA.

12 Christian Ihlen to Church Department, 20 September 1941, in "Kirken 1940–42," pp. 202–4, and box 29, Berggrav Papers, RA.

13 Copies in Berggrav, "Da 'Kirkens Grunn' ble til," appendix 2 and appendix 3, p. 2, KKS.

14 Berggrav, "Da 'Kirkens Grunn' ble til," appendix 3, pp. 13–14, KKS.

15 Karl Barth to Eberhard Bethge, 1967, quoted in Hockenos, *Church Divided*, 173.

16 For my more extensive analysis of the church's failure to protect Jews, which links the church's response to anti-pluralism and latent anti-Semitism, see Hassing, "The Churches of Norway and the Jews," 517–22.

17 Fleming, *Hitler and the Final Solution*, 44; for a detailed analysis of the evolution of the policy, see Browning, *The Origins of the Final Solution*, 253–415, particularly 371, for late September as when Hitler decided on the "physical destruction" of all European Jews.

18 Eidsivating lagmannsrett, "Rettsbok for Eidsivating lagmannsrett. Hovedforhandling: Den offentlige påtalemyndighet mot Wilhelm Artur Konstantin Wagner," 13 August 1946, pp. 26–28, Wagner War Crimes Trial Records, RA.

19 For von Moltke's movements, see von Moltke, *Briefe an Freya*, 407–09.

20 Mendelsohn, *1940–1985*, 74.

21 Ulstein, *Flyktningar til Sverige 1940–43*, 230; Bloch-Hoell, "Den norske kirke," 15.

22 For the latest statistics, I have used "Flukten til Sverige," website of Senter for studier av Holocaust og livssynsminoriteter [Center for Studies of the Holocaust and Worldview Minorities], Oslo, www.hlsenteret.no. Accessed 20 September 2012.

23 Gestapo Report, November 1942, Larsen, Sandberg, and Dahm, eds., *Meldungen*, vol. 2, 879.

24 "Rettsbok for Oslo forhørsrett, 16 May 1946," p. 29, Frøyland Treason Trial Records, RA.

25 Depositions of Sara Blomberg Heed and Ingebjorg Slettten, Frøyland Treason Trial Records, RA; Øybekk, "Lars Andreas Frøyland," 71.

26 Baptist periodical *Banneret* (16 June 1945): 4, Methodist periodical *Kristelig Tidende* (1 March 1946): 118–19.

27 Hallesby et al. to Quisling, Oslo, 10 November 1942, in Austad, *KM*, 222–23. For Mangers's refusal to sign, see Rieber-Mohn, "Vi var med," 94, and Eidsvig, "Den katolske kirke," 350.

28 Abrahamsen, "Holocaust in Norway," 134; Christie, *Kirke i kamp,* 269; Bloch-Hoell, "Den norske kirke," 15.

29 The following supported the protest: the University Theological Faculty and Seminary for Practical Theology, Free Faculty of Theology and Seminary for Practical Theology, Norwegian Lutheran Home Mission Society, Western Districts Home Mission Association, Norwegian Mission Society, Norwegian Lutheran China Mission Association, Santal Mission, Christian Buddhist Mission, Norwegian

Mission to Israel, Norway's Finn Mission Society, Norwegian Seamen's Mission, Seamen's Home Mission, Norwegian Mission among the Homeless, Norwegian Sunday School Association, Norwegian Christian Youth Association, Norway's Christian Student and Junior College Student League, Norway's Christian Student Movement, Norway's National Church League, Blue Cross, Christian Physicians Association, Norwegian Deacons Fraternal Association, Norwegian Baptist Society, Methodist Church, Norwegian Mission Association (Covenant Church), Norwegian Mission Alliance, Norwegian Sunday School Union, and the Salvation Army. The Pentecostal Assemblies had no central authority to speak for all congregations, but Osvald Orlien added his support later and informed Quisling of "the same deep sorrow" within Pentecostal churches; Osvald Orlien to Quisling, Oslo, 19 January 1943, KKS, and in Austad, *KM*, 223–24. For an example of parishes sending their own protests, see the case of Ålesund Church, where Leif Winsnes defended Jews from the pulpit, declared it a shame that the authorities confiscated Jewish property, and persuaded all but one of the 300 congregants to support his protest to the Church Department; Herlof Hansen to Nasjonal Samling Fylkesføreren, Ålesund, 2 November 1942, box 9, Feyling Papers, RA.

30 Abrahamsen, "Holocaust in Norway," 134; Christie, *Kirke i kamp,* 269.

31 "Martin Luthers mening om jødene" [Martin Luther's Opinion about Jews], *Aftenposten,* 24 November 1942; "Bort med jødene!" (Away with the Jews!], *Fritt Folk,* 25 November 1942.

32 Lars Frøyland to Church Department, Oslo, 26 November 1942, in Austad, *KM*, 224–25.

33 O. J. B. Kvasnes to Church Department, 4 December 1942, K.D. J. 7079, box 9, Feyling Papers, RA.

34 Ludvig D. Zwilgmeyer to Church Department, 27 November 1942, Zwilgmeyer Treason Trial Records, RA.

35 Mendelsohn, 1940–1985, 103–14.

36 Feyling to Hallesby et al., November 1942, Bispearkivet V: "Departementale skrivelser 1942–1945," SAS.

37 There is no evidence, to my knowledge, that Feyling thought Jews were to be deported to death camps; Feyling deposition, "Rapport til Oslo Politikammer (Landssvikavdelingen)," p. 12, Feyling Treason Trial Records, RA. This deposition is consistent with other statements.

38 Skancke, co-signed by Feyling, to Interior Department, 19 December 1942, "Div. Feyling saker fra serien: 'Opprydding blant presteskapet etter krigen 1941–46,'" box 10, Feyling Papers, RA.

39 Anna C. Andersen, Thoralf Bryne, and O. F. Olden for the Society of Friends to Schanche [sic], Stavanger, 31 December 1942, K.D. J. 0042, 4 January 1943, box 9, Feyling Papers, RA.

40 Oswald Orlien to Quisling, Oslo, 19 January 1943, KKS.

41 "Deportasjonen av de norske jødene," website of Senter for studier av Holocaust

og livssynsminoriteter [Center for Studies of the Holocaust and Worldview Minorities], Oslo, www.hlsenteret.no. Accessed 20 September 2012. See also Mendelsohn, *1940–1985*, 184–85, 223–41, 254.

16. AGAINST COMPULSORY LABOR SERVICE

1 Qtd. in Nøkleby, *Holdningskamp*, 250.
2 Gestapo Report, November 1942, in Larsen, Sandberg, and Dahm, eds., *Meldungen*, vol. 2, 909.
3 Roberts, *Storm of War*, 324, 344–45.
4 Calvocoressi and Wint, *Total War*, 401.
5 Semelin, *Unarmed*, 33.
6 Grimnes, *Hjemmefrontens ledelse*, 68.
7 For the letter, see Austad, *KM*, 232–33.
8 Full text in Christie, *Kirke i kamp*, 277–82; see also KKS.
9 Christie, *Kirke i kamp*, 278. On resistance to youth service, also see Nøkleby, *Holdningskamp*, 129–31
10 For an eyewitness account of the PCL's message read in church, see letter published in *Norsk Tidend*, 13 February 1943; the Church Department recorded 17 January as the date of the reading; *Aftenposten*, 13 February 1943. See also Christie, *Kirke i kamp*, 278.
11 Christie, *Kirke i kamp*, 282–83.
12 Ibid., 283.
13 Quisling, "Vidkun Quislings tale den 1 februar 1943," pp. 1–19. The section dealing with Christianity and the church was published as a separate brochure entitled "Ministerpresidenten uttaler seg om kirken og kristendommen," NU 907, NB.
14 Schjelderup, *Over bakkekammen*, 70.
15 Christie, *Kirke i kamp*, 287; Schübeler, *Kirkekampen*, 220.
16 Bohn, "Det tyske Reichskommissariat," 133, 129.
17 Bull, *Klassekamp*, 375; Fjørtoft, *Oppgjøret*, 201.
18 Schjelderup, *Over bakkekammen*, 72.
19 Ibid., 73.
20 Grimnes, *Hjemmefrontens ledelse* , 159–60.
21 Ibid., 154.
22 Ibid., 96, and 79 for membership in 1941–42.
23 Ibid., 192.
24 Gjelsvik, *Hjemmefronten*, 106.
25 Ibid, 105.
26 Christie, *Kirke i kamp*, 287.
27 Schübeler, *Kirkekampen*, 222.
28 Ibid., 220.
29 Christie, *Kirke i kamp*, 289.
30 Ibid., 288–89.

31 Ibid., 288.

32 Ibid., 289–90.

33 Report of March 1943, Larsen, Sandberg, and Dahm, eds., *Meldungen*, vol. 2, 1018, 1044.

34 Gjelsvik, *Hjemmefronten*, 108.

35 Tor Skjønsberg, qtd. in Gjelsvik, *Hjemmefronten*, 108.

36 Alex Johnson, qtd. in Gjelsvik , *Hjemmefronten*, 110.

37 Tor Skjønsberg, qtd. in Gjelsvik, *Hjemmefronten*, 109.

38 Gjelsvik, *Hjemmefronten*, 110.

39 Schübeler, *Kirkekampen*, 222.

40 Ibid., 223.

41 Ole Hallesby, cited by Schübeler, and Schübeler himself, in Schübeler, *Kirkekampen*, 221, 224; Handeland, *Kristent samråd*, 47.

42 For Hallesby's account of the arrest, see Schübeler, *Kirkekampen*, 224–27; for Hope's, see Handeland, *Ludvig Hope*, 233–34; for the protest's international distribution, see Schübeler, *Kirkekampen*, 222, 224.

43 Hallesby qtd. in Schübeler, *Kirkekampen*, 226.

44 Ibid.

17. BETWEEN THE TIMES

1 Paul Tillich, *Against the Third Reich*, 163.

2 Qtd. in Ryan, *Longest Day*, 150–51.

3 Dahl, *Fører for fall*, 435.

4 Quisling, *Ministerpresident Vidkun Quislings tale i Oslo den 14. mai 1944*, 2–3.

5 Kjeldstadli, *Hjemmestyrkene*, 211.

6 Vilhelm H. Günther, "Die Norwegischen Kirche in Erster Halbjahr 1943," 15 (137), Kleine Erwerbungen 298/5, V.H. Günther Papers, BA.

7 In the early 1900s, the state was too slow to build churches in response to urban migration, so the "small church" movement undertook to fund and build practical churches in high-growth urban areas.

8 Gestapo Report, July 1943, in Larsen, Sandberg, and Dahm, eds., *Meldungen*, vol. 2, 1170.

9 Schübeler, *Kirkekampen*, 229, 238–39.

10 Falck-Hansen to Quisling, quoted in report of April 1943, in Larsen, Sandberg, and Dahm, eds., *Meldungen*, vol. 2, 1066. Other NS members also suggested measures to be taken against the clergy: for a recommendation of three to four transfers a year, see Reidar Johansen to Bjørgvin Bishop (Georg C. Falck-Hansen), Stord, 24 March 1943, KKS; for a demand for more evictions, see Lars Kraggerud to Church Department, Lunner, 6 March 1943, KKS, and NS Personalkontor to Church Department, Oslo, 20 April 1943, KKS; for other suggestions, see Axel Aass to Skancke, Hamar, 21 July 1943, box 5, Feyling Papers, RA.

11 That Feyling was behind the policy seems clear from several documents; see his reply to the State Police, Oslo, 7 August 1943, J. 2203 A. 1943, in A. Kirke-Departementet, Kopibok 1943, 3. kvartal, 1639–2293, RA.

12 See "Hemmelig," report on Feyling's conference with State Police officer Lande-rud, 6 September 1943, box 19, Feyling Papers, RA; see also Skancke, co-signed by Feyling, "'Kirkestriden' og dens behandling," Oslo, 20 September 1943, KKS.

13 Feyling to Attorney General Jørgen Nordvik, Oslo, 2 September 1943, box 10, Feyling Papers, RA.

14 Feyling to Lederen av Statspolitiet, Oslo, 14 September 1943, J. 2567 A. 1943, in A. Kirkedepartmentet, Kopibok 1943, 3. kvartal, 1639–2293, 2187, RA.

15 Falck-Hansen proposed the group internment solution in a meeting with Feyling and Bergen State Police Inspector Granaas on 9 February 1943; see Granaas to Lederen av Statspolitiet (Karl Marthinsen), Bergen, 9 February 1943, Falck-Hansen Treason Trial Records, RA.

16 Carlsen, *Kirkefronten*, 205.

17 Names of the ordained are listed in Carlsen, *Kirkefronten*, 193; Krohn-Hansen, *Brente jord*, 189–92.

18 The figures on the expulsions are given in an article by H.C. Christie in *Aften-posten*, 15 and 17 August 1945; Norrman's figure is 127 in *Quislingkyrkan*, 216.

19 Fure, *Universitetet i kamp*, 59–62, 86–87.

20 Ibid., 199–201.

21 Schübeler, *Kirkekampen*, 228.

22 Brodersen, *Mellom frontene*, 71–73.

23 Bloch-Hoell, "Den norske kirke," 17–18.

24 Schübeler, *Kirkefronten*, 238–39.

25 Bloch-Hoell, "Den norske kirke," 19–20. On the basis of documents he discov-ered in the Norwegian School of Theology's archives, Bloch-Hoell corrects Einar Molland's account ascribing its closure to a student boycott.

26 Molland, "Kirkens kamp," 70.

27 Aulén, "Norska prästvigningar i Strängnäs domkyrka," 111–18.

28 "Kirkelig Rådsmøte 3. og 4. desember 1943," box 2, Feyling Papers, RA.

29 Norrman, *Quislingkyrkan*, 334.

30 Feyling to Leader of State Police, Oslo, 16 December 1943, "Thunem-Feyling saken," DMS.

31 Feyling to Quisling, 29 April 1944, "Utdrag av dokumenter i Mappe I i offentlig straffesak ved Eidsivating lagmanssrett," Feyling Treason Trial Records, RA.

32 Einar Amdahl to Landssvikpolitiet, Stavanger, "Erklæring angående forhenvæ-rende NS Biskop O. J. B. Kvasnes og Det Norske Misjonsselskap," 17 September 1946, Kvasnes Treason Trial Records, RA.

33 Ørnulf Skjæveland, "Utkast til meddelelse til N.T.B. Ad. Norsk Misjonsselskap. N.M.S.s Hovedstyre i en kritisk stilling," box 5, Feyling Papers, RA.

34 Amdahl to Landssvikpolitiet, Stavanger, "Erklæring angående forhenværende NS Biskop O. J. B. Kvasnes og Det Norske Misjonsselskap," 17 September 1946, Kvasnes Treason Trial Records, RA.

35 Feyling to Sikkerhetspoliti, Oslo, 6 June 1944, Feyling Treason Trial Records, RA.

36 Feyling to "kansellisjef" Lundestad, Oslo, 7 June 1944; Feyling to Foreningskontoret, Oslo, 8 June 1944, Feyling Treason Trial Records, RA.

37 Per Gjerstad to NS General Secretariat, Stavanger, 23 June 1944, KKS.

38 For a detailed analysis of Thunem and his actions, see Berge, "Skuffelser og svik," 187–263.

39 "Det norske Misjonsselskap har i lang tid drevet kommunistisk undergravingsarbeid," *Fritt Folk*, 6 July 1944.

40 Amdahl to Landssvikpolitiet, "Erklæring angående forhenværende NS Biskop O. J. B. Kvasnes og Det Norske Misjonsselskap," Stavanger, 17 September 1946, Kvasnes Treason Trial Records, RA.

41 Ibid.

42 On dissent within the church, see an untitled, undated letter from an unidentified group of clergy, "Rapporter fra Nidaros," KKS.

43 "The Grini Book, which lists Norwegians interned at Grini, has many examples of "utterances hostile to the state" or "utterances hostile to Germany" as reasons for internment; Lange and Schreiner, *Griniboken*.

44 Nøkleby, *Skutt*, 194.

45 Ibid., 146–51, 222–23. See also Bjønnes-Jacobsen's account in Schübeler, *Kirkekampen*, 340–42.

46 See "Fengslede," "Oversikter," KKS. This is not an entirely accurate list; it excludes, for example, the jurist, Kristian Hansson, who was a member of the PCL, imprisoned in Oslo and then placed under house arrest in Tjøme for the rest of the occupation.

47 For more on Boge, see Martinsen, "Ingolf Boge," www.kyrkja.net/boge.htm, a website that also has a photo of him taken on 12 April 1942 reading *The Foundation of the Church* to his congregants in Fjell, on the island of Stora Sotra, west of Bergen; accessed 15 September 2012. See also Carlsen, *Kirkefronten*, 184. For more on Thu, see the notice in "Kirken i Dag," dated (in pencil) August 1944, KKS.

48 PCL, "Kirken idag: Påske 1944," KKS.

49 There has been no detailed study based on the records of each clergyman. PCL lists occasionally include names without dates, hence the approximate figures; the records are accurate enough, however, to indicate the trend; see "Fengslede," KKS.

50 For first figure, see "Forviste" and "I Sv.," KKS; for the second, see Christie, *Kirke i kamp*, 325–26, and originals in KKS.

51 Christie, *Kirke i kamp*, 325–26, and originals in KKS.

52 "Kirken og overgangstiden," KKS.

53 PCL, "Hilsen mellom prestebrødre Pinsen 1944: Kristi kirke og dens gjerning," KKS.

54 Reports from the dioceses, KKS.

55 Andreas Seierstad to Gabriel Skagestad, 31 December 1944, KKS.

56 Wollert Krohn-Hansen to PCL, 19 August 1943, KKS.

18. THE RECKONING

1   For Steltzer's story, see his autobiography, *Sechzig Jahre Zeitgenosse.*

2   On Fjellbu's decision to flee to Sweden and the events leading to his arrival in Kirkenes, see Fjellbu, *Minner,* 166ff.

3   Skodvin, *Krig og okkupasjon,* 258.

4   Eriksen and Halvorsen, *Frigjøring,* 112.

5   Roberts, *Storm of War,* 520, 556–57. There are ongoing debates about World War II casualty statistics; some estimates rise to 70 million.

6   Dahl et.al., *Norsk krigsleksikon,* 228.

7   Feyling burned papers on 8 May and was arrested the next day; deposition of Sigmund Feyling taken by Jørund Kårstad, Oslo, 29 August 1945, Feyling Treason Trial Papers, RA.

8   Berg, *For godvilje,* 37.

9   Kolsrud, *En splintret stat,* 108–10.

10 Minutes of the Second Bishops' Conference, 15–21 June 1945, KUD A Kontoret, box 309, RA; "Den Midlertidige Kirkeledelse fremdeles i funksjon," *Dagen,* 30 June 1945; Berggrav, "Kirkeledelsens kompetanse," *Dagen,* 1 February 1946.

11 [Berggrav], "1945. De to første Bispemøter. Mai og juni 1945. A. Historikk siden sist. B. Første møte 9–12. mai 1945. C. Annet møte 15. og 21 juni 1945." KUD A Kontoret, box 309, RA.

12 [Berggrav], "1945. De to første Bispemøter" KUD A Kontoret, box 309, RA. For copies of telegraphic greetings from abroad, see "Utlandets kirker hilser Norge," *Vårt Land,* 31 August 1945. For reinstatement of resigned clergy, see Church of Norway's bishops to the Church of Norway's parishes and clergy, Circular 1, Oslo, 9 May 1945, box 309, KUD A Kontoret, RA. For the charges against NS clergy, see also *Dagen,* 25 June 1945.

13 Bishops to clergy and congregations, 11 May 1945, KKS.

14 Reports from the Baptist, Methodist, and Lutheran free churches, KKS.

15 On the legal basis, see Andenæs, *Vanskelige oppgjøret,* 105–13.

16 Berggrav, "Folkedommen over NS."

17 On the article's representativeness and centrality in the debate, see Andenæs, *Vanskelige oppgjøret,* 60–61, and Fjørtoft, *Oppgjøret,* 72–73.

18 Berggrav, "Folkdommen over NS," 40.

19 Inge Lønning, quoted and confirmed by Heiene, *Berggrav,* 379.

20 For the protest of the Society of Friends, see "Kvekerne mot dødstraff," *Dagen,* 22 June 1945; for the Methodists, see District Superintendents of the Methodist Church, "Tilsynsmennenes fellesrapport," 135.

21 Investigative Commission of 1945, *Innstilling,* 223–31. For a contemporary indictment, see Fjørtoft, *Oppgjøret,* 74.

22 Heiene, *Berggrav*, 377, 381.

23 Qtd. in Høidal, *Quisling*, 550.

24 Eidsivating lagstols landssvikavdeling, *Straffesak mot Vidkun Quisling*, 216–20.

25 Ibid., 366, 368, 370.

26 "Universistiske strøtanker," written at Akershus, 1–6 October 1945, ms. fol. 3920 IX, Quisling Papers, RA. *From the World of Prayer* was first published in 1928 and is still in print in Norwegian, German, and English, along with several other of Hallesby's devotional works (what we would now call works on spirituality).

27 Bratteli and Myhre, *Quislings siste dager*, 190.

28 "Universistiske strøtanker," Quisling Papers, RA; Bratteli and Myhre, *Quislings siste dager,* 185, 191; Quisling to Maria Quisling, undated letter, Akershus, 1945, ms. fol. 3920 IX 6, Quisling Papers, RA.

29 Unless otherwise specified, my account is extracted from the official record of the charges and sentencing published in *Norsk Retstidende* 113 (1947): 165–92.

30 Devik, "Ragnar Skancke," 446.

31 "Rettsbok for Eidsivating lagmannsrett, Oslo, 7 June 1949," Feyling Treason Trial Records, RA.

32 For the charges on which Feyling was sentenced, see "Rettsbok for Oslo forhørsrett," 21 March 1947, Feyling Treason Trial Records, RA.

33 Deposition of Feyling taken by Odd Kvalvik, Oslo, 16 September 1946, Feyling Treason Trial Records, RA.

34 Deposition of Sigmund Feyling taken by Odd Kvalvik, Oslo, 15 January 1946, Feyling Treason Trials Records, RA.

35 Larsen, "Rettsoppgjøret," 20.

36 Ibid., 32; Andenæs, *Vanskelige oppgjøret*, 229.

37 Larsen, "Rettsoppgjøret," 24; Oftestad, "..uverdige til å være evangeliets tjenere," 77.

38 Clergy who did not appeal to Romans 13:1 explained that they simply did not think the NS government was illegal or that it had committed acts that justified the church's non-cooperation. For examples, see deposition of Georg Christian Falck-Hansen taken by Ølvar Berven, "Rapport til herr politimesteren i Kongsvinger," Kongsvinger, 9 June 1945, Falck-Hansen Treason Trial Records, RA; and deposition of H. O. Hagen to Lars Lofthus, "Rapport til Oslo Politikammer (Landssvikavdelingen)," Oslo, 17 September 1945, Hagen Treason Trial Records, RA. See also Larsen, "Rettsoppgjøret," 14.

39 Larsen, "Rettsoppgjøret," 14–15.

40 When Berggrav had seemed to endorse the NS, in 1940, the Church of Norway did recognize the state, which is why Berggrav had to speak as he did. After the war, he explained that he gave the advice on the assumption that most would understand what he really meant; Larsen, "Rettsoppgjøret," 15.

41 Eidsivating lagmannsrett, *Straffesak mot Vidkun Quisling*, 369.

42 Dahl et. al., *Norsk krigsleksikon*, 180.

43 Aarflot, *Bisperåd*, 100n106.

EPILOGUE: LEGACIES

1 Austad considers the church's postwar era as ending in 1953, "Kirkekampen—et intermesso?," 21. In this section, I draw on Lundestad, "Hovedtendenser i norsk politikk," 451–519, who sees the political postwar era as ending in 1965.

2 Furre, *Norsk historie*, 142; Lundestad, "Hovedtendenser," 453–55.

3 Tschudi, *Norsk kirke*, 129–38; Wisløff, *Norsk kirkehistorie*, 475; Løsneslokken and Hjemdal, *På ditt ord*, 147; Rudvin, *Norske lutherske indremisjonsselskap*, 424–25.

4 Moe, *Levet og lært*, 161–62. Some clergy did realize the depth of the patriotic motives in support for the church. Thorleif Boman, for example, thought most of the monetary support for the clergy in eastern Norway after 5 April 1942 came from people who were seldom in church; see "Hvorfor ble Berggrav, Hallesby og Hope innesperret," *Dagen*, 10 November 1945.

5 Ronald Fangen expressed the disappointed mood in "Situasjon og oppgave," *Vårt Land*, 31 August 1945; Pryser, *Klassen og nasjonen*, 179; Arne Fjellbu, "Kirkens stilling og oppgaver i dag," *Vårt Land*, 31 August 1946.

6 Tschudi, *Norsk kirke*, 134–138, 142; Conrad Bonnevie-Svendsen, "Norges kirke idag," 12 October 1945.

7 Solum, *Kryssende spor*, 85.

8 Editorial, *Vårt Land*, 31 August 1945.

9 See Tønnessen's summary of Christian postwar anti-secularism in "'. . . et trygt og godt hjem?'" 360.

10 Arne Fjellbu, "Kirkens stilling og oppgaver i dag," *Vårt Land*, 31 August 1946.

11 Arne Fjellbu, cited in Wisløff, *Norsk kirkehistorie* , 475.

12 Norborg, *Vekkeren*, 212.

13 Løsnesløkken and Hjemdal, *På ditt ord*, 149.

14 Olav Valen-Sendstad, "Grunnstrømninger i den norske kirke i dag," *Dagen*, 5 October 1945; Tschudi, *Norsk kirke*, 125; Egil Brekke, "Kirkens oppgaver etter krigen," *Aftenposten*, 5 July 1945; Lavik, *Spenningen*, 215.

15 Berggrav, *Kirkens ordning*.

16 Løvlie, *Kirke, stat og folk*, 41.

17 Ibid., 45.

18 Ibid., 100.

19 Tønnessen, "'. . . et trygt og godt hjem for alle?,'" 285, 307–8.

20 Qtd. in "Kirken må være en bekjennelseskirke," *Vårt Land*, 20 September 1945.

21 My account of the Hell conflict is based on Løsnesløkken and Hjemdal, *På ditt ord*, 160–62, and Wisløff, *Norsk kirkehistorie*, 499–500. Schjelderup's side of the debate is also documented in Repstad, *Kristian Schjelderup*, 349–89.

22 Austad, *Kirkens Grunn*, 16.

23 Ibid., 231.

24 Ibid., 230–32.

25 Berggrav, *The Norwegian Church*, 15–17.

26 On the classical Lutheran positions on these issues, see Molland, *Konfesjonskunskap*, 192–94, 197, 212; see also Molland, "Kirkekampens historie, " 128–30.

27 Sanders, *Protestant Concepts*, 60–61, 66. Torleiv Austad has kept the theology of the Norwegian resistance at the forefront of the ongoing reformulations of doctrine in Lutheran and ecumenical theology; see Austad, "The Doctrine of God's Twofold Governance in the Norwegian Church Struggle from 1940 to 1945: Fifteen Theses."

28 PCL, "Hilsen mellom prestebrødre. Pinsen 1944. Kristi kirke og dens gjerning," KKS.

29 Berggrav, "Two Addresses Given at the Ecumenical Service in the Cathedral of St. Peter, Geneva," 20 February 1946, *The Christian News-Letter* no. 256, 20 March 1946, 7–9.

30 Molland, "Kirkekampens historie," 127.

31 Molland, "Den norske kirkekamps status," 180.

32 For more on this, see Hassing, "Ecumemical Aspects," and "Norwegian Free Churches."

33 Hallesby, "Bekjennelsestroskapen idag," *Dagen*, 6 October 1945.

34 The free churches and the board of *Vårt Land* reached agreement on free church participation in June 1947; see "Evangeliske Samfunns Fellesråd kaller Norges frikirkelige til effektiv innsats for Vårt Land," *Vårt Land*, 19 June 1947.

35 See Council of Autonomous Organizations' explanation in *Dagen*, 23 March 1946, and Ronald Fangen's opposition to it in "En 'bitter rot,'" *Vårt Land*, 13 February 1946 and "Guddomelig eller menneskelig strategi?," *Vårt Land*, 11 March 1946; editorial, *Dagen*, 27 January 1947.

36 Egil Brekke, "Vi trenger et økumenisk hjemmearbeid," *Dagen*, 26 September 1946; Berggrav quoted in "Spørsmålet om et kirkenes fellesråd under debatt," *Dagen*, 11 October 1946.

37 On the Contact Circle, see Bloch-Hoell, "Kontakt kretsen for kirkesamfunn," 114–27; Berggrav to Arnold Øhrn, Oslo, 21 June 1945, NKR (Note: I received a copy of this document from Norges frikirkeråd; presumably the archives containing this document were also transferred when Norges frikirkeråd fused with Norges kristne råd [NKR]); Bloch-Hoell, *Økumenikk*, 122.

38 Løsnesløkken and Hjemdal, *På ditt ord*, 155. The confessionalist Lutherans were also the major reason that free church Christians could not teach religion classes; Rudvin, *Indremisjonsselskap*, 424.

39 The estimate of the Contact Circle's importance comes from Bloch-Hoell, *Økumenikk*, 121.

40 Østnor, *Kirkens enhet*, 50.

41 Poulsen, "Uklare linjer," 320.

42 Poulsen, "Uklare linjer," 320–328.

43 Lauha, "Finland: Ansvar för folket förblir kyrkans kallelse," 54; Klemelä, "Finlands kyrka under andra världskriget," 329; Murtorinne, "Die nordischen Kirchen," 221–223.

44 Montgomery, "Den svenska linjen är den kristna linjen," 354–356.

45 On the Scandinavian bishops' conference, see Schörring, "Introduktion," 11–13.

46 Bishops of the Church of Norway to parish councils and clergy, Oslo, November 1946 ("Rundskriv 1946 om Norges kirke og det ekumeniske (mellom-kirkelige) arbeid."), in "Protokoll for Bispemøtet November 1946, box 309, KUD A Kontoret, RA.

47 Heiene, "Den norske kirke og økumenikken," 387.

48 *Time*, 25 December 1944.

49 Wilhelm Visser 't Hooft to Berggrav, 2 October 1945, General Secretariat Correspondence, WCC.

50 Sharp, "Technique of Nonviolent Action," 162, 164, 168; Skodvin, "Norwegian Non-Violent Resistance," 149–51; Semelin, *Unarmed*, 66–67.

51 Austad, "Pacifists," 399.

52 Barth, "The Protestant Churches," 269.

53 On the German church struggle as a lesson to both the Norwegian and Dutch churches in their resistance to Nazism, see Boyens, *Kirchenkampf und Ökumene 1939–1945*, 165–66.

54 Bracher, *German Dictatorship*, 389.

55 Austad, *Kirkens Grunn*, 20n22. I have drawn on Austad's list of comparisons and contrasts in *Kirkens Grunn*, 20–22.

56 Two experts, Stein Ugelvik Larsen and Torleiv Austad, disagree on the long-term effects of the church struggle, but not on its significance in the twentieth-century history of the church. Larsen, "Kirkekampens betydning," 131–48, and Austad, "Kirkekampen - et intermesso?" 20–35.

57 Burleigh, *Church History of Scotland*, 353. Interestingly, Burleigh does not mention the Church of Norway in 1942 as an analogous event to the Disruption, perhaps because it did not result in establishment of a free church, but he offers "parallel" examples from the nineteenth century Reformed tradition in Geneva (1849), Holland (1886), and two Swiss cantons, Vaud in 1845 and Neuchâtel in 1873.

58 On the Disruption and its significance in Scottish history, see Lynch, *Scotland*, 397–402.

59 Burleigh, *Church History of Scotland*, 361.

60 Boas, *Religious Resistance in Holland*, 11.

61 Warmbrunn, *The Dutch under German Occupation*, 156–64.

62 Scholars more knowledgeable than I will have to consider the Norwegian case in relation to the Roman Catholic resistance and that of minority Protestant churches, such as the French.

63 Lincoln, "Notes," 266–92.

64 Lincoln, "Notes," 277.

Bibliography

For reasons of space, the bibliography only includes archival collections referred to in the notes, published works cited in the text and notes, and a few additional works that have contributed to the book. Where primary sources have been published in books, I have used published versions in the notes.

ARCHIVAL COLLECTIONS

Austad Collection
    Torleiv Austad's private collection
Borgen Collection
    Peder Borgen's private collection
Bundesarchiv, Koblenz (BA)
    Vilhelm H. Günther Papers
Evangelisches Zentralarchiv, Berlin (EZ)
    Record Groups 5/130, 5/161, 5/198–200, 5/223. Includes correspondence and reports of V. H. Günther with Foreign Department of the German Evangelical Church, 1933–1941
Hoover Institution on War, Revolution and Peace, Palo Alto, California (HI)
    German Auswärtiges Amt (Foreign Office), Microfilm Collection
Landsarkivet, Uppsala (LA)
    Erling Eidem Papers
Nasjonalbiblioteket, Oslo (NB)
    Kirkekampens sentralarkiv (KKS). This is the most important collection of documents on the church resistance. The collection includes a large number of documents and copies of documents collected by the CCC and PCL during the occupation, including voluminous documents smuggled out of the Church Department. Many of these were collected in "Kirken 1940–1942," which is often cited

in the text. Also in the collection are accounts of the writing of *The Foundation of the Church* (Kirkens Grunn) and responses to a postwar questionnaire submitted by bishops, deans, and clergy about their experiences during the war. I understand that archivists have organized the collection since I studied it. Major documents have been published by Sigmund Feyling in *Kirkelig hvitbok* (Church White Papers), published in 1942, and by Torleiv Austad in *Kirkelig motstand*, published in 2005 with extensive notes and analysis.

   Manuscript collection

National Archives, Washington, D.C. (NA)

   Department of State Files. Diplomatic Branch

Nordiska Ekumeniska Institutet, Uppsala (NEI) Incoming Information EV: 2 1941–1942

Norges Hjemmefrontmuseum, Oslo (NHM)

   Conrad Bonnevie-Svendsen interview, 12 October 1972

   Kåre Norum interview, 25 August 1970

Norges Kristne Råd, Oslo (NKR)

   Archive

Det Norske Misjonsselskap, Stavanger (NMS)

   Einar Amdahl Papers

   Adolf Thunem-Sigmund Feyling Case Records

Public Record Office, London (PRO)

   Political Intelligence Department, Foreign Office Records

Riksarkivet, Oslo (RA)

   Private Papers

      Eivind Berggrav Papers

      Sigmund Feyling Papers

      Vidkun Quisling Papers

   Ministry of Church and Education Records

      Treason Trial Records:

         Falck-Hansen, Georg C.

         Feyling, Sigmund

         Frøyland, Lars

         Hagen, Hans O.

         Hansteen, Christian F.

         Kvasnes, Ole J. B.

         Landerud, Ole O.

         Quisling, Vidkun

         Riisnæs , Sverre

         Skancke, Ragnar

         Solberg, Nicolas O.K.

         Zwilgmeyer, Ludvig D.

   War Crimes Trial Records

      Wagner, Wilhelm A.K.

Riksarkivet, Stockholm (RAS)
  Utrikesdepartementet (Foreign Office) Records
Skodvin Collection
  Private collection of the late Magne Skodvin. This refers to a copy of a small por-
  tion of one of Alfred Huhnhäuser's postwar depositions that relates to the church;
  I have a copy courtesy of Magne Skodvin. Huhnhäuser's memoirs, which I have
  not read, are now in the Institut für Zeitgeschichte, Munich.
Statsarkivet, Hamar (SAH)
  Henrik Hille Papers.
Statsarkivet, Kristiansand (SAK)
  Skien Diocesan Records
Statsarkivet, Stavanger (SAS)
  Stavanger Diocesan Records
Universitetsbiblioteket, Lund (UBL)
  Gustaf Aulén Papers
Universitetsbiblioteket, Trondheim (UBT)
  Arne Fjellbu's Journal ("Dagbok"), 1940–1945
World Council of Churches Archives, Geneva (WCC)
  General Secretariat Records
  Nils Ehrenström Papers
  William Paton Papers

SECONDARY SOURCES

Aarflot, Andreas. *Bisperåd og kirkestyre: Bispemøtets rolle i den norske kirkestruk-turen 1917–1977* [Bishops' Council and Church Governance: The Role of the Bishops' Conference in the Norwegian Church Structure 1917–1977]. Bergen: Eide Forlag, 2011.

Aartun, Leiv Brynjulf and Sigurd Aartun. *Motstandskampen i skolene 1940–1942: Lærerstriden mot nazifiseringen* [The Resistance Struggle in the Schools 1940–1942: The Teachers' Battle Against Nazification]. Oslo: Orion Forlag, 2003.

Abrahamsen, Samuel. "The Holocaust in Norway." In *Contemporary Views on the Holocaust*, edited by Randolph L. Braham, 109–42. Boston, London, and The Hague: Kluver-Nijhoff Publishing Company, 1983.

———. *Norway's Response to the Holocaust: A Historical Perspective*. New York: Holocaust Library, 1991.

Ager, T. M. and Bjarne Høye. *The Fight of the Norwegian Church against Nazism.* New York: Macmillan Company, 1943.

Agøy, Nils Ivar. *Kirken og arbeiderbevegelsen: Spenninger, skuffelser, håp; Tiden fram til 1940* [The Church and the Labor Movement: Tensions, Disappointments, Hope; The Period to 1940]. Bergen: Fagbokforlaget, 2011.

Aker, Ivar [Ernst A. Schirmer]. "Nordendom og Austendom" [Northerndom and Easterndom]. *Ragnarok* 9, no. 1 (1943): 19–26.

Andenæs, Johannes. *Det vanskelige oppgjøret: Rettsoppgjøret etter okkupasjonen* [The Difficult Settlement: The Legal Settlement After the Occupation]. Oslo: Tanum, 1980.

Andenæs, Tønnes, ed. *The Constitution of Norway*. Oslo: Oslo University Press, 1960.

Aukrust, Knut. "'Ellers intet illegalt å bemerke': Om den politiske overvåkning av gudstjenester i Norge under 2. verdenskrig" ["Otherwise nothing illegal to note": About the Political Surveillance of Worship Services in Norway During the Second World War]. *Norsk Teologisk Tidsskrift* 90 (1990): 193–99.

Aulén, Gustaf. *Kan något kristet krav ställas på statslivet?* [Can Any Christian Condition Be Placed on State Life?]. Stockholm: Svenska Kyrkans Diakonistyrelses Bokförlag, 1940.

———. *Den norska kyrkostriden* [The Norwegian Church Struggle]. Världspolitikens dagsfrågor 1942 Nr. 5 [World Political Questions of the Day 1942 No. 5]. Stockholm: Utrikespolitiska institut, 1942.

———. "Norska prästvigningar i Strängnäs domkyrka" [Norwegian Ordinations in Strängnäs Church]. In *Festskrift til biskop Arne Fjellbu på 70-års dagen* [Festschrift to Bishop Arne Fjellbu On His 70th Birthday], edited by Johan B. Rian et al., 111–18. Oslo: Gyldendal Norsk Forlag, 1960.

Austad, Torleiv. "The Doctrine of God's Twofold Governance in the Norwegian Church Struggle from 1940 to 1945: Fifteen Theses." In *Lutheran Churches—Salt or Mirror of Society? Case Studies on the Theory and Practice of the Two Kingdoms Doctrine*, edited by Ulrich Duchrow in collaboration with Dorothea Millwood, 28–60. Geneva: Lutheran World Federation, 1977.

———. "Etikk under krigen: Kirkens etiske begrunnelse for den sivile motstand i Norge 1940–1945" [Ethics During the War: The Church's Ethical Justification for Its Civil Resistance in Norway 1940–1945]. In *Kyrkja under krigen: Bokutgåve av TKRS 1 1995* [The Church During the War: Book Edition av TKRS 1 1995], edited by Jan Ove Ulstein, 11–22. Volda: *Tidsskrift for Kirke, Religion og Samfunn*, Høgskulen i Volda, Møreforsking Volda, 1995.

———. "Kirkekampen—et intermesso?" [The Church Struggle—An Intermezzo?]. In *Statskirke i etterkrigssamfunn: Kirkehistoriske og sosiologiske synpunkter på Den norske kirke etter 1945* [State Church in Postwar Society: Church Historical and Sociological Perspectives on the Church of Norway After 1945], edited by Knut Lundby and Ingun Montgomery, 20–35. Oslo, Bergen, and Tromsø: Universitets-forlaget, 1981.

———. *Kirkelig Motstand: Dokumenter fra den norske kirkekamp under okkupasjonen 1940–45 med innledninger og kommentarer* [Church Resistance: Documents from the Norwegian Church Struggle During the Occupation 1940–45 with Introductions and Commentary]. Kristiansand: Høyskoleforlaget AS—Norwegian Academic Press, 2005.

———. *Kirkens Grunn: Analyse av en kirkelig bekjennelse fra okkupasjonstiden 1940–45* [The Foundation of the Church: Analysis of an Church Confession from the Occupation Era 1940–45]. Oslo: Luther Forlag, 1974.

————. "Pacifists in Nazi-Occupied Norway." In *Challenge to Mars: Essays on Pacifism from 1918 to 1945*, edited by Peter Brock and Thomas P. Socknat, 395–408. Toronto: University of Toronto Press, 1999.

————. "Der Widerstand der Kirche gegen den nationalsozialistischen Staat in Norwegen 1940–1945" [The Resistance of the Church to the National Socialist State in Norway 1940–1945]. *Kirchliche Zeitgeschichte* [Contemporary Church History] vol. 1, no. 1 (1988): 70–94.

————. "Sviktet kirken jødene under okkupasonen?" [Did the Church Betray the Jews During the Occupation?]. In *Dømmekraft i krise? Holdninger i kirken til jøder, teologi og NS under okkupasjonen* [Judgment in Crisis? Positions in the Church on Jews, Theology, and NS during the Occupation], by Torleiv Austad, Ottar Berge, and Jan Ove Ulstein, 17–109. *Kyrkjefag Profil nr. 18* [Church Subjects Profile No. 18.]. Trondheim: Akademika forlag, n.d. [2012].

Barnett, Victoria. *For the Soul of the People: Protestant Protest Against Hitler*. New York and Oxford: Oxford University Press, 1992.

Barth, Else Margarete. *Gud, det er meg: Vidkun Quisling som politisk filosof* [God, It's Me: Vidkun Quisling as Political Philosopher]. Oslo: Pax Forlag, 1996.

Barth, Karl. "The Protestant Churches in Europe." *Foreign Affairs* 21 (1942–1943): 260–75.

Berg, Paal. *For godvilje og rett: Taler og artikler* [For Good Will and Justice: Speeches and Articles]. Oslo: Gyldendal Norsk Forlag, 1947.

Berg, Pål A. *Kirke i krig: Den norske kirke under 2. verdenskrig 1940–45* [The Church in War: The Church of Norway During the Second World War 1940–1945]. Oslo: Genesis Forlag, 1999.

Berge, Ottar. "Skuffelser og svik" [Disappointment and Betrayal]. In *Dømmekraft i krise? Holdninger i kirken til jøder, teologi og NS under okkupasjonen* [Judgment in Crisis? Positions in the Church on Jews, Theology, and NS during the Occupation], by Torleiv Austad, Ottar Berge, and Jan Ove Ulstein, 187–265. *Kyrkjefag Profil nr. 18*. Trondheim: Akademika forlag, n.d. [2012].

Bergen, Doris. *Twisted Cross: The German Christian Movement in the Third Reich*. Chapel Hill: University of North Carolina Press, 1996.

Berger, Peter L. *The Sacred Canopy: Elements of a Theory of Religion*. Garden City, New York: Doubleday & Co.,1967.

Berggrav, Eivind. "Arresterte prester: Det dramatiske og det prinsipielle i tyske kirkekamp idag" [Arrested Pastors: The Dramatic and the Principled in the German Church Struggle Today]. *Kirke og Kultur* [Church and Culture] 42 (1935): 193–206.

————. *With God in the Darkness and Other Papers Illustrating the Norwegian Church Conflict*. Edited by George A.K. Bell. London: Hodder and Stoughton, 1943.

————. *Da kampen kom: Noen blad fra startåret* [When the Struggle Began: A Few Pages from the Opening Year]. Oslo: Land og Kirke, 1945.

————. "Folkedommen over NS: Hva vil være rett av oss?" [The People's Judgment on the NS: What Would Be Right of Us?]. *Kirke og kultur* [Church and Culture] 50 (1945): 6–44.

———. *Kirkens ordning i Norge: Attersyn og framblikk* [The Church's Polity in Norway: Retrospect and Prospect]. Oslo: Land og Kirke, 1945.

———. *Staten og mennesket: Oppgjør og framblikk* [The State and the Person: An Accounting and a Look Forward]. Oslo: Land og Kirke, 1945.

———. *The Norwegian Church in Its International Setting: The Burge Memorial Lecture.* London: SCM Press, 1946.

———. "Beretninginger om Den norske kirke i 1939, avgitt til det Kgl. Kirke- og Undervisningsdepartement av Den norske kirkes biskoper: I. Oslo bispedømme 1939" [Reports of the Church of Norway's Bishops in 1939, Provided to the Royal Ministry of Church and Education by the Church of Norway's Bishops: I. Oslo Diocese 1939]. In *Norvegia Sacra 1940: Aarbok til kunnskap om Den norske kirke i fortid og samtid 20* [Norvegia Sacra: Yearbook for Knowledge of the Church of Norway in the Past and the Present vol. 20], edited by Oluf Kolsrud, 150–65. Oslo: Den norske kirke, 1950.

———. *Man and State.* Translated by George Aus. Philadelphia: Muhlenberg Press, 1951.

———. "Stat og kirke idag etter luthersk syn: Foredrag på det lutherske verdensforbunds møte i Hannover 1952" [State and Church Today From a Lutheran Perspective: Lecture at the Lutheran World Federation's Conference in Hannover 1952," *Kirke og Kultur* [Church and Culture] 57 (1952): 449–462.

———. *Forgjeves for fred vinteren 1939–40: Forsøk og samtaler i Norden, Berlin og London* [In Vain for Peace in the Winter of 1939–40: Attempts and Conversations in the Nordic Countries, Berlin, and London]. Oslo: Land og Kirke, 1960.

———. *Front—fangenskap—flukt 1942–1945* [Front—Imprisonment—Escape 1942–1945]. Oslo: Land og Kirke, 1966.

Berggrav, Eivind, Ole Hallesby, Ludvig Hope, and J. Støren. *Under Guds veldige hånd: Taler i Calmeyergatens Misjonshus av O. Hallesby, J. Støren, L. Hope og E. Berggrav mandag 28. oktober 1940* [Under God's Mighty Hand: Speeches at the Calmeyer Street Mission Hall by O. Hallesby, J. Støren, L. Hope, and E. Berggrav, Monday, 28 October 1940]. Oslo: Gimnes, 1940.

Berglyd, Jostein. "Presten som ble landsforræder" [The Pastor Who Became a Traitor]. *Fast Grunn* 44 (1991): 329–34.

Bishops of the Church of Norway. "Neste fase i rettsoppgjøret: Biskopenes brev til justisministeren november 1946" [The Next Phase in the Legal Settlement: The Bishops' Letter to the Minister of Justice]. Oslo: Land og Kirke, 1946.

———."Beretninger om Den norske kirke i 1939" [Reports on the Church of Norway in 1939]. In *Norvegia Sacra: Aarbok til kunnskap om Den norske kirke i fortid og samtid* [Norvegia Sacra: Yearbook for Knowledge about the Church of Norway in the Past and the Present], 20 (1940), 150–204. Edited by Oluf Kolsrud. Oslo: Bishops of the Church of Norway, 1950.

Bloch-Hoell, Nils E. "Kontakt kretsen for kirkesamfunn" [Contact Circle for Church Communions]. *Tidsskrift for Teologi og Kirke* 45 (1974): 115–27.

———. *Økumenikk—fakta og meninger* [Ecumenics—Facts and Opinions]. Oslo: Land og Kirke and Gyldendal Norsk Forlag, 1976.

———. "Den norske kirke under okkupasjonen: Kirkekamp, illegal informasjonstjeneste og litt Mf-historie" [The Church of Norway During the Occupation: Church Struggle, Illegal Information Service, and a Little MF History]. *Tidsskrift for Teologi og Kirke* 66 (1995): 5–25.

Boas, J.H. *Religious Resistance in Holland.* London: The Netherlands Government Information Bureau, 1945.

Bohn, Robert. "Det tyske Reichskommissariet i Norge 1940–1945" [The German Reichskommissariat in Norway 1940–1945]. In *I krigens kjølvann: Nye sider ved norsk krigshistorie og etterkrigstid* [In the Wake of the War: New Aspects of Norwegian War History and the Postwar Era], edited by Stein Ugelvik Larsen, 119–33. Oslo: Universitetsforlaget, 1999.

———. *Reichskommissariat Norwegen: "Nationalsozialistische Neuordnung" under Kriegswirtschaft* [Reichskommissariat Norway: "National Socialist New Order" and Wartime Economy]. In *Beiträge zur Militärgeschichte* [Contributions to Military History], vol. 54. Munich: R. Oldenbourg Verlag, 2000.

Boman, Thorleif. "Kirken og dissenterne" [The Church and the Dissenters]. *Kirke og Kultur* 61 (1956): 565–72.

Bondurant, Joan V., ed., in association with Margaret W. Fisher. *Conflict: Violence and Nonviolence.* Chicago and New York: Aldine, Atherton, 1971.

Bonhoeffer, Dietrich. *Ethics. Dietrich Bonhoeffer Works*, vol. 6, general editor Wayne Whitson Floyd Jr. Edited by Ilse Tödt et al., English edition edited by Clifford J. Green. Translated by Reinhard Krauss, Charles C. West, and Douglass Stott. Minneapolis: Fortress Press, 2005.

Boyens, Armin. *Kirchenkampf und Ökumene 1933–1939: Darstellung und Dokumentation.* [Church Struggle and Ecumenism: Account and Documentation]. Munich: Chr. Kaiser Verlag, 1969.

———. *Kirchenkampf und Ökumene 1939–1945: Darstellung und Dokumentation unter besonderer Berücksichtigung der Quellen des Ökumenischen Rates der Kirchen.* [Church Struggle and Ecumenism: Account and Documentation With Special Attention to the Sources of the World Council of Churches]. Munich: Chr. Kaiser Verlag, 1973.

Bracher, Karl Dietrich. *The German Dictatorship: The Origins, Structure, and Effects of National Socialism.* Translated by Jean Steinberg. New York: Holt, Rinehart and Winston, 1970.

———. *The Age of Ideologies: A History of Political Thought in the Twentieth Century.* Translated by Ewald Osers. London: Methuen and Co., Ltd., 1984.

Bratteli, Tone, and Hans B. Myhre. *Quislings siste dager* [Quisling's Last Days]. Oslo: J.W. Cappelens Forlag, 1992.

Braw, Christian. "Quislings tro" [Quisling's Faith]. *Tidsskrift for Teologi og Kirke* 60 (1989): 1–18.

Breistein, Ingunn Folkestad. *Har staten bedre borgere?": Dissenternes kamp for religiøs frihet 1891–1969* [Does the State Have Better Citizens? The Dissenters' Struggle for Religious Freedom 1891–1959]. Trondheim: Tapir Akademisk Forlag, 2003.

Brodersen, Arvid. *Mellom frontene* [Between the Fronts]. Oslo: J.W. Cappelens Forlag, 1979.

Browning, Christopher R. *The Origins of the Final Solution: The Evolution of Nazi Jewish Policy, September 1939–March 1942.* Lincoln: University of Nebraska Press, 2004.

Bruknapp, Dag O. "Ideene splitter partiet" [The Ideas Split the Party]. In *Fra idé til dom: Noen trekk fra utviklingen av Nasjonal Samling* [From Idea to Verdict: A Few Aspects from the Development of National Union], edited by Rolf Danielsen and Stein Ugelvik Larsen, 9–47. Bergen, Oslo, and Tromsø: Universitetsforlaget, 1976.

Bull, Edvard. *Kommunisme og religion* [Communism and Religion]. Kristiania (Oslo): Det norske arbeiderpartis forlag, 1923.

Bull, Edvard (Jr.). *Klassekamp og felleskap 1920–1945* [Class Struggle and Solidarity 1920–1945]. *Norges historie* [Norway's History] vol. 13, edited by Knut Mykland. Oslo: Cappelens Forlag, 1979.

Bullock, Alan. *Hitler: A Study in Tyranny.* Revised edition. New York: Harper and Row, Publishers, 1962.

Burleigh, J.H.S. *A Church History of Scotland.* Edinburgh: Hope Trust, 1983.

Calvocoressi, Peter, and Guy Wint. *Total War: Causes and Courses of the Second World War.* Harmondsworth, UK: Penguin Books, 1974.

Carlsen, Ingvald B. *Kirkefronten i Norge under okkupasjonen 1940–1945* [The Church Front in Norway During the Occupation]. Oslo: H. Aschehoug & Co. (W. Nygaard), 1945.

Carsten, F. L. *The Rise of Fascism.* Berkeley: University of California Press, 1967.

Carter, April. "People Power and Protest: The Literature on Civil Resistance in Historical Context." In *Civil Resistance and Power Politics: The Experience of Nonviolent Action from Gandhi to the Present,* edited by Adam Roberts and Timothy Garton Ash, 25–42. Oxford: Oxford University Press, 2009.

Christensen, Chr. A.R. *Okkupasjonsår og etterkrigstid* [Occupation Years and Postwar Era]. *Vårt folks historie* [Our People's History] vol. 9, edited by Axel Coldevin, Thorleif Dahl, and Johan Schreiner. Oslo: H. Aschehoug & Co. (W. Nygaard), 1961.

Christie, H. C. *Den norske kirke i kamp* [The Church of Norway in Struggle]. Oslo: Land og Kirke, 1945.

Churchill, Winston S. *The Gathering Storm. The Second World War,* vol. 1. Boston: Houghton Mifflin Company, 1948.

Clark, Alan. *Barbarossa: The Russian-German Conflict, 1941–45.* New York: William Morrow and Company, 1965.

Cochrane, Arthur C. *The Church's Confession Under Hitler.* Pittsburgh Reprint Series no. 4, edited by Dikran Y. Hadidian. Pittsburgh: The Pickwick Press, 1976.

Conference at Oxford on Church, Community, and State. *The Churches Survey Their Task: The Report of the Conference at Oxford on Church, Community and State, July 1937.* London: Allen & Unwin, 1937. Note, in particular, reports 2 and 7 on church and state.

Conway, John S. *The Nazi Persecution of the Churches 1933–1945.* New York: Basic Books, 1968.

Dahl, Hans Fredrik. *Norge mellom krigene: Det norske samfunn i krise og konflikt 1918–1940* [Norway Between the Wars: Norwegian Society in Crisis and Conflict 1918–1914]. Oslo: Pax Forlag, 1971.

———. "Seks myter om okkupasjonen: En dokumentasjon ved Hans Fredrik Dahl" [Six Myths About the Occupation: A Documentation by Hans Fredrik Dahl]. In *Krigen i Norge* [The War in Norway], edited by Hans Fredrik Dahl, 175–94. Oslo: Pax Forlag A/S, 1974.

———. *Dette er London* [This is London]. *NRK i krig 1940–1945* [NRK (Norwegian Radio Corporation) in War], vol. 1. Oslo: J.W. Cappelens Forlag, 1978.

———. *Den norske nasjonalsosialismen: Nasjonal Samling 1933–1945 i tekst og billeder* [The Norwegian National Socialism: National Union 1933–1945 in Text and Pictures]. Oslo: Pax Forlag A.s, 1982.

———. *Vidkun Quisling: En fører blir til* [Vidkun Quisling: A Leader is Formed]. *Vidkun Quisling*, vol. 1. Oslo: H. Aschehoug & Co. (W. Nygaard), 1991.

———. *Vidkun Quisling: En fører for fall* [Vidkun Quisling: A Leader Before the Fall]. *Vidkun Quisling*, vol. 2. Oslo: H. Aschehoug & Co. (W. Nygaard), 1992.

———. "Fra Brand til Quisling: Litt om kirkekampens dramatis personae" [From Brand to Quisling: A Little About the Church Struggle's Dramatis Personae]. In *Kyrkja under krigen: Bokutgåve av TKRS 1 1995* [The Church During the War: Book Edition of TKRS 1 1995], edited by Jan Ove Ulstein, 3–9. Volda: *Tidsskrift for Kirke, Religion og Samfunn*; Høgskulen i Volda; Møreforsking Volda, 1995.

Dahl, Hans Fredrik et al. *Norsk krigsleksikon* [Norwegian War Dictionary]. Oslo: J.W. Cappelens Forlag A.S., 1995.

Dahl, Hans Fredrik, Bernt Hagtvet, and Guri Hjeltnes. *Den norske nasjonalsosialismen: Nasjonal Samling 1933–1945 i tekst og bilder* [The Norwegian National Socialism: Nasjonal Samling (National Union) 1933–1945]. Oslo: Pax Forlag, 1982.

Dale, Aasmund. "Kirken på vikende front i Norge? Forholdet mellom skole og kirke (i 30-årene)" [The Church On A Receding Front in Norway? The Relationship Between Church and School (in the 30s)]. In *Kirken, krisen og krigen* [The Church, the Crisis, and the War], edited by Ingun Montgomery and Stein Ugelvik Larsen, 82–86. Bergen, Oslo, and Tromsø: Universitetsforlaget, 1982.

Danbolt, Ove C. "Ronald Fangens kamp mot nazismen i 1930-årene" [Ronald Fangen's Fight Against Nazism]. *Fast Grunn* 21 (1968): 233–38.

Debes, Jan. *1940–45. Sentraladministrasjonens historie* [The Central Administration's History], vol. 5, edited by Torstein, Jens Eckhoff, Arup Seip, and Ingeborg Wilberg. Oslo: Universitetsforlaget, 1980.

"Den haugianske linje: En enquete" [The Haugean Line: A Survey]. *Norsk Kirkeblad* 37 (1940): 574–79, 598–600.

Devik, Olaf. "Skancke, Ragnar." In *Norsk biografisk leksikon* [Norwegian Biographical Dictionary], vol. 13: 442–47.

Dietrichson, Johannes Ø. "Trekk fra kampen mot ungdomstjenesten" [Aspects of the Struggle Against the Youth Service]. In *Norges krig 1940–1945* [Norway's War 1940], vol. 3, edited by Sverre Steen, 111–26. Oslo: Gyldendal Norsk Forlag, 1950.

Duchrow, Ulrich ed., in collaboration with Dorothea Millwood. *Two Kingdoms— The Use and Misuse of a Lutheran Theological Concept.* Geneva: Lutheran World Federation, 1977.

Dyrhaug, Tore. *Norge okkupert! Tysk etterretning om Norge og nordmenn 1942– 1945.* [Norway Occupied! German Intelligence on Norway and Norwegians 1942–1945]. Oslo: Universitetsforlaget, 1985.

Ehrenström, Nils. *Christian Faith and the Modern State: An Oecumenical Approach.* Translated by Denzil Patrick and Olive Wyon. London: Student Christian Movement Press, 1937.

———. "Movements for International Friendship and Life and Work, 1925–1948." In *A History of the Ecumenical Movement 1517–1948*, edited by Ruth Rouse and Stephen Charles Neill, 545–96. Second edition. Philadelphia: The Westminster Press, 1967.

———. "Nordiska Ekumeniska Institutet från Genèves horisont" [Nordic Ecumenical Institute from the Horizon of Geneva]. *Kristen Gemenskap* 44 (1971): 66–70.

Eide, Bernhard. *Det Vestlandske Indremisjonsforbund gjennom 50 år* [The Western Home Mission Association Through 50 Years]. Bergen: Det Vestlandske Indremisjonsforbund, 1948.

Eidsivating lagstols landssviksavdeling. *Straffesak mot Vidkun Abraham Lauritz Jonssøn Quisling* [Criminal Case Against Vidkun Abraham Lauritz Jonssøn Quisling]. Oslo: Eidsivating lagstols landssvikavdeling, 1946.

Eidssvig, Bernt I. "Den katolske kirke vender tilbake" [The Catholic Church Returns]. In *Den katolske kirke i Norge: Fra kristningen til i dag* [The Catholic Church in Norway: From the Christianization until Today], edited by John W. Gran, Erik Gunnes, and Lars Roar Langslet, 143–426. Oslo: H. Aschehoug & Co., (W. Nygaard), 1993.

Ellingsen, Terje. *Kirkestyre i historisk lys* [Church Governance in an Historical Light]. Stavanger: Nomi Forlag,1969.

Emberland, Terje. *Religion og rase: Nyhedenskap og nazisme i Norge 1933–1945* [Religion and Race: Neo-paganism and Nazism in Norway, 1933–1945]. Oslo: Humanist Forlag, 2003.

Engelsen, Nils J. "Økumenen på hjemmeplan" [Ecumenist at Home]. In *Eivind Berggrav: Brobygger og kirkeleder 1884–1984* [Eivind Berggrav: Bridge Builder and

Church Leader 1884–1984], edited by Per Voksø, 135–143. Oslo: Land og Kirke/ Gyldendal Norsk Forlag, 1984.

Ericksen, Robert P. *Complicity in the Holocaust: Churches and Universities in Nazi Germany*. Cambridge: Cambridge University Press, 2012.

Ericksen, Robert P., and Susannah Heschel, eds. *Betrayal: German Churches and the Holocaust*. Minneapolis: Augsburg Press, 1999.

Eriksen, Knut E., and Terje Halvorsen, eds. *Frigøring* [Liberation]. *Norge i krig: Fremmedåk og frihetskamp 1940–1945* [Norway at War: Foreign Yoke and Freedom Fight 1940–1945], vol. 8. Oslo: Aschehoug & Co. (W. Nygaard), 1987.

Eriksen, Trond B., et.al. *Jødehat: Antisemitismens historie fra antikken til i dag* [Hatred of Jews: Anti-Semitism's History from Antiquity to the Present]. N.p. [Oslo?]: N.W. Damm & Søn AS, 2005.

Fagerland, Ståle. "'Dagen' og fascismen 1933–36" [*Dagen* and Fascism 1933–36]. History thesis. University of Trondheim/Norges Lærerhøgskole, 1976.

Fen, Åke. *Nazis in Norway*. Harmondsworth, UK: Penguin Books,1943.

Feyling, Sigmund. "Den autoritære stat" [The Authoritarian State]. In Sigmund Feyling, *Stat og kirke: Kirken og den nye tid*, 25–40. Oslo: J.M. Stenersen's Forlag, 1941.

———. "Den norske kirke og det norske folk" [The Church of Norway and the Norwegian People]. In *Stat og kirke: Kirken og Den nye tid*, 19–24. Oslo: J.M Stensersens Forlag, 1941.

———. "Kirkens ja til tiddskiftet i vårt land" [The Church's Yes to the Changed Time in our Land]. In Sigmund Feyling, *Stat og kirke: Kirken og den nye tid*, 9–12. Oslo: J.M. Stenersen's Forlag, 1941.

———. *Stat og kirke: Kirken og Den nye tid* [State and Church: The Church and The New Age]. Oslo: J.M. Stenersens Forlag, 1941.

———. *Liv og lære: Kristenlære med øvinger* [Life and Doctrine: Christian Doctrine with Exercises]. Oslo: Centralforlaget, 1943.

Feyling, Sigmund, ed. *Kirkelig hvitbok: Utgitt på foranstaltning av Kirke- og Undervisningsdepartementet* [Church White Book: Published By Arrangement with the Ministry of Church and Education]. Oslo: I kommisjon hos Gunnar Stenersens Forlag, 1942.

Fischer, Klaus. *Nazi Germany: A New History*. New York: The Continuum Publishing Company, 1995.

Fjellbu, Arne. *Minner fra krigsårene* [Memories from the War Years]. Oslo: Land og Kirke, 1945.

Fjørtoft, Kjell. *Ulvetiden: Krig og samarbeid* [Time of the Wolves: War and Cooperation]. Oslo: Gyldendal Norsk Forlag, 1990.

———. *Oppgjøret som ikke tok slutt* [The Settlement That Never Ended]. Oslo: Gyldendal Norsk Forlag,1997.

Fleming, Gerald. *Hitler and the Final Solution*. Introduction by Saul Friedländer. Berkeley, Los Angeles, and London: University of California Press, 1984.

Foerster, R. Heinrich. *Die öffentliche Verantwortung der Evangelisch-lutherischen Kirche in einer Bekenntnissituation: Das Paradigma des norwegischen Kirchenkampfes* [The Public Responsibility of the Evangelical Lutheran Church in a Situation of Confession: The Paradigm of the Norwegian Church Struggle]. Veröffentlichungen der Luther-Akademie Ratzeburg, vol. 7. Erlangen: Martin Luther Verlag, 1984.

Forell, George W. "The State as Order of Creation." In *God and Caesar: A Christian Approach to Social Ethics*, edited by Warren A. Quanbeck, 31–52. Minneapolis: Augsburg Publishing House, 1959

Foss, Øivind. *Antijudaisme, kirke og misjon* [Anti-Judaism, Church, and Mission]. Oslo: ad Notam Gyldendal, 1994.

Fure, Jorunn Sem Fure. *Universitetet i kamp 1940–1945* [The University in Struggle, 1940–1945]. Oslo: Vidarforlaget, 2007.

Furre, Berge. *Norsk historie 1914–2000* [Norwegian History, 1914–2000]. Oslo: Det Norske Samlaget, 2000.

Gathorne-Hardy, G. M. *Norway and the War*. London: Humphrey Milford, Oxford University Press, 1941.

Gerlach, Wolfgang. *And the Witnesses Were Silent: The Confessing Church and the Persecution of the Jews*. Translated and edited by Victoria Barnett Lincoln. London: University of Nebraska Press, 2000.

Gjelsvik, Tore. *Hjemmefronten: Den sivile motstand under okkupasjonen 1940–1945* [The Civil Resistance During the Occupation, 1940–1945]. Oslo: J. W. Cappelens Forlag, 1977.

———. *Norwegian Resistance, 1940–1945*. Translated by Thomas K. Derry. London: C. Hurst, 1979.

Glenthøj, Jørgen. "Det Nordiske Økumeniske Instituts betydning under 2. verdenskrig" [The Nordic Ecumenical Institute's Significance During the Second World War]. *Kristen Gemenskap* 44 (1971): 71–76.

Goebbels, Joseph. *The Goebbels Diaries 1942–1943*. Edited and translated by Louis P. Lochner. Garden City, N.Y.: Doubleday & Company, Inc., 1948.

Goldhagen, Daniel J. *Hitler's Willing Executioners: Ordinary Germans and the Holocaust*. New York: Alfred A. Knopf, 1996.

Gram, Gerda. *Norske tilstande: Norge under 2. verdenskrig* [Norwegian Conditions: Norway During the Second World War]. Odense: Odense Universitetsforlag, 1986.

Grimnes, Ole Kristian. *Hjemmefrontens ledelse* [The Home Front's Leadership]. In *Norge og Den 2. verdenskrig: Studier i norsk samtidshistorie* [Norway and the Second World War]. Oslo: Universitetsforlaget, 1979.

———. *Overfall* [Attack]. *Norge i krig: Fremmedåk og frihetskamp 1940–1945* [Norway at War: Foreign Yoke and Freedom Fight 1940–1945], vol. 1. Oslo: Aschehoug & Co. (W. Nygaard), 1984.

———. "Kollaborasjon og oppgjør" [Collaboration and Reckoning]. In *I krigens kjølvann* [In the War's Wake], edited by Stein Ugelvik Larsen, 47–57. Oslo: Universitetsforlaget, 1999.

Hallesby, Ole. *Den kristelige sedelære* [Christian Ethics]. Oslo: Lutherstiftelsen, 1928.

Handeland, Oscar. *Det norske lutherske kinamisjonsforbund gjennom 50 år* [The Norwegian Lutheran China Mission Association], vols. 1–2. Oslo: Kinamisjonsforbundet, 1941–1946.

———. *Kristent samråd i kirkekampen* [The Christian Consultative Council in the Church Struggle]. Bergen: A.S. Lunde & Co.s Forlag, 1945.

———. *Ludvig Hope*. Bergen: A.S. Lunde & Co.s Forlag, 1955.

Handeland, Oscar, and Johannes Thorvaldsen. *I Herrens tjeneste: Misjonssambandet i Norge* [In the Lord's Service: The Mission Association in Norway], edited by Olav Uglem, Ivar Grimsmo, and Arne Aambø. [Bergen]: Lunde & Co.s Forlag, 1966.

Hansson, Kristian. *Norsk kirkerett* [Norwegian Church (Ecclesiastical) Law]. Oslo: H. Aschehoug & Co. (W. Nygaard), 1935.

———. *Stat og Kirke: Fredstider og kampår i Norge.* [State and Church: Times of Peace and Years of Struggle]. *Sak og Samfunn* [Cause and Society], vol. 2. Bergen: Christian Michelsens Institutt for Vitenskap og Åndsfrihet, 1945.

Hassing, Arne. "The Norwegian Free Churches and the Church of Norway 1940–1945." In *Context: Festskrift til Peder Johan Borgen* [Essays in Honour of Peder Johan Borgen], edited by Peter Wilhelm Bøckman and Roald E. Kristiansen, 75–88. "Relieff," Nr. 24. Trondheim: Tapir, 1987.

———. "The Core Ideas of the 'NS Church' in Occupied Norway 1940–45." *Studia Theologica* 42 (1988): 1–20.

———. "The Churches of Norway and the Jews, 1933–1943." *Journal of Ecumenical Studies* 26 (1989): 496–522.

———. "Ecumemical Aspects of the Norwegian Free-Church Experience in World War II." *Journal of Ecumenical Studies* 28 (1991): 18–38.

Hauge, Jens Christian. *Rapport om mitt arbeid under okkupasjonen* [Report on My Work During the Occupation]. Oslo: Gyldendal, 1995.

Heiene, Gunnar. "Ecumenist of Our Time: Eivind Berggrav." *Mid-Stream* 26, no. 1, (1987): 40–50.

———. *Eivind Berggrav: En biografi* [Eivind Berggrav: A Biography]. Oslo: Universitetsforlaget, 1992.

———. "Den norske kirke og økumeniken i etterkrigstiden" [The Church of Norway and Ecumenics in the Postwar Era]. In *Nordiske folkekirker i opbrud: National identitet og international nyorientering efter 1945* [Nordic Folk Churches in Disintegration: National Identity and New International Orientation after 1945], edited by Jens Holger Schjørring, 385–98. Aarhus: Aarhus Universitetsforlag, 2001.

Heling, Arnd. *Die Theologie Eivind Berggravs im norwegischen Kirchenkampf: Ein Beitrag zur politischen Theologie im Luthertum* [The Theology of Eivind Berggrav in the Norwegian Church Struggle: A Contribution to Political Theology in Lutheranism]. Historisch-Theologische Studien zum 19. und 20. Jahrhundert [Historical Theology Studies in the 19th and 20th Centuries], vol. 3. Edited by Gerhard Besier, Robert P. Ericksen, Frédéric Hartweg, and Ingun Montgomery. Neukirchen-Vluyn: Neukirchener Verlag des Erziehungsvereins GmbH, 1992.

Helland, Jacob. "Einar Høigård." In *Einar Høigård: Et minneskrift* [Einar Høigård: A Memorial], by Norges lærerinneforbund, Norges lærerlag, Norsk lektorlag, 7–12. Oslo: J.W. Cappelens Forlag, 1965.

Helmreich, Ernst C. *The German Churches Under Hitler: Background, Struggle, and People*. Detroit: Wayne State University Press, 1979.

Hestvold, Ole. *Alex Johnson: Et liv i spenningsfelt* [A Life in the Tension Zone]. Oslo: Universitetsforlaget, 1987.

Hjelmtveit, Nils. *Vekstår og vargtid* [Years of Growth and Time of Wolves]. Oslo: H. Aschehoug & Co. (W. Nygaard), 1969.

Hockenos, Matthew D. *A Church Divided: German Protestants Confront the Nazi Past*. Bloomington and Indianapolis: Indiana University Press, 2004.

Høidal, Oddvar K. *Quisling: En studie i landssvik* [Quisling: A Study in Treason]. Revised edition. Oslo: Orion Forlag, 2002.

Høigård, Einar og Herman Ruge. *Den norske skoles historie: En oversikt* [The History of the Norwegian School: A Survey]. Oslo: J.W. Cappelens Forlag, 1963.

Hope, Ludvig. *Kyrkja og guds folk* [The Church and the People of God]. Oslo: Lunde, 1923.

Hoprekstad, Olav. *Frå lærarstriden* [From the Teachers' Struggle]. Bergen: J.W. Eides Forlag, 1946.

Huhnhäuser, Albert. Untitled and undated statement written in prison. Copy courtesy of Professor Magne Skodvin.

Investigative Commission of 1945 (Undersøkelseskommisjonen av 1945). *Innstilling fra Undersøkelses-kommisjonen av 1945* [Report of the Investigative Commission of 1945]. Oslo: Stortinget, 1946.

Jäckel, Eberhard. *Hitler's World View: A Blueprint for Power*. Translated by Herbert Arnold. Cambridge: Harvard University Press, 1981.

Jensen, Magnus. "Kampen om skolen" [The Struggle for the Schools]. In *Norges krig 1940–1945* [Norway's War 1940–1945], vol. 3, edited by Sverre Steen, 73–110. Oslo: Gyldendal Norsk Forlag, 1950.

Johansen, Per Ole. *Oss selv nærmest: Norge og jødene 1914–1943* [Closest to Ourselves: Norway and the Jews 1914–1943]. Oslo: Gyldendal Norsk Forlag, 1984.

Karlström, Nils. "Movements for International Friendship and Life and Work, 1910–1925." In *A History of the Ecumenical Movement 1517–1948*, edited by Ruth Rouse and Stephen Charles Neill, 509–42. Second edition. Philadelphia: The Westminster Press, 1967.

Karsrud, Ravn K. "Prestene som støttet Quisling: En bakgrunnsundersøkelse" [The Pastors Who Supported Quisling: A Background Investigation]. *Teologiske arbeidshefter* 5 (1980): 1–60.

Keller, Adolf. *Church and State on the European Continent: The Social Service Lecture, 1936*. London: The Epworth Press, 1936.

Kershaw, Ian. *Hitler 1936–1945: Nemesis*. New York and London: W.W. Norton & Co., 2000.

Kirkens Informasjonstjeneste [The Church's Information Service]. *Kirkelig ordliste:*

Norsk-engelsk [*Ecclesiastical Word List: Norwegian-English*]. Second edition. Oslo: Kirkens Informasjonstjeneste, 1995.

Kjeldstadli, Knut. *Et splittet samfunn 1905–35* [A Divided Society 1905–35]. *Aschehougs Norges historie* [Aschehoug's History of Norway], vol. 10. Edited by Knut Helle. Oslo: H. Aschehough & Co. (W. Nygaard), 1994.

Kjeldstadli, Sverre. *Hjemmestyrkene: Hovedtrekk av den militære motstanden under okkupasjonen* [The Home Forces: Main Features of the Military Resistance During the Occupation]. Oslo: H. Aschehoug & Co. (W. Nygaard), 1959.

Klemelä, Esko. "Finlands kyrka under andra världskriget: Synpunkter på kyrkans utrikes- och inrikespolitiska roll" [Finland's Church During the Second World War: Perspectives on the Church's Domestic and Foreign Political Role]. In *Kirken, krisen og krigen* [The Church, the Crisis, and the War], edited by Stein Ugelvik Larsen and Ingun Montgomery, 329–34. Bergen, Oslo, Tromsø: Universitetsforlaget, 1982.

Kolb, Robert, and Timothy Wengert, eds. *The Book of Concord: The Confessions of the Evangelical Lutheran Church*. Translated by Charles Arand, Eric Gritsch, Robert Kolb, William Russell, James Schaaf, Jane Strohl, and Timothy Wengert. Minneapolis: Fortress Press, 2000.

Kolsrud, Ole. *En splintret stat: Regjeringskontorene 1940–1945* [A Splintered State: The Government Offices 1940–1945]. Adminstrasjon og arkiver III: Riksarkivaren skriftserie [Administration and Archives III: National Archives Publication Series], vol. 14. Oslo: Universitetsforlaget, 2004.

Kraglund, Ivar, and Arnfinn Moland. *Hjemmefront* [Home Front]. *Norge i Krig: Fremmedåk og frihetskamp 1940–1945* [Norway at War: Foreign Yoke and Freedom Fight 1940–1945]. Aschehougs Norges historie [Aschehoug's History of Norway], vol. 6. Oslo: Aschehoug & Co. (W. Nygaard), 1987.

Krohn-Hansen, Wollert. *Den brente jord: Dagboksoptegnelser fra krigen og kirkekampen i Nord-Norge* [The Scorched Earth: Diary Entries from the War and the Church Struggle in Northern Norway]. Oslo: H. Aschehoug & Co. (W. Nygaard), 1945.

Kullerud, Dag. *Ole Hallesby: Mannen som ville kristne Norge* [Ole Hallesby: The Man Who Wanted to Christianize Norway]. Oslo: Gyldendal Norsk Forlag, 1987.

Lange, August, and Johan Schreiner, eds. *Griniboken* [The Grini Book]. 2 vols. Oslo: Gyldendal, 1946–47.

Lange, Even. "*Samling om felles mål, 1933–1970*" [Uniting Around Common Goals, 1933–1970]. *Aschehougs Norges historie* [Aschehoug's History of Norway], vol. 11. Oslo: H. Aschehoug & Co. (W. Nygaard), 1998.

Larsen, Birger D. "Rettsoppgjøret mot NS-prestene" [The Legal Settlement Against the NS Pastors]. Church history thesis, Norwegian School of Theology, 1981.

Larsen, Stein Ugelvik. "Den norske kirkes politiske stilling belyst ved konflikten omkring 'den rette kirke' og NS-kirken under okkupasjonen" [The Church of Norway's Political Standing In Light of the Conflict About the 'Right Church' and the NS Church During the Occupation]. In *Religion och kyrka i 1930-talets sociala kris: Nordiska kyrkohistorikermötet i Uppsala 1974, Anföranden och rap-*

porter [Religion and Church in the Social Crisis of the 1930s: Nordic Church History Conference in Uppsala 1974; Papers and Reports], edited by Ragnar Norrman, 33–42. Uppsala: Almqvist & Wiksell, 1976.

———. "Kirkekampens betydning—i ettertid" [The Church Struggle's Significance—In the Future]. In *Kyrkja under krigen: Bokutgåve av TKRS 1 1995* [The Church During the War: Book Edition of TKRS 1 1995], edited by Jan Ove Ulstein, 131–48. Volda: Tidsskrift for Kirke, Religion og Samfunn; Høgskulen i Volda; Møreforsking Volda, 1995.

———. "The Social Foundations of Norwegian Fascism 1933–1945: An Analysis of Membership Data." In *Who Were the Fascists? Social Roots of European Fascism,* edited by Stein Ugelvik Larsen, Bernt Hagtvet, and Jan Petter Myklebust, 595–620. Oslo: Universitetsforlaget, 1980.

Larsen, Stein Ugelvik, Beatrice Sandberg, and Volker Dahm, eds. *Meldungen aus Norwegen 1940–1945* [Reports from Norway 1940–1945]. 3 vols. Munich: R. Oldenbourg Verlag. Texste und Materialen zur Zeitgeschichte [Texts and Materials for Contemporary History], vol. 6. Munich: Institut für Zeitgeschichte, 2008.

Lauha, Aila. "Finland: Ansvar för folket förblir kyrkans kallese" [Finland: Responsibility for the People Remains the Church's Calling]. In *Nordiske Folkekirker i opbrud: National identitet og international nyorientering efter 1945,* edited by Jens Holger Schørring, 53–64. Aarhus: Aarhus Universitetsforlag, 2001.

Lavik, Johannes. *Spenningen i norsk kirkeliv: Kirkehistoriske konturtegninger* [The Tension in Norwegian Church Life: Church Historical Contour Drawings]. Oslo: Gyldendal Norsk Forlag, 1946.

Lincoln, Bruce. "Notes Toward a Theory of Revolution." In *Religion, Rebellion, Revolution,* edited by Bruce Lincoln, 266–92. Houndmills, Basingstoke, Hampshire, and London: The Macmillan Press, 1985.

Lønning, Inge. "Arven fra Luther: Norsk-tyske kirkelige og religiøse forbindelseslinjer fra reformasjonen til i dag" [The Heritage from Luther: Norwegian-German Ecclesiastical and Religious Lines of Connection from the Reformation until the Present]. In *Tyskland-Norge: Den lange historien* [Germany-Norway: The Long History], edited by Jarle Simensen with Ole Kristian Grimnes, Rolf Hobson, Einhart Lorenz, 44–48. Oslo: Tano Aschehoug, 1999.

Loock, Hans-Dietrich. *Quisling, Rosenberg und Terboven: Zur Vorgeschichte und Geschichte der nationalsozialistischen Revolution in Norwegen* [Quisling, Rosenberg, and Terboven: Toward the Prehistory and History of the National Socialist Revolution in Norway]. In *Quellen und Darstellungen zur Zeitgeschichte* [Sources and Interpretations for Contemporary History], vol. 18. Stuttgart: Deutsche Verlags-Anstalt GmbH, 1970.

Løsnesløkken, Åge, and Kurt Hjemdal. *På ditt ord: Indremisjonsselskapets historie 1868–1993* [On Your Word: The Home Mission Society's History, 1868–1993]. Oslo: Luther Forlag, 1993.

Løvlie, Birger. *Kirke, stat og folk i en etterkrigstid: Kirkeordningsarbeid i Den norske kirke 1945–1984 i et strategisk perspektiv* [Church, State, and People in a Postwar

Era: Church Polity Efforts in the Church of Norway 1945–1984 from a Strategic Perspective]. Oslo: Luther Forlag, 1996.

Ludlow, Peter W. "Bischof Berggrav zum deutschen Kirchenkampf" [Bishop Berggrav on the German Church Struggle]. In *Zur Geschichte des Kirchenkampfes: Gesammelte Aufsätze II* [Toward the History of the Church Struggle: Collected Papers II], edited by Heinz Brunotte and Ernst Wolf, 221–258. *Arbeiten zur Geschichte des Kirchenkampfes* [Work on the History of the Church Struggle], vol. 26. Göttingen: Vendenhoeck & Ruprecht, 1971.

———.Protestants in WWII.

Lundby, Knut. "Norge" [Norway]. In *Religiös Förändring i Norden 1930–1980* [Religious Change in the Nordic Countries 1930–1980], edited by Göran Gustafsson, 154–95. Malmö: Liber Förlag; Copenhagen: Gyldendal; Reykjavík: Mál og menning; Helsinki: Söderström & Co.; Oslo: Universitetsforlaget, 1985.

Lundestad, Geir. "Hovedtendenser i norsk politikk" [Main Trends in Norwegian Politics]. In *Vekst og velstand. Norsk politisk historie 1945–1965. Regjering og opposisjon under Arbeiderpartistyre* [Growth and Welfare: Norwegian Political History 1945–1965; Government and Opposition Under Labor Party Rule], edited by Trond Bergh and Helge Ø. Pharo, 451–519. Oslo, Bergen, and Tromsø: Universitetsforlaget, 1977.

Lynch, Michael. *Scotland: A New History*. London: Pimlico, 1992.

MacCulloch, Diarmaid. *The Reformation: A History*. New York: Viking, 2003.

Mann, Michael. *Fascists*. Cambridge, U.K. and New York: Cambridge University Press, 2004.

Martin, Hugh, Douglas Newton, H. M. Waddams, and R. R. Williams. *Christian Counter-Attack: Europe's Churches Against Nazism*. London: Student Christian Movement Press, Ltd, 1943.

Martinsen, Svenn. "Ingolf Boge: Martyr under nazi-diktaturet" [Ingolf Boge: Martyr under nazi-diktaturet]. Website on Ingolf Anderson Boge at www.kyrkja.net/boge.htm, accessed 2 October 2012.

Marty, Martin, and Scott Appleby. *The Glory and the Power: The Fundamentalist Challenge to the Modern World*. Boston: Beacon Press, 1992.

McGovern, William Montgomery. *From Luther to Hitler: The History of Fascist-Nazi Political Philosophy*. Boston: Houghton Mifflin Company, 1941.

Mehren, Ivar Torgersen von. "Kristen Samling—et fenomen" [Christian Union—A Phenomenon]. In *Kyrkja under krigen: Bokutgåve av TKRS 1 1995* [The Church During the Occupation: Book Edition of TKRS 1 1995], edited by Jan Ove Ulstein, 43–63. Volda: Tidsskrift for Kirke, Religion og Samfunn; Høgskulen i Volda; Møreforsking Volda, 1995.

Melsom, Odd. *Fra kirke- og kulturkampen under okkupasjonen* [From the Church and Cultural Struggle During the Occupation]. In *Supplement til okkupasjonshistorien* [Supplement to the Occupation's History], vol. 3. Oslo: Institutt for Norsk Okkupasjonshistorie, 1980.

Mendelsohn, Oskar. *Jødenes historie i Norge gjennom 300 år* [The History of the

Jews in Norway Through 300 Years], vol. 1. Oslo, Bergen, Tromsø: Universitets-forlaget, 1969.

————. *1940–1985*. Vol. 2 of *Jødenes historie i Norge gjennom 300 år* [The History of the Jews in Norway Through 300 Years]. Oslo, Bergen, Stavanger, and Tromsø: Universitetsforlaget, 1986.

Methodist Church. "Tilsynsmennenes fellesrapport" [The District Superintendents' Common Report]. In *Årboken for Metodistkirkens årskonferanse i Norge avholdt i Trondheim 1.–5. august 1945* [Year Book of the Methodist Church's Annual Conference in Norway Held in Trondheim, 1–5 August 1945], 53–67. Oslo: Norsk Forlagsselskap, 1945.

Miller, William R. *Nonviolence: A Christian Interpretation*. New York: Association Press, 1964.

Moe, Olaf. *Levet og lært: Erindringer*. Oslo: Lutherstiftelsen, 1956.

Molland, Einar. "Den norske kirke—en luthersk folkekirke" [The Church of Nor-way—A Lutheran Folk Church]. *Kristen Gemenskap* [Christian Community] 8, no. 1 (1936): 8–16.

————. "Den norske kirkekamps status" [The Norwegian Church Struggle's Status]. *Kristen Gemenskap* 17 (1944): 169–81.

————. "Kirkekampens historie" [The History of the Church Struggle]. *Kirke og Kultur* 50 (1945): 113–30.

————. "Kirkens kamp." [The Church's Struggle]. In *Norges krig 1940–1945* [Norway's War, 1940–1945], vol. 3, 35–72. Oslo: Gyldendal Norsk Forlag, 1950.

————. *Fra Hans Nielsen Hauge til Eivind Berggrav: Hovedlinjer i Norges kirkehis-torie det 19. og 20. århundre* [From Hans Nielsen Hauge to Eivind Berggrav: Main Trends in Norwegian Church History in the 19th and 20th Centuries]. Oslo: Gyldendal Norsk Forlag, 1951

————. *Konfesjonskunnskap: Kristenhetens trosbekjennelser og kirkesamfunn* [Confessional Knowledge: Christianity's Creeds and Churches]. Second revised edition. Oslo: Forlaget Land og Kirke, 1961.

Moltke, Helmuth James von. *Briefe an Freya 1939–1945*. Edited by Beate Ruhm von Oppen. Munich: Verlag C.H. Beck, 1988.

Montgomery, Ingun. "Politisk ideologi og religiös forkynnelse: Norsk nasismes for-hold til kristendommen" [Political Ideology and Religious Proclamation]. In *Reli-gion och kyrka i 1930-talets sociala kris: Nordiska kyrkohistorikermötet i Uppsala 1974, Anföranden och rapporter* [Religion and Church in the Social Crisis of the 1930s: Nordic Church History Conference in Uppsala 1974; Papers and Reports], edited by Ragnar Norrman, 17–32. Uppsala: Almqvist & Wiksell, 1976.

————. "Den svenska linjen är den kristna linjen" [The Swedish Course is the Chris-tian Course]. In *Kirken, krisen og krigen* [The Church, the Crisis, and the War], edited by Stein Ugelvik Larsen and Ingun Montgomery, 353–60. Bergen, Oslo, Tromsø: Universitetsforlaget, 1982.

Montgomery, Ingun, and Stein Ugelvik Larsen, eds. *Kirken, krisen og krigen* [The

Church, the Crisis, and the War]. Skrifter utgitt av Nordisk institut för kyrkohistorisk forskning [Writings Published by the Nordic Institute for Church Historical Research], no. 5. Oslo: Universitetsforlaget, 1982.

Moulton, J. L. *The Norwegian Campaign of 1940*. London: Eyre & Spottiswoode, 1966.

Murtorinne, Eino. "Die nordischen Kirchen im zweiten Weltkrieg" [The Nordic Churches in the Second World War]. In *Nordische und deutsche Kirchen im 20. Jahrhundert: Referate auf der Internationalen Arbeitstagung in Sandbjerg/Dänemark 1981* [Nordic and German Churches in the Twentieth Century: Reports of the International Work Conference in Sandbjerg, Denmark, 1981], edited by Carsten Nicolaisen, 212–27. Göttingen: Vandenhoeck & Ruprecht, 1982.

Myklebust, Jan P., and Bernt Hagtvet. "Regional Contrasts in the Membership Base of the Nasjonal Samling: A Study of the Political Ecology of Norwegian Fascism 1933–1945." In *Who Were the Fascists?* edited by Stein Ugelvik Larsen, Bernt Hagtvet, and Jan Petter Myklebust, 621–50. Oslo: Universitetsforlaget, 1980.

Neocleous, Mark. "Racism, Fascism and Nationalism." In *The Fascism Reader*, edited by Aristotle A. Kallis, 349–58. London and New York: Routledge, 2003.

Nerman, Ture, ed. and trans. *Ande mot våld: Norges kyrka och skola 1940–42* [Spirit Against Violence: Norway's Church and School 1940–42]. Stockholm: Trots Allt!, 1942.

Nøkleby, Berit. *Nyordning* [New Order]. *Norge i krig: Fremmedåk og frihetskamp 1940–1945* [Norway at War: Foreign Yoke and Freedom Fight 1940–1945], vol. 2. Oslo: Aschehoug & Co. (W. Nygaard), 1985.

———. *Holdningskamp* [Attitude (Stance) Struggle]. *Norge i krig: Fremmedåk og frihetskamp 1940–1945* [Norway at War: Foreign Yoke and Freedom Fight 1940–1945], vol. 4. Oslo: Aschehoug & Co. (W. Nygaard), 1986.

———. *Josef Terboven—Hitlers mann i Norge* [Josef Terboven—Hitler's Man in Norway]. Oslo: Gyldendal norsk forlag, 1992.

———. *Skutt blir den: Tysk bruk av dødsstraff i Norge, 1940–1945* [Will Be Shot: German Use of the Death Penalty in Norway, 1940–1945]. Oslo: Gyldendal Norsk Forlag, 1996.

Norborg, Sverre. *Vekkeren fra Aremark: Ole Hallesbys livssaga* [Awakener from Aremark: Ole Hallesby's Life Saga]. Oslo: Luther Forlag, 1979.

Norderval, Øyvind. "Quisling, kirken og kristendommen: Quislings kirkepolitikk og verdensanskuelse" [Quisling, the Church, and Christianity: Quisling's Church Politics and Worldview]. *Norsk Teologisk Tidsskrift* 91 (1990): 215–31.

———. "Den norske kirke i etterkrigssamfunnet: Konflikt, nyorientering og reformer" [The Church of Norway in the Postwar Society: Conflict, New Orientation, and Reforms]. In *Nordiske Folkekirker i opbrud: National identitet og international nyorientering efter 1945* [Nordic Folk Churches in Dissolution: National Identity and International Reorientation After 1945], edited by Jens Holger Schjørring, 191–212. Aarhus: Aarhus Universitetsforlag, 2001.

Norrman, Ragnar. "Prästerna i norska kyrkan 1939–1945: Sosial struktur och ekonomiska villkor" [The Clergy in the Norwegian Church 1939–1945: Social Structure and Economic Conditions]. *Kyrkohistorisk årsskrift* [Church Historical Yearbook] 84 (1984): 173–209.

———. "Sverige och norska kyrkokampen—en översikt" [Sweden and the Norwegian Church Struggle—An Overview]. In *Kyrkja under Krigen* [The Church During the War], edited by Jan Ove Ulstein, 65–83. Bokutgåve av TKRS 1 1995 [Book Edition of TKRS 1 (1995)]. Volda: *Tidsskrift for Kirke, Religion og Samfunn*, Høgskolen i Volda, Møreforskning Volda, 1995.

———. *Quislingkyrkan: Nasjonal Samlings kyrkopolitik 1940–1945* [National Union's Church Politics 1940–1945]. Skellefteå, Sweden: Norma Bokförlag, 1998.

[Det] norske lutherske Kinamisjonsforbund. *Årbok 1941* [Year Book 1941]. Oslo: Forbundets forlag, 1941.

Oberman, Heiko O. *The Reformation: Roots and Ramifications*. Grand Rapids: Eerdmans Press, 1994.

Oftestad, Bernt T. *Kristentro og kulturansvar hos Ronald Fangen* [Christian Faith and Cultural Responsibility in Ronald Fangen]. Oslo: Land og Kirke, Gyldendal Norsk Forlag, 1981.

———. "'… uverdige til å være evangeliets tjenere': Landssvikoppgjøret med prestene i Den norske kirke" ["Unworthy to be Servants of the Gospel: The Treason Settlement with the Pastors in the Church of Norway]. *Tidsskrift for Kirke, Religion, og Samfunn* 10 (1997): 63–80.

———. *Den norske statsreligion: Fra øvrighetskirke til demokratisk statskirke* [The Norwegian State Religion: From Government (Authorities) Church to Democratic State Church]. Kristiansand: Høyskoleforlaget, 1998.

Østnor, Lars. *Kirkens enhet: Et bidrag til forståelsen av norske teologers oppfatning av det økumeniske problem i mellomkrigstiden* [The Church's Unity: A Contribution to the Understanding of Norwegian Theologians' Perception of the Ecumenical Problem in the Interwar Years]. Oslo: Solum Forlag, 1990.

Øybekk, Bjørnar Johnsen. "Lars Andreas Frøyland: En biografisk undersøkelse av mannen som ble NS-biskop i Oslo, med særlig vekt på okkupasjonsårene" [Lars Andreas Frøyland: A Biographical Investigation of the Man Who Became the NS bishop in Oslo with Special Attention to the Occupation Years]. Church history thesis, Norwegian School of Theology, Oslo, 2001.

Pierard, Richard. "Why did Protestants welcome Hitler?" *Fides et historia* 10, no. 2 (1978): 8–29.

Poulsen, Henning. "Uklare linjer: Dansk kirke under besættelsen" [Unclear lines: The Danish Church under Occupation]. In *Kirken, krisen, og krigen* [The Church, the Crisis, and the War], edited by Ingun Montgomery and Stein Ugelvik Larsen, 320–28, Publications issued by the Nordic Institute for Church Historical Research. Bergen, Oslo, Tromsø: Universitetsforlaget, 1982.

Pryser, Tore. *Klassen og nasjonen (1935–1946)* [The Class and the Nation 1935–1946)]. *Arbeiderbevegelsens historie* [The Labor Movement's History], vol. 4. Oslo: Tiden Norsk Forlag, 1988.

———. *Hitlers hemmelige agenter: Tysk etterretning i Norge 1939–1945* [Hitler's Secret Agents: German Intelligence in Norway 1939–1940] Oslo: Universitetsforlaget, 2001.

Quisling, Vidkun. *Quisling har sagt—citater fra taler og avisartikler* [Quisling Has Said—Quotations from Speeches and Newspaper Articles], vol 1. Oslo: I kommisjon hos J.M. Stenersens forlag, 1940.

———. *For Norges frihet og selvstendighet: Artikler og taler 9. april 1940–23. juni 1941* [For Norway's Freedom and Independence: Articles and Speeches 9 April 1940—23 June 1941]. Edited by H. N. Østbye. Oslo: NS Presse-og Propagandaavdeling, 1941.

———. *Ministerpresidenten uttaler seg om kirken og kristendommen* [The Minister President Speaks About Church and Christianity]. [Oslo]: [Nasjonal Samling], 1943.

———. *Vidkun Quislings tale den 1 februar 1943* [Vidkun Quisling's Speech on 1 February 1943]. N.p.: Riksspropagandaledelsen. 1943.

———. *Ministerpresident Vidkun Quislings tale i Oslo den 14. mai 1944* [Minister President's Speech in Oslo on 14 May 1944]. Oslo: Rikspropagandaledelsen, 1944.

Rasmussen, Tarald. "Det indre og det ytre: Noen hovedtemaer fra luthersk moraltradisjon" [The Inner and the Outer: Some Main Themes from the Lutheran Moral Tradition]. *Moralsk og moderne?* [Moral and Modern?], edited by Svein Aage Christoffersen, 17–39. Oslo: Ad Notam Gyldendal, 1999.

Repstad, Pål. *Mannen som ville åpne kirken: Kristian Schjelderups liv* [The Man Who Wanted to Open the Church: Kristian Schjelderup's Life]. Oslo: Universitetsforlaget, 1989.

Rieber-Mohn, Gottlieb W. "Vi var med: Glimt av den katolske kirke i Norge under okkupasjonen" [We Took Part: Glimpses of the Catholic Church in Norway During the Occupation]. *St. Olav* 57 (1945): 83–86, 93–95.

Ringdal, Nils Johan. *Mellom barken og veden: Politiet under okkupasjonen* [Between the Bark and the Wood: The Police During the Occupation]. Oslo: Aschehoug, 1987.

Riste, Olav. *1940–1942: Prøvetid* [Testing Time]. *"London-regjeringa.": Norge i krigsalliansen 1940–1945* ["The London Government": Norway in the War Alliance 1940–1945], vol. 1. Oslo: Det norske samlaget, 1973.

———. *Norway's Foreign Relations: A History*. Oslo: Universitetsforlaget, 2001.

Roberts, Adam, ed. *Civilian Resistance as a National Defense: Nonviolent Action Against Aggression*. Harrisburg, Pennsylvania: Stackpole Books, 1968.

Roberts, Andrew. *The Storm of War: A New History of the Second World War*. New York: HarperCollins Publishers, 2011.

Rokkan, Stein. "Geografi, religion og samfunnsklasse: Kryssende konfliktlinjer i norsk politikk; Essays i politisk sosiologi" [Geography, Religion, and Social Class: Crisscrossing Cleavages in Norwegian Politics; Essays in Political Sociology]. In *Stat, nasjon, klasse,* [State, Nation, Class], translated by Lars Alldén and Bernt Hagtvet, 111–89. Oslo: Universitetsforlaget, 1987.

Roon, Ger von. *German Resistance to Hitler: Count von Moltke and the Kreisau Circle*. Translated by Peter Ludlow. London: Van Nostrand Reinhold Company, 1971.

Rostrup, Eilert T. "Legionæropropet—et bidrag til forståelsen av forholdet mellom prester og statsledelsen under okkupasjonen 1940–1945" [The Legionnaire Appeal—A Contribution to the Understanding of the Relationship Between the Clergy and the State Leadership During the Occupation 1940–1945]. Church history thesis, Norwegian School of Theology, Oslo, 1981.

Rudvin, Ola. *Det norske lutherske indremisjonsselskap 1892–1968* [The Norwegian Lutheran Home Mission Society, 1892–1968]. *Indremisjonsselskapets historie* [The Home Mission Society's History], vol. 2. Oslo: Lutherstiftelsens forlag, 1970.

Ryan, Cornelius. *The Longest Day*. New York: Fawcett, 1959.

Sanders, Thomas G. *Protestant Concepts of Church and State: Historical Backgrounds and Approaches for the Future*. Garden City, NY: Doubleday & Co., Inc., 1964.

Sanengen, Alf. "Kampen mot A-t og arbeidsmobiliseringen" [The Struggle Against A-t (Labor Service) and Labor Mobilization]. In *Norges krig 1940–1945* [Norway's War 1940–1945], vol. 3, edited by Sverre Steen, 319–48. Oslo: Gyldendal Norsk Forlag, 1950.

Schjelderup, Ferdinand. *Fra Norges kamp for retten: 1940 i Høyesterett*. [From Norway's Struggle for Law: 1940 in the Supreme Court]. Oslo: Grøndahl & Søns Forlag, 1945.

———. *På bred front* [On a Broad Front]. Oslo: Grøndahl & Søns Forlag, 1947.

———. *Over bakkekammen 1943–1944* [Over the Crest of the Hill, 1943–1944]. Oslo: Gyldendal Norsk Forlag, 1949.

Schjelderup, Kristian. *På vei mot hedenskapet* [On the Path to Paganism]. Oslo: H. Aschehoug & Co. (W. Nygaard), 1935.

Schjørring, Jens Holger. "Introduktion" [Introduction]. In *Nordiske Folkekirker i opbrud: National identitet og international nyorientering efter 1945* [The Nordic Folk Churches in Disintegration: National Identity and New International Orientation after 1945], edited by Jens Holger Schjørring, 11–44. Aarhus: Aarhus Universitetsforlag, 2001.

Scholder, Klaus. *Preliminary History and the Time of Illusions, 1918–1934*. Vol. 1 of *The Churches and the Third Reich*. Translated by John Bowden. Philadelphia: Fortress, 1988.

———. *The Year of Disillusionment: 1934, Barmen and Rome*. Vol. 2 of *The Churches and the Third Reich*. Translated by John Bowden. Philadelphia: Fortress Press, 1988.

———. *A Requiem for Hitler and Other New Perspectives on the German Church Struggle*. Translated by John Bowden. London: SCM Press; Philadelphia: Trinity Press International, 1989.

Schübeler, Ludwig. *Kirkekampen slik jeg så den* [The Church Struggle As I Saw It]. Oslo: Lutherstiftelsens Forlag, 1945.

Seip, Didrik Arup. *Hjemme og i fiendeland 1940–1945* [At Home and in Enemy Country, 1940–1945]. Oslo: Gyldendal Norsk Forlag, 1946.

Semelin, Jacques. *Unarmed Against Hitler: Civilian Resistance in Europe 1939–1943*. Translated by Suzan Husserl-Kapit. Foreword by Stanley Hoffmann. Westport, Connecticut and London: Praeger Publishers, 1993.

Senter for studier av Holocaust og livssynsminoriter [Center for Studies of the Holocaust and Religious Minorities]. "Deportasjonen av de norsk jødene" [The Deportation of the Norwegian Jews]. http://www.hlsenteret.no, accessed 20 September 2012.

———. "Flukten til Sverige" [The Escape to Sweden]. http://www.hlsenteret.no, accessed 20 September 2012.

Sharp, Gene. *The Politics of Nonviolent Action*. 3 vols. Boston: Porter Sargent, Boston, 1981.

Shirer, William L. *The Rise and Fall of the Third Reich: A History of Nazi Germany*. New York: Simon and Schuster, 1960.

Singer, Kurt D. ed. *White Book of the Church of Norway on Its Persecution by the German Occupation Forces and the Quisling Regime in Norway*. New York: Pictorial Publishing Company, 1941.

Skodvin, Magne. "Det store fremstøt" [The Great Advance]. In *Norges krig 1940–1945* [Norway's War 1940–1945], vol. 2, edited by Sverre Steen, 573–734. Oslo: Gyldendal Norsk Forlag, 1948.

———. *Striden om okkupasjonsstyret i Norge fram til 25. september 1940* [The Conflict Over Occupation Rule in Norway to 25 September 1940]. Oslo: Det Norske Samlaget, 1956.

———. "Norwegian Non-Violent Resistance." In *The Strategy of Civilian Defense: Non-violent Resistance to Aggression*, edited by Adam Roberts, 136–53. London: Faber and Faber Ltd., 1967.

———. *Krig og okkupasjon 1939–1945* [War and Occupation 1939–1945]. Oslo: Det Norske Samlaget, 1990.

Smemo, Johannes. "Norsk kristendom" [Norwegian Christianity]. In *Den norske kirke 1930: Et jubileumsskrift*, edited by Sven Svensen, Laurentius Koren, and Andreas Jakobsen. Oslo: Selskapet til kristelige andaktsbøkers utgivelse, 1930.

Solum, Erik S. *Kryssende spor: Hamar-bispene Kristian Schjelderup og Alex Johnson* [Crisscrossing Tracks: The Hamar Bishops Kristian Schjelderup and Alex Johnson]. Oslo: Land og Kirke and Gyldendal norsk forlag, 1983.

Sørensen, Øystein. *Hitler eller Quisling: Ideologiske brytninger i Nasjonal Samling 1940–1945* [Hitler or Quisling: Ideological Conflicts in National Union 1940–1945]. Oslo: Cappelen, Oslo, 1989.

Steen, Sverre. "Riksrådsforhandlingene" [The National Council Negotiations]. In *Norge og den 2. verdenskrig: 1940 – Fra nøytral til okkupert* [Norway and the Second World War: 1940—From Neutral to Occupied], edited by Helge Paulsen, 127–283. Studier i norsk samtidshistorie. Oslo: Universitetsforlaget, 1969.

Steltzer, Theodor. *Sechzig Jahre Zeitgenosse* [Sixty Years Contemporary]. Munich: List Verlag, 1966.

Stridsklev, Inger Cecilie. "Kristen Samlings historie" [Christian Union's History]. In *Kyrkja under krigen: Bokutgåve av TKRS 1 1995* [The Church During the War: Book Edition of TKRS 1 1995], edited by Jan Ove Ulstein, 23–41. Volda: *Tidsskrift for Kirke, Religion og Samfunn*; Høgskulen i Volda; Møreforsking Volda, 1995.

Sundkler, Bengt. *Nathan Söderblom: His Life and Work.* Lund: Gleerups, 1968.

Svendsen, H. S. Blom. *Den norske kirkes presteforening 1900–1950* [The Church of Norway's Clergy Association]. Oslo: Den norske kirkes presteforening, 1950.

Tillich, Paul. *Against the Third Reich: Paul Tillich's Wartime Addresses to Nazi Germany.* Edited by Ronald H. Stone and Matthew Lon Weaver. Translated by Matthew Lon Weaver. Louisville, KY: Westminster John Knox Press, 1998.

Tønnessen, Aud V. *". . . et trygt og godt hjem for alle"?: Kirkelederes kritikk av velferdsstaten etter 1945* [". . . a safe and good home for all"?: Church Leaders' Critique of the Welfare State After 1945]. KIFO Perspektiv: Forskning i kirke, religion, samfunn. Skriftserie utgitt av Stiftelsen Kirkeforskning Nr. 7 [KIFO Perpectiv: Research in Church, Religion, Society. Series Published by the Church Research Foundation No. 7]. Trondheim: Tapir Akademisk Forlag, 2000.

Tschudi, Stephan. *Norsk kirke i dag: Oppgjør og program* [The Norwegian Church Today: Settlement and Agenda]. Oslo: Land og kirke, 1945.

Ulstein, Jan Ove, ed. *Kyrkja under krigen: Bokutgåve av TKRS 1 1995* [The Church During the War: Book Edition of TKRS 1 1995]. Volda: *Tidsskrift for Kirke, Religion, og Samfunn*, Høgskulen i Volda, and Møreforsking Volda, 1995.

———. "Teologi i kontekst under krigen: Nokre linjer i ei innfløkt historie" (Theology in Context during the War: A Few Lines in a Complicated History). In *Dømmekraft i krise? Holdninger i kirken til jøder, teologi og NS under okkupasjonen* [Judgment in Crisis? Positions in the Church on Jews, Theology, and NS during the Occupation], by Torleiv Austad, Ottar Berge, and Jan Ove Ulstein, 111–86. *Kyrkjefag Profil nr. 18.* Trondheim: Akademika forlag, n.d. [2012].

Ulstein, Ragnar. *Flyktningar til Sverige 1940–43* [Refugees to Sweden 1940–43]. Vol. 1 of *Svensketraffikken* [The Swedish Traffic]. Oslo: Det norske samlaget, 1974.

Van Dusen, Henry P. *What IS the Church Doing?* New York: Scribner's Sons, 1943.

Voksø, Per. *Krigens dagbok: Norge 1940–1945* [War Diary: Norway 1940–1945]. Oslo: Forlaget Det Beste, 1984.

Warmbrunn, Werner. *The Dutch under German Occupation, 1940–1945.* Stanford, California: Stanford University Press; London: Oxford University Press, 1963.

Welle, Ivar. "Inntrykk fra Tyskland" [Impressions from Germany]. *Luthersk Kirketidende* 70 (1933): 465–70, 508–13, 536–39, 568–72.

———. "Den norske folkekirke [The Norwegian People's Church]. In *Den kristne arbeidsfront i Norge* [The Christian Work Front in Norway], edited by D. Munkejord, 7–34. Oslo: Lutherstiftelsens forlag, 1938.

Wheal, Elizabeth-Anne, Stephen Pope, and James Taylor, eds. *A Dictionary of the Second World War.* New York: Peter Bedrick Books, 1990.

Williams, R.R. "The Church in Norway and the Pastorals." In *No Other Gospel: The Church Conflict on the Continent*, by J.O. Cobham, A.G. Herbert, F. Hildebrandt, N. Micklem, A.R. Vidler, and R.R. Williams, 43–51. London: Student Christian Movement Press Ltd., 1943.

Wisløff, Carl F. *Norsk kirkehistorie* [Norwegian Church History], vol. 3. Oslo: Luther-stiftelsen, 1971.

————. *Norsk kirkedebatt gjennom 100 år* [Norwegian Church Debate Over 100 Years]. N.p.: Lunde Forlag, 1979.

Wisløff, Fredrik, and Ola Rudvin. *Sokneprest Joh. M. Wisløff: Mannen og verket* [Reverend Joh. M. Wisløff: The Man and the Work]. Oslo: Indremisjonsforlaget A/S., 1950.

Wyller, Thomas C. *Fra okkupasjonsårenes maktkamp: Nasjonal Samlings korporative nyordningsforsøk 9. april 1940 – 1. februar 1942* [From the Power Struggle of the Occupation Years: National Union's Efforts to Create a New Corporate Order]. Oslo: Johan Grundt Tanum, 1953.

————. *Nyordning og motstand: Organisasjonenes politiske rolle under okkupasjonen.* [New Order and Resistance: The Political Role of the Organizations During the Occupation]. Oslo: Universitetsforlaget, 1958.

Index

Absolutism, 19

Abwehr, 85–86

Act of State at Akershus, 120, 218–19

Administrative Council: formation of, 48–50, 126; and invasion of Norway, 43–46; and Jews, 205; and National Council Negotiations, 52–54, 248; and Terboven, 49–50, 52; and treason debate, 248

Aftenposten, 115

Agder Diocese, 20, 184–85

Agrarian Party government, 39

Aker, Ivar. *See* Schirmer, Ernst A.

Akershus County, 45, 53

Ålesund, 63, 223, 313n29

Allies, 41, 97, 109, 119, 169; and Battle of the Bulge, 230; media of, 212, 223; in Norway, 243–45; and Omaha Beach, 230; and postwar era, 267, 269; Supreme Command, 230, 244; and Sweden, 267; and victory, 176–77, 244–45; Western Front, 216, 229–30. *See also names of Allied countries*

Althaus, Paul, 6, 14, 84, 193, 264

ambassador, German, 41, 43–46

Amdahl, Einar, 21, 155–56, 236, 288n16, 304n6; arrest/imprisonment of, 236; and Stavanger manifesto, 175–76

"A Mighty Fortress Is Our God" (hymn), 122

Andersen, Johannes, 105, 297n6

Annunciation Day protest, 140–41, 155

anti-Judaism, 30

anti-Semitism, 7, 10, 29–31, 33; as anti-Christian, 29, 33, 271–72; and Confessing Church, 17, 272, 282n49; Constitutional exclusion of from Norway, 29, 207–8; and Feyling, 194, 213–14; and German Lutheranism, 7, 14–17, 271–72, 282n49; and Luther, 16–17, 212–14, 281n48; and Netherlands, 274; and NS church, 191, 193–94, 213, 310n17; and NS state, 30–31, 39–40, 206–9; and treason trials, 254–55; and yellow "Jewish business" signs, 205–6

Apostles' Creed, 8, 12, 18, 23, 57

"Appeal to the Norwegian People" (Feyling), 109–10, 297n6

Arbeiderbladet (newspaper), 248

Arnesson, Nikolas, 160, 305n24

Aryan theology, 7, 29; Aryan Christ, 14–15, 194

Athanasian Creed, 18–19

atheists, 187

Augsburg Confession, 15–16, 19–20, 57; Article 16, 15; Article 28, 16; and NS church system, 97; and Valen-Sendstad, 156

Aulén, Gustaf, 80, 235, 267

Auschwitz, 209, 214–15

Austad, Torleiv, 30, 261–62, 322n27, 323n56

authoritarian state, 13, 84–86; and NS church, 194, 197–99, 201; and polity (church order), 110–12, 197–99; and treason trials, 253. *See also names of authoritarian parties and states*

autonomous church, 180–90; administration of, 181–82; and arrests/ imprisonments/deportations, 238–39; claiming parishes for, 186–88, 200–201; and communication, 182–84, 308n12; establishing, 170–71, 174, 176–77; finances for, 184–86, 189; and *The Foundation of the Church*, 158; and "ice front" of social non-cooperation, 99, 186, 199–200, 311n37; and mission societies, 188–89; newsletters of, 201; and non-cooperation policy, 180–81, 186, 196, 199–200; and PCL, 170–71, 174, 180–84; and politics, 187, 189–90; spies in, 187

baptisms, 19–20, 131, 159; and autonomous church, 181, 186; and Jews, 211; and NS church, 186, 188

Baptists, 21, 133, 211

Barbarossa, 108–10, 120, 172, 244, 295n13, 297n6; and Finland, 109, 172, 266; and Jews, 206–7

Barmen Declaration, 8–9, 74, 209, 261; Jews excluded from, 209

Barth, Karl, 8, 24, 209, 268, 270

Bastiansen, Alf, 151*fig.*, 196, 231

Bavaria, 8–9

BBC (Norwegian), 48, 100, 131,

290n10; and compulsory labor service, 226; and Jewish persecution, 212

Beck, Wilhelm, 288n16

Belgium, invasion of, 51

Bentzen, Amund, 80

Berg, Paal, 44–46, 52, 123, 126, 286n21, 289n25; and Circle (*Kretsen*), 105; and clergy's resignations, 157; and liberation, 245; and professional organizations, 72

Bergen, 91, 135–36, 185, 187, 238, 295n37; and *The Foundation of the Church*, 155–56, 208–9

Bergersen, Birger, 72, 289n25

Berggrav, Eivind J., 144*fig.*, 146*fig.*, 148*fig.*; Asker cottage of, 146*fig.*, 158, 163, 178; as Bishop of Oslo, 19, 32, 37, 54, 107, 113–15, 234; and Bishops' Conference, 19, 56–57, 110, 112–14; and bishops' resignations, 123–28; Burge Memorial Lecture, 262–63; and CCC, 58–64, 73–75, 107, 117, 190, 272–73, 288n19; as Christian hero of Nazi era, 268, 272–73; and Church Order Commission, 260; and Church's Consultative Council, 117; and Circle (*Kretsen*), 105–7, 221, 297n46; and civilian casualties, 46–48; as civil servant, 44, 47; and compulsory youth service, 131–33, 135, 141, 302n12; and conscience, 71–73, 104, 160, 254, 290n13; and Coordination Committee, 107, 297n46; on death penalty, 248; and diocesan communication networks, 183; and duty of disobedience, 80–81; and ecumenical movement, 32, 37–38, 48, 57, 64, 92, 164, 263–69; escape from house arrest, 246; and exclusion of Jews, 156, 205–6, 208–9; and "the folk church," 25; and *The Foundation of the Church*,

156–57, 160, 162, 208; German language fluency of, 29, 43, 52, 268; and Gestapo, 76, 79, 88; as Günther's source, 88; and Hallesby, 37–38, 57–58, 117; health of, 248; house arrest of, 88, 141, 158, 162–64, 170–71, 177–79, 184, 249, 259; Hygen as representative of, 170; imprisonment of, 162–63, 221, 301n30; and invasion, 42–48, 248; Johnson as protégé of, 93, 107; and just state, 78–81; and Lambeth Cross, 268; liberal mindset of, 37, 57; in Lovisenberg Hospital, 131; and Mangers, 134, 263–64; on moral fiber of Norwegians, 105; and National Council Negotiations, 52–53, 248; national rehabilitation of, 77; and Nidaros Cathedral incident, 123, 127, 131; NS assault on, 112–14; and NS assault on polity (church order), 110–12, 115–16; and NS church negotiations, 177–79; and NS church system, 84, 93, 99–100, 294n25; optimism of, 117; and organists, 115; and Oslo coalition, 43–46, 248; and parish council elections, 111; and *Pastoral Letter*, 75–79; and PCL, 170, 182, 184; and peace mediation (1939), 37–39, 57, 120; and postwar era, 246, 259–60, 262–66, 270, 272; and Prayer of Intercession, 71, 246, 251, 254, 290n10; as presiding bishop, 114–15; public attacks on, 47–48; and Quisling, 42–45, 76, 125–26, 158, 160, 162–63, 177, 189, 219, 248–49; radio appeals of, 46–48; reaction to National Socialism, 29; and rehabilitation of Luther, 262; and religious broadcasts, 99–100; and religious instruction in schools, 103; resignation of, 125–26, 140; and ringing of church bells, 246;

Seip as brother-in-law, 48; and Steltzer, 92, 162–64; and teachers' front, 72, 135–37; and Terboven, 113, 120, 163; and *Time* magazine, 268; and treason debate, 247–48; and treason trials, 249, 253–54, 320n40; and two realms doctrine, 79–81, 172, 291n45; and unified church front, 57–64, 127–28; visit to Finland, 39, 42; and Youth Campaign Day, 112

Berggrav, Kathrine, 80

Berg-Hansen, Kaare, 301n43

Berg internment camp, 236, 238

Berlin: and compulsory youth service, 136; Olympic Games, 10; and peace mediation (1939), 38, 120; and Quisling, 40, 119; Reich Chief Security Office, 87; and Terboven, 86

Bernhardt, Eilert, 64

Beronka, Johan A., 105, 172, 297n6

Bible: Acts 17:26, 211; Acts 5:29, 72, 211; eliminating Jewishness of, 7, 110, 194; literal interpretation of, 20; New Testament, 7; and NS church, 193; Old Testament, 7, 101; Romans 13, 5, 15, 72, 97, 193, 251, 253, 264, 320n38; sales of, 117

Bible Belt, 20

birth records, 181

bishops, German, 8–9; and Confessing Church, 9; and German church struggle, 7–11; and NS church, 172; public declaration of support, 8, 11. *See also names of German bishops*

bishops, Norwegian, 146*fig.*; and autonomous church, 170, 181–82; and Barbarossa, 109–10; and Bishops' Conference, 19, 56–58, 110, 112–14; and CCC, 58–64, 73–75, 272, 288n16; and church conflict (1920s), 23–25; and Church of Finland, 39; and Church's Consultative Council, 117; and compulsory youth service, 131,

bishops, Norwegian *(continued)*
133–34, 136; educated at German
universities, 28; and *The Foundation
of the Church*, 161, 305n35; as Freemasons, 198, 311n34; house arrests
of, 158, 238; indicting NS state for
abuse of rights, 87; and Nidaros
Cathedral incident, 122, 124, 126–
27, 130–32; NS assault on, 112–14;
NS assault on polity (church order),
110–12, 114–16; NS bishops, 90,
127–28, 155, 172–75, 181, 195–98,
200, 210–12, 214, 252, 294n32,
311n34; NS bishops, imprisonment/
forced labor of, 252; NS bishops,
treason trials of, 252; and NS internment policy, 232–33; ordination rights
of, 19, 116, 124–25, 172–73; and
organists, 115; and parish council
elections, 111; and *Pastoral Letter*,
75–82; and PCL, 170–71, 182–83;
and Prayer of Intercession, 71; and
protests of Jewish arrests, 210–11;
and religious broadcasts, 100; resignations of, 73, 76, 78, 81–82, 123–
27, 130–33, 137, 140, 155, 160, 172,
196; retirement of, 112–13, 127;
review of religious textbooks used
in schools, 101–3; salaries of, 19; as
senior civil servants, 19, 112; statistics of repression against, 238–39,
318n49; and unified church front, 57–
64, 127–28. *See also name of bishops*
bishops, Scandinavian, 11, 172, 267–68
bishops, Swedish, 212, 267
Bishops' Conference, 19, 56–58, 110,
112–14, 157; abolition of, 172, 195;
and autonomous church, 188; and
bishops' resignations, 123; and postwar era, 246, 268; and treason trials,
253, 255
Bjørgvin Diocese, 187
blasphemy laws, 26

Blehr, Eivind, 171
Blessing-Dahle, Peder, 88–89, 99, 105,
121, 297n6
Bloch-Hoell, Nils, 184, 234, 308n7
Block, Carl, 267
Blücher (German cruiser), 41
Blue Cross, 313n29
Boge, Ingolf, 238
Böhme, Franz, 244
Bolshevism: and compulsory labor ser-
vice, 218–19; and Jewish persecution,
206–7; struggle against, 108–10, 113,
218–19, 230; threat to Christianity,
193; and treason trials, 252–53
Boman, Thorleif, 28, 282n52, 321n4
Bonhoeffer, Dietrich, 9, 11–12, 268; and
Berggrav's arrest, 162–63, 305n36;
"everyone who acts responsibly
becomes guilty," 48; execution of,
243
Boniface VIII, 264
Bonnevie-Svendsen, Conrad: and Coor-
dination Committee, 106–7, 158,
183, 221; and courier services, 107,
183; escape to Sweden, 183, 238,
246; and *The Foundation of the
Church*, 158, 162; as Minister of
Church and Education, 245, 247;
pastor to deaf/hearing-impaired,
106, 182–83
Bormann, Martin, 163
Bräuer, Curt, 41, 43–46, 48–49
Bredtvedt Prison, 162–63
Brekke, Egil, 265
Brodersen, Arvid, 92–93, 234
Brotherhood of St. Michael, 92–93
Brun, Johan Lyder, 23, 63
Bull, Edvard, 27
Burge Memorial Lecture, 262–63

Calmeyer Street Mission Hall (Oslo),
23, 60, 283n19
Calvin, John, 8, 264

Can Any Christian Demand Be Placed on State Life? (Aulén), 80
Canaris, Wilhelm W., 162–63, 243
cannibalism, 26
capitalism, 22, 126, 258
Carlsen, Ingvald B., 99, 148*fig.*, 288n16, 288n19; imprisonment of, 162
Castberg, Tycho, 298n24
cathedral deans, 73, 78, 111–12, 124–25, 128–29, 298n24; and autonomous church, 181; NS deans, 155, 181, 196, 198, 200; resignations of, 128–29
Cathedral of St. Peter (Geneva), 264
CCC (Christian Consultative Council), 58–65, 73–75, 117–18, 148*fig.*, 190, 288n16, 288n19, 289n29; and bishops' resignations, 123; and clergy's resistance, 302n22; and compulsory youth service, 131, 135, 138, 140–41; and courier services, 61–62, 93, 106–7, 138; exclusion of free churches, 64; and *The Foundation of the Church*, 155–58, 160–62, 208–9, 305n35; and "Haugean course," 60–64; as illegal organization, 61; and just state, 73–75, 77; letter to Skancke, 73–75; and NS church system, 93, 292n2; and *Pastoral Letter*, 76–77, 82; and postwar era, 240, 261; and secrecy, 61, 73; for Stavanger Diocese, 155–56, 174–77, 303n2, 304n6; and Stavanger manifesto, 174–77; unable to function, 170
censorship, German, 48, 63; and autonomous church, 187; and NS church system, 98–100; and paper rationing, 183; and PCL, 183; and Reichskommissariat, 86; and Stavanger manifesto, 176
chauffeurs' school (Svelvik), 223
"The Chosen People" (Luther), 214
Christensen, Ingolf E., 45, 53, 289n25

Christian Buddhist Mission, 313–14n29
Christian Democratic Party, 259
Christian Gymnasium, 288n19
Christianity, 11–12; and Barbarossa, 109–10; and cross, 103; "finest hour" of, 275; and individualism, 18, 22, 27, 32, 138; and Jews, 211–12; national element in, 101–3; Norwegian Christianity, 18, 22, 27, 32, 101–3, 138, 271–73; and NS church/church system, 32, 101–3, 194, 201, 271–72; and postwar era, 258, 271–72; and swastika, 101–3
"Christianity—The Tenth National Plague" (Øverland), 26
Christian Labor Party, 27
Christian Physicians Association, 313n29
Christian Union, 192–93, 199, 310n7; newspaper of, 192
Christian V, King of Norway, 19
Christie, Hartvig C., 62–63
christological theme, 74
Church Advisory Conference (NS), 172–73, 195, 199, 231
church and state, 11, 24–26; and Disruption, 273–74; and ecumenical movement, 31, 74; and *The Foundation of the Church*, 157–60; in Germany, 13, 16–17; and invasion, 43; and letter to Skancke, 73–75; and NS church, 171–79; and postwar era, 240, 259–60, 262–63; and *The Temporal and the Eternal* (Berggrav), 55–56. *See also* two realms doctrine
"Church and *Volkstum*" (Althaus), 6
church bells, 113, 298n25
Church for the Deaf, 182
Churchill, Winston, 42, 96–97, 217
Church of Denmark, 266
Church of England, 48, 172
Church of Finland, 39, 172, 176, 266–67

Church of Norway, xx*fig*., 17, 18–
26, 170, 218; accommodation
to Nazism, 17, 32, 71; and anti-
Semitism, 206–9; apostolic succession not retained in, 172; and
autonomous church, 170, 180–90;
and Barbarossa, 108–10; and church
attendance, 20, 77, 98, 117, 160,
187–88, 257, 304n18, 309n30; and
church conflict (1920s), 23–25, 57,
60, 62–64, 117, 240, 260, 283nn19–
20; Clergy Association, 184, 104–5;
and compulsory labor service, 224–
25; and compulsory youth service,
130–42; and confessions, 18–19, 21,
23–24, 28, 50, 55, 59–61, 116–17,
157–60, 178, 189, 193, 208–9, 240,
260–66, 268, 322n38; and Danish
Law of 1683 (King Christian V),
19; disestablishment of, 273; and
ecumenical movement, 32, 37–38,
134, 164, 264–66, 268; "finest hour"
of, 275; as "the folk church," 20, 25;
and *The Foundation of the Church*,
155–65, 182, 193; and "Hell Controversy," 261; and inner person, 55–
56; and liberation, 245–46; material
costs of occupation, 247; and non-
violent resistance, 269; and Norwegian Law (1687), 19; and NS church/
church system, 83–94, 97–98, 104–
5, 195; and NS negotiations, 173–75,
177–79, 195–96, 217, 307n29; passive members in, 20, 188, 282n8; and
polity (church order), 19, 110–12,
114–17; and postwar era, 239, 257,
259–66, 268–69, 273; and Prayer of
Intercession, 71, 238, 246, 251, 254,
290n10; protest against Jewish persecution, 210–12, 214–15, 313n29;
reconstitution of, 246–47; seal of
confessional, 71, 73, 75; and state
servility, 17, 26, 33, 77, 263, 270,

272; and Stavanger manifesto, 174–
76; and two realms doctrine, 25, 33,
55–56, 74, 77–81, 132, 157–59, 171–
73, 262–63, 270; and unified church
front, 57–65, 127–28, 158, 163–64,
184, 239–40, 261; and Winter War,
39. *See also* bishops, Norwegian;
clergy, Norwegian
Church of Scotland, 273–74
Church of Sweden, 93, 172, 176, 267
Church Order Commission, 259–60
Church's Consultative Council, 117–18,
170
*The Church's Organization in Norway:
Retrospect and Prospect* (Berggrav),
259
"The Church's Yes to the Changed
Times in Our Land" (Feyling), 84
"The Church Today" (PCL newspaper),
183–84
Circle (*Kretsen*), 105–7, 217, 297n46;
arrests/exile of members, 106; and
Berggrav, 105–7, 221, 297n46; and
compulsory labor service, 220–21;
and compulsory youth service, 135;
and teachers' front, 135
civilian casualties, 46–48
civil servants, Norwegian: Berggrav
as, 44, 47; bishops and clergy as, 19,
33, 71, 99; and conscience, 71–72;
and invasion, 43–44; Oftenæs as, 70,
83; retirement age lowered, 70, 112–
13; senior civil servants, 19, 112–13.
See also bishops, Norwegian; clergy,
Norwegian
class, social, 256; and NS church, 192
clergy, German, 8, 10–13, 15; and
Brotherhood of St. Michael, 92–93.
See also names of German clergy
clergy, Norwegian, 155, 321n4; and
autonomous church, 181–87, 196–97,
308n5; banning of public readings
by, 141–42, 196; and Barbarossa,

109–10, 297n6; and Bishops' Conference, 113; and bishops' resignation, 125, 128–29, 137; and CCC, 61–62, 65; and church conflict (1920s), 23–25; as civil servants, 33, 71, 184; Clergy Association, 104–5; collections for, 184–87, 189, 321n4; and compulsory labor service, 221–23; and compulsory youth service, 132, 135, 140–42, 155, 302n22; and conscience, 71–72, 104–5, 141, 176, 208, 254; and diocesan communication networks, 183; and dismissals, 140, 155, 161–62, 195–98, 222, 239, 252; educated at German universities, 28; expulsion from parishes, 179, 182, 187, 232, 238–39, 252; and *The Foundation of the Church*, 155–61, 193, 305n35; house arrests of, 158, 238; and National Labor Service Law, 221–23; and Nidaros Cathedral incident, 121–23; NS clergy, 88–92, 98–101, 103–5, 109–10, 117, 121–23, 125, 129, 152*fig.*, 171, 173–74, 181, 186, 192–93, 196, 198–200, 239–40, 245, 253–55, 297n6, 308n5, 320n38; NS clergy, imprisonment of, 253; NS clergy, treason trials of, 253–54, 320n38; and NS internment policy, 232–33; opposition clergy, 90, 98–99, 140, 173, 196–98, 222; and ordination, 104, 156–57, 173, 182, 189, 198, 233, 235; and organists, 115; and *Pastoral Letter*, 81; and PCL, 181–84, 218, 315n10; and postwar era, 239–40, 272; and Prayer of Intercession, 71; protest against Jewish persecution, 205, 210, 212; reinstatement of, 245, 255; and religious broadcasts, 98–100; and religious instruction in schools, 72, 101, 103; resignations of, 129, 141, 155–57,

160–64, 170, 176, 180, 184, 198, 222, 273, 301n43, 305n25, 305n43; and resistance, 71–72, 104–5, 141, 302n22; salaries of, 170, 181, 184–87, 189, 199; as school board members, 101, 103; and seal of confessional, 71, 73, 75; and state servility, 33, 272; statistics of repression against, 238–39, 318n49; and Stavanger manifesto, 175; views on German Christian movement, 29. *See also names of Norwegian clergy*

clergy, Swedish, 267

Clergy Association, 104–5, 184, 196

collaboration, German, 5; and Godesberg Declaration, 10–11; ideological collaboration, 10–11; and Pastors' Emergency League, 8

collaboration, Norwegian, 43–48, 52–54; administrative collaboration, 43–46; and Berggrav, 43–48, 248; economic collaboration, 54, 220; ideological collaboration, 42, 44; and NS church, 240; and Oslo coalition, 43–46, 248; political collaboration, 52–54; and Quisling, 42, 44, 46; and Støren, 127

Commissarial Council, 56, 59, 69, 71, 73, 177, 253

"Common Platform," 256

communion, 20

Communism, 11, 22, 31; and Barbarossa, 108–10; *Friheten* (newspaper), 248; and Gestapo, 89; and NMS takeover, 236; and NS church, 193–95; and NS state, 30, 39–40, 126. *See also* Communists

Communism and Religion (Bull), 27

Communists, 6; and autonomous church, 187; and compulsory labor service, 224; and *The Foundation of the Church*, 160; Øverland as, 26. *See also* Communism compulsory labor service, 219–26; and clergy, 221–23; and military mobilization, 218, 221, 223–25; and university students, 220

compulsory youth service, 127, 130–42, 201, 232, 302n12, 303n39; and clergy, 132, 135, 140–42, 155, 302n22; and *The Foundation of the Church*, 159; and parents, 131–33, 137–41, 159; and PCL, 218; and teachers, 131–40; and treason trials, 251; voluntary participation in, 307n29

concentration camps, 10, 170, 234, 238–39; Auschwitz, 209, 214–15

Confessing Church, 8–10, 29, 31; and anti-Semitism, 17, 282n49; arrest of leaders, 10; and Finland, 267; as legitimate national church, 9; as "Nazi-free space," 9; Norwegians sided with, 29, 59; and postwar era, 267, 270–71

confessions: and CCC, 60–61, 156–58; and church conflict (1920s), 23–24, 57, 189, 240, 260, 265; and Church of Norway, 18–19, 21, 23–24, 28, 50, 55, 59–61, 116–17, 157–60, 178, 189, 193, 208–9, 240, 260–66, 268, 322n38; and *The Foundation of the Church*, 158–60, 208–9, 261–62; and German church struggle, 8; and Hallesby, 21, 57, 178, 260; and NS church, 178, 193; and postwar era, 260–66, 268, 322n38; and religious instruction in schools, 28. *See also names of confessions and creeds*

confirmations, 19–20, 72, 186, 188, 199

conflict resolution, 257

conscience, 55, 59, 71–74, 79, 115; and Berggrav, 71–73, 104, 160, 254, 290n13; and church conflict (1920s), 240; and clergy, 71–72, 104–5, 141, 176, 208, 254; and compulsory labor

service, 224–25; and *The Foundation of the Church*, 159–60; freedom of, 178, 190; and Jewish persecution, 211, 213; and parents, 138, 218; and PCL, 218; and professional organizations, 104–5; and Stavanger manifesto, 175; and teachers, 72, 104, 136–38, 290n13; and treason trials, 254

Constitution, Norwegian, 24–26, 41; Article 2, 26, 98, 141, 159, 207; and blasphemy laws, 26; and church-state relationship, 55, 73; exclusion of Jews, 29, 207–8; and "extraordinary circumstances," 45, 286n21; and *The Foundation of the Church*, 159–60; and invasion, 43–45; king as head of Church, 24–25; and NS church/church system, 97–98, 196, 245; signing of (1814), 41; and treason trials, 247, 249, 252

constitutional democracy, 256

Contact Circle for Church Communions, 265–66, 322n39; boycott of, 266

Conventicle Law, 20

Coordination Committee, 93, 105–7, 217, 297n46; and compulsory labor service, 220–23, 226; and courier services, 106–7, 182–83, 304n19; and *The Foundation of the Church*, 158; and parents, 138; and PCL, 182–83; and professional organizations, 106, 221; and teachers, 106, 135, 137–38

Copenhagen bishops' conference, 267

Council of Autonomous Organizations, 21, 58, 188, 288n16, 288n19; and Church's Consultative Council, 117; and compulsory youth service, 133; and PCL, 170, 231; and postwar era, 265

courts, 26, 70, 73; German Law Court,

70; and NS church system, 86; NS
People's Court, 70, 162. *See also*
Supreme Court, Norwegian
Covenant Church, 313n29

Dagbladet (newspaper), 248
Dagen (Christian newspaper), 28–29,
63, 84, 265, 287n6
Dahlemites, 8–10
Deaconess Home, 210
deaf/hearing impaired, 106, 183; Church
for the Deaf, 182
death penalty, 247–48, 250; Berggrav's
stand against, 248; and Gestapo,
238; and NS state, 210
Delbrügge, Hans, 52–53
Denmark: Danish Christianity, 18;
Danish Law of 1683 (King Christian
V), 19; invasion of, 40–41, 266; Jews
immigrated from, 29; and Reichs-
kommissariat, 49
Diakonhjemmet Hospital, 183
Dibelius, Otto, 10, 124, 157, 270; arrest
of, 10
Dietrichson, Johannes Ø., 88, 140–41,
151*fig.*, 158, 182, 231
Diocesan Council Law (1933), 19–20
disobedience, duty of, 31, 80–81
Disruption, 273–74, 323n57
Dissenter Law (1845), 21, 104, 273;
amended, 172
Dissenter Parliament, 21, 133, 164, 211,
302n12, 306n44
Donau aus Bremen, S/S, 214–15
Dönitz, Karl, 244

Easter (1942): and clergy's resignations,
160–62, 164, 180, 184, 254, 273;
and *The Foundation of the Church,*
155, 157–58, 160, 162; and NS church,
179, 192–93, 195–96, 198–99, 201;
reprisals from, 169–70, 174; and
treason trials, 254

"Ecclesiastical White Book" (Feyling),
161
economic depression: in Germany, 6–7;
in Norway, 22
economic justice, 27
ecumenical movement, 31–32; and
Berggrav, 32, 37–38, 48, 57, 64,
92, 164, 263–69; and CCC, 74;
and compulsory youth service,
134; Faith and Order branch, 32,
268; and *The Foundation of the
Church,* 164; international, 266–
69; Life and Work branch, 32,
268; Nordic Ecumenical Institute,
93, 164, 267; and Norwegian
School of Theology, 282n5; and
NS church system, 92; and Oxford
Conference (1937), 31–32; and peace
mediation (1939), 37–38, 57; and
postwar era, 263–69; and reconciliation, 37, 267–68; World Alliance for
International Friendship Through
the Churches branch, 32; and World
Council of Churches, 11, 93, 267–
69
education: and civil resistance, 61;
closing of church schools, 10; as
cultural order, 14; and German
language, 28; and NS church, 173;
and postwar era, 259; and Reichskommissariat, 86. *See also* religious
instruction in schools; teachers
Education Council, 134
Education Department, 101
Ehrenström, Nils, 11, 15
Eide, Kåre, 258
Eidem, Erling, 11, 267
Eidsivating lagmannsrett (district court
of appeals), 248–49
Eisenhower, Dwight D., 244
El Alamein (Egypt), 216
Eldal, J., 103
elections, German, 7

elections, Norwegian, 27–28, 39; and
female voters, 27; and NS, 39–40;
and postwar era, 259
Elert, Werner, 14
Elverum, 188; Elverum Authorization,
41, 53
Engelbrecht, Erwin, 47–48
engineers, 72, 106
English Channel, 51
Enlightenment, 12
Erichsen, Christian, 298n24
Eriksen, Leif, 184
eternal realm. *See* spiritual realm
Evangelical Lutheran Church, 10, 18,
24–26
Evangelical Lutheran Free Church, 133,
302n12, 306n44
Evanston Assembly (1954), 269
evolution of species, 108

Falck-Hansen, Georg, 213, 232, 297n6
Falstad internment camp, 238
Fangen, Ronald, 28, 120, 265
Fascism, 22, 25, 31, 284n48. *See also
names of Fascist states*
Fascist National Union Party. *See* NS
state
Fatherland Song, 158
Fehlis, Heinrich, 209; suicide of, 245
Feyling, Sigmund, 83–85, 88–94,
149*fig.*, 292n2, 293n6, 294n32; as
anti-Semitic, 194, 213–14; arrest
of, 319n7; assault on bishops, 112–
14; assault on polity (church order),
110–12, 114–17; *Aula* speech of,
141–42; and Barbarossa, 109–10,
193, 297n6; biography of, 84; and
bishops' resignations, 123, 126–29;
burning of papers, 245, 319n7; and
Christian NS conference, 112; and
Church Advisory Conference, 172;
and clergy's resignations, 141–42,
251, 305n25; and compulsory labor

service, 222; death of, 252; and *The
Foundation of the Church*, 159–61,
305n35; guilty verdict of, 251–52,
254–55; and "ice front" of social
non-cooperation, 311n37; imprisonment of, 251–52; and internment
policy, 232–33, 317n11; and Jewish
persecution, 207, 212–14, 313n29;
and National Labor Service Law,
222; and NMS takeover, 235–37;
and NS church/church policy, 97–98,
172–75, 177–79, 193–201, 232–33,
311n23, 317n11; and professional
organizations, 104–5; and "The Protest of the Forty-Three," 104–5; and
religious broadcasts, 98–100, 295n7;
and religious textbooks, 101–3,
296n24; revised catechism of, 135;
and school reform, 101–3; and
Støren, 112–14; and theological
faculties, 234; treason trial of, 250–
52, 254–55; and Youth Campaign
Day, 111–12
Finland, 38–39; archbishop of, 172; and
Barbarossa, 109, 172, 266; Church
of Finland, 39, 172, 176, 266–67;
defeat of, 39, 266; invasion of, 38–
39; military aid to, 38–39; military
alliance with Germany, 172, 267
Finnmark, 154*fig.*, 243, 247
Fjelberg, Arne, 151*fig.*, 231
Fjellbu, Arne: and assault on bishops,
110; as bishop of Finnmark, 154*fig.*,
244, 258; and church conflict (1920s),
63; and dismissal, 123, 126, 128,
140; escape to Sweden, 238, 244;
expulsion/banishment of, 197, 244;
and Nidaros Cathedral incident,
121–23, 126; and *Pastoral Letter*,
77; and postwar era, 258
Fjell Parish, 238
Fleischer, Andreas, 124, 126, 146*fig.*,
187, 295n37

Fløystad, Gjerulf, 184
forced labor. *See* compulsory labor
　service
For Church and Culture (journal),
　247–48
"For the Church and the Christian Faith
　Against Bolshevism" (Feyling), 110
Fortress Norway, 169, 243
Fosse, Harald, 200
*The Foundation of the Church: A Con-
　fession and a Declaration*, 155–65;
　and autonomous church, 182, 193;
　Bergen draft of, 155–56, 208–9; and
　Berggrav, 156–57, 160, 162, 208;
　and clergy, 155–61; drafts of, 155–
　58; Easter Sunday for reading of,
　155, 157–58, 160, 162, 164; Jews
　excluded from, 155–56, 208–9; NS
　response to, 160–63, 165; and ordi-
　nation, 157, 159; and PCL, 182;
　and postwar era, 245, 261–62;
　Stavanger CCC draft of, 155–56,
　303n2, 304n6; and theological facul-
　ties, 234; and treason trials, 253;
　and unified church front, 159, 163–
　64, 261; and "we condemn," 157–58
"Four Cardinal Points," 135
Fourth Commandment, 102, 132
France: capitulation of, 53; casualty
　statistics for, 244; invasion of, 51;
　and Norway, 41–42, 51; and Winter
　War, 39
Frankfurt am Main (Germany), 206
free churches, 10, 21, 283nn13–14; and
　clergy's resignations, 164; and com-
　pulsory youth service, 132–33, 164;
　exclusion of, 64, 265–66, 322n34,
　322n38; and Jews, 211–12; Justice
　Department, 91; and liberation, 247;
　material costs of occupation, 247;
　and NS church/church system, 91,
　104, 193; and *Pastoral Letter*, 75,
　133, 164; and postwar era, 263–66,

322n34, 322n38; as "sects," 10, 21,
　142, 283n13; and Stavanger mani-
　festo, 176–77, 237
Free Faculty of Theology, 19, 233–35,
　282n5; and Bloch-Hoell, 184, 234;
　and boycotts, 235; and church con-
　flict (1920s), 21, 23; closing of, 234–
　35; and compulsory labor service,
　220; and Feyling, 84; protest against
　Jewish persecution, 313n29; and
　Seierstad, 80, 231; Seminary for
　Practical Theology, 231, 235; and
　Smemo, 231; and treason trials,
　253; and Vold, 62
free folk church, 175–77, 237
Freemasons, 87, 198, 311n34
Free Norwegian Lutheran Folk Church,
　175, 236
Friheten (newspaper), 248
Fritt Folk (NS newspaper), 84, 120,
　236
Frogner Church (Oslo), 141, 182, 231
From the World of Prayer (Hallesby),
　249
Frøyland, Lars Andreas: and Barba-
　rossa, 297n6; and Clergy Associa-
　tion, 104–5; illegal ordinations
　by, 310n9; imprisonment of, 252;
　and Jews, 210–12; and religious
　broadcasts, 99; as replacement
　bishop of Oslo, 173, 175, 198,
　234; and theological faculties,
　234; treason trial of, 252
"fuel holiday," 137, 139–40
Fuglesang, Rolf, 126, 194
fundamentalism, 23, 64, 283n19
funerals, 19–20, 186
Fyresdal parsonage, 249

Gau Aachen, 49
Geelmuyden, Knut, 297n6
Gerhardsen, Einar, 47, 105, 169, 245,
　256, 259–60, 289n25

German church struggle, 5, 7–12, 29; accommodation to state ideology, 14; and Confessing Church, 8–10, 17, 29, 31, 59, 267, 270–71, 282n49; and Dahlemites, 8–10; and German Christian movement, 7–14, 29, 194; and Godesberg Declaration, 10–11; and intact churches, 8–9; and Lutheran bishops' declaration, 11; Norwegian church struggle compared to, 270–73; reaction to in Norway, 29, 57, 59–60, 123; and Reich Church, 7–9; Scholder as preeminent scholar of, 6; and Terboven, 49–50

German Evangelical Church, 5, 7, 16, 32, 50; and Finland, 267; and postwar era, 263, 267–68. *See also* German Lutheranism

German language: Berggrav fluent in, 29, 43, 52, 268; taught in Norwegian schools, 28

German Lutheranism, 5–8, 11–17; abdicated responsibility for political/social problems, 15–16; accommodation to Nazism, 12, 16–17; and anti-Semitism, 7, 14–17, 271–72, 282n49; and Barbarossa, 108–9; and concept of God, 12–13; "declaration of bankruptcy," 11; and Holocaust, 16–17; and inwardness, 14–15; natural theology of, 14; and Nazism, 6–7, 12, 16–17, 32, 50, 57; and orders of creation, 6, 8, 11–14; and state servility, 13–17, 270, 272; theological authority of state, 13–15; trinitarian conception lacking in, 12; and two realms doctrine, 14–17, 25, 270; and *Volk*, 12–14. *See also* German church struggle

German uniforms, 223

Germany: and Barbarossa, 108–10, 120, 172, 206–7, 244, 295n13; and Battle of the Bulge, 230; Brotherhood of St. Michael, 92–93; brutality of invasion, 47; capitulation of, 237, 243–44; casualty statistics for, 244; Enabling Act (1933), 7; and "Final Solution," 209; Foreign Office, 212; Hitler Youth, 130; invasions, 11, 20, 37, 40–51, 88, 108, 266; and Jewish persecution, 6–7, 10–12, 16–17, 29–30, 209, 212–13, 281n48, 282n49; and Non-Aggression Pact (1939), 108; and Norwegian executions, 126, 210; and NS church system, 85–86; and Omaha Beach, 230; police agencies in Norway, 87; Reichstag, 7; retreat from Norway, 243–44; Sixth Army surrender, 216, 219; and Stalingrad, 216–17, 219, 229; and submarines, 119

Gestapo, 9–10; arrests of university students, 93; and autonomous church, 186, 188; Bergen chief/assistant killed, 169–70; and Berggrav, 120, 163; and capitulation, 245; and clergy's resignations, 142; and compulsory labor service, 223, 225; and compulsory youth service, 134, 136, 142; Consultant on World View Issues, 87; and Coordination Committee, 106–7; and German church struggle, 9–10; informants of, 88–89; intelligence reports, 77, 216, 231; and Jewish persecution, 206, 209–10; and Mangers, 133–34; and Milorg, 170; and NS church/church system, 85–89, 93, 178; and *Pastoral Letter*, 76–77, 79; "Reports from Norway," 89, 294n25; Security Police and Security Service, 87, 92, 250–51; and Terboven, 69, 120, 170; and violence, 59, 93

Giverholt, Arne, 29, 284n38

Gjerdi, Andreas, 88–89, 99, 105, 112, 297n6

Gjerstad, Per, 236
Gjessing, Marcus, 297n6
Glasgow (cruiser), 42
Gleditsch, Jens, 25
Godal, Tord, 151*fig.*, 231
Godesberg Declaration, 10–11
"God's Call to Us Now" (newspaper article), 38
Goebbels, Josef, 86, 109, 136
Gogarten, Friedrich, 14
Good Friday service, 158, 304n18
Göring, Hermann, 38, 49
Göteborgs Handels- och Sjöfartstidning, 48, 78
Gothenburg Diocese Times, 267
Gothenland, S/S, 215
government, Norwegian, 25, 28; and capitulation, 51–52; and Circle (*Kretsen*), 105; and compulsory labor service, 220; Defense High Command, 217; and Home Front, 217, 220–21, 245; and invasion, 41–47; and liberation, 243, 245; in London, 51–53, 55, 95–97, 217; and military aid to Finland, 38–39; and National Council Negotiations, 53–54, 248; and *Pastoral Letter*, 77–78; and PCL, 171, 246; prayer for, 71; and Prayer of Intercession, 290n10; and Stavanger manifesto, 176; and treason trials, 253; in Tromsø, 51
"Greetings Between Clergy Brothers" (PCL newspaper), 183, 308n12
Grimnes, Ole Kristian, 44
Grini internment camp, 96, 153*fig.*, 169, 226, 238, 246, 318n43
Grossmann, Klaus, 87
Gudbrandsdalen, 41
"Guidelines for the Use of the Organ in Worship" (Church Dept.), 115
Günther, Christian, 38
Günther, Vilhelm Hermann, 77, 88, 178, 231

Haakon VII, King of Norway, 41–43, 45–46, 50–51, 56, 95; and liberation, 245; prayer for, 71; refusal to abdicate, 53–54
Haga, Sigurd, 297n6
Hagelin, Albert Viljam, 104, 126
Hagen, Hans Olaf, 105, 297n6
Hague Convention, 47, 49, 54–55, 76, 81, 104; Article 43, 55; and compulsory labor service, 224; and treason trials, 253
Halifax, Viscount (Edward F. L. Wood), 38, 120
Hallesby, Ole, 21, 26, 28, 145*fig.*, 148*fig.*, 283nn19–20; arrest/deportation of, 226, 230–31, 237; and autonomous church, 170, 184; and Berggrav, 37–38, 57–58, 117; and CCC, 60, 62–63, 288n16, 288n19; and church conflict (1920s), 23, 57, 60, 62–63, 260–61; and Church Order Commission, 260; and compulsory labor service, 220, 222, 225–26; and *The Foundation of the Church*, 157, 162; as Günther's source, 88; liberation of, 246; and NS church, 193; and NS church negotiations, 174–75, 177–79; and PCL, 170, 174–76, 184, 218, 220, 222, 225–26, 237; and peace mediation (1939), 37–38, 57; and postwar era, 257, 259–61, 265; protest against Jewish persecution, 211; and Stavanger manifesto, 175–76; and Terboven, 225–26, 230–31; and treason debate, 248; and treason trials, 253
Hålogaland Diocese, 129, 188, 301n43
Halvorsen, Hans, 105
Hamar Diocese, 41, 114, 198, 248; bishop of, 261
Hambro, Carl J., 44–45
Hammersen, Fridtjof, 163, 249

Hansson, Kristian, 63, 148*fig.*, 156, 288n16, 288n19, 318n46; assumed Feyling's position, 245; house arrest of, 162

Hansteen, Christian, 110, 297n6

Haraldsson, Olav, 56

Harbek, Ole F., 52

Hartmann, Paul, 105

Håskoll, Rasmus, 186

Haslie, Johannes, 105

Hauge, Dagfinn, 151*fig.*, 231; and "small church" movement, 231

Hauge, Hans Nielsen, 20–21, 56, 272; and "Haugean course," 60–64; imprisonment of, 20–21; and NS church, 193; as spiritual father of mission societies, 21

Hauge, Jens Christian, 92

Haugen, Erling, 301n43

Helgøya internment, 232–33, 237

"Hell Controversy," 261

Helsen, Olaf, 289n25

High Council, 61, 289n25

Hille, Henrik, 146*fig.*; and dismissal, 126; health of, 128; and Helgøya internment, 232–33; and PCL, 170, 218; resignation of, 124, 126, 128

Himmler, Heinrich, 50–51, 76–77, 87, 163

Hird (NS paramilitary organization), 69–70, 76–77, 289n2; and Jewish persecution, 206; and Nidaros Cathedral incident, 121; and treason trials, 251

Hirsch, Emanuel, 14

Hitler, Adolf, 5; and Administrative Council, 49; attempted assassination of (July 1944), 93, 243; and Barbarossa, 108–10, 295n13; and Battle of Britain, 95; belief in distinctiveness of races, 108; belief in evolution of species, 108; belief in survival of fittest, 108; at Brenner Pass meeting, 38; direct line from Luther, 12; and Fortress Norway, 169, 243; Führer Directive, 49–50, 70; and German church struggle, 7–13; and invasion of Norway, 40–43, 48; and Jewish persecution, 201, 209, 213; mobilizing for total war, 216–17; Norwegian reaction to, 28–29; paranoia of, 243; policy of not provoking churches, 12, 50, 86, 194, 269–70, 295n7; preparing for Allied invasion through Norway, 169, 243; and Quisling, 40, 42–43, 45, 59, 109, 119, 164, 218; suicide of, 244; and Terboven, 49–51, 70

Hitler Youth, 130

Hjelmtveit, Nils, 28, 78, 246, 260, 284n35

Høeg, Hans, 60, 184, 288n16, 288n19

Hoel, Adolf, 234

Hoem, Øivind, 99, 297n6

Høigård, Einar, 134–35, 233; arrest and death of, 135

Høivik, Hans, 184. *See also* Høeg, Hans

Holocaust, 16–17

Home Front, 97; and Berggrav, 163; and Hallesby, 246; and Jewish persecution, 209, 215; and Norwegian government, 217, 220–21, 245; and Østlid, 83–84, 292n2; and PCL, 182–83; and theological faculties, 234. *See also* Circle (*Kretsen*); Coordination Committee

Home Front Leadership, 61, 93, 97, 217, 246; and compulsory labor service, 220–21, 223–24; and liberation, 245

Hooft, Willem Visser't, 268

Hope, Ludwig, 21, 58, 117, 148*fig.*; arrest/deportation of, 226, 230–31, 237; and autonomous church, 170, 184; and CCC, 60, 62–63, 288n16, 288n19; and compulsory labor service, 222, 225–26; and *The Founda-tion of the Church*, 157, 162; and Grini internment camp, 153*fig.*, 226; liberation of, 246; and PCL, 170, 184, 218, 222, 225–26, 237; and Terboven, 226, 230–31

Hoprekstad, Olav, 135–36

Hovdin, Haakon, 297n6

Høyem, Brage, 298n24

Høyer, Ansgar N., 222, 297n6

Huhnhäuser, Alfred, 86, 293n14

human rights violations, 12, 75, 211, 234–35, 245, 269, 271

Hygen, Johannes, 111–12, 170; as Berggrav's representative, 170; as Günther's source, 88; and NS church negotiations, 174–75, 177–79; and PCL, 170, 174–76, 218; and Stavan-ger manifesto, 175–76

The Idea of the Holy (Otto), 79

Ihlen, Christian, 207

Imperial Commissioner. *See* Reichskommissariat

individualism: and mission societies, 20; and Norwegian Christianity, 18, 22, 27, 32, 138

Indrebø, Ragnvald, 148*fig.*, 231, 288n16, 288n19; imprisonment of, 162

informants: and Gestapo, 87–88; and NS church/church system, 87–91, 98, 113–14, 196–97. *See also* spies

Ingier, C. J., 297n6

Inter-Church Aid, 5; European Central Bureau, 5

international ecumenical movement, 266–69

international press, 10, 75–77, 164; and treason trials, 248–49

internment camps, 238–39; Berg intern-ment camp, 236, 238; Falstad intern-ment camp, 238; Grini internment camp, 96, 153*fig.*, 169, 226, 238, 246, 318n43

internment policy (NS), 231–33, 237, 317n11; Helgøya internment, 232–33, 237; Lillehammer internment, 232–33, 237

Ivarsson, Eirik, 305n24

Jacob Church (Oslo), 231, 288n19

Jäger, August, 9

Jahn, Gunnar, 105, 289n25

Japan, 108, 119

Jesus, 43; and Althaus, 264; Aryan Christ, 14–15, 194; and church con-flict (1920s), 57; Feyling's views on, 84, 102; and *The Foundation of the Church*, 160; and German Lutheran-ism, 7–9, 14–15; Ihlen's views on, 207; and letter to Skancke, 74; and protests of Jewish arrests, 211–12; Quisling's views on, 250; and unified church front, 59, 63

"Jewish problem," 30, 201, 205–7, 213

"Jewish question," 29–31, 205, 213–14, 254–55

Jews, Danish, 266

Jews, German, 6–7, 10–12; arrests of, 10; "betrayal" of, 17, 282n49; and *Kristallnacht*, 10, 281n48; persecution of, 12, 16–17, 29–30; and Prussian Confessional Synod (Breslau), 11

Jews, Norwegian, 22, 29–31, 205–15; arrests of, 206, 209–15, 254; asylum for, 29–30; and Barbarossa, 206–7; and Berggrav, 156, 205–6, 208–9; and Bolshevism, 206–7; casualty sta-tistics for, 244–45; confiscation of property, 205, 210, 213–14, 313n29; deportation to death camps, 193, 214–15, 218, 255, 313n29; escape to Sweden, 206, 209–10, 215; exclusion from country, 29, 207–8; expulsion

Jews, Norwegian *(continued)*
of, 209–10; and Feyling, 194, 207, 212–14; and *The Foundation of the Church*, 155–56, 208; and Freemasons, 311n34; Günther's wife as, 88; indifference to in prewar period, 30, 208; internment of, 209, 214–15, 218, 222; "J" stamped on identity cards, 207; and Lund, 302n33; and marriages, 207, 254–55; and mission societies, 207, 211–12; and NS church, 191, 193–94, 212–14; and NS state, 40, 101, 206–9; persecution of, 205–7, 209–15, 218, 312n2; prayer for, 212; and Quisling, 206–8, 210, 212; and registration of property, 207, 254; sent to Auschwitz, 209, 214–15; and stateless Jews, 206; and Terboven, 205–6, 221, 231n4; and Wagner, 87, 206; and yellow "Jewish business" signs, 205–6. *See also* anti-Semitism; Holocaust
Johanson, Harry, 267
Johnson, Alex, 93, 106–7, 221–23, 258
Jørgensen, Herman E., 290n10
Jøssings, 216, 222
June negotiations. *See* National Council Negotiations
Justice Department, 75, 288n19, 296n16; and clergy's resignations, 160–61; and free churches, 91, 104; and Jewish persecution, 207; and NS church, 187; and religious broadcasts, 99–100, 288n16
just state, 73–75, 77–82

Kaila, Erkki, 172
Kampen Church (Oslo), 196, 231
Keller, Adolf, 5, 17
Kirchenkampf. *See* German church struggle
kirkekamp. *See* Norwegian church struggle

Kirkenes, 169, 243–44
Knab, Werner, 76
Knutzen, Sam, 184–85
Kohlrep, Walter, 87
Koht, Halvdan, 43, 47, 96
Koren, Laurentius, 104–5
Koritzinsky, Harry, 231n4
Kornelius, Kornelius O., 155–56, 304n6
Kreisau Circle, 12, 93, 162–63, 209, 249
Kreutz, R. S., 297n6
Kristallnacht, 10, 281n48
Kristelig Tidende, 64
Kristiansand, 155, 189, 303n2
Kristiansen, Cay Børre, 238
Kristiansund, 188
Krohn-Hansen, Wollert, 146fig.; and autonomous church, 188, 308n5; and compulsory youth service, 136, 138; and Helgøya internment, 232–33; and Norwegian government, 51; and postwar era, 240; resignation of, 123–24, 126
Krokskogen, 46–48
Kühlewein, Julius, 11
Kvam, Aksel, 297n6
Kvasnes, Ole J. B.: and Barbarossa, 297n6; considered for Feyling's position, 83; and Jewish persecution, 212–13; and NMS takeover, 235–37; NS acting bishop of Stavanger, 177, 198; and NS internment policy, 232; and NS theological "college," 235; treason trial of, 252

labor movement, Norwegian, 22, 25–26, 43, 257
Labor Party, 26–28, 256; anti-religion stance of, 27, 100; *Arbeiderbladet* (newspaper), 248; and autonomous church, 189; and Circle (*Kretsen*), 105; deportation of Gerhardsen, 169; forming government, 19, 27–28, 57;

and Home Front Leadership, 97,
217; and liberation, 245; and Nidaros Cathedral incident, 122; and
postwar era, 258–60; and school
reform, 27, 100–101; and Socialism,
40. *See also* government, Norwegian
labor service. *See* compulsory labor
service
laity, 20, 28, 30, 32–33, 65, 92–93, 110–
11, 113; and NS church, 192–93, 199
Land og Kirke (publishing house), 258
Larsen, Stein Ugelvik, 323n56
Lavik, Johannes, 29, 265
Lawyers Association, 79
Lehtonen, Aleksi, 39
"Letter to the German Nobility"
(Luther), 173
Liberal Party, 189, 272
liberal theology, 19, 22–26; and Berg-
grav, 37, 57; and CCC, 62–64; and
church conflict (1920s), 23–25, 57,
60, 62–64, 260–61, 283nn19–20;
and church-state relationship, 24–26;
and Gleditsch, 25; and modernity,
23; and postwar era, 240, 260–61
Lie, Jonas, 91, 126, 162
Lie, Trivet, 96
Lie, Trygve, 257
Life and Doctrine (Feyling), 102–3
Lillehammer internment, 232–33, 237
Lincoln, Bruce, 275
Lindheim, Egil, 121–22
Ljostveit, Henrik Kristian, 99
Lofoton islands, 96, 169
London: Blitz, 95; Norwegian govern-
ment in, 51–53, 55, 95–97, 217; and
peace mediation (1939), 38, 120;
radio, 76
London News, 223
Lothe, Einar, 123, 128, 173, 252, 297n6
Lothe, L., 177
Lothe, Odd, 301n43
Lovisenberg Hospital, 131

Luftwaffe, 249
Lund, Sigrid Helliesen, 137, 302n33
Lunde, Gulbrand, 99, 109–10
Luther, Martin, 11–13; and anti-Semitism,
16–17, 212–14, 281n48; and Church
of Norway, 19, 79–81, 211–12;
direct line to Hitler, 12; and Fourth
Commandment, 132; and "Luther
arsenal," 80–81, 291n45; and NS
church, 172–73, 193, 237; and postwar era, 262–64; and state servility,
17, 263, 282n52; and statism, 13;
and two realms doctrine, 16, 79–81,
159, 172, 291n45; and tyranny, 125;
"the young" Luther, 172–73
Lutheran Council, 9
Lutheranism, 21–26, 64; confessional
Lutheranism, 21, 240, 260, 266,
268, 322n38; and Godesberg Declaration, 10–11; and NS church, 191;
and postwar era, 260, 262–64, 266–
68, 270–73, 322n38. *See also* Church
of Norway; German Lutheranism
Lutheran World Federation, 268, 367
Luthersk Kirketidende, 117

MacCulloch, 281n48
Majavatn, 209–10
Malde, Karl, 235
Måløy (Lofoton islands) raids/sabotage,
169
Mamen, Hans C., 210
Manders, Olav, 114
Mangers, Jacob, 133–34, 211; and Berg-
grav, 134, 263–64; and deportation
threat, 133–34
Mann, Michael, 13
Marahrens, August, 11
Maroni, James, 146*fig.*; and bishops'
resignations, 124; and CCC, 73–
74; and dismissal, 112, 126; and
Helgøya internment, 232–33; and
PCL, 170, 218

marriages, 20, 181; and Jewish persecution, 207, 254–55. *See also* weddings
Marstrander, Peter E., 234
Marthinsen, Karl A., 91–92, 128, 214, 295n37
Marxism: as anti-Christian, 272; and Bastiansen, 196; and Gestapo, 89; Marxist labor movement, 25, 27
McGovern, William, 13
media, German, 10
media, international, 10, 75–77, 164; and treason trials, 248–49
media, Norwegian, 30–31; and anti-Semitism, 30–31; and Barbarossa, 109; and bishops' resignations, 126; and CCC, 61–62, 289n29; and civil resistance, 61; and compulsory labor service, 225–26; and compulsory youth service, 131, 138; illegal press, 212, 226; and Jews, 212; and mutuality ploy, 116–17; and National Labor Service Law, 225–26; NS media, 30–31, 77, 84, 90, 115, 120, 232; and *Pastoral Letter*, 76–77; and PCL, 183–84, 308n12; and Reichskommissariat, 86; religious media, 86, 88, 109; and treason debate, 248; and treason trials, 248–49
media, Swedish, 164
Megrund, Conrad, 298n24
Mein Kampf (Hitler), 108
Meiser, Hans, 9, 11
Methodists, 21, 64, 122, 313n29; Annual Conference, 248
Milorg, 89, 92, 96–97, 170, 217, 221, 230, 238, 244
Minister President, 120–21, 130, 163, 171, 195, 222. *See also* Quisling, Vidkun
Ministry of Church and Education, 25; assault on bishops, 112–14; assault on polity (church order), 110–12, 114–17; Auditing Office for Public

Foundations, 83; and autonomous church, 181, 183; and bishops' resignations, 123–29; and censorship, 98–100; Church Office, 83; and church conflict (1920s), 261; and clergy's resignations, 141–42, 161–64; and Commissarial Council, 69; and compulsory labor service, 222; and compulsory youth service, 130–42; "cracks" in, 93; and "Ecclesiastical White Book" (Feyling), 161; and Hjelmtveit, 28, 78, 246, 260, 284n35; and internment policy, 231–33; and Jewish persecution, 214, 313n29; and letter to Skancke, 73; and liberation, 245–47; Management Division, 83, 199; Ministers' Meetings, 90, 125; and mutuality ploy, 116–17; and National Labor Service Law, 222; and Nidaros Cathedral incident, 121–24, 126, 130; and NMS takeover, 235–36; and Norway's Teacher Association, 130–31, 136–37, 140; and NS church, 171–73, 197–200; and NS church system, 85, 89–90, 250; and Oftenæs, 70, 83; and organists, 114–15; and postwar era, 239–40, 246–47, 260–61; and protests of Jewish arrests, 214; and religious broadcasts, 98–100, 295n7; and religious instruction in schools, 101–3; review of religious textbooks used in schools, 103; and Seip, 48; spies in, 75, 83–84, 91, 114, 292n2; State Secretary, 90; and teachers, 136, 140; and teachers' front, 137; and theological faculties, 233–35; and Youth Campaign Day, 111–12; and Youth Corps (NSUF), 111–12, 130–31, 135–40. *See also* Feyling, Sigmund; NS church system; Skancke, Ragnar
Ministry of Culture and Public Information, 194

Ministry of Justice. *See* Justice Department

Ministry of Labor Service and Sports, 139

Ministry of the Interior, 171; Associations Office, 236

Mission Covenant Church, 21

mission societies, 20–21, 30, 282n10, 283n12; and autonomous church, 182, 185, 188–89; and CCC, 60–64; and church attendance, 189, 257; and church conflict (1920s), 23–25, 57, 60, 62–64, 260–61, 283nn19–20; and Church's Consultative Council, 117–18; and clergy's resignations, 164; and compulsory youth service, 132–34; and courier services, 237; domestic missions, 21, 188; finances for, 185, 189; foreign missions, 21, 188; and *The Foundation of the Church*, 159; Hallesby as leader of, 21, 57, 265; Hauge as spiritual father of, 21; Hope as leader of, 21, 58; low-church orthodoxy of, 20, 23, 26, 29; and Mission to Israel, 207; and NMS takeover, 235–37; and NS church/church system, 85, 91, 192–93, 198; as "the organizations," 20; and *Pastoral Letter*, 75; and PCL, 182, 189; and politics, 27–28; and postwar era, 257, 265–66, 272; protest against Jewish persecution, 211–12, 313n29; and revivals, 189; and Stavanger manifesto, 176; and unified church front, 57–65, 189. *See also* orthodox theology; *names of mission society bishops and clergy*

modernity, 23, 258, 261

Modvar, O. J., 297n6

Molde, 41–42, 63

Molland, Einar, 77, 79, 93, 233, 235, 260, 264

Molland, Eivind, 93

morality: and conscience, 73; higher morality, 6; moral responsibility, 56

Mørland, Arnt, 184–85

Morocco, 216

Mosaic Society, 254

Müller, Georg Wilhelm, 86

Müller, Ludwig, 7–8

Munk, Kaj, 266

Mussolini, Benito, 38

Narvik, 42, 123, 188

Nasjonal Samling. *See* NS state

National Assembly (*Riksting*), 130, 140, 164

National Convention of Friends, 265

National Council Negotiations, 52–54; as "June negotiations," 248; and treason debate, 248

nationalism: and compulsory youth service, 138–39; and German Protestantism, 7, 13; and NS church, 194, 198

National Labor Service Law, 219–26

National Socialism, 5–7; and Church of Norway, 59; and compulsory youth service, 132; and German Lutheranism, 17, 263; "nation-statism" as ideological core of, 13; and Nazification, 7, 11; and NS state, 30–31, 39–40, 194, 284n48; and postwar era, 258, 262–63, 270; and Quisling, 219; reaction to in Norway, 28–29; and Roman Catholic Church, 134; Terboven's views on, 120; and treason trials, 251; and Wagner, 87; and Wehrmacht, 93. *See also* NS state

National Socialist German Labor Party, 7, 49

National Synod (Wittenberg), 7

National Union party. *See* NS state

National Youth Service Law (1942), 130–32, 136–37, 141. *See also* compulsory youth service

"nation-statism," 13
NATO (North Atlantic Treaty Organization), 257
Nazi Church. *See* NS church Nazification, 7, 11; and compulsory youth service, 132; and *The Foundation of the Church*, 157; and NS church system, 56, 59, 97–98, 101, 105, 107, 132; and professional organizations, 105; and religious instruction in schools, 101; and theological faculties, 233; and treason trials, 250–51
Nazism, 5–7, 10–11; and autonomous church, 189–90; and Bolshevism, 108–10, 113; and compulsory labor service, 220; and compulsory youth service, 134–35; and Finland, 266–67; and German Lutheranism, 16–17, 270–72; and mission societies, 189; Nazi revolution, 7, 28–29, 31, 233; and NS church, 181, 194, 201, 213; and postwar era, 239, 257, 262, 270–74; and Quisling, 206; and Sweden, 267; and teachers' resistance, 134–35; and Terboven, 49; and theological faculties, 28, 233; and treason trials, 249–51, 253–54
neo-Pietist confessionalist, 240
Netherlands, 38, 270, 274, 323n57; invasion of, 51; and Reichskommissariat, 49
Nicene Creed, 18
Nidaros Cathedral (Trondheim), 63; cathedral incident, 121–24, 126–27, 130–32, 150fig.
Nidaros Diocese, 20, 25, 112, 160; and NS church, 173, 197–98
Niemöller, Martin, 8–10, 268; arrest of, 10
Nilsen, E. Anker, 122
Nome, John, 237
non-cooperation: and autonomous church, 180–81, 186, 196; and church conflict (1920s), 23, 58; and compulsory labor service, 224, 226; and NMS takeover, 237; and parish council elections, 111; and *Pastoral Letter*, 77; and teachers, 136
non-violence: and autonomous church, 190; and *The Foundation of the Church*, 157; and postwar era, 257, 269; and women's organizations, 137
Nordic Ecumenical Institute, 93, 164, 267
Norsk Kirkeblad, 197
Norsk Skuleblad (teachers' periodical), 102–3, 135
North Africa, 119, 216
"Northerndom and Easterndom" (Schirmer), 194
Norum, Kåre, 102–3, 135–36
Norway: accommodation to Nazism, 22, 32, 53–54, 71; and Barbarossa, 108–10; bombing of heavy water production plant, 230; capitulation of, 50–52, 95, 120, 188, 253; casualty statistics for, 244; Christian history of, 56; and civilian casualties, 46–48; close historic ties with Germany, 28; commando operations inside, 96–97; as corporate state, 130; economy of, 220, 256, 258; and executions by Germans/NS, 126, 210, 238, 243; Fortress Norway, 169, 243; German military installations in, 54, 209, 220–21; and "German work," 54, 220; as homogeneous country, 30, 208; independence (1905), 189; invasion of, 20, 40–51, 88, 133, 188, 205, 249, 266; king of, 19, 41–43, 45–46, 50–51, 53–54, 56; and liberation, 96, 217, 231, 240, 243–45, 247–48, 257, 265; and merchant marine, 95, 244; military forces of, 243; morale in, 96; national anthem of, 122; and

national coalition government, 245, 256; and NATO, 257; and neutrality, 38–39, 95; nine centuries of Christianity in, 18; and NS military mobilization, 218, 221, 223–25, 244–45; "Operation Jupiter," 97; Penal Code, 247; rail system in, 106, 109; reaction to National Socialism, 28–29; restrictive immigration/refugee policy, 30; and Stalingrad, 216–17, 219; and United Kingdom, 41–42, 51, 95–97, 169, 243–44; and United Nations, 257; Wehrmacht retreat from, 243–45; and Winter War, 38–39; and xenophobia, 30. *See also* Church of Norway; government, Norwegian

Norway's Christian Student and Junior College Student League, 313n29

Norway's Christian Student Movement, 313n29

Norway's Finn Mission Society, 313n29

Norway's National Church League, 313n29

Norway's Teacher Association, 130–31, 136–37, 140

Norwegian Army, 42, 46–48, 51; Sixth Division, 51

Norwegian Baptist Society, 313n29

Norwegian Broadcasting Service, 42, 246, 288n19

Norwegian China Mission Association, 21, 58, 183, 231, 283n12, 288n16, 313n29

Norwegian Christian Youth Association, 184, 313n29

Norwegian Church Order Law (1953), 260

Norwegian church struggle, 24–25; beginning of end of, 230–32; and compulsory youth service, 140; and free churches, 133; German church struggle compared to, 270–73; as

historic event, 273; and NMS takeover, 236; and NS church/church system, 90, 94, 171, 194, 230; and postwar era, 258–60, 262, 264, 323n56; and religious broadcasts, 99; and Støren, 127; and theological faculties, 233; and treason trials, 251

Norwegian Deacons Fraternal Association, 313n29

Norwegian Female Teachers Association, 135

Norwegian Institute of Technology, 70, 290n4

Norwegian Law (1687), 19

Norwegian Lutheran Home Mission Society, 21, 23, 58, 188, 259, 283n12, 288n16, 313n29

Norwegian Lutheran Mission Federation, 283n12

Norwegian Mission Alliance, 313n29

Norwegian Mission among the Homeless, 313n29

Norwegian Missionary Society (NMS), 21, 235–37; and Amdahl, 155–56, 175, 236, 288n16; and autonomous church, 185; and detainment/hard labor, 237; NS takeover of, 235–37; and Provisional Mission Administration, 237; and Smebye, 288n19

Norwegian Mission Association, 313n29

Norwegian Mission to Israel, 207, 313n29

Norwegian Radio Corporation (NRK), 98–100

Norwegian Santal Mission, 283n12

Norwegian School of Theology, 282n5, 313n29. *See also* Free Faculty of Theology

Norwegian Seamen's Mission, 198, 246, 313n29

Norwegian Secondary School Teachers' League, 135

Norwegian State Police. *See* State Police

Norwegian Student Association, 220

Norwegian Sunday School Association, 313n29

Norwegian Sunday School Union, 313n29

Norwegian Teachers' League, 135

Norwegian University of Science and Technology, 70, 290n4

NS church, 171–76, 182, 191–201; and anti-Semitism, 191, 193–94, 213, 310n17; and apostolic succession, 172; appointment of bishops by Quisling, 173, 175; and archbishops, 172, 197–98; and autonomous church, 180–81, 183, 186–90, 195–97; boycotts of, 186, 188, 199; and Church Advisory Conference, 172–73, 195, 199, 231; and Church Council, 197; and Church Parliament, 197; and compulsory labor service, 222; core ideas of, 193–95; and ecclesiastical legitimacy, 172; and internment policy, 231–33, 237, 316n10, 317n11; intimidation of worshippers in, 186, 199, 309n29; and Jewish persecution, 191, 193–94, 212–14; law prohibiting collections for resigned clergy, 185; legitimacy of, 180–81; membership profile of, 191–93, 310n3; and National Labor Service Law, 222; as Nazi church, 181, 194, 201; and NMS takeover, 235–37; and office of archbishop, 172; and polity (church order), 197–99, 218; publications of, 192, 194, 212; and Stavanger manifesto, 174–76; ten dioceses in, 172–73, 198; and theological "college," 235; and theological faculties, 233–35

NS church system, 83–94; assault on bishops, 112–14; assault on polity (church order), 110–12, 114–17; and bishops' resignations, 126–28; and CCC, 64–65, 73–75; and censorship, 98–100; and Church Advisory Conference, 172; and church policy, 97–98, 231–33, 237, 316n10, 317n11; and *The Foundation of the Church*, 156–57, 160–63, 165; and leadership principle, 197–98; and Nazification, 56, 59, 97–98, 101, 105, 107, 132; and NS bishops, 90, 127–28, 155, 172–75, 181, 195–98, 200, 210–12, 214, 294n32, 311n34; and NS clergy, 88–92, 98–101, 103–5, 109–10, 117, 121–23, 125, 129, 152*fig.*, 171, 173–74, 181, 186, 192–93, 196, 198–200, 239–40, 245, 255, 297n6, 308n5; and NS deans, 155, 181, 196, 198, 200; and *Pastoral Letter*, 76–77, 81, 100; and Prayer of Intercession, 71, 290n10; and religious broadcasts, 98–100; and religious instruction in schools, 101–3; and seal of confessional, 71, 73, 75; suspension of NS clergy, 245; and theological faculties, 233. *See also* Church and Education Department; NS church

NS Relief Fund, 254

NS state, 28, 174; and anti-Semitism, 30–31, 39–40, 206–9; and Barbarossa, 109–10; and capitulation, 230, 245; Christian faction of, 30–31, 40; and coercion, 99–100, 140, 195, 201, 218, 250–51; Commissarial Council, 56, 59, 69, 71; and compulsory labor service, 219–22; and compulsory youth service, 127, 130–42, 218, 232; confiscation of radios, 100; executions by, 126, 210; fragmenting of, 230; General Secretariat, 111–12, 236; and *Hird* (paramilitary organization), 69–70, 76–77, 121, 158, 206, 251, 289n2; "ice front" against, 99,

186, 199–200, 311n37; and invasion of Norway, 40, 42, 44; and Jewish persecution, 40, 101, 206–9, 254–55; and "Jøssings," 216, 222; legality of, 177–79; and National Labor Service Law, 219–22; National Socialist faction of, 30–31, 39–40, 194, 284n48; as "New Age," 40, 69, 121, 206–7, 287n6; and new order, 40, 73, 77, 85, 90, 99, 159, 252; newspaper of, 84; and Norway's Teacher Association, 130–31, 136–37, 140; and PCL negotiations, 173–75, 177–79, 195–96, 217, 307n29; and PCL's New Year's message (1943), 217–18; People's Court, 70, 162; and postwar era, 256, 259, 263, 269, 271–72; and professional organizations, 65, 69, 72, 206; and Quisling, 30, 39–40, 42, 44, 50, 56, 120, 219; and racism, 31, 39; return to power, 54, 56, 65; "rowing club" out of party, 230; settlement with, 247–55; and state terror, 218, 225; and teachers, 135–36; and treason debate, 247–48; and treason trials, 247, 249–55; and violence, 65, 69–70, 73–77, 121, 124–25; Youth Campaign Day, 111–12; Youth Corps (NSUF), 111–12, 130–31, 135–38, 140. *See also* NS church; NS church system

Nygaardsvold, Johan, 28, 47, 245
Nygren, Anders, 267
Nystedt, Olle, 105

Odland, Sigurd, 23, 253
Oftenæs, Søren, 70, 83
Ohm, Karl, 163
Øhrn, Arnold T., 133, 211
Øksfjord (Finnmark), 96
Olav, Crown Prince, 41, 76
Olav, Saint, 121, 250
Olay, A. M., 297n6

Old Aker Church, 288n19
Old Testament: as "Jewish" stories, 101; struck from Christian scriptures, 7, 101
Olsen, Peder, 234, 249
Olympic Games (Berlin), 10
On the Jews and Their Lies (Luther), 16–17
On the Order of the Church: The Bishops' Position on Matters of Worship, 115–16
Operation Weser, 40–41, 51, 205
orders of creation, 6, 8, 11–14; biological orders, 14; and compulsory youth service, 132; cultural orders, 14; existed as hierarchy of authority/obedience, 14; father and family, 14; king and subjects, 14; *Volk* as supreme order, 6, 12–14. *See also* two realms doctrine
ordination: by Aulén in Sweden, 235; and autonomous church, 182, 189; and bishops, 19, 116, 124–25, 172–73, 198, 311n34; and clergy, 104, 156–57, 173, 182, 189, 198, 233, 235; and *The Foundation of the Church*, 156–57, 159; and Helgøya internment, 233; illegal ordinations, 240, 245, 310n9; and NS church, 172–73, 192, 198–99, 245, 310n9, 311n34; and *On the Order of the Church*, 116; and theological faculties, 235
Ording, Hans, 240
Ording, Johannes, 23
Ordo Crucis (Order of the Cross), 93
Orlien, Oswald, 214, 313n29
orthodox theology, 19, 23–26; and autonomous church, 189; and CCC, 62–64; and church conflict (1920s), 23–25, 57, 60, 62–64, 260–61, 283nn19–20; and church-state relationship, 24–26; and mission societies, 20, 23, 26, 29,

orthodox theology *(continued)*
189; neo-orthodox theology, 24; and
NS church, 192; and postwar era,
240, 260–61, 272
Oslo: Akershus castle, 120; Cathedral,
111–12, 158, 304n18; and compulsory
youth service, 140–41; and *The Foundation of the Church*, 158; Frogner
Church, 141, 182, 231; German congregation in, 88; German embassy
in, 50; Grini internment camp, 96,
153*fig.*, 169, 226, 238, 246, 318n43;
harbor of, 120; and invasion, 42–
46; Jacob Church, 231, 288n19; Jews
in, 30, 210, 215; Kampen Church,
196, 231; and NS church, 210–11;
and PCL, 175–76, 178, 181–82,
184–85; Philadelphia Church, 214;
political Oslo milieu, 44, 52–54;
Sagene Church, 185; State Police
headquarters, 91; St. Mark's Church,
61; St. Olav's Street, 181–82; street-
cars in, 37; Swedish congregation in,
80, 164; Swedish embassy in, 164;
taxis in, 77; and Teachers' Action
Committee, 135; and Terboven, 50
Oslo Cathedral School, 134
Oslo coalition, 43–46, 248
Oslo County, 45, 53
Oslo Diocese, 19, 288n16, 288n19;
bishop of, 19, 32, 37, 54, 107, 113–
15, 234; and CCC, 60–62; and NS
church, 173
Østlid, Henry O., 83–84, 292n2
Østnor, Lars, 266
Otto, Rudolf, 79
Øverland, Arnulf, 26, 169
Oxford Conference on Church, Com-
munity, and State (1937), 31–32, 37
Oxford Group Movement, 24

paganism, 28–29, 219; neo-paganism,
31, 194

parents, 46, 103; and compulsory youth
service, 131–33, 137–41, 218; and
conscience, 138, 218; and *The Foundation of the Church*, 159; prayer
for, 218; and resistance, 137–40, 218
Parish Council and Parish Meetings
Law (1920), 19, 111
Parish Council Law (1942), 252
parish councils, 19–20; and autonomous church, 181; and bishops'
resignations, 128–29; and clergy's
resignations, 164, 170; and NS
church, 173, 175, 181, 200–201;
and *Pastoral Letter*, 75; publicly
elected, 19, 111; reinstatement of,
245; and Stavanger manifesto, 175;
and Youth Campaign Day, 111–12
parliamentary democracy, 22
*Pastoral Letter to Our Congregations
from the Bishops of the Church of
Norway (February 1941)*, 75–82,
99–100, 133; attempt to confiscate,
76–77, 99; BBC's reports on, 100;
as framework for resistance, 77–82,
269; and postwar era, 269; spiritual/
moral capital of, 174
Pastors' Emergency League, 8
Pasvik River, 243
patriotism, German, 11
patriotism, Norwegian, 56, 105, 187–
88, 199; and aid to Jews, 211; Christian patriotism, 56, 187–88, 199,
257, 321n4; and postwar era, 257,
271
PCL (Provisional Church Leadership):
arrest/deportation of Hallesby and
Hope, 226, 230–31; and autonomous
church, 170–71, 174, 180–84, 187;
and compulsory labor service, 221–
22, 224, 226; and compulsory youth
service, 225; and courier services,
182–84; and diocesan communication networks, 183; Easter message

(1944), 238; exclusion of free churches, 265; hidden records of, 182; "holding out" policy of, 231, 234–35, 237; as illegal organization, 171, 183–84; and liberation, 246; members of, 181, 221; and mission societies, 182, 189; and National Labor Service Law, 221–22, 224–26; National Plan, 245; newspapers of, 183–84, 308n12; New Year's message (1943), 217–18, 315n10; and NS negotiations, 174–75, 177–79, 195–96, 217, 307n29; Pentecost message (1944), 239, 264; and postwar era, 239–40, 261, 264; protest against Jewish persecution, 211–12, 214, 218, 222, 254; and purging NS church personnel, 246; and reconstituting the Church, 246; and registration of property, 218; and repression statistics, 238–39, 318n46, 318n49; reputation abroad, 229; as Secret Church Leadership, 231; and Stavanger manifesto, 175–76; "ten commandments" of, 180–81; and theological faculties, 234–35; and treason trials, 253; and unified church front, 237

peace mediation (1939), 37–39, 57

Pedersen, Ole B., 90

Penal Code, 247; and Feyling's treason trial, 250; and NS bishops' treason trials, 252; and Quisling's treason trial, 249, 254; Section 86, 247, 250, 252, 254; Section 98, 247, 252; Section 222, 252; Section 233, 254; and Skancke's treason trial, 250; and war crimes, 247

Pentecostalists, 21, 306n44; Pentecostal Assemblies, 214, 313n29

Pharo, Håkon, 122

Philadelphia Church (Oslo), 214

Phony War, 37, 57

Pietism, 15

Pluskat, Werner, 230

Poland, invasion of, 11, 37, 49, 108

police. *See* State Police

politics, German, 6–7, 10–13, 15–16

politics, Norwegian: and Administrative Council, 49–50, 54; and anti-Semitism, 30; and autonomous church, 187, 189–90; ban on political parties, 103; and Berggrav, 42–45, 57, 59, 76, 110, 120, 125–26, 163; and bishops' resignations, 125–26; and Church of Norway, 19, 21, 26–28, 31, 50, 57, 59, 64, 70–71, 89, 98–100; and "Common Platform," 256; and courts, 70; and *The Foundation of the Church*, 157, 159–60; framework for German occupation, 54, 56, 59; and invasion, 42–45; and Jewish persecution, 211; and national coalition government, 245, 256; and Nidaros Cathedral incident, 126; and NMS takeover, 236; and NS church, 171–74, 193, 195–96, 199, 201; and NS church system, 84, 86–87, 89–92, 98–104, 250; and PCL, 170–71; political parties/leaders, 52–53, 65, 103; political speech, 89, 98–100; and postwar era, 258–62; and Prayer of Intercession, 71; and professional organizations, 104–5; and "The Protest of the Forty-Three," 104–5; and religious broadcasts, 98–100; and religious instruction in schools, 100–103; and Stavanger manifesto, 176; and Terboven, 50, 59, 70, 86; and treason trials, 250–51, 253; and Youth Campaign Day, 111–12

polity (church order), 19, 110–12, 114–17; and NS church, 197–99, 218; and Stavanger manifesto, 176

Polmak Church (Finnmark), 154*fig.*

Pope Innocent III, 305n24

Pope Pius XII, 133–34
pornography, 7
postal service, Norwegian, 106, 233
postwar church, 239–40, 256–75,
    321n1; and accountability, 239; and
    Christian culture, 257–59; and church-
    state relationship, 240, 259–60, 262–
    63; and cultural awakening, 256–59;
    and ecumenical movement, 263–69;
    and forgiveness, 239; and *The Foun-
    dation of the Church*, 245, 261–62;
    and justice, 239; and rehabilitation of
    Luther, 262–64; and unified church
    front, 260–61; and war weariness,
    257
Prayer Book, 115
Prayer of Intercession, 71, 246, 290n10;
    meaningful pause in, 71; and NS
    church, 173; and Thu, 238; and trea-
    son trials, 251, 254
Presbyterians, 273–74, 323n57
prime minister, Norwegian: and inva-
    sion, 41, 43, 45, 47; and Quisling, 43
professional organizations, 65, 69, 72,
    103–6; and conscience, 104–5; and
    Coordination Committee, 106, 221;
    and postwar era, 257; protest against
    Jewish persecution, 206
"professor case," 23
propaganda, German, 59; anti-Christian,
    9, 110; and Barbarossa, 109–10; and
    Berggrav's radio appeals, 48, 286n34;
    and Jewish persecution, 206, 213; and
    Reichskommissariat, 86; and state
    radio network, 100; and teachers,
    135; and total war, 217
prostitution, 7
"The Protest of the Forty-Three," 104–5
Provisional Church Leadership, 151*fig.*,
    259, 302n22
Prussian Confessional Synod (Breslau), 11
Prussian Union Church, 29; "Brown
    Synod," 29

Quakers, 21
"Quisling," 46, 48
Quisling, Vidkun, 39–40, 147*fig.*; and
    Act of State at Akershus, 120, 218–
    19; and Agrarian Party, 39; anniver-
    sary of return to power, 218–19;
    and anti-Semitism, 30, 39–40; and
    assault on bishops, 113; and Berg-
    grav, 42–45, 76, 107, 125–26, 158,
    160, 162–63, 177, 189, 219, 248–49;
    and bishops' resignations, 123, 125–
    26, 129; and capitulation, 230; and
    Church Advisory Conference, 172;
    and clergy's resignations, 142, 251,
    305n25; and compulsory labor ser-
    vice, 218–20, 222, 224–25; and com-
    pulsory youth service, 130–31, 136,
    139–40, 142; coup attempt of, 42–
    45; execution of, 250; and *The Foun-
    dation of the Church*, 158, 160–63;
    and "fuel holiday," 137, 139–40;
    guilty verdict of, 249–50, 254; and
    Hitler, 40, 42–43, 45, 59, 109, 119,
    164, 218; and invasion of Norway,
    40, 42–45; and Jewish persecution,
    206–8, 210–12, 218, 313n29; last
    radio broadcast of, 245; law prohib-
    iting collections for resigned clergy,
    185; as Minister President, 120–21,
    195; and National Assembly, 130;
    and National Labor Service Law,
    219–20, 222, 224–25; and Nidaros
    Cathedral incident, 121, 123; and
    NMS takeover, 236; and Norway's
    Teacher Association, 130–31, 136–
    37, 140; and NS church/church
    system, 89–90, 99, 171–72, 174,
    177–79, 185, 195–98; ordered death
    penalty for helping Jews escape, 210;
    and peace accord with Germany,
    218; prayer for, 71; removal from
    office, 48, 54, 61, 107, 120, 189,
    248; return to power, 54, 56, 59,

89, 119–21; surrender of, 245; and
Terboven, 50, 59, 119–20, 164; and
theological faculties, 234; as traitor,
40, 42; treason trial of, 248–50, 254;
and Universism, 40, 249–50, 285n8;
vision of corporate state, 130; and
Youth Corps (NSUF), 130–31, 136,
139–40, 164
Quisling church. *See* NS church

racism, 11, 14, 29, 31, 33, 39, 108, 213,
271–72. *See also* anti-Semitism
radio broadcasts: and Berggrav, 47–
48; and Bonnevie-Svendsen, 247;
boycott of, 99–100, 196; of church
services, 71, 98–100, 210–11, 261,
288n16; and coercion, 99–100; confiscation of radios, 100, 205; and
Feyling, 97–100; and Hallesby, 261;
in London, 76; and protests of Jewish arrests, 210–11; and Quisling,
245
Raeder, Erich, 40
Rediess, Wilhelm, 76, 87; suicide of,
245
Reformation, 6, 15, 19, 79, 115, 212,
240, 273; and CCC, 60–61; and NS
church, 172; and postwar era, 264
"Reformation of the Church in the
Spirit of 'the Young Luther,'" (Feyling), 172–73
Reformed tradition, 5–6, 8–9, 273–74,
323n57
Reich Chief Security Office (Berlin), 87
Reich Security Main Office, 87
Reichskommissariat, 49–51, 56, 69–71;
administration (I) department, 86;
and assault on bishops, 113; and
Berggrav's arrest, 162–63; and capitulation, 245; and compulsory labor
service, 223; economy (II) department, 86; and Jewish persecution,
205; and NS church system, 85–89,

93, 98, 104, 295n7; and parish council elections, 111; and "The Protest
of the Forty-Three," 104; public
information and propaganda (III)
department, 86, 109, 205, 293n14;
and suicides, 245; technology (IV)
department, 86; and treason trials,
251; and Wehrmacht, 93
Reine (Lofoton islands) raids/sabotage,
169
Reinhardt, Helmuth, 87
"Religion and Law" (Berggrav), 79
religious instruction in schools, 20, 24,
26–28, 100–103; and compulsory
youth service, 131–39; and postwar
era, 322n38; reform of, 27, 100–103;
textbooks used in, 101–3
resistance, Danish, 266
resistance, German: and Berggrav, 162;
and the Church, 49–50; and Confessing Church, 9–10, 270–71; and
Jews, 209; and postwar era, 270–71;
and Terboven, 49. *See also* German
church struggle; Kreisau Circle
resistance, Norwegian, 28, 31–33; and
BBC, 100; and bishops' resignations,
123; and CCC, 61–62, 65; church
resistance, 54, 56, 61–62, 65, 89–91,
94, 105–7, 164–65, 171, 186, 188–
90, 197, 229, 268–74; civil resistance, 61, 69–70, 72, 78, 93, 97, 104,
269; and clergy, 71–72, 104–5, 141,
302n22; and compulsory labor service, 220–26; and compulsory youth
service, 131–39, 302n22; and conscience, 72, 104–5, 136–37, 290n13;
and courier services, 61–62, 93, 106–
7, 138, 182–84, 232–33, 237, 304n19;
and deportations, 169; and ecumenical movement, 31–32; and expulsion
of clergy, 197, 232; and *The Foundation of the Church*, 162–63; "Four
Cardinal Points" of teachers' resis-

resistance, Norwegian *(continued)*
tance, 135; and Gestapo, 85, 88–89;
and High Council, 61, 289n25; and
Høigård, 134–35, 233; and invasion,
42, 44, 48; and Jews, 209–10; justification for, 78; and king's refusal to
abdicate, 54, 95; and Labor Party, 28;
military resistance, 69, 85–86, 89, 92,
96–97, 169–70, 217, 221, 230, 238,
244; and NMS takeover, 236–37;
and non-violence, 137, 157, 190, 257,
269; and Norwegian government,
95–96; and NS church system, 85,
88–94; and parents, 137–39, 218;
Pastoral Letter as framework for,
77–82, 269; and popular opinion,
77–78; and postwar era, 258, 268–
69; and professional organizations,
65, 69, 72, 104–6; and "The Protest
of the Forty-Three," 104; setting fire
to *Aula*, 234; and teachers, 72, 102–
3, 134–40, 269, 302n22; and theological faculties, 233–34; trivial acts
of dissidence, 238, 318n43; underground, 105; violent resistance, 93;
and women's organizations, 137–
38. *See also* Home Front; Milorg;
Norwegian church struggle
Rhedin, Ivar, 267
Rheims (France), 244
Rhineland, 49–50
Riisnæs, Sverre, 70, 126, 162, 207,
305n25
Rjukan, bombing of, 230
Roman Catholic Church, 21–22, 280n2,
305n24; and compulsory youth service, 133–34, 142; and Godesberg
Declaration, 11; and Jews, 211; and
Netherlands, 274; and papacy, 133–
34; and postwar era, 263, 273–74,
323n62; and Terboven, 49–50, 133;
and von Moltke, Helmuth, 162
Romanticism, 14

Rosef, Nils, 114
Rosenberg, Alfred, 59
rule of law, 69–70, 73, 271
rural deans, 83–84, 111–12, 123, 161,
183, 198
rural dialect movement, 134
rural folk movement, 21
Russian famine (1920s), 39
Russian revolution (1917), 22, 25, 27

sabotage, 45–47, 96, 169, 209, 217,
224, 230
Sæbø, Per Eivind, 161
Sæbø Church, 152*fig.*
Sæther, Orvar, 140
Sagene Church (Oslo), 185
Salvation Army, 133, 313n29
Sami (Lapp), 207, 255
Sande, Hans, 184
Sandsvær parish, 222
Santal Missions, 288n16, 288n19,
313n29
Sasse, Hermann, 14
Scharffenberg, Johan, 289n25
Schirmer, Ernst A., 194
Schjelderup, Ferdinand, 261; and Circle
(*Kretsen*), 105, 107, 297n46; and
compulsory labor service, 220;
and Coordination Committee, 107,
297n46; and High Council, 289n25;
and professional organizations, 72;
and teachers, 72, 137, 290n13
Schjelderup, Harald, 220
Schleswig-Holstein, 29, 92
Scholder, Klaus, 6, 12–13
school boards, 101, 103, 140
Schübeler, Lilly, 182
Schübeler, Ludwig, 151*fig.*, 183, 189, 231
Scotland, 273–74, 323n57
Secret Church Leadership, 151*fig.*, 231.
See also PCL (Provisional Church
Leadership)
Secret Finance Leadership, 185

secret police. *See* Gestapo

"sects," 10, 21, 142, 283n13

secularism, 16, 22–24; and church conflict (1920s), 23–24, 261; and compulsory youth service, 134; and Labor Party, 27–28; and postwar era, 257–61

Security Police and Security Service, 87; administrative (I and II) departments, 87; Criminal Police (V) department, 87; Gestapo (IV) department, 87–89; intelligence (III and IV) departments, 87; intelligence (III and VI) departments, 87

Segerstedt, Torgny, 48

Seierstad, Andreas, 63, 80, 151*fig.*, 184, 231, 240

Seip, Didrik Arup, 48, 169

Semelin, Jacques, 78

Shirer, William, 13, 281n48

Short Catechism (Luther), 19

Signal (Wehrmacht's magazine), 48

Sivertsen, Jørgen E., 198, 297n6

Skagestad, Gabriel, 146*fig.*; and assault on bishops, 114; and dismissal, 126; and Feyling, 84, 114; and *The Foundation of the Church*, 155–57, 304n6; health of, 123, 128; and Helgøya internment, 232–33; and *Pastoral Letter*, 77; resignation of, 123–24, 128

Skancke, Ragnar, 70–75, 83–86, 88–90, 149*fig.*, 293n6; and anti-Semitism, 207; assault on bishops, 113, 250; assault on polity (church order), 117, 250; banning of public readings by clergy, 141–42; and bishops' resignations, 126, 129; and Church Advisory Conference, 172; and clergy's resignations, 251, 305n25; and compulsory labor service, 222–23; and compulsory youth service, 131–32, 134, 139; execution of, 250; guilty verdict of, 250, 254; and National Labor Service Law, 222–23; and Norway's Teacher Association, 131, 136–37; and NS church, 172, 177–79, 194–95, 250; and religious broadcasts, 98–99; and religious instruction in schools, 101, 103, 250; and theological faculties, 234–35, 250; treason trial of, 250, 254

Skaugum (Crown Prince Olav's residence), 76

Skien Diocese, 173, 192, 200

Skjånes, Ivar, 122

Skjerstad (coastal steamer), 169

Skjønsberg, Tor, 105, 107, 221, 223–24

Skodvin, Magne, 290n13

"small church" movement, 231, 316n7

Smebye, Einar, 288n16, 288n19

Smemo, Johannes, 18, 22, 32, 151*fig.*, 231; escape to Sweden, 240

smoking, 182

snipers, 45–47

social democratic welfare state, 26–28, 256, 259–60

Socialism, 40, 258

Society of Friends, 21, 214, 248

Söderblom, Nathan, 57

SOE (Special Operations Executive), 96

Solberg, Nicolas, 90

Soviet Union, 119, 216; and Barbarossa, 108–10, 120, 172, 206–7, 244, 295n13, 297n6; casualty statistics for, 244; invasion of Finland, 38–39, 266; and Non-Aggression Pact (1939), 108; and Norway, 96–97, 243–44; and NS church, 193–95; and Socialism, 40; and Stalingrad, 216–17, 219, 229

spies, 83–84, 90–91, 114, 292n2. *See also* informants

spiritual realm, 16, 25, 55, 79–81, 171; and *The Foundation of the Church*, 157, 159; and NS church, 172–73, 201; and PCL, 171

SS: and capitulation, 245; and Jewish persecution, 205; in Norway, 50–51, 245; and Terboven, 50–51, 205; and Wagner, 87

Stalingrad, 216–17, 219, 229

St. Andrew's Church (Edinburgh), 273–74

St. Andrew's University, 268

Stang, Alex, 139

State Police, 69; and arrests/internments of teachers, 140; and autonomous church, 181–83, 185; and Berggrav's arrest, 163, 249; and bishops' resignations, 125, 128, 301n30; and compulsory labor service, 220; and compulsory youth service, 140, 218; Division III, 92; Division V-A, 91–92, 295n37; and *The Foundation of the Church*, 158, 160–62; and Jewish persecution, 210, 214, 254; and Nidaros Cathedral incident, 121–22; and NMS takeover, 236–37; and NS church/church system, 86–87, 90–92, 174, 179, 196–97, 232, 294n32, 295n37; and NS internment policy, 232; and *Pastoral Letter*, 76–77; and PCL, 218; political police, 69, 289n2; regional police, 91; and Reichskommissariat, 86–87; and seal of confessional, 73, 75; and Secret Finance Leadership, 185; and theological faculties, 234; and treason trials, 250–51

state servility: and Church of Norway, 17, 26, 33, 77, 263, 270, 272; and German Lutheranism, 13–17, 270, 272; and Luther, 17, 263, 282n52; and NS church, 194–95

statism, 13, 19

Stavanger, 91, 109; CCC (Christian Consultative Council), 155–56, 174–75, 237, 303n2, 304n6; and NMS takeover, 235, 237; and NS church, 198, 200, 212–13, 235; and revenue collection organizations, 185; Society of Friends, 214; and Stavanger manifesto, 174–77, 208–9, 237

Steltzer, Theodor: and Berggrav's arrest, 162–64; condemned to death, 243; and *The Foundation of the Church*, 158; and Kreisau Circle, 92–93, 209, 249; and theological faculties, 234; and warning to Jews, 209

Stene, Aasta, 137

Stene, Helga, 137

St. Mark's Church (Oslo), 61; Communication Service, 61

Stockholm, 42, 45, 93

Stockholm Conference (1925), 31–32

Støren, Johan, 73–74, 112–14, 121–24, 126–28, 146*fig.*, 172

Storting (Parliament), 25; building of, 104, 225; elections, 27–28, 259; Elverum Authorization, 41, 53; and invasion, 41, 43–45; Investigative Commission, 248; and liberation, 245, 248; National Assembly as replacement for, 130, 140, 164; and National Council Negotiations, 52–54, 248; and postwar era, 260; prayer for, 71; Presidium, 53, 287n2; and treason debate, 248; and treason trials, 251

sun cross. *See* swastika

Supreme Court, Norwegian, 19; and invasion, 43–45, 286n21; and NS appointees, 112; resignation of, 70, 73, 78–79, 107, 123, 289n3; retirement age lowered, 112

survival of fittest, 108

Svelvik chauffeurs' school, 223

Sverdrup, Edward, 23

Sverre Sigurdsson, King of Norway, 120, 305n24

Svolvær (Lofoton islands), 96

swastika, 101–2

Sweden: archbishop of, 11; and Aulén, 80; Church of Sweden, 93, 172, 176, 267; and compulsory labor service, 222–23, 225–26; escape to, 183, 206, 209–10, 215, 235, 238–40, 244, 246; Foreign Office, 267; and *The Foundation of the Church*, 164; German military transport through, 267; and iron ore exports, 42; and Jews, 206, 209–10, 212, 215; media in, 76, 78, 219, 222–23, 225–26; and neutrality, 267; and postwar era, 263, 267; and Steltzer, 93; and theological faculties, 235; views on Norwegians, 105; and Winter War, 39
Swiss Evangelical Press Service, 11
synagogues, 10, 22, 30, 214, 255

Tælavåg fishing village, 170
teachers: arrests/internments of, 140, 169; and Berggrav, 72, 135–37; and compulsory youth service, 131–40; and conscience, 72, 104, 136–38, 290n13; and Coordination Committee, 106, 135, 137–38; female teachers, 135; and Høigård, 134–35, 233; and NS church system, 90, 102–3; and PCL, 182; profession as calling, 72, 134, 140, 290n13; and Reichskommissariat, 86; and resistance, 72, 102–3, 134–40, 269, 302n22; salaries of, 136, 140; teaching in private homes, 137, 140
Teachers' Action Committee, 135–36
teachers' organizations, 72, 134–35
telegraphic service, Norwegian, 131, 161, 163, 233, 246
temperance movement, 134, 272
The Temporal and the Eternal (Berggrav), 54–56, 73, 253, 287nn6–7
temporal realm, 14–17, 55, 79; and *The Foundation of the Church*, 157, 159
Terboven, Josef, 49–52, 147*fig.*; arrest

of 43 organization leaders, 104–5; arrests/deportation of faculty/students, 234–35; arrests/internments of teachers, 140, 169; and assault on bishops, 113; banning of political parties, 103; banning of professional organizations, 104–5, 107; and Berggrav, 113, 120, 163; and bishops' resignations, 125–26; and compulsory labor service, 219–20, 225–26; and compulsory youth service, 133; confiscation of church bells, 113, 298n25; deportations of resistance leaders, 169; and *The Foundation of the Church*, 161, 163; and Gestapo, 69; and Göring, 49; and Hallesby, 225–26, 230–31; and Hope, 226, 230–31; and Jewish persecution, 205–6, 221, 231n4; and Lofoton retaliations, 96, 169; and Majavatn retaliation, 209–10; and National Labor Service Law, 219–20, 225–26; and NS church system, 86–87, 89–90, 99, 103–5; and NS Commissarial Council, 56, 59, 69; and *Pastoral Letter*, 76–77, 99; policy of not provoking churches, 50, 55, 77, 86, 89, 98–100, 109, 113, 206, 232, 269–70, 295n13; and Prayer of Intercession, 71; and Quisling, 50, 59, 119–20, 164; razing of Tælavåg, 170; as *Reichskommissar*, 49–51, 56, 69–71, 84, 86–87, 89, 96, 232; and religious broadcasts, 98–99; and Rhineland, 49–50; and Roman Catholic Church, 49–50, 133; ruthlessness of, 119; suicide of, 245
Theisen, Otto, 74, 83–84, 110, 172, 195, 199–200
theological faculties: and arrests/deportations, 234; and boycotts, 234–35; and church conflict (1920s), 23; and clergy's resignations, 163;

theological faculties *(continued)*
closing of, 233–35; educated at German universities, 28, 233; escape to Sweden, 235; and letter to Skancke, 132; protest against Jewish persecution, 212, 313n29; review of hymnals/liturgical changes, 116; review of religious textbooks used in schools, 101–2. *See also* Free Faculty of Theology; Theological Faculty (Univ. of Oslo)

Theological Faculty (Univ. of Oslo), 19, 233–35; and admissions requirements, 234; and arrests/deportations, 234–35; and *Aula* fire, 234; and boycotts, 234; and church conflict (1920s), 23–24; closing of, 233–35; and Mission to Israel, 207; and Molland, 233; and NS church, 192; and "professor case," 23; protest against Jewish persecution, 207, 313n29; Seminary for Practical Theology, 234

theological students, 183–84, 210, 222; arrests/deportation of, 234–35; and boycotts, 234–35; escape to Sweden, 235; executions of, 238

Third Reich, 8–10, 133. *See also* Germany; Nazism

Thomle, Erling, 151*fig.*, 181–82, 231; arrest of, 231

Thommessen, Øystein, 105

Thu, Arne, 238

Thunem, Adolf, 236–37

Tillich, Paul, 229

Time magazine, 268

Tønsberg, 236, 238

totalitarianism: Althaus's views on, 6, 280n8; and Church of Norway, 25, 275; and ecumenical movement, 31–32; Feyling's views on, 85; and Luther, 27; and postwar era, 260, 270, 275; in service to God, 6–7, 280n8

trade unions, 65, 69, 103, 206

Trægde, Tomas Per, 238

treason: and Berggrav, 47, 162; debate about, 247–48; and Hallesby, 226; and postwar era, 247–48, 271; and Quisling, 40, 42; treason laws, 247. *See also* treason trials

Treason Decree (1944), 247, 252, 254

treason trials, 220, 247–55; Feyling's trial, 250–52, 254–55; and "Jewish question," 254–55; of NS bishops, 252; of NS clergy, 253–54, 320n38; Quisling's trial, 248–50, 254; Skancke's trial, 250; statistics on, 255

Trinity Church, 288n19

Tromsø, 42, 51, 91, 123, 197

Trøndelag, 42, 70, 80; and Jewish persecution, 210

Trondenes, bishop of, 198

Trondheim, 189, 209; and CCC, 63; deportations from, 169; and *The Foundation of the Church*, 160; and invasion, 41–42; Jews in, 30, 210, 215; Nidaros Cathedral, 63, 114, 121–24, 126–27, 130–32; Norwegian Institute of Technology, 70; and State Police, 91

Tschudi, Stephan, 257–58

two realms doctrine: and Church of Norway, 25, 33, 55–56, 74, 77–81, 132, 157–59, 171–73, 262–63, 270; and compulsory youth service, 132; and *The Foundation of the Church*, 157–59; and German Lutheranism, 14–17, 25, 270; and just state, 74, 77–81; and NS church, 172–73, 191, 201; and PCL, 171; and postwar era, 259, 262–63, 270; reinterpretation of, 79–81. *See also* spiritual realm; temporal realm

Ukranian famine (1920s), 39

Ulleland, Peder, 297n6

unemployment, 22

United (Lutheran/Reformed) churches, 5–6

United Kingdom: Battle of Britain, 95; Blitz, 95; bombing in Norway, 230; casualty statistics for, 244; declared war on Germany, 37; and El Alamein victory, 216; Foreign Office, 38; and *The Foundation of the Church*, 164; intelligence reports, 187; Lambeth Cross, 268; Lofoton islands raids/sabotage, 169; mining operations, 41; morale in, 96; and Norway, 41–42, 51, 95–97, 169, 243–44; and postwar era, 268; sabotage operations in Norway, 96, 169, 217, 230; SOE (Special Operations Executive), 96; Special Operations Executive, 230; St. Andrew's University, 268; Western Front, 216, 229–30; Winter War, 39

United Nations, 257; Secretary General, 257

United States, 108; casualty statistics for, 244; and *The Foundation of the Church*, 164; and Norway, 96–97, 243; and Pearl Harbor, 108, 119; and Western Front, 216, 229–30

Universism, 40, 249–50, 285n8

University of Erlangen, 6

University of Oslo, 92; deportation of Seip, 169; and "professor case," 23. *See also* Theological Faculty (Univ. of Oslo)

University of Uppsala, 235, 267

Uppsala Conference (1917), 31–32

Vågen, Tormod, 151*fig.*, 183, 231, 288n16

Valen-Sendstad, Olav, 156, 175, 208–9, 303n2, 304n6

Vårt Land (Christian newspaper), 258, 265, 322n34

Versailles, Treaty of, 6

Vold, Karl, 62

Volk, 6–8, 11–14; Norwegian reaction to, 29; as supreme order of creation, 6, 12–14

Volkstrum movement, 6–7, 11–15; and Aryan Christ, 14–15

von Falkenhorst, Nikolaus, 46, 85, 92–93, 162–63, 234, 244, 249

von Moltke, Helmuth: and Berggrav's arrest, 162–63, 305n36; execution of, 243; and Kreisau Circle, 162, 209; and warning to Jews, 209

von Ribbentrop, Joachim, 43–45

von Stauffenberg, Claus, 243

von Weizsäcker, Ernst, 38

Wagner, Wilhelm Artur Konstantin, 87–90, 92, 115–17; biography of, 87; and compulsory labor service, 225; and "Ecclesiastical White Book" (Feyling), 161; and internment policy, 232; and Jewish persecution, 87, 206, 214; and NS church, 178, 197

war crimes/criminals, 239, 247; foreign war criminals, 247

weddings, 19, 186, 188, 199. *See also* marriages

Weebe, Axel, 164

Wegener, Paul, 163, 249

Wehrmacht: Abwehr of, 85–86; and autonomous church, 186, 188; and counterintelligence, 162; High Command, 48; intelligence reports, 77; invasion of Norway, 41, 45–48; lucrative contracts/high wages offered by, 54, 220; and NS church system, 85–86, 93; retreat from Norway, 243–45; and Steltzer, 92, 158, 162–63; and theological faculties, 234; and von Moltke,, 162

Weimar Republic, 6

Welhaven, Kristian, 46

Welle, Ivar, 20, 29, 298n24

Welsh, David, 273–74

Weserübung. See Operation Weser

Western Home Mission Association, 21, 189

When the Struggle Began (Berggrav), 248

"When the Driver Is Out of His Mind: Luther on the Duty of Disobedience" (Berggrav), 80–81, 292n49

Winsnes, Leif, 313n29

Winter War, 38–39, 266

Wisløff, Hans E., 133, 148*fig.*, 288n19, 302n12; imprisonment of, 162; and PCL, 170, 218

Wisløff, Johan M., 23, 283n19, 288n16

women's organizations, 137–38

Wood, Edward F. L. (Viscount Halifax), 38, 120

World Council of Churches, 11, 93, 267–69; Berggrav as president of, 268–69

World War I, 6, 49

World War I, post, 14; and church conflict (1920s), 23–25; as "the crisis," 22; economic depression, 22; "the hard thirties," 22; interwar era, 22–27

World War II: Barbarossa, 108–10, 120, 172, 206–7, 295n13, 297n6; Battle of Britain, 95; Battle of the Bulge, 230; Blitz, 95; casualty statistics of, 244, 319n5; D-Day, 230, 244; Eastern Front, 109, 119, 216, 244–46; end of, 176–77, 198, 238, 243–45; invasion of Denmark, 40–41; invasion of Finland, 38–39; invasion of Norway, 20, 40–51, 88, 133, 188, 205; invasion of Poland, 11, 37; Lofoton islands raids/sabotage, 169; Non-Aggression Pact (1939), 108; North Africa, 119, 216; Omaha Beach, 230; Operation Weser, 40–41; in Pacific, 244; Pearl Harbor, 108, 119; and Phony War, 37, 57; Stalingrad victory, 216–17, 219, 229; VE-Day, 244; Western Front, 216, 229–30, 244; and Winter War, 38–39, 266

Wormdal, Reidulf, 297n6

Würm, Theophil, 9, 11

Würtemberg, 8–9

xenophobia, 30

Yad Vashem (Jerusalem), 302n33

"Yes, We Love This Country" (national anthem), 122

Young Reformation Movement, 8

Youth Corps (NSUF), 111–12, 130–40, 164, 251. *See also* compulsory youth service

Zwilgmeyer, Dagfinn, 297n6

Zwilgmeyer, Ludvig Daae, 173, 195, 198, 200, 213, 297n6